FROMMER'S

Easy Guide

TO

Rome, Florence & Venice

By

Eleonora Baldwin, Stephen Keeling & Donald Strachan

Easy Guides are ✦ Quick To Read ✦ Light To Carry
✦ For Expert Advice ✦ In All Price Ranges

FrommerMedia LLC

Published by
FROMMER MEDIA LLC

Copyright © 2016 by Frommer Media LLC. All rights reserved. No part of this publication may be reproduced, stored in a retrieval system, or transmitted in any form or by any means, electronic, mechanical, photocopying, recording, scanning or otherwise, except as permitted under Sections 107 or 108 of the 1976 United States Copyright Act, without the prior written permission of the Publisher. Requests to the Publisher for permission should be addressed to customer_service@FrommerMedia.com.

Frommer's is a registered trademark of Arthur Frommer. Frommer Media LLC is not associated with any product or vendor mentioned in this book.

ISBN 978-162887-200-2 (paper), 978-162887-201-9 (e-book)

Editorial Director: Pauline Frommer
Editor: Melissa Klurman
Production Editor: Erin Geile
Cartographer: Liz Puhl
Photo Editor: Dana Davis
Cover Design: Howard Grossman

For information on our other products or services, see www.frommers.com.

Frommer Media LLC also publishes its books in a variety of electronic formats. Some content that appears in print may not be available in electronic formats.

Manufactured in the United States of America

5 4 3 2 1

FROMMER'S STAR RATINGS SYSTEM

Every hotel, restaurant and attraction listed in this guide has been ranked for quality and value. Here's what the stars mean:

★ Recommended
★★ Highly Recommended
★★★ A must! Don't miss!

AN IMPORTANT NOTE

The world is a dynamic place. Hotels change ownership, restaurants hike their prices, museums alter their opening hours, and busses and trains change their routings. And all of this can occur in the several months after our authors have visited, inspected, and written about, these hotels, restaurants, museums, and transportation services. Though we have made valiant efforts to keep all our information fresh and up-to-date, some few changes can inevitably occur in the periods before a revised edition of this guidebook is published. So please bear with us if a tiny number of the details in this book have changed. Please also note that we have no responsibility or liability for any inaccuracy or errors or omissions, or for inconvenience, loss, damage, or expenses suffered by anyone as a result of assertions in this guide.

A foreword TO THIS EASY GUIDE TO ROME, FLORENCE & VENICE

BY

ARTHUR FROMMER

Friends:

I was overwhelmed by my first contact with Italy. I was so affected by its visual sights that in a guidebook designed to deal with dry, dollars-and-cents matters (as my *Europe on $5 a Day* was initially planned to do), I grew lyrical in a chapter dealing with Venice. Arriving there by night, I wrote that "little clusters of candy-striped mooring poles emerge from the dark; the reflection of a slate-grey church bathed in a blue spotlight, shimmers in the water as you pass by." I was literally turned on.

And the people! Unlike the laid-back, reticent, soft-spoken types of northern Europe (much like us Americans), here were those who wore emotions on their sleeves. I gloried in the sounds of Italy, in the excitability of shopkeepers, the shouts of merchants and customers, the warm embraces of friends meeting on the street, the happy seniors playing bocce balls in parks and open spaces, the swaggering fashionistas both male and female. I marveled at the giant Roman ruins, the elaborate statuary more numerous than in any other country, the resplendent churches with frescoes by artists of genius. I loved the food, the endless varieties of pasta, the chiantis that accompanied the meals and the espressos that ended them.

For the first-time visitor to Italy, there is a classic itinerary that can't be equaled, and that forms the heart of this guidebook: Rome, Florence, Venice. While countless other areas, cities, and villages are almost—that's "almost"—as compelling, it is these magical three places that overawe all others, that can be easily reached by inexpensive train, and will never fail to excite. From Rome to Florence is only 2 hours by express train, from Florence to Venice is another 2-or-so hours, and each city is an overwhelming touristic experience.

The highlights are, of course, legendary: In Rome, the Roman Forum best reached by first ascending the Capitoline steps designed by Michelangelo, the Vatican, the Colosseum, the Pantheon and the Piazza Navona, the Via Veneto; in Florence, the original of Michelangelo's David in the Accademia Museum, the Uffizi and the Pitti Palace, the Medici Chapels and the Ghiberti Doors; in Venice, the Piazza San Marco, the Ducal Palace and the Rialto, a ride by vaporetto along the canals.

And these and more are colorfully described and appraised in this book by three distinguished authors. Eleonora Baldwin, American-born but Italian-raised, lives in Rome, where she is one of the city's foremost experts on Italian cuisine and local restaurants. She is, among numerous other writing credits, the force behind the popular "foodie" blog "Aglio, Olio e Peperoncino" and "Rome Every Day." What a joy to have her contribute so much to our chapter on hotels, restaurants, sights, and shops of Rome!

Donald Strachan, who lives much of the year in Italy, has written books and articles about Italy and Italian cities for more than 20 years; we spotted his work at an early time, and immediately enlisted him to prepare a great many of our guidebooks to Italy. Stephen Keeling, one of his two co-authors, is an Oxford graduate who has largely devoted his career to travel writing and was awarded in 2008 a much-coveted journalism prize for *Frommer's Guide to Tuscany & Umbria.* It would be hard to find a more knowledgeable and talented trio of travel writers on Italy, and we at Frommer's are immensely proud of having Eleonora, Donald, and Stephen as our main partners to Italy.

Now, on your return trip to Italy, you may well decide to branch out to Milan and Bologna, Pisa, Siena and Lucca, Naples and the Amalfi Coast, Sicily, Tuscany and Umbria, and you may also decide to use our 576-page *Complete Guide to Italy,* our *Easy Guide to Florence & Tuscany,* our *Venice Day by Day,* or several other Easy Guides to various Italian locations that will be appearing momentarily in the bookstores. Italy can support a lifetime of travel, and many avid travelers make countless repeat trips there. But for the three major Italian destinations covered in this book, we believe our Easy Guide approach will prove just the right thing!

From all of us at Frommer's: *Buon Viaggio!*

Cordially,

Arthur Frommer

CONTENTS

ABOUT THE AUTHORS

Eleonora Baldwin, American-born but Italian raised, lives in Rome, where she divides her time between food and guidebook writing, and designing custom food, wine, and cooking experiences for curious travelers in Italy.

Stephen Keeling has been traveling to Italy since 1985 (when a serving of gelato was 1,000 lire) and covering his favorite nation for Frommer's since 2007. He has written for *"the Independent," "Daily Telegraph,"* and various travel magazines, has authored the award-winning Frommer's family travel guide to Tuscany and Umbria; and researched numerous travel guides in Europe, Asia, and the Americas. Stephen lives in New York City.

Donald Strachan is a writer and journalist who has written about Italy for publications worldwide including *"National Geographic Traveller," "The Guardian," "The Sunday Telegraph," "The Independent,"* and others; see www.donaldstrachan.com.

ABOUT THE FROMMER TRAVEL GUIDES

For most of the past 50 years, Frommer's has been the leading series of travel guides in North America, accounting for as many as 24% of all guidebooks sold. I think I know why.

Though we hope our books are entertaining, we nevertheless deal with travel in a serious fashion. Our guidebooks have never looked on such journeys as a mere recreation, but as a far more important human function, a time of learning and introspection, an essential part of a civilized life. We stress the culture, lifestyle, history, and beliefs of the destinations we cover, and urge our readers to seek out people and new ideas as the chief rewards of travel.

We have never shied from controversy. We have, from the beginning, encouraged our authors to be intensely judgmental, critical—both pro and con—in their comments, and wholly independent. Our only clients are our readers, and we have triggered the ire of countless prominent sorts, from a tourist newspaper we called "practically worthless" (it unsuccessfully sued us) to the many rip-offs we've condemned.

And because we believe that travel should be available to everyone regardless of their incomes, we have always been cost-conscious at every level of expenditure. Though we have broadened our recommendations beyond the budget category, we insist that every lodging we include be sensibly priced. We use every form of media to assist our readers, and are particularly proud of our feisty daily website, the award-winning Frommers.com.

I have high hopes for the future of Frommer's. May these guidebooks, in all the years ahead, continue to reflect the joy of travel and the freedom that travel represents. May they always pursue a cost-conscious path, so that people of all incomes can enjoy the rewards of travel. And may they create, for both the traveler and the persons among whom we travel, a community of friends, where all human beings live in harmony and peace.

Arthur Frommer

THE BEST OF ITALY

I taly is a country that needs no fanfare to introduce it. The mere name conjures up vivid images: The noble ruins of Ancient Rome, the paintings and palaces of Florence, the secret canals and mazelike layout of Venice. For centuries, visitors have headed to Italy looking for their own slice of the good life, and these three cities supply the highpoint of any trip around the country.

Nowhere in the world is the impact of the Renaissance seen more fully than in its birthplace, **Florence,** the repository of artistic works left by Masaccio, Botticelli, Leonardo, Michelangelo, and many others. Much of the "known world" was once ruled from **Rome,** a city supposedly founded by twins Romulus and Remus in 753 B.C. Its fortunes have fallen, of course, but it remains timeless. There's no place with more artistic monuments—not even **Venice,** an impossible floating city that was shaped by its merchants and centuries of trade with the Byzantine world farther east.

And there's more. Long before Italy was a country, it was a loose collection of city-states. Centuries of alliance and rivalry left a legacy dotted across the hinterlands of these three great cities, and much of it lies within easy day-trip distance. It is a short hop from the former maritime republic to the "Venetian Arc": **Verona,** with its romance and its intact Roman Arena; and **Padua** and its sublime Giotto frescoes. In **Siena,** the ethereal art and Gothic palaces survive, barely altered since the city's heyday in the 1300s. The eruption of Vesuvius in A.D. 79 preserved **Pompeii** under volcanic ash for 2 millennia. It remains the best place to get close-up with the world of the ancients.

ITALY'S best AUTHENTIC EXPERIENCES

o **Dining Italian Style:** The most cherished pastime of most Italians is eating—and each region and city has its own recipes handed down through generations. If the weather is fine and you're dining outdoors, perhaps with a view of a medieval church or piazza, you'll find the closest thing to food heaven. *Buon appetito!*

- **Catching an Opera at Verona's Arena:** Summertime opera festivals in Verona are produced on a scale more human than those in such cities as Milan—and best of all, they are held under the stars. The setting is the ancient **Arena di Verona,** a site that's grand enough to accommodate as many elephants as required for a performance of "Aïda." See p. 291.
- **Cicchetti and a Spritz in Venice:** *Cicchetti*—tapaslike small servings, usually eaten while standing at a bar—are a Venetian tradition. Accompany the *cicchetti* with a spritz made with Aperol and sparkling Prosecco wine from the Veneto hills, to make the experience complete. See p. 239.
- **Exploring Rome's Mercato di Testaccio:** In 2012, old Testaccio Market made way for a glass-paneled, modernist beauty across the street from a slaughterhouse-turned-museum. Mingle with busy signoras whose trolleys are chock-full of celery, carrots, and onions for the day's *ragù*. Grab a slice of focaccia or some Roman street food, and pick up a genuine flavor of the Eternal City. See p. 125.

ITALY'S best RESTAURANTS

- **Pizza Rustica, Rome:** Chef-entrepreneur Gabriele Bonci elevates the simple slice of pizza to extraordinary levels. There's nothing fussy about the place, or the prices, but every single ingredient that goes onto or into a Pizza Rustica creation is carefully sourced and expertly prepared. It shows from the first bite. See p. 60.
- **Ora d'Aria, Florence:** For all its historic location in an alleyway behind Piazza della Signoria, Florence's best dinner spot is unshakably modern. Head chef Marco Stabile gives traditional Tuscan ingredients a fresh (and lighter) makeover. See p. 157.
- **Ai Artisti, Venice:** Venice's culinary rep is founded on the quality of the fish sold at its famous market. Both *primi* and *secondi* at Ai Artisti feature the freshest catch from the lagoon and farther afield. See p. 246.
- **Il Gelato Bistrò, Rome:** Savory ice cream may sound nuts—and occasionally it contains nuts—but gelato maestro Claudio Torcè pulls it off. For evening *aperigelato* or a light lunch, pair natural flavors such as *sesamo nero* (black sesame) with Parma ham served in a savory pancake. It really works. See p. 60.

ITALY'S best HOTELS

- **La Dimora degli Angeli, Florence:** You walk a fine line when you try to bring a historic *palazzo* into the 21st century, and this place walks it expertly. Rooms are split over two floors, with contrasting characters—one romantic, and modern-baroque in style; the second characterized by sharp, contemporary lines and Scandinavian-influenced design. See p. 148.
- **Villa Spalletti Trivelli, Rome:** All-inclusive can be exclusive, especially when the experience of staying in an Italian noble mansion is part of the

package. Opulence and impeccable service comes at a price, of course. When our lottery numbers come up, we will be booking a stay here. See p. 52.

o **Continentale, Florence:** Echoes of *la dolce vita* fill every sculpted corner of this modern hotel, and rooms are flooded in natural light. If you want to relax away from your 1950s-styled bedroom, there are day beds arranged by a huge picture window facing the Ponte Vecchio, and on the roof, La Terrazza is Florence's best gathering spot for evening cocktails. See p. 149.

o **Metropole, Venice:** The Grand Old Lady of Venetian hospitality was transformed from a medieval building into a luxury hotel in the 19th century. Today it remains a chic choice, filled with antiques and Asian art. See p. 232.

ITALY'S best FOR FAMILIES

o **Climbing Pisa's Wonky Tower:** Are we walking up or down? Pleasantly disoriented kids are bound to ask as you spiral your way to the rooftop viewing balcony atop one of the world's most famous pieces of botched engineering. Pisa is an easy day trip from Florence, and 8 is the minimum age for heading up its *Torre Pendente,* or Leaning Tower. See p. 212.

o **Boat Tripping on the Venice Lagoon:** Who doesn't like a day boating on a lake, any lake? Throw in the floating city and its bell tower of San Marco as permanent fixtures on the horizon and you have one unforgettable family moment. See p. 279.

o **Attending a Fiorentina Soccer Match:** Forget lions battling gladiators in Rome's Colosseum, or Guelphs fighting Ghibellines in Florence's medieval lanes. For a modern showdown, hit a Florence soccer game. Home side Fiorentina plays Serie A matches at the city's Stadio Comunale alternate weekends from September to June. Wear something lilac—the team's nickname is *i viola* ("the purples"). See p. 200.

o **Taking a Trip to an Artisan Gelateria:** Fluffy heaps of gelato, however pretty, are built with additives, stabilizers, and air pumped into the blend. Blue "Smurf" or bubblegum-pink flavors denote chemical color enhancement, and ice crystals or grainy texture are telltale signs of engineered gelato—so steer clear. Authentic artisan *gelaterie* produce good stuff from scratch daily, with fresh ingredients and less bravado. See "Gelato," p. 72, 164, and 251.

o **Visiting Rome's Centrale Montemartini:** Where industrial archaeology became a museum: The restored rooms of Rome's first public electricity plant now house Greek and Roman statues from the city collection. The museum always has drawing and painting materials onsite, and guided tours for children are available on request. Plus on Sundays, there's free admission for kids under 12. See p. 114.

ITALY'S best MUSEUMS

- **Vatican Museums, Rome:** The 100 galleries that constitute the Musei Vaticani are loaded with papal treasures accumulated over the centuries. Musts include the Sistine Chapel, such ancient Greek and Roman sculptures as "Laocoön" and "Belvedere Apollo," and the frescoed "Stanze" executed by Raphael, among which is his "School of Athens." See p. 76.

- **Galleria degli Uffizi, Florence:** This U-shaped High Renaissance building designed by Giorgio Vasari was the administrative headquarters, or *uffizi* (offices), for the Medici dukes of Tuscany. It's now the crown jewel of Europe's art museums, housing the world's greatest collection of Renaissance paintings, including icons by Botticelli, Leonardo da Vinci, and Michelangelo. See p. 173.

- **Accademia, Venice:** The "Academy" houses an incomparable collection of Venetian painting, exhibited chronologically from the 13th to the 18th century. It's one of the most richly stocked museums in Italy, displaying works by Bellini, Carpaccio, Giorgione, Titian, and Tintoretto. See p. 264.

- **Galleria Borghese, Rome:** Housed amid the frescoes and decor of a 1613 palace in the heart of the Villa Borghese gardens, this gem of a building is merely the backdrop for its collections, which include masterpieces of baroque sculpture by a young Bernini and Canova, and paintings by Caravaggio and Raphael. See p. 108.

- **Santa Maria della Scala, Siena:** The building is as much the star as the artworks. This was a hospital from medieval times until the 1990s, when the building was closed and its frescoed wards, ancient chapels and sacristy, and labyrinthine basement floors were gradually opened up for public viewing. See p. 209.

ITALY'S best FREE THINGS TO DO

- **Getting Rained on in Rome's Pantheon:** People often wonder whether the 9m (30-ft.) oculus in the Pantheon's dome has a glass covering. Visit the ancient temple in the middle of a downpour for your answer: The oculus is open to the elements, transforming the Pantheon into a giant shower on wet days. In light rain, the building fills with mist, and during a full-fledged thunderstorm, the drops come down in a perfect 9m-wide shaft, splattering on the polychrome marble floor. Come on Pentecost to get rained on by a cloud of rose petals. See p. 100.

- **Basking in the Lights of the Renaissance:** At dusk, make the steep climb up to the ancient church of San Miniato al Monte, Florence. Sit down on the steps and watch the city begin its evening twinkle. See p. 195.

- **Getting Gothic on the Streets of Siena:** The shell-shaped Piazza del Campo stands at the heart of one of Europe's best-preserved medieval cities. Steep, canyonlike streets, icons of Gothic architecture like the Palazzo Pubblico, and ethereal Madonnas painted on shimmering gold altarpieces transport you back to a time before the Renaissance. See p. 207.

o **Gazing in Wonder at Caravaggio's Greatest Paintings:** Rome's French church, San Luigi dei Francesi is home to three panels by bad-boy of the baroque, Michelangelo Merisi da Caravaggio. His "Calling of St. Matthew" was painted at the height of his fame (and powers), and incorporates the uncompromising realism and *chiaroscuro* (extremes of light and dark) style that was Caravaggio's trademark. See p. 100.

o **Getting Hopelessly Lost in Venice:** You haven't experienced Venice until you've turned a corner convinced you're on the way somewhere, only to find yourself smack against a canal with no bridge, or in a little courtyard with no way out. All you can do is shrug, smile, and give the city's maze of narrow streets another try. Because getting lost in Venice is a pleasure. See p. 219.

undiscovered ITALY

* **San Frediano, Florence:** Most Florentines have abandoned their *centro storico* to the visitors, but on the Arno's Left Bank in San Frediano, you'll find plenty of local action after dark. Dine at **iO** (p. 163), slurp a gelato by the river at **La Carraia** (p. 165), then drink until late at **Diorama** (p. 205) or catch an acoustic gig at **Volume** (p. 204). See "Where to Eat" and "Entertainment & Nightlife" in chapter 6.

o **The Aperitivo Spots and Craft Beer Bars in Rome:** Don't confuse *aperitivo* with happy hour: Predinner cocktails tickle appetites, induce conversation and flirting, and allow free access to all-you-can-eat buffets if you buy one drink. And Romans are increasingly turning to artisan-brewed beers for that one drink. See "Entertainment & Nightlife" in chapter 4.

o **The *Cicchetti*-Filled Bacari of Venice:** At *bacari* (neighborhood bars) throughout Venice, locals nibble on tapas-like *cicchetti,* small fried bites, served alongside regional drinks such as Prosecco, spritz (Prosecco mixed with Aperol), or beer. It's finger food at its best: quick, inexpensive, tasty, and fun, and an easy way to meet the residents who call Venice home. See "Where to Dine" in chapter 8.

o **Florence's Vegetarian Dining Scene:** The days when you had to be a carnivore to fully enjoy a meal in the Renaissance city are long gone. The modern menu at **Vagalume** (p. 163) is populated with veggie dishes to fit any appetite. And vegans, as well as celiacs, are looked after by the dishes at **Brac** (p. 162) and **Konnubio** (p. 160).

SUGGESTED ITINERARIES

Italy is so vast and treasure-filled that it's hard to resist the temptation to pack in too much in too short a time. It's a dauntingly diverse and complex destination, and you can't even skim the surface in 1 or 2 weeks—so relax, don't try. If you're a first-time visitor with very little touring time on your hands, we suggest you go just for the classic nuggets: Rome, Florence, and Venice could be packed into 1 very busy week, better yet in 2.

How can you accomplish that? Well, Italy ranks with Germany and France in offering mainland Europe's best-maintained super-highways (called *autostrade*). You'll pay a toll to drive on them (p. 297), but it's much quicker to use them than to trust your limited time to the array of minor roads, which can be *much* slower going.

The country also boasts one of the fastest and most efficient high-speed rail networks in the world. Rome and Milan are the key hubs of this 21st-century transportation empire—for example, from Rome's Termini station, Florence can be reached in only 91 minutes. In fact, if you're city-hopping between Rome, Florence, and Venice, you need never rent a car. Upgrades to the rail network mean that key routes are served by comfortable, fast trains; the key connections include the Venice–Florence–Rome line. You'll only really require a rental car if you plan rural detours.

The following itineraries take you to some of our favorite places. The pace may be a bit breathless for some visitors, so skip a stop occasionally to have some chill-out time—after all, you're on vacation. Of course, you can also use any of our itineraries as a jumping-off point to develop your own adventure.

ROME, FLORENCE & VENICE IN 1 WEEK

Let's be realistic: It's impossible to see Italy's three iconic cities fully in a week. However, an efficient, fast rail network along the Rome–Florence–Venice axis means it's surprisingly easy to see some of the best they offer. This weeklong itinerary treads the familiar highlights, but these are the most visited because time after time they provide memories to last a lifetime.

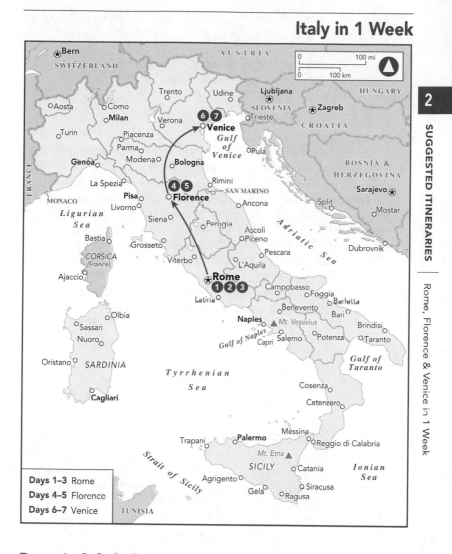

Days 1–3 Rome
Days 4–5 Florence
Days 6–7 Venice

Days 1, 2 & 3: Rome ★★★

You could spend a month touring the Eternal City, but 3 days is enough to get a flavor of it. There are two essential areas to focus on in a short visit. The first is the legacy of Imperial Rome, such as the **Forum, Campidoglio,** and **Colosseum** (p. 88). Bookend your day with the Forum and Colosseum (one first, the other last) to avoid the busiest crowds; the same ticket is good for both. On **Day 2,** tackle **St. Peter's Basilica** and the **Vatican Museums** (p. 80), with a collection unlike any other in the world that includes Michelangelo's **Sistine Chapel.** On your third day, it's a toss-up: Choose between the underground catacombs of the **Via Appia**

Antica (p. 116); treading the streets of Rome's ancient seaport at **Ostia Antica** (p. 130); or visiting some of the capital's quieter museum collections, including the **Palazzo Massimo alle Terme** (p. 113). Spend your evenings in the bars of **Campo de' Fiori** or **Monti** (p. 128), and the restaurants of **Trastevere** (p. 69) or **Testaccio** (p. 70). Toward the end of **Day 3,** catch the late train to Florence.

Days 4 & 5: Florence: Cradle of the Renaissance ★★★

You have 2 whole days to explore the city of Giotto, Leonardo, Botticelli, and Michelangelo. Start with their masterpieces at the **Uffizi** (you should definitely have booked admission tickets ahead; see p. 173), followed by the **Duomo** complex (p. 171): Scale Brunelleschi's ochre dome, and follow up with a visit to the adjoining **Battistero di San Giovanni, Museo Storico dell'Opera del Duomo,** and **Campanile di Giotto** (p. 167). Start the next day with "David" at the **Accademia** (p. 188). For the rest of your time, spend it getting to know the art at the **Palazzo Pitti** (p. 193), the intimate wall paintings of **San Marco** (p. 189), and Masaccio's revolutionary frescoes at the **Cappella Brancacci** (p. 196). In the evenings, head south of the Arno for lively wine bars and better restaurants (p. 163). Leave via an early train on the morning of **Day 6.**

Days 6 & 7: Venice: The City That Defies the Sea ★★★

You'll ride into the heart of Venice on a *vaporetto* (water bus), taking in the **Grand Canal,** the world's greatest main street. Begin your sightseeing at **Piazza San Marco** (p. 254): The **Basilica di San Marco** is right there, and after exploring it, visit the nearby **Palazzo Ducale** (**Doge's Palace;** p. 259) before walking over the **Bridge of Sighs.** Begin your evening with the classic Venetian *aperitivo,* an Aperol spritz (Aperol with sparkling wine and soda) followed by *cicchetti* (Venetian tapas) before a late dinner. Make your second day all about the city's unique art: the **Gallerie dell'Accademia** (p. 264), the modern **Peggy Guggenheim Collection** (p. 267), and **San Rocco** (p. 270). Catch the latest train you can back to Rome. Or add another night—you can never stay too long in Venice.

A 2-WEEK ITINERARY

It's obviously difficult to see the top sights of Italy—and to see them properly—in just 2 weeks. But in the itinerary below, we lead you around the best of it all in 14 days. We'll go beyond the well-trodden (and spectacular) Rome–Florence–Venice trail to include the southern region of Campania, specifically Pompeii, which has Italy's most complete Roman ruins. Additional stops in the center and north are Pisa (for the Leaning Tower and more), Padua (with its Giotto frescoes), and Verona (city of lovers since "Romeo and Juliet").

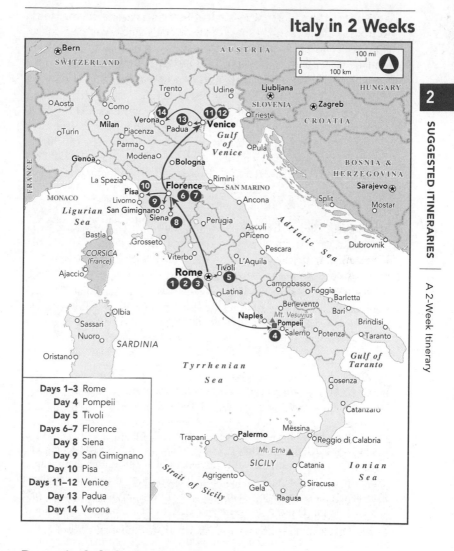

Italy in 2 Weeks

Days 1–3 Rome
Day 4 Pompeii
Day 5 Tivoli
Days 6–7 Florence
Day 8 Siena
Day 9 San Gimignano
Day 10 Pisa
Days 11–12 Venice
Day 13 Padua
Day 14 Verona

Days 1, 2 & 3: Rome ★★★

Follow the itinerary suggested in "Italy in 1 Week," above. Because an
extra week allows you to add a day trip to Pompeii, on **Day 4,** choose
your third day from between the catacombs of the **Via Appia Antica**
(p. 116) and Rome's less visited museums. Using Rome as a base for the
first part of a longer stay means you should consider apartment rental
rather than a hotel room in the capital; see "Self-Catering Apartments,"
p. 45.

Day 4: Pompeii: Europe's Best-Preserved Roman Ruins ★★

On **Day 4,** take the high-speed Frecciarossa or Italo train from Rome to Naples, then the Circumvesuviana train 24km (15 miles) southeast of Naples to spend a day wandering the archaeological remains at **Pompeii** (p. 132). It's better if you have packed water and some lunch, because onsite services aren't especially enticing. The city was buried for 2,000 years, having suffered total devastation when nearby Vesuvius erupted in A.D. 79. Some of the great archaeological treasures of Europe—including the remarkable patrician villa **Casa dei Vettii** and the frescoed **Villa dei Misteri**—are found here. Return to Rome for overnighting: This is a very long day. Alternatively, you can do the trip as an escorted visit by bus from Rome. Several operators offer it; ask at your hotel or at one of Rome's tourist information points (see "Visitor Information," p. 134).

Day 5: Tivoli: A Day Trip to Rome's Imperial Villa ★★

Take your foot off the gas with a more relaxed day trip, 32km (20 miles) northeast of Rome to **Tivoli** (p. 135). It was out here that Emperor Hadrian built his serene rural retreat, known now as the **Villa Adriana** (p. 135). It is the grandest retirement residence you'll ever see, complete with theaters, baths, fountains, and gardens. This emperor had an eye for design.

Days 6 & 7: Florence ★★★

Follow the itinerary suggested in "Rome, Florence & Venice in 1 Week," above.

Day 8: A Day Trip to Gothic Siena ★★★

It's just over an hour to **Siena** (p. 207) on the *rapida* bus. Leave early and set out immediately on arrival for **Piazza del Campo,** the shell-shaped main square, including its art-filled **Museo Civico** (inside the **Palazzo Pubblico**). This is a flying visit, but you still have time to squeeze in a fast look at the **Duomo** and **Museo dell'Opera Metropolitana,** where you'll find Sienese master Duccio's giant "Maestà." Stop on the Campo for a late afternoon drink and then head to a restaurant in Siena's atmospheric back streets. Reserve an early table: The last bus back to Florence departs at 8:45pm, arriving back in Florence at 10pm.

Day 9: San Gimignano: A Town Stuck in the 1300s ★★

It's another long day on the buses, but well worth it to see one of the most perfectly preserved Gothic towns in Europe. You'll change buses in Poggibonsi for the last, ridiculously pretty leg through the vine-clad hills to **San Gimignano** (p. 213). The "city of beautiful towers" had over 70 of the things spiking the sky in its medieval heyday. Now just a handful remain, including the **Torre Grossa** (which you can climb). The frescoed **Collegiata** is the essential art stop. You can dine early at **Chiribiri** (it's open all day), then leave on the late bus. Also consider renting a car: The roads of central Tuscany are pretty at any time of year, and parking on the outskirts of San Gimignano is well provisioned and signposted.

Day 10: Pisa & Its Leaning Tower ★★

The set-piece piazza here is one of the most photographed slices of real estate on the planet. Pisa's **Campo dei Miracoli** ("Field of Miracles") is home to the **Leaning Tower** (p. 212), of course. You can visit the **Duomo**, with its Arab-influenced Pisan-Romanesque facade; the **Battistero** with its carved pulpit and crazy acoustics; and the rest of the piazza's monuments and museums on the same combination ticket. You should book a slot ahead of time if you want to climb the Leaning Tower, however. For dining *alla pisana*, head away from the touristy piazza. The "real Pisa" lies in the warren of streets around the market square, **Piazza delle Vettovaglie**. Finish your visit with a stroll along the handsome promenade beside the **River Arno**.

Days 11 & 12: Venice ★★★

Follow the itinerary suggested in "Rome, Florence & Venice in 1 Week," above.

Day 13: Padua & Its Giotto Frescoes ★

Lying only 40km (25 miles) to the west, **Padua** (p. 288) is a straightforward day trip by train. In one fairly relaxed day, you can visit the **Basilica di Sant'Antonio** (p. 289) with its Donatello bronzes and the **Cappella degli Scrovegni** (p. 289), or Arena Chapel, with its Giotto frescoes—perhaps the most important paintings in the history of Italian art. Also look next door at the **Chiesa degli Eremitani**. One of the saddest sights in Italian art is here, the Ovetari Chapel, where Mantegna's frescoes were almost totally destroyed by a World War II bomb. Return to Venice for the night.

Day 14: Verona: City of Lovers & Gladiators ★★★

Although he likely never set foot in the place, Shakespeare placed the world's most famous love story here, "Romeo and Juliet." Wander **Piazza dei Signori** and take in another square, **Piazza delle Erbe,** before descending on the **Arena di Verona** (p. 291): Evoking Rome's Colosseum, it's the world's best-preserved gladiatorial arena, still used for monumental opera performances in summer months. Head back to Venice for the night. It is well worth booking your tickets for the high-speed Frecciabianca train ahead of time. The journey is just 1 hour, 10 minutes, compared with over 2 hours for the slower regional service.

ITALY FOR FAMILIES

Italy is probably the friendliest family vacation destination in all of Europe. Practically, it presents few challenges. But if you're traveling by rental car with young children, be sure to request safety car seats ahead of time. Let the rental company know the age of your child (up to 12), and they will arrange for a seat that complies with EU regulations. Rail travelers should remember that reduced-price family fares are available on much of the high-speed network; ask when you buy your tickets or contact a booking agent.

As you tour, don't go hunting for "child-friendly" restaurants or special kids' menus. There's always plenty available for little ones, even dishes that aren't on offer to grown-up patrons. Never be afraid to ask if you have a fussy eater in the family. Pretty much any request is met with a smile.

Perhaps the main issue for travelers with children is spacing your museum visits so that you get a chance to see the masterpieces without having young kids suffer a meltdown after too many paintings of saints and holy *bambini*. Remember to punctuate every day with a **gelato** stop—Italy makes the world's best ice cream. You will even find creative *soya* flavors for anyone with lactose intolerance. We also suggest planning fewer long, tiring day trips out of town, especially by public transportation. And end your trip in Venice, which many children may assume was dreamed up by Walt Disney anyway.

Day 1: Rome's Ancient Ruins ★★★

History is on your side here: The wonders of **Ancient Rome** (p. 86) should appeal as much to kids (of almost any age) as to adults. There are plenty of gory tales to tell at the **Colosseum** (p. 88), where the bookshop has a good selection of city guides aimed at kids. After that, little ones can let off steam wandering the **Roman Forum** and the **Palatine Hill.** (The roadside ruins of the **Imperial Forums** can be viewed at any time.) Cap the afternoon by exploring the **Villa Borghese** (p. 108), a monumental park in the heart of the city. You can rent bikes, and there is also a small zoo in the northeast of the grounds. For dinner, head for some fluffy crusts at an authentic Roman **pizzeria,** such as **Li Rioni** (p. 62).

Day 2: Rome: Living History ★★★

Head early to **St. Peter's Basilica** (p. 78), before the lines form. Kids will find it spooky wandering the Vatican grottoes, and few can resist climbing up to Michelangelo's dome at 114m (375 ft.). After time out for lunch, begin your assault on the **Vatican Museums** and the **Sistine Chapel** (be sure to book advance tickets; it's worth the 4€ to avoid the lines). Even if your kids don't like art museums, they will probably gawk at the grandeur. Later in the day, head for the **Spanish Steps** (a good spot for some upscale souvenir shopping; see p. 123) before wandering over to the **Trevi Fountain.** Give the kids coins to toss into the fountain, which

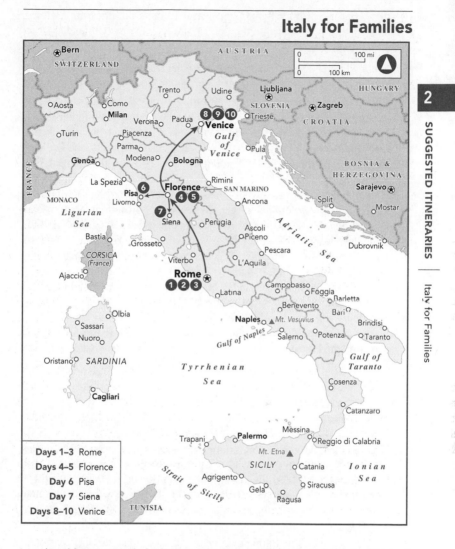

Days 1–3 Rome
Days 4–5 Florence
Day 6 Pisa
Day 7 Siena
Days 8–10 Venice

is said to ensure their return to Rome—perhaps when they are older and can better appreciate the city's many more artistic attractions.

Day 3: Rome: Underground ★★★

There are, literally, layers of history below the city streets, and kids will love to explore the catacombs of the **Via Appia Antica** (p. 116), the first cemetery of Rome's Christian community, and where the devout practiced their faith in secret during periods of persecution. **Context Travel** (p. 120) runs an excellent tour of the city's subterranean layers, which takes in San Clemente (p. 95) and SS. Giovanni e Paolo. It costs 255€ per party. Eat more **pizza** before you leave; Rome's pizzerias are bettered only by those in Naples, to the south. And the next recommended stops all lie to the north.

Days 4 & 5: Florence: City of the Renaissance ★★★

Take the early train to Florence. It is usually thought of as more of an adult city, but there's enough here to fill 2 family days, plus a couple of day trips. With 4 nights here, you should take an apartment rather than a hotel room, to give you all the more space to spread out. Check out **GoWithOh.com** for a good range of quality places. Close to the Duomo, **Residence Hilda** (p. 152) is a family-friendly hotel that rents large, apartment-style rooms. Begin with the city's monumental main square, **Piazza della Signoria,** now an open-air museum of statues. The **Palazzo Vecchio** (p. 180) dominates one side; you can all tour it with special family-friendly guides, including a docent dressed as Cosimo de' Medici. You won't want to miss the **Uffizi.** With young children, you could turn your visit into a treasure trail of the museum's collection by first visiting the shop to select some postcards of the key artworks. On the second morning, kids will delight in climbing to the top of Brunelleschi's dome on the **Duomo** for a classic panorama. Get there as early as possible— lines lengthen very rapidly. You'll still have time to climb the 414 steps up to the **Campanile di Giotto,** run around in the **Giardino di Boboli,** and stroll the **Ponte Vecchio** at dusk. Add the following two day trips—to Pisa and Siena—on to your Florence stay, returning each evening to your Florence apartment.

Day 6: Pisa & Its Leaning Tower ★★

If your kids are 7 or under, you should consider skipping **Pisa** (p. 210): 8 is the minimum age for the disorienting ascent up the bell tower of Pisa's cathedral, which more commonly goes by the name the **Leaning Tower.** Elsewhere in the city, kids will love the hyperreal monuments of the **Campo dei Miracoli** and learning about the city's Galileo links: He was born here, and supposedly discovered his law of pendulum motion while watching a swinging lamp inside the **Duomo.** Before heading back to Florence, take them to taste a local specialty, *cecina*—a pizzalike, garbanzo bean–flour flatbread served warm—at popular slice parlor **Il Montino.** Rail connections between Florence and Pisa are fairly fast (1 hr., 20 min.), frequent, and affordable (around 8€ each way).

Day 7: Gothic Siena ★★★

Count yourself lucky if you can visit **Siena** (p. 207) around July 2 or August 16 for the famous 4-day **Palio** celebrations, when horses race at breakneck speed around **Piazza del Campo.** Year-round, a couple of epic climbs will thrill the kids. The **Torre del Mangia**—the bell tower of the **Palazzo Pubblico**—ends in a dramatic view of the city and the enveloping countryside. Through the **Museo dell'Opera Metropolitana,** they can scale the "Facciatone" for an alternative, dizzying view down into the Campo. At **Santa Maria della Scala,** they will find **Bambimus,** the art museum for kids, where paintings are hung at child-friendly heights. The zebra-striped **Duomo** is jazzy enough to pique their curiosity. Siena's many bakeries are famed for their sweet treats. Take the bus back to Florence after an early dinner.

Days 8, 9 & 10: Venice, City on the Lagoon ★★★

Leave Florence early for Venice, the most kid-pleasing city in Italy. The fun begins the moment you arrive and take a *vaporetto* ride along the **Grand Canal.** Head straight for **Piazza San Marco** (p. 254), where kids delight in feeding the pigeons and riding the elevator up the great **Campanile.** Catch the mosaics inside the **Basilica di San Marco,** which dominates the square. At the **Palazzo Ducale,** kids can walk over the infamous **Bridge of Sighs** after checking out the pint-size knight's armor. As in Florence, make time for the priority art: Visit the **Gallerie dell'Accademia** (p. 264) and **San Rocco,** where kids view the episodic Tintoretto paintings like a picture book. Take a modern break at the **Peggy Guggenheim Collection** for pop art, open courtyard, and rooftop cafe. In summer, save time for the beach at the **Lido** (p. 277) and for getting a different angle on Venice's canals from the seat of a **gondola** (p. 270).

ITALY IN CONTEXT

3

As with any destination, a little background reading can help you to understand more. Many Italy stereotypes are accurate—children are feted wherever they go, food and soccer are treated like religion, the north–south divide is real, bureaucracy is part of daily life. Some are wide of the mark—not every Italian you meet will be open and effusive. Occasionally they do taciturn pretty well, too.

The most important thing to remember is that, for a country with so much history—3 millennia and counting—Italy has only a short history *as a country*. Only in 2011 did it celebrate its 150th birthday. Prior to 1861, the map of the peninsula was in constant flux. War, alliance, invasion, and disputed successions caused that map to change color as often as a chameleon crossing a field of wildflowers. Republics, mini-monarchies, client states, Papal States and city-states, as well as Islamic emirates, colonies, dukedoms, and Christian theocracies, roll on and off the pages of Italian history with regularity. In some regions, you'll hear languages and dialects other than Italian. It's part of an identity that is often more regional than it is national.

This confusing history explains why your Italian experience will differ wildly if you visit, say, Rome rather than Venice. (And why you should visit both, if you can.) The architecture is different; the food is different; the important historical figures are different, as are the local issues of the day. And the people are different: While the north–south schism is most often written about, cities as close together as Florence and Siena can feel very dissimilar. This chapter aims to help you understand why.

ITALY TODAY

The big Italian news for many travelers is the favorable movement in exchange rates. In last year's edition of this guide, the U.S. dollar/euro exchange rate was $1.37. At the time of writing, it's $1.10. Everything in Italy just became 20% cheaper for visitors from across the Atlantic. (The Canadian dollar has moved less dramatically, but also in the right direction—from $1.49 to $1.35.) So, congratulations: You picked a great time to visit.

cuisine AROUND THE COUNTRY

Italians know how to cook—just ask one. But be sure to leave plenty of time: Once an Italian starts talking food, it's a while before they pause for breath. Italy doesn't really have a unified, national cuisine; it's more a loose grouping of regional cuisines that share a few staples, notably pasta, bread, tomatoes, and pig meat cured in endless ways.

Rome can be the best place to introduce yourself to Italian food, because it boasts restaurants from every region. On a Roman vacation, you'll also encounter authentic local specialties such as *saltimbocca alla romana* (literally "jump-in-your-mouth"—thin slices of veal with sage, cured ham, and cheese) and *carciofi alla romana* (tender artichokes cooked with herbs, such as mint and garlic), and a dish that's become ubiquitous, *spaghetti alla carbonara*—pasta coated in a white sauce of cured pork (cheek, if it's authentic), egg, and *Pecorino romano* (ewe's milk cheese).

To the north, in **Florence and Tuscany,** you'll find seasonal ingredients served simply; it's almost the antithesis of "French" cooking, with its multiple processes. The main ingredient for almost any savory dish is the local olive oil, feted for its low acidity. The typical Tuscan pasta is wide, flat *pappardelle,* generally tossed with a game sauce such as *lepre* (hare) or *cinghiale* (boar). Tuscans are fond of their own strong ewe's milk cheese, Pecorino, made most famously around the Val d'Orcia town of Pienza. Meat is usually the centerpiece of the *secondo:* A *bistecca alla fiorentina* is the classic main, a T-bone-like slab of meat. An authentic *fiorentina* should be cut only from the white Chianina breed of cattle. Sweet treats are also good here, particularly Siena's *panforte* (a dense, sticky cake), *biscotti di Prato* (hard, almond-flour biscuits for dipping in dessert wine), and *miele* (honey) from Montalcino.

Venice is rarely celebrated for its cuisine. Fresh seafood is usually excellent, however, and figures heavily in the Venetian diet. Grilled fish is often served with red radicchio, a bitter lettuce that grows best in nearby Treviso. Two classic nonfish dishes are *fegato alla veneziana* (liver and onions) and *risi e bisi* (rice and fresh peas). The traditional carbohydrate up here isn't pasta but *risotto* (rice), flavored with seasonal ingredients.

One gastronomic trend to watch out for as you travel is the booming popularity of artisanal beer, especially among the young. Although supermarket shelves are still stacked with mainstream brands Peroni and Moretti, smaller stores and bars increasingly offer craft microbrews. Italy had fewer than 50 breweries in 2000. That figure is now well over 400, and is still rising fast.

Many Italians have not been so lucky. One reason for the euro's plunge is a stubbornly slow European recovery from the global financial crisis—known here as the *Crisi.* It had a disastrous effect on Italy's economy, causing the deepest recession since World War II. Public debt grew to alarming levels, and for a decade economic growth has been almost nonexistent. As a result, 2011 and 2012 saw Italy pitched into the center of a European banking crisis, which almost brought about the collapse of the euro currency. However, by 2015, many Italians were beginning to see light at the end of their dark economic tunnel—a little, at least. Yet even here, a stark north–south divide lingers: The south's economy shrank faster during recession, unemployment rose quicker, and at the time of writing, economic recovery has been somewhere between marginal and invisible. Unsurprisingly, net migration from south to north continues.

Populism has become a feature of national politics. A party led by comedian Beppe Grillo—the *MoVimento 5 Stelle* (5 Star Movement)—polled around a quarter of the vote in 2013 elections. In 2014, Matteo Renzi swapped his job as *Partito Democratico* (PD; Democratic Party) mayor of Florence to become Italy's youngest prime minister, age 39, heading a center-left coalition. One of his first big moves was the abolition—from 2015—of Italy's *province*. This layer of government, between *comune* (town or city) and *regione* (region, e.g., Tuscany), has been deemed one bureaucracy too far for the 21st century. Voters seem cautiously optimistic about Renzi: At elections in 2014, his PD trounced Grillo's antisystem party. Opinion polling through mid-2015 showed Italians still favoring Renzi's reformism over rivals' policies. From top to toe, highlands to islands, fingers are firmly crossed that the good times are coming round again.

Italy's population is aging, and a youth vacuum is being filled by immigrants, especially those from Eastern Europe, notably Romania (whose language is similar to Italian), and Albania, as well as from North Africa. In a number of high-profile tragedies, overloaded boats coming from Africa have sunk in the Mediterranean Sea, with appalling loss of life. In addition, Italy doesn't have the colonial experience of Britain and France, or the "melting pot" history of the New World; tensions were inevitable, and discrimination is a daily fact of life for many minorities. Change is coming—in 2013, Cécile Kyenge became Italy's first black government minister, and black soccer player Mario Balotelli is one of the country's biggest sports stars. But it is coming too slowly for some.

THE MAKING OF ITALY

Etruscans & Villanovans: Prehistory to the Rise of Rome

Of all the early inhabitants of Italy, the most significant legacy was left by the **Etruscans.** No one knows exactly where they came from, and the inscriptions that they left behind (often on graves in necropolises) are of little help—the Etruscan language has never been fully deciphered by scholars. Whatever their origins, within 2 centuries of appearing on the peninsula around 800 B.C., they had subjugated the lands now known as **Tuscany** (to which they left their name) and Campania, along with the **Villanovan** tribes that lived there. They also made Rome the governmental seat of Latium. "Roma" is an Etruscan name, and the ancient kings of Rome had Etruscan names: Numa, Ancus, and even Romulus.

The Etruscans ruled until the **Roman Revolt** around 510 B.C., and by 250 B.C. the Romans and their allies had vanquished or assimilated the Etruscans, wiping out their language and religion. However, many of the former rulers' manners and beliefs remained, and became integral to what we now understand as "Roman culture."

Rome's **Museo Nazionale Etrusco** (p. 111) and the Etruscan collection in Rome's **Vatican Museums** (p. 80) are a logical start-point if you want to see the remains of Etruscan civilization. Florence's **Museo Archeologico** (p. 188) houses one of the greatest Etruscan bronzes yet unearthed, the "Arezzo Chimera."

The Roman Republic: ca. 510–27 B.C.

After the Republic was established around 510 B.C., the Romans continued to increase their power by conquering neighboring communities in the highlands and forming alliances with other Latins in the lowlands. They gave to their allies, and then to conquered peoples, partial or complete Roman citizenship, with the obligation of military service. Citizen colonies were set up as settlements of Roman farmers or veterans—including both **Florence** and **Siena.** The all-powerful Senate presided as Rome defeated rival powers one after the other and came to rule the Mediterranean.

No figure was more towering during the late Republic, or more instrumental in its transformation into Empire (see below), than **Julius Caesar,** the charismatic conqueror of Gaul—"the wife of every husband and the husband of every wife." After defeating the last resistance of the Pompeiians in 45 B.C., he came to Rome and was made dictator and consul for 10 years. Conspirators, led by Marcus Junius Brutus, stabbed him to death in the Senate on March 15, 44 B.C., the "Ides of March."

Their motivation was to restore the power of the Republic and topple dictatorship. But they failed: **Mark Antony,** a Roman general, assumed control. He made peace with Caesar's willed successor, **Octavian,** and (after the Treaty of Brundisium, which dissolved the Republic) found himself married to Octavian's sister, Octavia. This didn't prevent him from also marrying Cleopatra in 36 B.C. The furious Octavian gathered western legions and defeated Antony at the **Battle of Actium** on September 2, 31 B.C. Cleopatra fled to Egypt, followed by Antony, who committed suicide in disgrace a year later. Cleopatra, unable to retain her rule of Egypt, followed suit with the help of an asp. The permanent end of the Republic was nigh.

Many of the standing buildings of Ancient Rome date to periods after the Republic, but parts of the **Roman Forum** (p. 91) date from the Republic, including the **Temple of Saturn.** The adjacent **Capitoline Hill** and **Palatine Hill** have been sacred religious and civic places since the earliest days of Rome. Rome's best artifacts from the days of the Republic are housed inside the **Musei Capitolini** (p. 93).

The Roman Empire in Its Pomp: 27 B.C.–A.D. 395

Born Gaius Octavius in 63 B.C., and later known as Octavian, **Augustus** became the first Roman emperor in 27 B.C. and reigned until A.D. 14. His autocratic reign ushered in the *Pax Romana,* 2 centuries of peace. In Rome, you can still see the remains of the **Forum of Augustus** (p. 89) and admire his statue in the **Vatican Museums** (p. 80).

By now, Rome ruled the entire Mediterranean world, either directly or indirectly, because all political, commercial, and cultural pathways led straight to Rome, the sprawling city set on seven hills: the Capitoline, Palatine, Aventine, Caelian, Esquiline, Quirinal, and Viminal. It was in this period that **Virgil** wrote his best-loved epic poem, "The Aeneid," which supplied a grandiose founding myth for the great city and empire; **Ovid** composed his erotic poetry; and **Horace** wrote his "Odes."

The emperors brought Rome to new heights. But without the countervailing power of the Senate and legislatures, success led to corruption. The centuries witnessed a steady decay in the ideals and traditions on which the Empire had been founded. The army became a fifth column of unruly mercenaries, the tax collector became the scourge of the countryside, and for every good emperor (Augustus, Claudius, Trajan, Vespasian, and Hadrian, to name a few) there were several cruel, debased, or incompetent tyrants (Caligula, Nero, Caracalla, and many others).

After Augustus died (by poison, perhaps), his widow, **Livia**—a shrewd operator who had divorced her first husband to marry Augustus—set up her son, **Tiberius,** as ruler through a number of intrigues and poisonings. A long series of murders and purges ensued, and Tiberius, who ruled during Pontius

10 EARLY ROMAN emperors

Augustus (ruled 27 B.C.–A.D.14): First, "divine" emperor to whom all later emperors aspired

Tiberius (r. A.D. 14–37): Former general whose increasingly unpopular reign was gripped by fear and paranoia

Caligula (r. A.D. 37–41): Young emperor whose reign of cruelty and terror ended when he was assassinated by his Praetorian Guard

Claudius (r. A.D. 41–54): A sickly man who turned out to be a wise and capable emperor, as well as the conqueror of Britain

Nero (r. A.D. 54–68): The last emperor of the Julio-Claudian dynasty was another cruel megalomaniac who killed his own mother and may have started the Great Fire of Rome (A.D. 64)

Vespasian (r. A.D. 69–79): First emperor of the Flavian dynasty, who built the Colosseum and lived as husband-and-wife with a freed slave, Caenis

Domitian (r. A.D. 81–96): Increasingly paranoid populist and authoritarian who became fixated on the idea that he would be assassinated—and was proven right

Trajan (r. A.D. 98–117): Virtuous soldier-ruler who presided over the moment Rome was at its geographically grandest scale, and also rebuilt much of the city

Hadrian (r. A.D. 113–138): Humanist, general, and builder who redesigned the Pantheon and added the Temple of Venus and Roma to the Forum

Marcus Aurelius (r. A.D. 161–180): Philosopher-king, and the last of the so-called "Five Good Emperors," whose statue is exhibited in the Musei Capitolini

Pilate's trial and crucifixion of Christ, was eventually murdered in his late 70s. Murder was so common that a short time later, **Domitian** (ruled A.D. 81–96) became so obsessed with the possibility of assassination that he had the walls of his palace covered in mica so that he could see behind him at all times. (He was killed anyway.)

Excesses ruled the day—at least, if you believe surviving tracts written by contemporary chroniclers infused with all kinds of bias: **Caligula** supposedly committed incest with his sister, Drusilla; appointed his horse to the Senate; lavished money on egotistical projects; and proclaimed himself a god. Caligula's successor, his uncle **Claudius,** was poisoned by his final wife, his niece Agrippina, to secure the succession of **Nero,** her son by a previous marriage. Nero's thanks were later to murder not only his mother but also his wife, Claudius's daughter, and his rival, Claudius's son. The disgraceful Nero, an enthusiastic persecutor of Christians, committed suicide with the cry, "What an artist I destroy!" By the 3rd century A.D., corruption and violence had become so prevalent that there were 23 emperors in 73 years. Few, however, were as twisted as **Caracalla** who, to secure control, had his brother Geta slashed to pieces while Geta was in the arms of his mother, former empress Julia Domna.

Constantine the Great became emperor in A.D. 306, and in 330, he made Constantinople (or Byzantium) the new capital of the Empire, moving the administrative functions away from Rome altogether, partly because the menace of possible barbarian attacks in the west had increased. Constantine was the first Christian emperor, allegedly converting after he saw the True Cross in a dream, accompanied by the legend, IN THIS SIGN SHALL YOU CONQUER. He defeated rival emperor Maxentius and his followers at the **Battle of the Milivan Bridge** (A.D. 312), a victory that's remembered by Rome's triumphal **Arco di Costantino** (p. 86). Constantine ended the persecution of Christians with the **Edict of Milan** (A.D. 313).

It was during the Imperial period that Rome flourished in architecture. **Classical orders** were simplified into types of column capitals: **Doric** (a plain capital), **Ionic** (a capital with a scroll), and **Corinthian** (a capital with flowering acanthus leaves). Much of this development in building prowess was because of the discovery of a form of concrete and the fine-tuning of the arch, which was used with a logic, rhythm, and ease never before seen. Some of the monumental buildings still stand in Rome, notably **Trajan's Column** (p. 91), the **Colosseum** (p. 88), and Hadrian's **Pantheon** (p. 100), among many others. Elsewhere in Italy, Verona's **Arena** (p. 291) bears witness to the kinds of crowds that the brutal sport of gladiatorial combat could draw—Ridley Scott's 2000 Oscar-winning movie "Gladiator" isn't all fiction. Three **Roman cities** have been preserved, with street plans and, in some cases, even buildings remaining intact: doomed **Pompeii** (p. 132) and its neighbor **Herculaneum,** both buried by Vesuvius's massive A.D. 79 eruption; and Rome's ancient seaport, **Ostia Antica** (p. 130). It was at Herculaneum that one of Rome's greatest writers perished, **Pliny the Elder** (A.D. 23–79). It's thanks to him; his nephew, **Pliny the Younger;** the historians **Tacitus, Suetonius, Cassius Dio,**

ALL ABOUT vino

Italy is the largest **wine**-producing country in the world; as far back as 800 B.C., the Etruscans were vintners. However, it wasn't until 1965 that laws were enacted to guarantee consistency in winemaking. Quality wines are labeled **"DOC"** (Denominazione di Origine Controllata). If you see **"DOCG"** on a label (the "G" stands for G*arantita*), that denotes an even better-quality wine region. **"IGT"** (Indicazione Geografica Tipica) indicates a more general wine zone—for example, Umbria—but still with some quality control.

Below we've cited a few of the best Italian wines around Venice, Rome, and Florence. Rest assured that there are hundreds more, and you'll have a great time sampling them to find your own favorites. Sometimes you don't want the marquee labels: A pitcher of the local *vino della casa* (house wine) to wash down lunch in a trattoria can be a delight.

Tuscany: Tuscan red wines rank with some of the finest in world. **Sangiovese** is the king of grapes here, and **chianti** from the hills south of Florence is the most widely known sangiovese wine. The best zone is **Chianti Classico,** where a lively ruby-red wine partners a bouquet of violets. The Tuscan south houses two even finer DOCGs: mighty, robust **Brunello di Montalcino,** a garnet red ideal for roasts and game; and almost purple **Vino Nobile di Montepulciano,** which has a rich, velvet body. End a meal with the Tuscan dessert wine called **vin santo,** which is usually accompanied by *biscotti* that you dunk into your glass.

The Veneto: Reds around Venice vary from light and lunchtime-friendly **Bardolino** to **Valpolicella,** which can be particularly intense if the grapes are partially dried before fermentation to make an **Amarone.** White, garganega-based **Soave** has a pale amber color and a peachlike flavor. **Prosecco** is the classic Italian sparkling white, and the base for both a Bellini and a Spritz—joints that use Champagne are doing it wrong.

Latium: Many of Rome's local wines come from the Castelli Romani, the hill towns around the capital. These wines are best drunk when young, and they're most often white, mellow, and dry. The golden wines of **Frascati** are the most famous.

and **Livy;** and satirist **Juvenal** that much of our knowledge of ancient Roman life and history was not lost.

The surviving Roman **art** had a major influence on the painters and sculptors of the Renaissance (see p. 25). In Rome itself, look for the marble *bas-reliefs* (sculptures that project slightly from a flat surface) on the **Arco di Costantino** (p. 86); the sculpture and mosaic collections at the **Palazzo Massimo alle Terme** (p. 113); and the gilded equestrian statue of Marcus Aurelius at the **Musei Capitolini** (p. 93). The Florentine Medici were avid collectors of Roman statuary, some now at the **Uffizi** (p. 173).

The Fall of the Empire, Byzantine Italy & the "Dark Ages"

The Eastern and Western sections of the Roman Empire split in A.D. 395, leaving the Italian peninsula without the support it had once received from east of the Adriatic. When the **Goths** moved toward Rome in the early 5th century, citizens in the provinces, who had grown to hate the bureaucracy set up by **Diocletian,** welcomed the invaders. And then the pillage began.

Rome was first sacked by **Alaric I,** king of the Visigoths, in 410. The populace made no attempt to defend the city (other than trying vainly to buy him off, a tactic that had worked 3 years earlier); most people fled into the hills. The feeble Western emperor **Honorius** hid out in **Ravenna** the entire time, which from 402 he had made the new capital of the Western Roman Empire.

More than 40 troubled years passed. Then **Attila the Hun** invaded Italy to besiege Rome. Attila was dissuaded from attacking, thanks largely to a peace mission headed by Pope Leo I in 452. Yet relief was short-lived: In 455, **Gaiseric,** king of the **Vandals,** carried out a 2-week sack that was unparalleled in its savagery. The empire of the West lasted for only another 20 years; finally, in 476, the sacks and chaos ended the once-mighty city, and Rome itself was left to the popes, though ruled nominally from Ravenna by an Exarch of Byzantium (aka Constantinople).

Although little of the detailed history of Italy in the post-Roman period is known—and few buildings survive—it's certain that the spread of **Christianity** was gradually creating a new society. The religion was probably founded in Rome about a decade after the death of Jesus, and gradually gained strength despite early (and enthusiastic) persecution by the Romans. The best way today to relive the early Christian era is to visit Rome's Appian Way and its Catacombs, along the **Via Appia Antica** (p. 116). According to Christian tradition, it was here that an escaping Peter encountered his vision of Christ. The **Catacombs** were the first cemeteries of the Christian community of Rome, and they house the remains of early popes and martyrs.

We have Christianity, along with the influence of Byzantium, to thank for the appearance of Italy's next great artistic style: the **Byzantine.** Painting and mosaic work in this era was very stylized and static, but also ornate and ethereal. The most accomplished examples of Byzantine art are found in Ravenna, but later churches in the Byzantine style include Venice's **Basilica di San Marco** (p. 254).

The Middle Ages: From the 9th Century to the 14th Century

As a ravaged Rome entered the Middle Ages, its people scattered in rustic exile. A modest population started life again in the swamps of the **Campus Martius,** while the seven hills—now without water because the aqueducts were cut—stood abandoned and crumbling.

The pope turned toward Europe, where he found a powerful ally in **Charlemagne,** king of the Franks. In 800, Pope Leo III crowned him emperor. Although Charlemagne pledged allegiance to the church and looked to Rome and its pope as the final arbiter in most religious and cultural affairs, he launched northwestern Europe on a course toward bitter opposition to the meddling of the papacy in temporal affairs.

The successor to Charlemagne's empire was a political entity known as the **Holy Roman Empire** (962–1806). The new Empire defined the end of the Dark Ages but ushered in a long period of bloody warfare. Magyars from Hungary invaded northeastern Lombardy and, in turn, were defeated by an increasingly powerful **Venice**. This was the great era of Venetian preeminence in the eastern Mediterranean; it defeated naval rival Genoa in the 1380 Battle of Chioggia; its merchants reigned over most of the eastern Mediterranean, and presided over a Republic that lasted for a millennium; great buildings like the **Doge's Palace** (p. 259) were built.

Rome during the Middle Ages was a quaint, rural town. Narrow lanes with overhanging buildings filled many areas that had once been showcases of Imperial power. The forums, mercantile exchanges, temples, and theaters of the Imperial era slowly disintegrated. As the seat of the Roman Catholic Church, the state was almost completely controlled by priests, and began an aggressive expansion of Church influence and acquisitions. The result was an endless series of power struggles.

In the mid–14th century, the **Black Death** ravaged Europe, killing perhaps a third of Italy's population; the unique preservation of Tuscan settlements like **San Gimignano** (p. 213) and **Siena** (p. 207) owes much to the fact that they never fully recovered after the devastation dished out by the 1348 plague. Despite such setbacks, Italian city-states grew wealthy from Crusade booty, trade, and **banking**.

The medieval period marks the beginning of building in stone on a mass scale. Flourishing from A.D. 800 to 1300, **Romanesque** architecture took its inspiration and rounded arches from Ancient Rome. Its architects concentrated on building large churches with wide aisles to accommodate the masses. Pisa's **Piazza dei Miracoli** (1153–1360s; p. 210) is typical of the Pisan-Romanesque style, with stacked arcades of mismatched columns in the cathedral's facade (and wrapping around the famous **Leaning Tower of Pisa**), and blind arcading set with diamond-shaped lozenges. The influence of Arab architecture is obvious—Pisa was a city of seafaring merchants.

Romanesque **sculpture** was fluid but still far from naturalistic. Often wonderfully childlike in its narrative simplicity, the work frequently mixes biblical scenes with the myths and motifs of local pagan traditions. The 48 relief panels on the bronze doors of the **Basilica di San Zeno Maggiore** in Verona (p. 291) are among the greatest remaining examples of Romanesque sculpture in Italy.

As the appeal of the Romanesque and Byzantine faded, the **Gothic** style flourished from the 13th to the 15th centuries. In architecture, Gothic was characterized by flying buttresses, pointed arches, and delicate stained-glass windows. These engineering developments freed architecture from the heavy, thick walls of the Romanesque and allowed ceilings to soar, walls to thin, and windows to proliferate.

Although the Gothic age continued to be religious, many secular buildings also arose, including an array of palaces designed to show off the prestige and wealth of various ruling dynasties. Siena's civic **Palazzo Pubblico** (p. 208) and many of the great buildings of **Venice** (see chapter 8) date from this period. **San Gimignano** (p. 213), in Tuscany, has a remarkably preserved Gothic center.

Painters such as **Cimabue** (1251–1302) and **Giotto** (1266–1337), in Florence, **Pietro Cavallini** (1259–ca. 1330) in Rome, and **Duccio di Buoninsegna** (ca. 1255–1319) in Siena began to lift art from Byzantine rigidity and set it on the road to realism. Giotto's finest work is his fresco cycle at Padua's **Cappella degli Scrovegni** (p. 289); he was the true harbinger of the oncoming Renaissance, which would forever change art and architecture. Duccio's 1311 "Maestà," now in Siena's **Museo dell'Opera del Duomo** (p. 209), influenced Sienese painters for generations. Ambrogio Lorenzetti painted the greatest civic frescoes of the Middle Ages—his "Allegories of Good and Bad Government" in Siena's **Palazzo Pubblico** (p. 208)—before he succumbed to the Black Death, along with almost every great Sienese artist of the time.

The medieval period also saw the birth of literature in the Italian language, which itself was a written version of the **Tuscan dialect,** primarily because the great writers of the age were all Tuscans. Florentine **Dante Alighieri** wrote his "Divine Comedy" in the 1310s. Boccaccio's "Decameron"—kind of a Florentine "Canterbury Tales"—appeared in the 1350s.

Renaissance & Baroque Italy: The 1400s to the 1700s

The story of Italy from the dawn of the Renaissance in the early 15th century to the Age of Enlightenment in the 17th and 18th centuries is as fascinating and complicated as that of the rise and fall of the Roman Empire.

During this period, **Rome** underwent major physical changes. The old centers of culture reverted to pastures and fields, and great churches and palaces were built using the stones of Ancient Rome. This construction boom did more damage to the temples of the Caesars than any barbarian sack had done. Rare marbles were stripped from the Imperial-era baths and used as altarpieces or sent to limekilns. So enthusiastic was the papal destruction of Imperial Rome that it's a miracle anything is left.

This era is best remembered because of its art, and around 1400 the most significant power in Italy was the city where the Renaissance began: **Florence** (see chapter 6). Slowly but surely, the **Medici** family rose to become the most powerful of the city's ruling oligarchy, gradually usurping the powers of the guilds and republicans. They reformed law and commerce, expanded the city's power by taking control of neighbors such as **Pisa,** and also sparked a "renaissance," a rebirth, in painting, sculpture, and architecture. Christopher Hibbert's "The Rise and Fall of the House of Medici" (2001) is the most readable historical account of the era.

Under the patronage of the Medici (as well as other powerful Florentine families), innovative young painters and sculptors pursued a greater degree of expressiveness and naturalism. **Donatello** (1386–1466) cast the first free-standing nude since antiquity (a bronze now in Florence's **Museo Nazionale del Bargello, p.** 177). **Lorenzo Ghiberti** (1378–1455) labored for 50 years on two sets of doors on Florence's **Baptistery** (p. 166), the most famous of which were dubbed the "Gates of Paradise." **Masaccio** (1401–28) produced the first painting that realistically portrayed linear perspective, on the nave wall of **Santa Maria Novella** (p. 186).

Next followed the brief period that's become known as the **High Renaissance:** The epitome of the Renaissance man, Florentine **Leonardo da Vinci** (1452–1519), painted his "Last Supper," in Milan, and an "Annunciation" (1481), now hanging in Florence's **Uffizi** (p. 173) alongside countless Renaissance masterpieces from such great painters as Paolo Uccello, Sandro Botticelli, Piero della Francesca, and others. **Raphael** (1483–1520) produced a sublime body of work in his 37 short years of life.

Skilled in sculpture, painting, and architecture, **Michelangelo** (1475–1564) and his career marked the apogee of the Renaissance. His giant "David" at the **Galleria dell'Accademia** (p. 188) in Florence is the world's most famous statue, and the **Sistine Chapel** frescoes have lured millions to the **Vatican Museums** (p. 76) in Rome.

The father of the Venetian High Renaissance was **Titian** (1485–1576); known for his mastery of color and tonality, he was the true heir to Venetian painters **Gentile Bellini** (1429–1507), **Giorgione** (1477–1510), and **Vittore Carpaccio** (1465–1525). Many of their masterpieces can be seen throughout **Venice** (see chapter 8).

As in painting, Renaissance architectural rules stressed proportion, order, classical inspiration, and mathematical precision. In the early 1400s, **Filippo Brunelleschi** (1377–1446) grasped the concept of "perspective" and provided artists with ground rules for creating the illusion of three dimensions on a flat surface. Ross King's "Brunelleschi's Dome" (2000) tells the story of his greatest achievement, the crowning of Florence's cathedral with its iconic ochre dome. **Michelangelo** (1475–1564) took up architecture late in life, designing the Laurentian Library (1524) and New Sacristy (1524–34) at Florence's **Basilica di San Lorenzo** (p. 185). He moved south (just as art's center of gravity did) to complete his crowning glory, the soaring dome of Rome's **St. Peter's Basilica** (p. 78).

The third great Renaissance architect—possibly the most influential of them all—was **Andrea Palladio** (1508–80), who worked in a classical mode of columns, porticoes, pediments, and other ancient temple–inspired features. His masterpieces include fine churches in Venice.

In time, the High Renaissance stagnated, paving the way for the **baroque.** Stuccoes, sculptures, and paintings were carefully designed to complement each other—and the space itself—to create a unified whole. Its spiritual home was Rome, and its towering figure was **Gian Lorenzo Bernini** (1598–1680), the greatest baroque sculptor, a fantastic architect, and no mean painter. Among many fine sculptures, you'll find his best in Rome's **Galleria Borghese** (p. 108) and **Santa Maria della Vittoria** (p. 113).

RENAISSANCE reading

Whole libraries have been written on the Renaissance. The most accessible introductions include Peter and Linda Murray's "The Art of the Renaissance" (1963), Michael Levey's "Early Renaissance" (1967), and Evelyn Welch's "Art in Renaissance Italy 1350–1500" (2000)—it's certainly worth acquainting yourself with some of the themes and styles before you visit. Giorgio Vasari's "Lives of the Artists" was first published in 1550, and it remains the definitive work on the Renaissance artists, written by one who knew some of them personally. It's also surprisingly readable. On the buildings, Peter Murray's "The Architecture of the Italian Renaissance" (1969) is a good read. In "The Stones of Florence" (1956), Mary McCarthy mixes architectural insight with no-holds-barred opinions.

In **music**, most famous of the baroque composers is Venetian **Antonio Vivaldi** (1678–1741), whose "Four Seasons" is among the most regularly performed classical compositions of all time. In painting, the baroque often mixed a kind of super-realism based on using peasants as models and an exaggerated use of light and dark—a technique called *chiaroscuro*—with compositional complexity and explosions of fury, movement, color, and figures. The period produced many fine artists, most notably **Caravaggio** (1571–1610). Among his masterpieces are a "St. Matthew" (1599) cycle in Rome's **San Luigi dei Francesi** (p. 100). The baroque also had an outstanding female painter in **Artemisia Gentileschi** (1593–1652): Check out her brutal "Judith Slaying Holofernes" (1620) in Florence's **Uffizi** (p. 173).

Frothy, ornate, and chaotic, **rococo** art was the baroque gone awry—and has few serious proponents in Italy. **Giambattista Tiepolo** (1696–1770) was arguably the best of Italy's rococo painters, and specialized in ceiling frescoes and canvases with cloud-filled heavens of light. He worked extensively in and around Venice. For rococo building—more a decorative than an architectural movement—look no further than Rome's **Spanish Steps** (p. 106) or the **Trevi Fountain** (p. 107).

At Last, a United Italy: The 1800s

By the 1800s, the glories of the Renaissance were a fading memory. From Turin to Naples, chunks of Italy had changed hands many, many times—between the Austrians, the Spanish, and the French; among autocratic thugs and (relatively) enlightened princes; between the noble and the merchant classes. The 19th century witnessed the final collapse of many of the Renaissance city-states. The last of the Medici, Gian Gastone, had died in 1737, leaving Tuscany in the hands of Lorraine and Habsburg princes. French emperor **Napoleon** brought an end to a millennium of Republic in **Venice** in 1797, and installed puppet or client rulers across the Italian peninsula. During the **Congress of Vienna** (1814–15), which followed Napoleon's defeat by an alliance of the British, Prussians, and Dutch, Italy was once again divided.

The A-List of Italian Novels Available in English

- Alessandro Manzoni, "The Betrothed" (1827)
- Alberto Moravia, "The Conformist" (1951)
- Giuseppe Tomasi di Lampedusa, "The Leopard" (1958)
- Elsa Morante, "History: A Novel" (1974)
- Italo Calvino, "If on a Winter's Night a Traveler" (1979)
- Umberto Eco, "Foucault's Pendulum" (1988)
- Niccolo Ammaniti, "I'm Not Scared" (2001)

Political unrest became a part of Italian life, some of it spurred by the industrialization of the north and some by the encouragement of insurrectionaries like **Giuseppe Mazzini** (1805–72). Europe's year of revolutions, **1848,** rocked Italy, too, with violent risings in Lombardy and Sicily. After decades of political machinations and intrigue, and thanks to the efforts of statesman **Camillo Cavour** (1810–61) and rebel general **Giuseppe Garibaldi** (1807–82), the Kingdom of Italy was proclaimed in 1861 and **Victor Emmanuel (Vittorio Emanuele) II** of Savoy became Italy's first monarch. The kingdom's first capital was **Turin** (1861–65), seat of the victorious Piedmontese, followed by **Florence** (1865–71).

The establishment of the kingdom, however, didn't signal a complete unification of Italy, because Latium (including Rome) was still under papal control and Venetia was held by Austria. This was partially resolved in 1866, when Venetia joined the rest of Italy after the **Seven Weeks' War** between Austria and Prussia. In 1871, Rome became the capital, after the city was retaken on September 20, 1870. Present-day **Via XX Settembre** is the very street up which patriots advanced after breaching the city gates. The **Risorgimento—** the "resurgence," Italian unification—was complete.

Political heights in Italy seemed to correspond to creative depths in art and architecture. Among the more notable practitioners was Venetian **Antonio Canova** (1757–1822), Italy's major neoclassical sculptor, who became notorious for painting both Napoleon and his sister Pauline as nudes. His best work is in Rome's **Galleria Borghese** (p. 108). Tuscany also bred a late-19th-century precursor to French Impressionism, the **Macchiaioli** movement; see their works in the "modern art" galleries at Florence's **Palazzo Pitti** (p. 193).

If art was hitting an all-time low, **music** was experiencing its Italian golden age. And it's bel canto **opera** for which the 19th century will largely be remembered. **Gioachino Rossini** (1792–1868) was born in Pesaro, in the Marches, and found success with his 1816 "The Barber of Seville." The fame of **Gaetano Donizetti** (1797–1848), a prolific native of Bergamo, was assured when his "Anna Bolena" premiered in 1830. Both were perhaps overshadowed by **Giuseppe Verdi** (1813–1901), whose works such as "Rigoletto" and "La Traviata" have become some of the most whistled on the planet.

The 20th Century: Two World Wars & One Duce

In 1915, Italy entered **World War I** on the side of the Allies, joining Britain, Russia, and France to help defeat Germany and the traditional enemy to the north, now the Austro-Hungarian Empire, and so to "reclaim" Trentino and Trieste: Mark Thompson's "The White War" (2008) tells the sorry tale of Italy's catastrophic campaign. In the aftermath of war and carnage, Italians further suffered with rising unemployment and horrendous inflation. On October 28, 1922, **Benito Mussolini,** who had started his Fascist Party in 1919, knew the country was ripe for change. He gathered 30,000 Black Shirts for his **March on Rome.** Inflation was soaring and workers had just called a general strike, so rather than recognizing a state under siege, **King Victor Emmanuel III** (1900–46) proclaimed Mussolini as the new leader. In 1929, Il Duce—a moniker Mussolini began using from 1925—defined the divisions between the Italian government and the pope by signing the Lateran Treaty, which granted political, territorial, and fiscal autonomy to the microstate of **Vatican City.** During the Spanish Civil War (1936–39), Mussolini's support of Franco's Fascists, who had staged a coup against the elected government of Spain, helped seal the Axis alliance between Italy and Nazi Germany. Italy was inexorably and disastrously sucked into **World War II.**

Deeply unpleasant though their politics were, the Fascist regime did sponsor some remarkable **architecture.** It's at its best in Rome's planned satellite community, **EUR.** In a city famed for classical works, Florence's **Santa Maria Novella station** (1934) is also a masterpiece of modernism. The station has a plaque commemorating Jews who were sent from the terminus to their deaths in Nazi Germany. The era's towering figure in music was **Giacomo Puccini** (1858–1924); such operas as "Tosca" (1900) and "Madama Butterfly" (1904) still pack houses worldwide.

After defeat in World War II, Italy voted for the establishment of the First Republic—overwhelmingly so in northern and central Italy, which helped to counterbalance a southern majority in favor of keeping the monarchy. Italy quickly succeeded in rebuilding its economy, in part because of U.S. aid under the **Marshall Plan** (1948–52). By the 1960s, as a member of the European Economic Community (founded by the **Treaty of Rome** in 1957), Italy had become one of the world's leading industrialized nations, and prominent in the manufacture of automobiles and office equipment. Fiat (from Turin), Ferrari (from Emilia-Romagna), and Olivetti (from northern Piedmont) were known around the world.

The country continued to be plagued by economic inequality between the prosperous industrial north and a depressed south, and during the late 1970s and early 1980s, it was rocked by domestic terrorism: These were the so-called **Anni di Piombo (Years of Lead),** during which extremists of the left and right bombed and assassinated with impunity. Conspiracy theories became the Italian staple diet; everyone from the state to shady Masonic lodges to the CIA was accused of involvement in what became in effect an undeclared civil war. The most notorious incident of the Anni di Piombo was the kidnap and murder of Prime Minister **Aldo Moro** in 1978. You'll find a succinct account of these murky years in Tobias Jones's "The Dark Heart of Italy" (2003).

The postwar Italian **film industry** became respected for its innovative directors. **Federico Fellini** (1920–93) burst onto the scene with his highly individual style, beginning with "La Strada" (1954) and going on to such classics as "The City of Women" (1980). His "La Dolce Vita" (1961) defined an era in Rome.

WHEN TO GO

The best months for traveling in Italy are from **April to June** and **mid-September to October**—temperatures are usually comfortable, rural colors are richer, and crowds aren't too intense (except around Easter). From **July through early September** the country's holiday spots teem with visitors. **Easter, May,** and **June** usually see the highest hotel prices in Rome and Florence.

August is the worst month in many places: Not only does it get uncomfortably hot, muggy, and crowded, but seemingly the entire country goes on vacation, at least around August 15—and many Italians take off the entire month. Many family-run hotels, restaurants, and shops are closed (except at the spas, beaches, and islands, where most Italians head). Paradoxically, Florence in August can seem empty of locals, and hotels there (and in Rome) are sometimes heavily discounted. Just be aware that fashionable restaurants and nightspots are usually closed for the whole month.

From **late October to Easter,** many attractions operate on shorter (sometimes *much* shorter) winter hours, and some hotels are closed for renovation or redecoration, though that is less likely if you are visiting cities. Many family-run restaurants take a week or two off sometime between **November and February;** spa and beach destinations become padlocked ghost towns.

Weather

It's warm all over Italy in summer; it can be very hot in the south, and almost anywhere inland—landlocked cities on the northern plains and in Tuscany can feel stifling during a July or August hot spell. The higher temperatures (measured in Italy in degrees Celsius) usually begin everywhere in May, often lasting until sometime in October. Winters in the north of Italy are cold, with rain and snow, and a biting wind whistles over the mountains into Venice. In Rome and the south the weather is warm (or at least, warm-ish) all year, averaging 10°C (50°F) in winter. The rainiest months almost everywhere are October and November.

Italy's Average Daily High Temperature & Monthly Rainfall

		JAN	FEB	MAR	APR	MAY	JUNE	JULY	AUG	SEPT	OCT	NOV	DEC
ROME	Temp. (°F)	55	56	59	63	71	77	83	83	79	71	62	57
	Temp. (°C)	12	13	15	17	21	25	28	28	26	21	16	13
	Rainfall (in.)	3.2	2.8	2.7	2.6	2	1.3	.6	1	2.7	4.5	4.4	3.8
FLORENCE	Temp. (°F)	49	53	60	68	75	84	89	88	81	69	58	50
	Temp. (°C)	9	11	15	20	23	28	31	31	27	20	14	10
	Rainfall (in.)	1.9	2.1	2.7	2.9	3	2.7	1.5	1.9	3.3	4	3.9	2.8
VENICE	Temp. (°F)	42	47	54	61	70	77	81	81	75	65	53	44
	Temp. (°C)	6	8	12	16	21	25	27	27	24	18	11	7
	Rainfall (in.)	2.3	2.1	2.2	2.5	2.7	3	2.5	3.3	2.6	2.7	3.4	2.1

Public Holidays

Offices, government buildings (though not usually tourist offices), and shops in Italy are generally closed on: January 1 (*Capodanno,* or New Year); January 6 (*La Befana,* or Epiphany); Easter Sunday (*Pasqua); Easter Monday (*Pasquetta*); April 25 (Liberation Day); May 1 (*Festa del Lavoro,* or Labor Day); June 2 (*Festa della Repubblica,* or Republic Day); August 15 (*Ferragosto,* or the Assumption of the Virgin); November 1 (All Saints' Day); December 8 (*L'Immacolata,* or the Immaculate Conception); December 25 (*Natale,* Christmas Day); and December 26 (*Santo Stefano,* or St. Stephen's Day). You'll often find businesses closed for the annual daylong celebration dedicated to the local saint (for example, on January 31 in San Gimignano, Tuscany).

Italy Calendar of Events

FEBRUARY

Carnevale, Venice. At this riotous time, theatrical presentations and masked balls take place throughout Venice and on the islands in the lagoon. The balls are by invitation only (except the Doge's Ball), but the street events and fireworks are open to everyone. www.carnevale.venezia.it. The week before Ash Wednesday, the beginning of Lent.

MARCH

Festa di San Giuseppe, the Trionfale Quarter, north of the Vatican, Rome. The heavily decorated statue of the saint is brought out at a fair with food stalls, concerts, and sporting events. Usually March 19.

APRIL

Holy Week, nationwide. Processions and ceremonies—some from pagan days, some from the Middle Ages—are staged. The most notable procession is led by the pope, passing the Colosseum and the Roman Forum; a torch-lit parade caps the observance. Beginning 4 days before Easter Sunday.

Easter Sunday (Pasqua), Piazza San Pietro, Rome. In an event broadcast around the world, the pope gives his blessing from the balcony of St. Peter's.

Scoppio del Carro (Explosion of the Cart), Florence. A cart laden with flowers and fireworks is drawn by three white oxen to the Duomo, where at the noon Mass a mechanical dove detonates it from the altar. Easter Sunday.

MAY

Maggio Musicale Fiorentino (Florentine Musical May), Florence. Italy's oldest and most prestigious music festival emphasizes music from the 14th to the 20th centuries, but also presents ballet and opera. www.maggiofiorentino.it. Late April to end of June.

Concorso Ippico Internazionale (International Horse Show), Piazza di Siena, Rome. Top-flight international show jumping at the Villa Borghese. www.piazzadisiena.org. Late May.

JUNE

Festa di San Ranieri, Pisa, Tuscany. The city honors its patron saint with candlelit parades, followed the next day by eight-rower teams competing in 16th-century costumes. June 16 and 17.

Calcio Storico (Historic Football), Florence. A revival of a raucous 15th-century form of football, pitting four teams in medieval costumes against one another. The matches usually culminate on June 24, feast day of St. John the Baptist. Late June.

Gioco del Ponte, Pisa, Tuscany. Teams in Renaissance costume take part in a long-contested push-of-war on the Ponte di Mezzo, which spans the Arno. www.giocodelpontedipisa.it. Last Sunday in June.

La Biennale di Venezia (International Exposition of Contemporary Art), Venice. One of the most famous regular art events in the world takes place during alternate odd-numbered years. www.labiennale.org. June to November.

JULY

Il Palio, Piazza del Campo, Siena, Tuscany. Palio fever grips this Tuscan hill town for a wild and exciting horse race from the Middle Ages. Pageantry, costumes, and the celebrations of the victorious *contrada* (sort of a neighborhood social club) mark the spectacle. It's a "no rules" event: Even a horse without a rider can win the race. July 2 and August 16.

Festa del Redentore (Feast of the Redeemer), Venice. This festival marks the lifting of the plague in 1576, with fireworks, pilgrimages, and boating. www.redentorevenezia.it. Third Saturday and Sunday in July.

AUGUST

Venice International Film Festival, Venice. Ranking after Cannes, this festival brings together stars, directors, producers, and filmmakers from all over the world to the Palazzo del Cinema on the Lido. www.labiennale.org. Late August to early September.

SEPTEMBER

Regata Storica, Grand Canal, Venice. A maritime spectacular: Many gondolas participate in the canal procession, although gondolas don't race in the regatta itself. www.regatastoricavenezia.it. First Sunday in September.

DECEMBER

Christmas Blessing of the Pope, Piazza di San Pietro, Rome. Delivered at noon from the balcony of St. Peter's Basilica, the pope's words are broadcast to the faithful around the globe. December 25.

ROME

Once it ruled the Western World, and even the partial, scattered ruins of that awesome empire are today among the most overpowering sights on earth. To walk the Roman Forum, to view the Colosseum, the Pantheon, and the Appian Way—these are among the most memorable, instructive, and humbling experiences in all of travel.

Equally thrilling are the sights of Christian Rome, which speak to the long and complex domination by this city of one of the world's major religions. Yet it's important to remember that Rome is not just a place of the past, but one that lives and breathes and buzzes with Vespas in the here and now.

As a visitor to Rome, you will be constantly reminded of this extraordinary history. Take the time to get away from the tourist masses to explore the intimate piazzas and lesser basilicas in the backstreets of Trastevere and the *centro storico*. Indulge in gastronomic pursuits and stuff your days with cappuccino, pizza, wine, and gelato. Have a picnic in Villa Borghese, take a vigorous walk along the Gianicolo, or nap in the grass against a fallen granite column at the Baths of Caracalla. Rome is so compact that without even planning too much, you'll end up enjoying both its monuments and its simpler pleasures.

Walk the streets of Rome, and the city will be yours.

ESSENTIALS

Getting There

BY PLANE   Most flights arrive at Rome's **Leonardo da Vinci International Airport** (www.adr.it; © **06-65951**), popularly known as **Fiumicino,** 30km (19 miles) from the city center. (If you're flying from other European cities, you might land at Ciampino Airport, discussed below.) There is a tourist information office at the airport's Terminal B, International arrivals, open daily from 9am to 6pm.

A *cambio* (money exchange) operates daily from 7am to 11pm, offering good rates, and there are ATMs in the airport.

There's a **train station** in the airport. To get into the city, follow the signs marked TRENI for the 31-minute shuttle ride to Rome's main station, **Stazione Termini.** The shuttle (the Leonardo Express) runs from 5:52am to 11:36pm, every 30 minutes, for 14€ one-way.

4

On the way, you'll pass a machine dispensing tickets, or you can buy them in person near the tracks if you do not have change or small bills on you. *Tip:* When you arrive at Termini, get out of the train quickly and grab a baggage cart: It's a long schlep from the track to the exit or to other train connections, and baggage carts can be scarce.

A **taxi** from da Vinci airport to the city costs a flat-rate 48€ for the 1-hour trip, depending on traffic (hotels tend to charge 50€–60€ for a pick-up service). The expense might be worth it if you have a lot of luggage. Note that the flat rate is applicable from the airport to central Rome and vice versa, but only if your central Rome location is inside the Aurelian Walls (most hotels are). Otherwise, standard metered rates apply, which can be 75€ or higher.

If you arrive instead at **Ciampino Airport** (www.adr.it/ciampino; ✆ 06-65951), you can take a Terravision bus (www.terravision.eu; ✆ 06-4880086) to Stazione Termini. This takes about 45 minutes and costs 4€. A **taxi** from here to Rome costs 30€, a flat rate that applies as long as you're going to a destination within the old Aurelian Walls. Otherwise, you'll pay the metered fare, but the trip is shorter (about 40 minutes).

BY TRAIN OR BUS   Trains and buses (including trains from the airport) arrive in the center of old Rome at **Stazione Termini,** Piazza dei Cinquecento. This is the train, bus, and subway transportation hub for all of Rome; it is surrounded by many hotels, especially budget ones.

If you're taking the **Metropolitana** (subway), follow the illuminated red-and-white M signs. To catch a bus, go straight through the outer hall and enter the sprawling bus lot of **Piazza dei Cinquecento.** You will also find a line of **taxis** parked out front.

The station is filled with services. There is an exchange window close to the end of platform 14 where you can change money, and an ATM at the end of platform 24. **Informazioni Ferroviarie** (in the outer hall) dispenses information on rail travel to other parts of Italy. There are also a **tourist information booth,** baggage services, newsstands, and snack bars.

BY CAR   From the north, the main access route is the **Autostrada A1.** Once called "Motorway of the Sun," the highway links Milan with Naples via Bologna, Florence, and Rome. At 754km (469 miles), it is the longest Italian autostrada and is the "spinal cord" of Italy's road network. All the autostrade join with the **Grande Raccordo Anulare,** a ring road encircling Rome, channeling traffic into the congested city. *Tip:* Long before you reach this road, you should study a map carefully to see what part of Rome you plan to enter and mark your route accordingly. Route markings along the ring road tend to be confusing.

Warning: Return your rental car immediately, or at least get yourself to a hotel, park your car, and leave it there until you leave Rome. Think twice before driving in Rome—the traffic can be nightmarish. In any case, most of central Rome is a ZTL (**Zona Traffico Limitato),** off limits for nonresidents (hotels can issue temporary permits), and rigorously enforced by cameras. You will almost certainly be fined.

If you plan to do serious sightseeing in Rome (and why else would you be here?), the **Roma Pass** (www.romapass.it) is definitely worth considering. For 36€, valid for 3 days, you get free entry to the first two museums or archaeological sites you visit; free admission to Museo della Repubblica Romana, Museo Bilotti, Museo Canonica, Museo delle Mura, Museo Napoleonico, and Villa di Massenzio; discounted entry to all other museums and sites; free use of the city's public transportation network (bus, Metro, and railway lines; airport transfers not included); express entry to the Colosseum; a free map; and free access to a special smartphone app. There's also a 48-hour version for 28€ that grants free entry to the first museum or archaeological site you visit, plus the same benefits as the 3-day version for 2 days. Note that the **Vatican Museums** are not part of either pass plan. Buy the passes online and pick them up at one of the Tourist Information Points (below).

An alternative is the **Archaeologia Card,** which for 25€ gives free admission to 9 sites for up to 7 days: the Colosseum, Palatine Museum and Roman Forum, Palazzo Massimo alle Terme, Palazzo Altemps, Crypta Balbi, Baths of Diocletian, Cecilia Metella, Villa dei Quintili, and Baths of Caracalla. These cards are sold at any of the above monuments' ticket booths. Transportation is not included in the Archaeologia Card, so if you plan to do a lot of sightseeing, the Roma Pass is a much better value.

Finally, if you are a return visitor or have an interest in Rome's well-stocked niche archaeological museums, the **Museo Nazionale Romano** combo ticket is the one to buy; it includes entry to the Palazzo Massimo alle Terme, Palazzo Altemps, Crypta Balbi, and Baths of Diocletian for just 7€ (plus 3€ when special exhibitions are on). You can buy online at www.coopculture.it, but it's just as easy to buy in the first museum of the four you enter. It is valid for 3 days. Note that the first Sunday of each month all Museo Nazionale Romano sites are free of charge.

Visitor Information

Information, Internet, maps, and the Roma Pass (see box above) are available at "Tourist Information Points" maintained by **Roma Capitale** (www.turismo roma.it) at various sites around the city. They're staffed daily from 9:30am to 7pm, except the one at Termini (daily 8am–7:30pm), located in "Centro Diagnostico" hall (Building F) next to platform 24; there's often a long line at this one, so if you're staying near other offices listed here, skip Termini: Lungotevere Vaticano (Piazza Pia) near the Castel Sant'Angelo; Via Nazionale 183, near the Palazzo delle Esposizioni; on Piazza delle Cinque Lune, near Piazza Navona; on Via dei Fori Imperiali (for the Forum); at Via Santa Maria del Pianto 1, in the old Jewish Quarter; and on Via Marco Minghetti, near Via del Corso. All phone calls for Roma Capitale are directed through a centralized number: ℰ **06-060608** (www.060608.it). Call daily between 9am and 9pm.

Local travel agency **Enjoy Rome,** Via Marghera 8a, 3 blocks north of Termini (www.enjoyrome.com; ℰ **06-4451843**), is also helpful, dispensing

Rome at a Glance

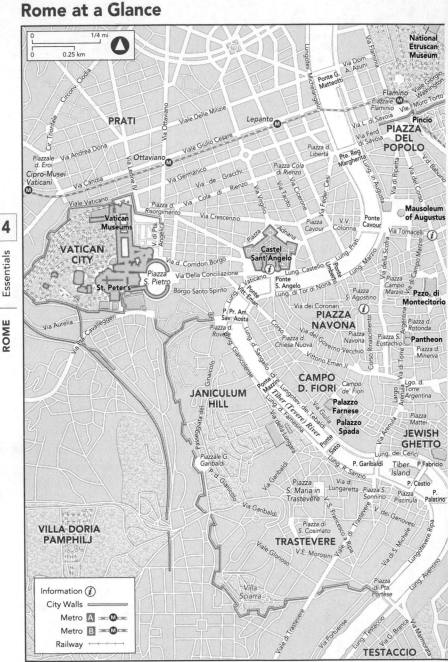

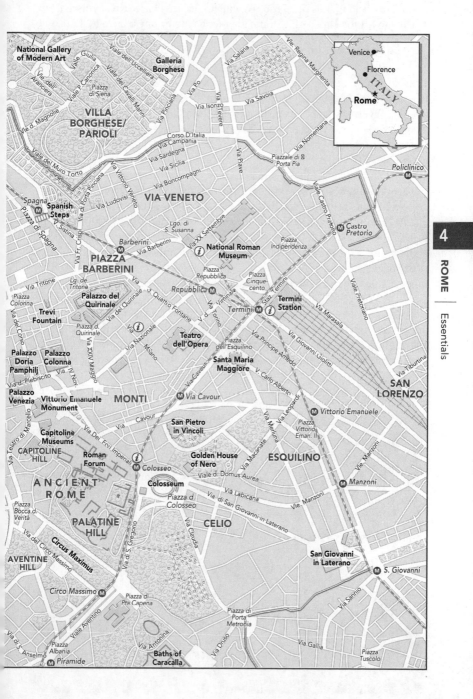

National Gallery
of Modern Art

Galleria
Borghese

VILLA
BORGHESE/
PARIOLI

Via Giulia
Viale dell'Uccelliera
Vie. delli
Aranciera
Viale P. Canonica
Piazza
di Siena
Viale dei Cavalli Marini
Via Pinciana
Via Po
Vle. Regina Margherita
Via Salaria
Via Savoia
Via Isonzo
Via Tevere
Via d. Magnolie
Viale del Muro Torto
Corso D'Italia
Via Campania
Via Sardegna
Via Sicilia
Via Boncompagni
Via Piave
Via Nomentana
Piazzale di ⊠
Porta Pia

Policlinico Ⓜ

Spagna
Spanish
Steps
Piazza
di Spagna
Via di Porta Pinciana
Via Vittorio Veneto
Via Ludovisi
VIA VENETO
Viale Castro Pretorio
Castro
Pretorio

V. Sistina
Via Fr. Crispi
Barberini
Via Barberini
Lgo. di
S. Susanna
Via XX Settembre
Piazza
Indipendenza

PIAZZA
BARBERINI
ⓘ National Roman
Museum

Via Tritone
Lg. de
Tritone
Via
Piazza
Repubblica
Piazza
Cinque-
cento
Piazza
Colonna
Palazzo del
Quirinale
Via del Quirinale
V. Quattro Fontane
Repubblica Ⓜ
Piazza del
Quirinale
Trevi
Fountain
Via d. Torno
V. d. Torno
Termini Ⓜ
Termini
Station
Via Marasala
Viale Pretoriano

Via del Corso
Via Nazionale
Via Milano
Teatro
dell'Opera
Piazza
dell'Esquilino
Via Principe Amedeo
Via Giovanni Giolitti

Palazzo
Doria
Pamphilj
Palazzo
Colonna
Via IV Nov.
Santa Maria
Maggiore
V. Carlo Alberto
SAN
LORENZO

Palazzo
Venezia
Via d. Plebiscito
Vittorio Emanuele
Monument
MONTI
Via Cavour
Ⓜ Via Cavour
Piazza
Vittorio
Eman. II.
Ⓜ Vittorio Emanuele
Via Merulana
Via Leopardi
Vle. Manzoni

Capitoline
Museums
Via del Teatro di Marcello
Via Del Fori Imperiali
San Pietro
in Vincoli
ESQUILINO

CAPITOLINE
HILL
Roman
Forum
ⓘ
Ⓜ Colosseo
Golden House
of Nero
Via di San Giovanni in Laterano
Ⓜ Manzoni

ANCIENT
ROME
Colosseum
Viale d. Domus Aurea
Via Labicana

Piazza
Bocca d.
Verità
Piazza d.
Colosseo
CELIO

PALATINE
HILL
Via di S. Gregorio
Via Claudia
San Giovanni
in Laterano
Ⓜ S. Giovanni

AVENTINE
HILL
Via del Circo Massimo
Circus Maximus

Circo Massimo Ⓜ
Viale Aventino
Piazza di
Pta Capena
Piazza di
Porta
Metronia
Via Sannio

Via di S. Anselmo
Piazza
Albania
Ⓜ Piramide
Via Antonina
Via Druso
Via Gallia
Piazza
Tuscolo

Baths of
Caracalla

Venice ●
Florence ●
ITALY
Rome ★

information and finding hotel rooms, with no service charge (in anything from a hostel to a three-star hotel). Hours are Monday to Friday 9am to 5:30pm and Saturday 8:30am to 2pm.

City Layout

The bulk of what you'll want to visit—ancient, Renaissance, and baroque Rome (as well as the train station)—lies on the east side of the **Tiber River (Fiume Tevere),** which meanders through town. However, several important landmarks are on the other side: **St. Peter's Basilica** and the **Vatican,** the **Castel Sant'Angelo,** and the colorful **Trastevere** neighborhood. With the exception of those last sights, I think it's fair to say that Rome has the most compact and walkable city center in Europe.

That doesn't mean you won't get lost from time to time (most newcomers do). Arm yourself with a detailed street map of Rome (or a smartphone with a hefty data plan; see p. 302). Most hotels also hand out a pretty good version of a city map. And know that street addresses in Rome can be frustrating. Numbers usually run consecutively, with odd numbers on one side of the street and evens on the other; however, in the old districts, the numbers sometimes run up one side and then run back in the opposite direction on the other side. Therefore, #50 could be opposite #308.

Finally, remember that much of the historic core of Rome does not fall under easy or distinct neighborhood classifications. Instead, most people's frame of reference, when describing a location within the centro, is the name of the nearest large monument or square, like St. Peter's or Piazza di Spagna.

St. Peter's Basilica.

The Neighborhoods in Brief

Where should you stay and where are the major attractions? Read on.

Vatican City & the Prati Although in practice it is just another part of Rome, **Vatican City** is technically a sovereign state. The **Vatican Museums, St. Peter's,** and the **Vatican Gardens** take up most of the land area, and the popes have lived here for 6 centuries. The neighborhood north of the Vatican—called "Borgo Pio"—contains some good hotels (and several bad ones), but it is removed from the more happening scene of ancient and Renaissance Rome, and getting to and from those areas can be time-consuming. Borgo Pio is also rather dull at night and contains few, if any, of Rome's finest restaurants. The white-collar **Prati** district, a middle-class suburb just east of the Vatican, is possibly a better choice, thanks to its smattering of affordable hotels, its shopping streets, and the fact that it boasts some excellent places to eat.

Centro Storico & the Pantheon One of the most desirable (and busiest) areas of Rome, the **Centro Storico** ("Historic Center") is a maze of narrow streets and cobbled alleys dating from the Middle Ages, and filled with churches and palaces built during the Renaissance and baroque eras. The only way to explore it is on foot. Its heart is **Piazza Navona,** built over Emperor Domitian's stadium and bustling with sidewalk cafes, *palazzi,* street artists, musicians, and pickpockets.

Rivaling Piazza Navona—in general activity, the cafe scene, and the nightlife—is the area around the **Pantheon,** which remains from ancient Roman times and is surrounded by a district built much later. South of Corso Vittorio Emanuele and centered on **Piazza Farnese** and the square of **Campo de' Fiori,** many buildings in this area were constructed in Renaissance times as private homes. West of Via Arenula lies one of the city's most intriguing districts, the old Jewish **Ghetto,** where the increasingly fashionable dining options far outnumber the hotels.

Ancient Rome, Monti & Celio Although no longer the heart of the city, this is where Rome began, with the **Colosseum, Palatine Hill, Roman Forum, Imperial Forums,** and **Circus Maximus.** This area offers only a few hotels—most of them inexpensive to moderate in price—and not a lot of great restaurants. Many restaurant owners have their eyes on the cash register and the tour-bus crowd, whose passengers are often herded in and out of these restaurants so fast that they don't know whether the food is any good. Just beyond the Circus Maximus is the **Aventine Hill,** south of the Palatine and close to the Tiber, now a leafy and rather posh residential quarter—with great city views. You will get much more of a neighborhood feel if you stay in **Monti** (Rome's oldest rione, or quarter) or **Celio,** respectively located north and south of the Colosseum. Both also have good dining, aimed at locals as well as visitors, and Monti, especially, has plenty of life from aperitivo o'clock and into the wee hours of the night.

Tridente & the Spanish Steps The northern part of Rome's center is sometimes known as the Tridente on account of the trident shape of the roads leading down from the apex of **Piazza del Popolo**—Via di Ripetta, Via del Corso, and Via del Babuino. The star here is unquestionably **Piazza di Spagna,** which attracts Romans and tourists alike to idly sit on its celebrated **Spanish Steps.** Some of Rome's most upscale shopping streets fan out from here, including **Via Condotti.** In fact, this is the most upscale part of Rome, full of expensive hotels, designer boutiques, and chic restaurants.

Via Veneto & Piazza Barberini In the 1950s and early 1960s, **Via Veneto** was the swinging place to be, as celebrities of the Dolce Vita paraded along the tree-lined boulevard to the delight of the paparazzi. The street is still the site of luxury hotels, cafes, and restaurants, although it's no longer such a happening spot and the restaurants are mostly overpriced and overcrowded tourist traps.

To the south, Via Veneto comes to an end at **Piazza Barberini,** and the magnificent **Palazzo Barberini,** begun in 1623 by Carlo Maderno and later completed by Bernini and Borromini.

Villa Borghese & Parioli We would call **Parioli** an area for connoisseurs, attracting those who shun the Spanish Steps and the overly commercialized Via Veneto. It is, in short, Rome's most elegant residential section, a setting for some of the city's finest restaurants, hotels, museums, and public parks. Geographically, Parioli is in fact framed by the green spaces of the **Villa Borghese** to the south and the **Villa Glori** and **Villa Ada** to the north. It lies adjacent to Prati but across the Tiber to the east; it's considered one of the safest districts in the city. All that being said, Parioli is not exactly central, so it can be a hassle as a base if you're dependent on public transportation.

Around Stazione Termini The main train station, **Stazione Termini,** adjoins **Piazza della Repubblica,** and is for many visitors their first introduction to Rome. Much of the area is seedy and filled with gas fumes from all the buses and cars, plus a fair share of weirdos. If you stay here, you might not get typical Roman charm, but you'll have a lot of affordable options and a convenient location, near the transportation hub of the city and not far from Ancient Rome. There is a fair amount to see here, including the **Basilica di Santa Maria Maggiore,** the artifacts at **Palazzo Massimo alle Terme,** and the **Baths of Diocletian.**

The neighborhoods on either side of Termini (Esquilino and Tiburtino) have been slowly cleaning up, and some streets are now attractive. Most budget hotels on the Via Marsala side of the station occupy a floor or several floors of a *palazzo* (palace); many of their entryways are drab, although upstairs they are often charming or at least clean and livable. In the area to the left of the station as you exit, the streets are wider, the traffic is heavier, and the noise level is higher. The area requires you to take just a little caution late at night.

Trastevere In a Roman adaptation of the Latin "Trans Tiber," Trastevere means "across the Tiber." This once medieval working-class district has been gentrified and is now filled with visitors from all over the world. It started to transform in the 1970s when expats and other bohemians discovered its rough charm. Since then, Trastevere has been filling up with tour buses, dance clubs, offbeat shops, sidewalk vendors, pubs, and little *trattorie* with menus printed in English. There are even places to stay— mostly rather quaint rentals and AirBnB's— but as of yet it hasn't burgeoned into a major hotel district. There are some excellent restaurants and bars here as well.

The area centers on the ancient churches of **Santa Cecilia** and **Santa Maria in Trastevere,** and remains one of Rome's most colorful quarters, even if a bit overrun.

Testaccio & Southern Rome In A.D. 55, Emperor Nero ordered that Rome's thousands of broken amphorae and terra-cotta roof tiles be stacked in a pile to the east of the Tiber, just west of today's Ostiense Railway Station. Over the centuries, the mound grew to a height of around 61m (200 ft.) and then was compacted to form the centerpiece for one of the city's most unusual working-class neighborhoods, **Testaccio.** Houses were built on the perimeter of the terra-cotta amphorae mound, and caves were dug into its mass to store wine and foodstuffs. Once home to slaughterhouses and Rome's former port on the Tiber, Testaccio is now known for its authentic Roman restaurants. It's also one of Rome's liveliest areas after dark.

Farther south and east, the **Via Appia Antica** is a 2,300-year-old road that has witnessed much of the history of the ancient world. By 190 B.C., it extended from Rome to Brindisi on the southeast coast. Its most famous sights are the **Catacombs,** the graveyards of early Christians and patrician families (despite what it says in "Quo Vadis," they weren't used as a place for Christians to hide while fleeing persecution). This is one of the most historically rich areas of Rome, great for a day trip, but not a convenient place to stay.

Getting Around

Central Rome is perfect for exploring on foot, with sites of interest often clustered together. Much of the inner core is traffic-free, so you will need to walk whether you like it or not. However, in many parts of the city, walking is uncomfortable because of the crowds, uneven cobblestones, heavy traffic, and narrow (if any) sidewalks. The hectic crush of urban Rome is considerably less during August, when many Romans leave town for vacation (and many restaurants and businesses close).

BY SUBWAY The **Metropolitana,** or **Metro** for short (www.roma metropolitane.it; ✆ **06-454640100**), is the fastest means of transportation, operating 5:30am to 11:30pm Sunday to Thursday, and until 1:30am on Friday and Saturday. A big red M indicates the entrance to the subway. If your destination is close to a Metro stop, hop on, because your journey will be much faster than surface transportation. There are currently three lines: Line A (orange) runs southeast to northwest via Termini, Barberini, Spagna, and several stations in Prati near the Vatican; Line B (blue), runs north to south via Termini and stops in Ancient Rome; and a third line, Line C (green), which is currently under construction and should be completed by 2020, runs from Monte Compatri in the southeast to San Giovanni (on Line A). The portion running from Monte Compatri in the Eastern outskirts of the city is currently connected as far as Centocelle, further extending to Piazza Lodi by the end of 2015.

Tickets are 1.50€ and are available from *tabacchi* (tobacco shops), many newsstands, and vending machines at all stations. Booklets of tickets are available at newsstands, *tabacchi,* and in some terminals. You can also buy a **pass** on either a daily or a weekly basis (see "By Bus & Tram," below). To open the subway barrier, insert your ticket. If you have a Roma Pass (p. 35), touch it against the yellow dot and the gates will open.

BY BUS & TRAM Roman buses and trams are operated by an organization known as **ATAC** (Agenzia del Trasporto Autoferrotranviario del Comune di Roma; www.atac.roma.it; ✆ **06-57003**). **Wi-Fi** is gradually being rolled out across the public transport network: Look for the "Atac Wi-Fi" sticker on the

---

Two Bus Warnings

Any map of the Roman bus system will likely be outdated before it's printed. Many buses listed on the "latest" map no longer exist; others are enjoying a much-needed rest, and new buses suddenly appear without warning. There's always talk of renumbering the whole system, so be aware that the route numbers we've listed might have changed by the time you travel.

Take extreme caution when riding Rome's overcrowded buses—pickpockets abound! This is particularly true on bus no. 64, a favorite of visitors because of its route through the historic districts and thus also a favorite of Rome's pickpocketing community. This bus has earned various nicknames, including the "Pickpocket Express" and "Wallet Eater."

Rome's Key Bus Routes

Although routes change, a few old reliable bus routes have remained valid for years in Rome:

- o **40 (Express):** Stazione Termini to the Vatican via Via Nazionale, Piazza Venezia and Piazza Pia, by the Castel Sant'Angelo
- o **64:** The "tourist route" from Termini, along Via Nazionale and through Piazza Venezia and along Via Argentina to Piazza San Pietro in the Vatican
- o **75:** Stazione Termini to the Colosseum
- o **H:** Stazione Termini via Piazza Venezia and the Ghetto to Trastevere via Ponte Garibaldi

tram/subway doors. To access the service, connect to the "Atac Wi-Fi" network and select "free navigation"; you can then register for free on the RomaWireless website, but you only get 1 hour of surfing, though access to transport help websites like **www.muoversiaroma.it** is unlimited.

For 1.50€, you can ride to most parts of Rome on buses or trams, although it can be slow going in all that traffic, and the buses are often very crowded. A ticket is valid for 100 minutes, and you can get on many buses and trams during that time by using the same ticket (plus one journey on the Metro). Tickets are sold in *tabacchi*, at newsstands, and at bus stops, but there are seldom ticket-issuing machines on the vehicles themselves.

At Stazione Termini, you can buy **special timed passes: BIG** (*biglietto giornaliero* or 1-day ticket) costs 6€, and a **CIS** (*carta settimanale*) is 24€ for 1 week. The **BTI** (*bigletto turistico,* or "tourist ticket") is 16.50€ for 3 days. If you plan to ride public transportation a lot—and if you are skipping between the *centro storico,* Roman ruins, and Vatican, as you likely will—these passes save time and hassle over buying a new ticket every time you ride. Purchase the appropriate pass for your length of stay in Rome. All the passes allow you to ride on the ATAC network, and are also valid on the Metro (subway). On the first bus you board, place your ticket in a small machine, which prints the day and hour you boarded, and then withdraw it. Do the same on the last bus you take during the valid period of the ticket. One-day and weekly tickets are also available at *tabacchi,* many newsstands, and at vending machines at all stations.

Buses and trams stop at areas marked FERMATA. At most of these, a yellow or white sign will display the numbers of the buses that stop there and a list of all the stops along each bus's route in order so you can easily search out your destination. In general, they're in service daily from 5am to midnight. After that and until dawn, you can ride on special night buses (they have an N in front of their bus number), which run only on main routes. It's best to take a taxi in the wee hours—if you can find one. The **bus information booth** at Piazza dei Cinquecento, in front of Stazione Termini, offers advice on routes.

BY TAXI Don't count on hailing a taxi on the street or even getting one at a stand. If you're going out, have your hotel call one. At a restaurant, ask the waiter or cashier to dial for you. If you want to phone for yourself, try the city taxi service at ✆ **06-0609** (which will redirect to the nearest taxi rank, after you say the name of your location to an automated service), or one of these radio taxi numbers: ✆ **06-6645,** 06-3570, or 06-4994. Taxis on call incur a surcharge of 3.50€.

The meter begins at 3€ (Mon–Fri 6am–10pm) for the first 3km (1¾ miles) and then rises 1.10€ per kilometer. The first suitcase is free. Every additional piece of luggage costs 1€. On Saturday and Sunday between 6am and 10pm, the meter starts at 4.50€; from 10pm to 6am every day, the meter starts at 6.50€. Trips from Termini incur a 2€ surcharge. Avoid paying your fare with large bills; invariably, taxi drivers claim that they don't have change, hoping for a bigger tip. In reality, a small tip is fine, but not necessary: Italians, at most, will simply "round up" to the nearest euro. If the driver is really helpful, a tip of 1€ to 2€ is sufficient. Many taxis accept credit cards, but it's best to check before getting in.

BY CAR All roads might lead to Rome, but you don't want to drive once you get here. Because the reception desks of most Roman hotels have at least one English-speaking person, call ahead to find out the best route into Rome from wherever you are starting out. You will want to get rid of your rental car as soon as possible, or park in a garage.

You might want to rent a car to explore the countryside around Rome or drive to another city. You will save the most money if you reserve before leaving home. But if you want to book a car here, **Hertz** is at Via Giovanni Giolitti 34 (www.hertz.com; ✆ **06-4740389;** Metro: Termini), and **Avis** is at Stazione Termini (www.avis.com; ✆ **06-4814373;** Metro: Termini). **Maggiore,** an Italian company, has an office at Stazione Termini (www.maggiore.it; ✆ **06-4880049;** Metro: Termini). There are also branches of the major agencies at the airport.

BY BIKE Other than walking, the best way to get through the medieval alleys and small piazzas of Rome is perched on the seat of a bicycle. Despite being hilly, the heart of Ancient Rome is threaded with bicycle lanes to get you through the murderous traffic. The most convenient place to rent bikes is **Bici & Baci,** Via del Viminale 5 (www.bicibaci.com; ✆ **06-4828443**), lying 2 blocks west of Stazione Termini, the main rail station. Prices start at 4€ per hour or 11€ per day.

[Fast FACTS] ROME

Banks In general, banks are open Monday to Friday 8:30am to 1:30pm and 3 to 4pm. Some banks keep afternoon hours from 2:45 to 3:45pm.

Dentists For dental work, go to **American**

Dental Arts Rome, Via del Governo Vecchio 73 (www. adadentistsrome.com; ✆ 06-6832613; Bus: 41,

4

ROME | Fast Facts: Rome

44, or 46B), which uses all the latest technology, including laser dental techniques.

Doctors   Call the U.S. Embassy at ℂ **06-46741** for a list of doctors who speak English. All big hospitals have a 24-hour first-aid service (go to the emergency room, *pronto soccorso*). You'll find English-speaking doctors at the privately run **Salvator Mundi International Hospital,** Viale delle Mura Gianicolensi 67 (www.salvatormundi.it; ℂ **06-588961;** Bus: 75). For medical assistance, the **International Medical Center** is on 24-hour duty at Via Firenze 47 (www.imc84.com; ℂ **06-4882371;** Metro: Repubblica). You could also contact the **Rome American Hospital,** Via Emilio Longoni 69 (www.hcir.it/romeamericanhospital; ℂ **06-22551**), with English-speaking doctors on duty 24 hours. A more personalized service is provided 24 hours a day by **Medi-Call Italia,** Via Cremera 8 (www.medi-call.it; ℂ **06-8840113;** Bus: 86). It can arrange for a qualified doctor to make a house call at your hotel or anywhere in Rome. In most cases, the doctor will be a general practitioner who can refer you to a specialist if needed. Fees begin at around 100€ per visit and can go higher if a specialist or specialized treatments are necessary.

Embassies & Consulates   See chapter 10.

Emergencies   To call the police, dial ℂ 113; for an ambulance ℂ 118; for a fire ℂ 115.

Internet Access   Wi-Fi is standard in all Rome hotels these days and is available for free in many cafes and information points. If you need a terminal, try **Internet Train,** Piazza Sant'Andrea della Valle, 3 (www.internettrain.it; ℂ **06-97273136;** Bus: 3, 71, or 492). It is open Monday to Friday 9am to 1am, Saturday 2pm to 1am, and Sunday 2pm to midnight. Thirty minutes online costs 2€.

Mail   You can buy special stamps at the **Vatican City Post Office,** adjacent to the information office in St. Peter's Square; it's open Monday to Friday 8:30am to 7pm and Saturday 8:30am to 6pm. Convenient post offices in the old city are located in Via Monterone 1 (near the Pantheon); Via Cavour 277; at Via Marsala 29 (on the north side of Termini); and at Via Molise 2, near Piazza Barberini. Most are open Monday to Friday 8:30am to 3:30pm, with the Termini branch open Monday to Friday 8:20am to 7:05pm and Sat 8:20am to 12:35pm.

Newspapers & Magazines   You can buy major publications including the "International New York Times" and the "London Times" at most newsstands. The English language expat

magazine (in English), "Wanted in Rome" (www.wantedinrome.com) comes out every 2 weeks and lists current events and shows. If you want to try your hand at reading Italian, "Time Out" now has a Rome edition.

Pharmacies   A reliable pharmacy is **Farmacia Internazionale,** Piazza Barberini 49 (www.farmint.it; ℂ **06-4825456;** Metro: Barberini), open 24 hours. Most pharmacies are open from 8:30am to 1pm and 4 to 7:30pm. In general, pharmacies follow a rotation system, so several are always open on Sunday.

Police   Dial ℂ 113.

Safety   Pickpocketing is the most common problem. Men should keep their wallets in their front pocket or inside jacket pocket. Purse snatching happens occasionally, with young men on Vespas who ride past you and grab your purse. To avoid trouble, stay away from the curb and keep your purse on the wall side of your body and place the strap across your chest. Don't place anything valuable on outdoor tables or chairs, where it can be grabbed up. Groups of child pickpockets have long been a particular menace, although the problem isn't as severe as in years past. They might approach you with pieces of cardboard hiding their stealing hands. Just keep repeating a firm *no!*

4

ROME | **Fast Facts: Rome**

WHERE TO STAY

Rome's standard hotels are notoriously overpriced. So, when you stay here, unusual solutions—rental apartments, B&Bs, even convents and monasteries—have two great virtues: They're cheaper than standard facilities and, often, more memorable.

Breakfast in all but the highest echelon of hotels is usually a buffet with coffee, fruit, rolls, and cheese. It's not always included in the rate, so check the listing carefully. If you are budgeting and breakfast is a payable extra, skip it and go to a nearby cafe-bar. It will likely be much cheaper.

Nearly all hotels are heated in the cooler months, but not all are air-conditioned in summer, which can be vitally important during a stifling July or August. The deluxe and first-class ones are, but after that, it's a toss-up. Be sure to check before you book a stay in the dog days of summer, if you suffer in the heat.

Self-Catering Apartments

Anyone looking to get into the local swing of things should stay in a short-term rental apartment. A centrally located, "economical" double room in a Rome hotel goes for about 120€ per night, and it may be cramped and dark, with few amenities. For the same price or less, you could have your own spacious one-bedroom apartment with a terrace, washing machine, air-conditioning, and a fridge to keep your wine in. Properties of all sizes and styles, in every price range, are available for stays of 3 nights to several weeks.

Nearly every rental apartment in Rome is owned and maintained by a third party (that is, not the rental agency). That means that the decor and flavor of the apartments, even in the same price range and neighborhood, can vary widely. Every reputable agency, however, puts multiple photos of each property they handle on its website, so that you'll have a sense of what you're getting into. The photos should be accompanied by a list of amenities, so if air-conditioning and a washing machine are important to you, but you can live without Wi-Fi, be sure to check for those features. (In the summer, you'll want to opt for that air-conditioning.) Note also that **www.airbnb.com**, the platform that allows individuals to rent their own apartments to guests, covers Rome.

ABOUT THE MONEY

It's standard practice for local rental agencies to collect 30% of the total rental amount upfront to secure a booking. When you get to Rome and check in, the balance of your rental fee is often payable in cash only. Upon booking, the agency should provide you with detailed "check-in" procedures. Sometimes, you're expected to call a cell or office phone when you arrive in Rome, and then the keyholder will meet you at the front door of the property at the agreed-upon time. *Tip:* Before the keyholder disappears, make sure you have a few numbers to call in case of an emergency. Otherwise, most apartments come with information sheets that list neighborhood shops and services. Beyond that, you're on your own, which is what makes an apartment stay such a great way to do as the Romans do.

RECOMMENDED AGENCIES

Cross Pollinate (www.cross-pollinate.com; ✆ 06-99369799) is a multi-destination agency but with a decent roster of apartments and B&Bs in Rome. It was created by the American owners of The Beehive Hotel in Rome, and they and their staff personally inspect the properties they offer.

GowithOh (www.gowithoh.com; ✆ 800/567-2927 in the U.S.) is a hip rental agency that covers 12 European cities, Rome among them. The website is fun to navigate and has sections on how to save money as well as over 400 apartments for rent in the city.

Eats & Sheets (www.eatsandsheets.com; ✆ 06-83515971) is a small boutique collective comprising two B&Bs (near the Vatican and Colosseum), and 11 beautiful apartments for rent, most in the Centro Storico but in a variety of sizes and types.

Roman Reference (www.romanreference.com; ✆ 06-48903612) offers no-surprises property descriptions (with helpful and diplomatic tags like "better for young people") and even includes the "eco-footprint" for each apartment (how much energy it consumes). You can expect transparency and responsiveness from the plain-dealing staff.

Rental in Rome (www.rentalinrome.com; ✆ 06-69905533) has an alluring website—with video clips of the apartments—and the widest selection of midrange and luxury apartments in the prime *centro storico* zone (there are less expensive ones, too).

Bed & Breakfast Association of Rome (www.b-b.rm.it) handles both self-catering apartments and rooms for rent within private apartments, some of which charge as little as 30€.

Monasteries & Convents

Staying in a convent or a monastery can be a great bargain and a unique experience if you're seeking a mellow, contemplative trip to the Eternal City. But remember, these are religious houses, which means the decor is most often stark and the rules are extensive. Cohabiting is almost always frowned upon—though marriage licenses are rarely required—and unruly behavior is not tolerated (so, no staggering in after too much *limoncello* at dinner). Plus, there's usually a curfew. Most rooms in convents and monasteries do not have private bathrooms, but ask when making your reservation in case some are available. The place to start is **www.monasterystays.com**, which essentially lays out all your monastic options for the Eternal City and can make all the bookings for you.

HOTELS BY PRICE

EXPENSIVE

Babuino 181 ★★, p. 52

Capo d'Africa ★★, p. 49

Deko Rome ★★★, p. 54

Del Sole al Pantheon ★, p. 50

The Inn at the Roman Forum ★★★, p. 49

The Inn at the Spanish Steps ★★★, p. 52

Raphael ★★, p. 51

Residenza Cellini ★★, p. 55

Residenza Paolo VI ★★, p. 47

Villa Laetitia ★★★, p. 47

Villa Spalletti Trivelli ★★★, p. 52

MODERATE

Arco del Lauro ★★, p. 57

Capitolium Rooms ★, p. 55

Daphne Trevi & Daphne Veneto ★, p. 54

Duca d'Alba ★★, p. 49

Hotel Adriano ★★★, p. 53

Hotel Condotti ★, p. 53

Lancelot ★, p. 50

La Residenza ★, p. 55

Nicolas Inn ★★, p. 50

QuodLibet ★★★, p. 48

Residenza in Farnese ★★, p. 51

Rome Armony Suites ★★, p. 48

San Francesco ★, p. 58

Seven Kings Relais ★★, p. 56

Teatro di Pompeo ★★, p. 51

INEXPENSIVE

Aphrodite ★, p. 56

The Beehive ★★, p. 56

Euro Quiris ★, p. 56

Panda ★, p. 53

Parlamento ★, p. 53

Around Vatican City & Prati

For most visitors, this is a rather dull area to be based in. It's well removed from the ancient sites, and not a great restaurant neighborhood. But if the main purpose of your visit centers on the Vatican, you'll be fine here, and you will be joined by thousands of other pilgrims, nuns, and priests.

EXPENSIVE

Residenza Paolo VI ★★   The only hotel actually within the Vatican state, the property is tucked into the walls of the venerated Augustinian Order headquarters, where it's been based since 1886. As a result, there's no city sales tax. Taking breakfast on the rooftop terrace is a special treat, because this narrow strip overlooks St. Peter's Square–if the timing's right, you'll see the pope himself blessing crowds (usually on Sunday). As for the rooms, they all are done with simple elegance, with tile or hardwood floors, heavy drapes and oriental rugs, and quality beds. The downside? Just like their in-Rome-proper rival hotels, space is at a premium in many of the guestrooms. There's a 15% discount on bookings of 3 or more nights.

Via Paolo VI 29. www.residenzapaolovi.com. (C) **06-684870.** 35 units. 135€–599€ double. Rates include breakfast. Parking nearby from 20€. Metro: Ottaviano. **Amenities:** Bar; babysitting; room service; Wi-Fi (15€ per day).

Villa Laetitia ★★★   This elegant hotel overlooking the River Tiber is the work of Anna Fendi, member of the Roman fashion dynasty and a nifty designer in her own right. Thanks to Signora Anna, the rooms are anything but traditional, although they're set in a 1911 villa, surrounded by tranquil gardens. Expect touches like bold, checkerboard patterns on the coverlets and floors, and works of modern art on the walls. The Stendhal Room is our favorite, with black-and-white floor tiles matching the bedspread, transparent plastic furniture (that's a chic-looking, transparent plastic), a small kitchenette painted in red, and a secluded balcony that catches the morning sun. Signora Fendi is often wandering the premises, so you may bump into her.

Lungotevere delle Armi 22–23. www.villalaetitia.com. ℂ **06-3226776.** 14 units. 200€–280€ double. Parking nearby 20€. Metro: Lepanto. **Amenities:** Bar; airport transfer (55€); babysitting; fitness room; restaurant; room service; spa; Wi-Fi (free).

MODERATE

QuodLibet ★★★   The name is Latin for "what pleases" and everything is pleasing here. This upscale B&B is a delight, with spacious rooms, gorgeous artwork and furnishings, and generous breakfasts (bread and croissants come from the bakery just next door). All the rooms are set on the fourth floor of an elegant building (with elevator and air-conditioning), so it's quieter than many places. It's located just a 10-minute walk from the Vatican Museums, and a block from the Metro (so you can zip to other parts of the city easily). Host Gianluca is a gem, a man with charm to spare and a deep knowledge of both Rome and what interests visitors. A top pick!

Via Barletta 29. www.quodlibetroma.com. ℂ **06-1222642.** 4 units. 70€–180€ double. Rates include breakfast. Metro: Ottaviano. **Amenities:** Wi-Fi (free).

Rome Armony Suites ★★   A warning: Rome Armony Suites is almost always booked up months in advance, so if you're interested in it staying here, book early! Popularity boils down to stellar service; owner Luca and his son Andrea are brilliant, sensitive hosts, who are especially good with first-time visitors to Rome: Luca virtually organizes guests' entire trips. As for the rooms, they're plush, big, clean and modern, with minimalist-style decor, tea and coffee facilities, and a fridge in each. For breakfast, you get a voucher to use in the Brown & Co. cafe around the corner. Final perk: the excellent location.

Via Orazio 3. www.romearmonysuites.com. ℂ **348-3305419.** 6 units. 120€–260€ double. Rates include breakfast. Metro: Ottaviano. **Amenities:** Wi-Fi (free).

Ancient Rome, Monti & Celio

There aren't many hotel rooms on Earth with a view of a 2,000-year-old amphitheater, so there's a definite "only in Rome" feeling to lodging on the edge of the ancient city. The negative side to residing in this area—and it's a big minus—is that the streets adjacent to those ancient monuments have little life outside tourism. There's a lot more going on in **Monti,** Rome's oldest "suburb" (only 5 min. from the Forum). It is especially lively after dark (so expect noisy streets until late). **Celio** has even more of a neighborhood vibe and a local, gentrified life quite separate from tourism.

If you are after a little more space than an affordable hotel room usually provides, **Residenza Leonina** ★, Piazza degli Zingari 4 (www.residenza leonina.com; *©* **06-48906885**), offers a few modern, spacious apartments in the heart of Monti. Prices range approximately 120€ to 200€ per night; you can get better deals if you book direct. *Tip:* One of central Rome's best gelato vendors is literally on the doorstep (see "Gelato," p. 72). Temptation will be hard to resist.

EXPENSIVE

Capo d'Africa ★★ This exquisite boutique hotel, located in the heart of Imperial Rome, set in a 20th century Palazzo, offers a unique lodging experience. With sweeping vistas from the roof terrace (the hotel's top perk; you eat breakfast up there), elegant design and upscale ambiance, guests are welcome as they would in any Roman home. The rooms, too, are magnificent: light-filled, spacious, sharp and modern, with cherrywood furniture, touches of glass and chrome accents, unusually comfy beds, marble bathrooms, and plenty of storage space, so you need never see your bags after you arrive.

Via Capo d'Africa 54. www.hotelcapodafrica.com. *©* **06-772801.** 65 units. 380€–430€ double. Rates include breakfast. Parking 45€. Bus: 53, 85, or 117. **Amenities:** Restaurant; bar; exercise room; room service; Wi-Fi (free).

The Inn at the Roman Forum ★★★ The name doesn't lie. This small hotel is tucked down a medieval lane on the edge of Monti, with the forums of several Roman emperors as neighbors. The midsize rooms are sumptuously decorated, with designs that fuse the contemporary and baroque traditions of the city. The two rooms on the top floor have private gardens, which offer total tranquility, plus there's a shared roof terrace where *aperitivo* is served each evening with unforgettable views of the Vittoriano and the Palatine Hill. The ground floor even has its own archaeological dig. The Inn isn't cheap, but the view alone more than makes up for the costs.

Via degli Ibernesi 30. www.theinnattheromanforum.com. *©* **06-69190970.** 12 units. 390€–990€ double. Rates include breakfast. Parking 30€. Metro: Cavour. **Amenities:** Bar; concierge; room service; Wi-Fi (10€ per day).

MODERATE

Duca d'Alba ★★ Monti doesn't have many full-service hotels—at least, not yet. The Duca d'Alba is right on one of the main drags, with all the nightlife and authentic dining you'll need on your doorstep. Rooms in the main building are cozy (read: small) and contemporary, with modern furniture and gadgetry, but even smaller bathrooms. The annex rooms next door have a *palazzo* character, with terra-cotta tiled floors, oak and cherry wood furniture, and more space; street-facing rooms are soundproofed. Those on the second floor are the brightest. *Tip:* If you offer to pay in cash, you'll receive a 12% discount.

Via Leonina 14. www.hotelducadalba.com. *©* **06-484471.** 33 units. 120€–412€ double. Rates include breakfast. Metro: Cavour. **Amenities:** Bar; babysitting (prebooking essential); Wi-Fi (free).

Lancelot ★ Expect warmth and hospitality from the minute you walk in the door. The English-speaking staff, who have all been here for years, are the heart and soul of Lancelot, and the reason why the hotel has so many repeat guests. It's not the room decor certainly, which is simple, a bit dated, and unremarkable (although most of the units are spacious, immaculately kept, and light-filled, thanks to large windows). Ask for the 6th-floor units that have private terraces overlooking Ancient Rome—they're well worth the 20€ extra you pay. What makes this place truly remarkable are the genteel, chandelier-lit common areas for meeting other travelers, "Room with a View"–style. Unusual for Rome, there's also private parking, for which you'll need to book ahead.

Via Capo d'Africa 47. www.lancelothotel.com. ℂ **06-70450615.** 61 units. 130€–196€ double. Rates include breakfast. Parking 10€ (prebooking essential). Bus: 53, 85, or 117. **Amenities:** Restaurant (set dinner 25€ incl. wine); bar; babysitting; Wi-Fi (free).

Nicolas Inn ★★ This tiny bed-and-breakfast, run by a welcoming American–Lebanese couple, makes the perfect base if you want to concentrate on Rome's ancient sights—the Colosseum is 1 (long) block in one direction, with the Forum just about 3 blocks in the other. Rooms are well proportioned, adequately air-conditioned, and decorated with sweet touches like wrought iron beds and heavy wooden furniture. Best of all, light floods in through large windows. Guests take breakfast at a local cafe—with unlimited espresso. Downers: no children under 5 years, and no credit cards accepted.

Via Cavour 295. www.nicolasinn.com. ℂ **06-97618483.** 4 units. 100€–180€ double. Rates include breakfast (at nearby cafe). Metro: Cavour or Colosseo. **Amenities:** Airport transfer (60€); concierge; Wi-Fi (free).

The Centro Storico & Pantheon

Travelers who want to immerse themselves in the atmosphere of Rome's lively Renaissance heart will prefer staying in this area over the more commercial Tridente district or quieter Vatican. You'll be looking at a lot of walking, but that's the reason many visitors come here in the first place—to wander and discover the glory that was and is Rome. You're also within walking distance of the Vatican and the ruins of Ancient Rome. Many restaurants and cafes are within an easy walk of all the hotels located here.

EXPENSIVE

Del Sole al Pantheon ★ Dating back, incredibly, to 1467, this place oozes history. Famous guests have included Jean-Paul Sartre and Simone de Beauvoir, as well as 15th-century poet Ludovico Ariosto and 19th-century composer Pietro Mascagni, among others. Rooms are decorated with lavish, period decor, lots of brocade drapery, fine fabrics, and traditional furniture. Each unit comes equipped with air-conditioning and satellite TV, and some feature unbeatable views of the Pantheon.

Piazza della Rotonda 63. www.hotelsolealpantheon.com. ℂ **06-6780441.** 32 units. 240€–422€ double. Rates include breakfast. Parking nearby 45€. Bus: 64. **Amenities:** Airport transfer (60€); bar; babysitting; room service; Wi-Fi (5€ per day; not available in annex building).

Raphael ★★ Planning on proposing? This ivy-covered palace, just off Piazza Navona, is just the kind of special-occasion place to choose, with luxurious rooms, enthusiastic staff, and a roof terrace with spectacular views across Rome. It's a gorgeous hotel, with all sorts of 20th-century artwork inside, including Picasso ceramics displayed in the lobby and paintings by Mirò, Morandi, and de Chirico scattered across the property. The standard rooms are all decorated in Victorian style, with antique furnishings and hardwood floors. But for many, the real attraction here is the chance to stay in the quirky executive suites designed by architect Richard Meier, which feature oak paneling, contemporary art, and Carrara marble in a style that blends contemporary and Asian design.

Largo Febo 2, Piazza Navona. www.raphaelhotel.com. ℂ **06-682831.** 50 units. 280€–730€ double. Rates include breakfast. Valet parking 50€. Bus: 64. **Amenities:** Restaurant; bar; babysitting; concierge; exercise room; room service; sauna; Wi-Fi (free).

MODERATE

Residenza in Farnese ★★ This little gem is tucked away in a stunning 15th-century mansion, within stumbling distance of the Campo de' Fiori. Most rooms are spacious and artsy, with colorful comforters and wallpaper, tiled floors, and a vaguely Renaissance theme. Standard rooms are a little smaller. If you book via the website with 21 days advance, a 10% discount is applied on every day of your stay. Other perks: the downright generous spread of fresh fruit, cheese, ham, egg, and yogurt for breakfast; and nearby cheap parking.

Via del Mascherone 59. www.residenzafarneseroma.it. ℂ **06-68210980.** 31 units. 92€–310€ double. Rates include breakfast. Parking 15€ (reservations essential). Bus: 64, 70, 81 and 87. **Amenities:** Airport transfer (free with stay of 4 nights or more); bar; concierge; room service; Wi-Fi (free).

Teatro di Pompeo ★★ History buffs will appreciate this small B&B, literally built on top of the ruins of the 1st-century Theater of Pompey, where on the Ides of March Julius Caesar was stabbed to death (p. 19). The lovely breakfast area beneath the lobby is actually part of the arcades of the old theater, with the original Roman stone walls. The large rooms themselves feel plush, with exposed, wood-beam ceilings, cherry-wood furniture, and terracotta tiled floors. Some rooms feature a view of the internal courtyard while others overlook the small square; all are quiet. The Campo de' Fiori is right behind the hotel. Staff members are extremely helpful and all speak good English. *Tip:* Avoid "Trattoria Der Pallaro" restaurant next door; it's a true tourist trap.

Largo del Pallaro 8. www.hotelteatrodipompeo.it. ℂ **06-68300170.** 13 units. 165€–220€ double. Rates include breakfast. Bus: 46, 62, or 64. **Amenities:** Bar; babysitting; room service; Wi-Fi (free).

Tridente & the Spanish Steps

The heart of the city is a great place to stay if you're a serious shopper or enjoy the romantic, somewhat nostalgic locales of the Spanish Steps and Trevi

Tourists gather on the Spanish Steps.

Fountain. But expect to part with a lot of extra euro for the privilege. This is one of the most elegant areas in Rome.

EXPENSIVE

Babuino 181 ★★ Leave Renaissance and baroque Italy far behind at this sleek, contemporary hotel, with relatively spacious rooms featuring Frette linens, iPod docks, and even a Nespresso machine for espresso lovers. The bathrooms are heavy on the marble and mosaics, and shuttered windows with hefty curtains provide a perfectly blacked out and quiet environment for light sleepers. The breakfast buffet is an additional 18€.

Via del Babuino 181. www.romeluxurysuites.com/babuino. ② **06-32295295.** 24 units. 250€–680€ double. Metro: Flaminio. **Amenities:** Bar; airport transfer (65€); babysitting; concierge; room service; Wi-Fi (free).

The Inn at the Spanish Steps ★★★ Set in one of Rome's most desirable locations on the famed Via dei Condotti shopping magnet, this lavish guesthouse is the epitome of luxe. Rooms are fantasias of design and comfort, some with parquet floors and cherubim frescoes on the ceiling, others decked out with wispy fabrics draping plush, canopied beds. Swank amenities include flatscreen TVs, iPod docks, a computer lending program, Jacuzzi tubs, and so on. Note that some rooms are located in the annex building, and these tend to be larger than the ones in the main building. The perfectly manicured rooftop garden provides beautiful views, to be enjoyed at breakfast—where there's a generous buffet spread—or at sunset, frosted glass of *vino* in hand.

Via dei Condotti 85. www.atspanishsteps.com. ② **06-69925657.** 24 units. 370€–750€ double. Rates include breakfast. Metro: Spagna. **Amenities:** Bar; babysitting; airport transfer (55€); concierge; room service; Wi-Fi (free).

Villa Spalletti Trivelli ★★★ This really is an experience rather than a hotel—an early 20th-century neoclassical villa revamped into an exclusive 12-room guesthouse, where guests mingle in the gardens or magnificent great hall, as if invited by an Italian noble for the weekend. There is no key for the entrance door; ring a bell and a staff member will open it for you, often offering you a glass of complimentary Prosecco as a welcome. Onsite is a Turkish bath, a sizeable and modern oasis for those who want extra pampering, while rooms feature elegant antiques and Fiandra damask linen sheets on the beds, with a sitting area or separate lounge, REN toiletries, and satellite LCD TV. And the minibar? All free, all day. There's no "nickel-and-diming" here, which makes a relaxing change.

Via Piacenza 4. www.villaspalletti.it. ℰ **06-48907934.** 12 units. 450€–710€ double. Rates include breakfast. Free parking. Metro: Barberini. **Amenities:** Restaurant; bar; concierge; exercise room; room service; spa; sauna; Wi-Fi (free).

MODERATE

Hotel Adriano ★★★ Secluded in a maze of small alleyways, but just 5 minutes from the Pantheon, the Adriano occupies an elegant 17th-century *palazzo*. The rooms boast an incredibly stylish and trendy modern design, with blond wood built-ins and designer furniture carefully chosen for each room. The hotel drips with atmosphere, but note that the Wi-Fi can be unstable, and that if you opt for an "annex" room it is quite a different experience, more akin to a self-catering apartment.

Via di Pallacorda 2. www.hoteladriano.com. ℰ **06-68802451.** 77 units. 90€–220€ double. Rates include breakfast. Parking nearby 40€. Bus: 175 or 492. **Amenities:** Bar; babysitting; bikes; concierge; gym; Wi-Fi (free).

Hotel Condotti ★ A cozy guesthouse that can be a tremendously good deal depending on when you stay and when you book. (*Hint:* Those who book well in advance and through a discounter get the best rates). For your money, you'll get a clean, unpretentious room, though the common areas aspire higher with marble floors, antiques, tapestries, and a Venetian-glass chandelier. Overall, it's worth considering for its proximity to the Spanish Steps, great deals online (especially during off-season), and free Internet (with terminals in the lobby for those traveling without their own computers).

Via Mario de' Fiori 37. www.hotelcondotti.com. ℰ **06-6794661.** 16 units. 150€ and way up. Rates include breakfast. Metro: Spagna. **Amenities:** Airport transfer (65€); bar; babysitting; bikes; room service; Wi-Fi (free).

INEXPENSIVE

Panda ★ Panda has long been popular among budget travelers, and its rooms book up quickly. Rooms are spare, but not without a bit of old-fashioned charm, like characteristic Roman *cotto* (terra-cotta) floor tiles and exposed beams. The cheaper singles and doubles don't have private bathrooms; only triples come with full private bath. The en-suite bathrooms tend to be cramped, however. Right outside the doorstep are several great cafes and wine bars where you can start the day with an espresso or end the night with a glass of vino.

Via della Croce 35. www.hotelpanda.it. ℰ **06-6780179.** 28 units (8 with bathroom). 68€–78€ double without bathroom; 90€–130€ double with bathroom. Metro: Spagna. **Amenities:** A/C; Wi-Fi (free).

Parlamento ★ Set on the top floors of a 17th-century *palazzo*, this is the best budget deal in the area, because all of its rooms have private bathrooms and are equipped with flatscreen satellite TVs, desks, exposed beams, and parquet or terra-cotta floors. Overall, it's basic and showing its vintage feel, but that keeps the prices lower. And the level of cleanliness and the quality of the beds is indisputable. Breakfast is served on the rooftop terrace—you can also chill up there with a glass of wine in the evening. Note that air-conditioning usually costs a little extra. The Trevi Fountain, Spanish Steps, and Pantheon are all within 5- to 10-minute walk.

Via delle Convertite 5 (at Via del Corso). www.hotelparlamento.it. ℰ **06-69921000.** 23 units. 124€–210€ double. Rates include breakfast. Parking nearby 30€. Metro: Spagna. **Amenities:** Airport transfer (55€); bar; concierge; room service; Wi-Fi (free).

Via Veneto & Piazza Barberini

If you stay in this area, you definitely won't be on the wrong side of the tracks. Unlike the streets around the train station, this is a beautiful and upscale commercial neighborhood, near some of Rome's best shopping.

EXPENSIVE

Deko Rome ★★★ Honeymooners love Deko Rome, but then, so does everyone who stays here. It is, quite simply, an exceptionally warm and welcoming place, a true boutique hotel (just nine rooms) occupying the second floor of an elegant early 20th-century *palazzo*. The interior blends antiques, vintage '60s pieces, and contemporary design for rooms that are chic in a way that's happily retro and quite comfortable; as a bonus, each room comes with an iPad and flatscreen TV. Throw in the friendly, fun owners (Marco and Serena) and excellent location, close to Via Veneto, and Deko is understandably hugely popular. It fills up quickly—reservations many months in advance are essential. Save 20€ if you pay in cash.

Via Toscana 1. www.dekorome.com. ℰ **06-42020032.** 9 units. 210€–250€. Rates include breakfast. Parking (nearby) 25€. Bus: 910 (from Termini). **Amenities:** Airport transfer (50€); bar; babysitting; Wi-Fi (free).

MODERATE

Daphne Trevi & Daphne Veneto ★ These jointly managed B&B properties, minutes from the Trevi fountain, are a relatively good value, even in the summer. Daphne Trevi occupies an 18th-century building with a range of en suite rooms, and Daphne Veneto is a 19th-century structure with en suite single rooms and larger doubles. In both locations the staff is super helpful—first time visitors will appreciate their hand-drawn maps, suggested walks, and reservation service. The rooms are also similar in both: cozy and clean (but no TVs), with small showers and desktop or laptop computers for guest use. Note, however, that Wi-Fi is not great in most rooms (first floor is best). The main difference between the two is location: Trevi lies on an older, quiet, cobblestone street, and Veneto lies on a wider, more businesslike thoroughfare (and rooms on its third and fourth floors have rooftop views).

Via di San Basilio 55. www.daphne-rome.com. ℰ **06-87450086.** 8 units. 130€–230€ double. Rates include breakfast. Nearby parking 30€. Metro: Barberini. **Amenities:** Airport transfers (55€); Wi-Fi (free).

La Residenza ★   Considering its location, just off Via Veneto, this hotel is a smart deal, with renovated, modern rooms, all relatively spacious with a couple of easy chairs or a small couch in addition to a desk. Families are especially well catered for, with quad rooms and junior suites on the top floor with a separate kids' alcove with two sofa beds, and an outdoor patio. In addition to free Wi-Fi in the rooms, there are terminals in the lobby where you can check the Internet. The breakfast buffet is excellent: a good choice of quality charcuterie and cheeses, breads, and pastries. There are a couple of welcome perks: free Friday cocktails and a welcome fruit basket on arrival.

Via Emilia 22–24. www.hotel-la-residenza.com. ℂ **06-4880789.** 29 units. 120€–250€ double. Rates include buffet breakfast. Parking (limited) 20€. Metro: Barberini. **Amenities:** Bar; babysitting; room service; Wi-Fi (free).

Around Termini

Known for its concentration of cheap hotels, the Termini area is about the only part of the center where you can score a high-season double for under 100€. The streets around **Termini** station are not the most picturesque, and parts of the neighborhood are downright seedy. But it's very convenient for transportation and access to most of Rome's top sights: Termini is the only spot where Rome's main Metro lines intersect, and buses and trams leave from the concourse outside to every part of the city.

There are some upscale hotels around here, but if you have the dollars to spend on a truly luxe hotel, choose a prettier neighborhood.

EXPENSIVE

Residenza Cellini ★★   For every rule, there is an exception. In this case, the lovely Cellini is the exception to the "don't spend top dollar to stay near Termini" rule. The feeling of refinement begins the second you walk through the door to find a vase of fresh lilies in the elegant, high-ceilinged hall. Antique-styled rooms are proudly traditional, with thick walls (so no noise from your neighbors), solid Selva furniture, and handsome parquet wood floors. It's not all about the past, however: Beds have orthopedic mattresses topped with memory foam, everything is made from anti-allergenic, natural materials, and there's satellite TV, splendid bathrooms with Jacuzzi tubs or hydro-jet showers, and air-conditioning to keep rooms cool all summer. The service here is top-notch and wonderfully personal.

Via Modena 5. www.residenzacellini.it. ℂ **06-47825204.** 11 units. 95€–250€ double. Rates include breakfast. Parking 35€. Metro: Repubblica. **Amenities:** Babysitting (pre-booking essential); Wi-Fi (free).

MODERATE

Capitolium Rooms ★   An intimate bed-and-breakfast occupying the second-floor wing of a handsome town house. The rooms are well lit, with antique-style white furniture and beds with soft mattresses. Sure, the decor is a little old-fashioned, but so is the warmth of the welcome. Pricing, especially out of high season (Apr–June) is negotiable—e-mail them directly and strike a deal, but insist on one of the five rooms with a view over the leafy colonial square. A couple of units are also large enough for families.

Via Montebello 104. www.capitoliumrooms.com. Ⓒ **06-4464917.** 7 units. 50€–210€ double. Rates include breakfast. Parking 15€–22€. Metro: Termini or Castro Pretorio. **Amenities:** Wi-Fi (free).

Seven Kings Relais ★★ There's a hipster retro feel to the decor of this striking hotel, kitted out with dark wooden furniture, chocolate-brown bedspreads, and modern tiled floors. Rooms are also unusually large—especially nos. 104, 201, and 205. Despite its location right on one of Rome's busiest thoroughfares, there's no noise: An external courtyard and modern soundproofing see to that. Breakfast is a 24-hour self-service bar with tea, coffee, and biscuits, and the reception staff works around the clock

Via XX Settembre 58A. www.7kings.eu. Ⓒ **06-42917784.** 11 units. 90€–220€ double. Metro: Repubblica. **Amenities:** Babysitting (prebooking essential); Wi-Fi (free).

INEXPENSIVE

Aphrodite ★ It's all about value and location at this oasis of tranquillity right across the street from the chaos of Termini station—though there *is* a high convenience/poor character tradeoff. Still, these modern rooms are spotless, with wide-plank wood floors and high-quality bathrooms boasting sinks with polished travertine counters. The California-style rooftop terrace and friendly service are another bonus. Need more convincing? The Terravision airport bus stops right outside. One warning: If you are a light sleeper, request a room at the back, or pack powerful earplugs.

Via Marsala 90. it.hotelaphrodite.com. Ⓒ **06-491096.** 60 units. 110€–205€ double. Rates include breakfast. Metro: Termini. **Amenities:** Bar; babysitting (prebooking essential); concierge; Wi-Fi (free).

The Beehive ★★ Conceived as part hostel/part hotel, The Beehive is a unique lodging experience. The eco-minded American owners have decorated the place with art pieces and flea-market treasures, and all are available for a variety of budgets. Some have private bathrooms, others have shared facilities or are actual six-bed dorms—all are decorated with flair. The garden with trees and quiet reading/relaxing areas is another strong point. There's also a walk-in American breakfast, open to all-comers, where you can get fruit, oatmeal, or eggs any way you like, as well as weekend brunches, and vegan buffets some evenings (8€ including a glass of wine).

Via Marghera 8. www.the-beehive.com. Ⓒ **06-44704553.** 12 units. 70€–80€ double; dorm beds 25€–35€. Metro: Termini or Castro Pretorio. **Amenities:** Restaurant; Wi-Fi (free).

Euro Quiris ★ There's not a frill in sight at this government-rated one star a couple of blocks north of the station. Rooms are on the fifth floor and simply decorated with functional furniture, but they are spotless, and mattresses are a lot more comfortable than you have a right to expect in this price bracket. Bathrooms are a good size, too. The friendly reception staff dispense sound local knowledge, including tips on where to have breakfast in cafes nearby, and the Beehive's American breakfast is just around the corner (see above). No credit cards accepted.

Via dei Mille 64. www.euroquirishotel.com. © **06-491279.** 9 units. 40€–160€ double. Metro: Termini. **Amenities:** Wi-Fi (free).

Trastevere

This was once an "undiscovered" neighborhood—but no longer. Being based over here does give some degree of escape from the busy (and pricy) *centro storico,* however. And there are bars, shops, and restaurants galore among Trastevere's narrow cobblestone lanes. The panorama from the **Gianicolo** (p. 90) is also walkable from pretty much everywhere in Trastevere.

MODERATE

Arco del Lauro ★★ Hidden in Trastevere's snaking alleyways, this serene little bed-and-breakfast is divided over two adjacent sites on the ground floor of a shuttered pink *palazzo.* Rooms have parquet floors and simple decor, with a mix of modern and period dressers and tables, and modern plush beds and armchairs. None is large, but they all have a feeling of air and space thanks to original, lofty wood ceilings. Breakfast is taken at a nearby cafe; there's also coffee and snacks laid out round the clock. Credit cards not accepted.

Via Arco de' Tolomei 29. www.arcodellauro.it. © **06-97840350.** 6 units. 85€–145€ double. Rates include breakfast (at nearby cafe). Bus: 125/Tram: 8. **Amenities:** Babysitting (2 weeks' prebooking essential); Wi-Fi (free).

A hidden alleyway in Trastevere.

San Francesco ★ There's a local feel to staying here that has disappeared from much of Trastevere, perhaps because it's at the very edge of the neighborhood, close to the Porta Portese gate in an area that hasn't been gentrified or over-exploited. All rooms are bright, with colorwashed walls and modern tiling. Doubles are fairly small, but the bathrooms are palatial. The grand piano in the lobby adds a touch of old-time charm; a top-floor garden with a bar overlooks terra-cotta rooftops and the church bell towers.

Via Jacopo de Settesoli 7. www.hotelsanfrancesco.net. © **06-48300051.** 24 units. 80€–184€ double. Price includes breakfast. Parking 20€–25€. Bus: 44 or 125. **Amenities:** Bar; babysitting (prebooking essential); Wi-Fi (free).

WHERE TO EAT

Rome remains a top destination for food lovers and has more dining diversity today than ever. Many of its *trattorie* haven't changed their menus in a quarter of a century, but there are an increasing number of creative eateries with chefs willing to experiment and revisit tradition to embrace modernity.

Restaurants generally serve lunch between 1 and 2:30pm, and dinner between about 8 and 10:30pm. At all other times, most restaurants are closed—though a new generation is moving toward all-day dining, with a limited service at the "in-between" time of mid-afternoon.

If you have your heart set on any of these establishments below, we seriously recommend *reserving ahead of arrival.* Hot tables go quickly, especially on high-season weekends—often twice: once for the early dining tourists, and then again by locals, who dine later, typically around 9pm.

A *servizio* (tip or service charge) is almost always added to your bill, or included in the price. Sometimes it is marked on the menu as *pane e servizio* (bread, cover charge, and service). You can of course leave extra if you wish— a couple of euros as a token. Don't go overboard on the tipping front, and watch out for sharp practices. More than once we have overheard waitstaff telling foreign tourists that service *wasn't* included, when the menu clearly stated (in Italian) that it was.

RESTAURANTS BY CUISINE

BAKERY
Antico Forno Roscioli ★★, p. 64
Panificio Bonci ★★, p. 60

CONTEMPORARY ROMAN
Café Romano ★, p. 64
Glass ★★★, p. 69
Pipero al Rex ★★★, p. 67

EMILIANA-ROMAGNOLA
Colline Emiliane ★★, p. 66

GELATO
Come il Latte ★★★, p. 73
Fatamorgana ★★★, p. 73
Fior di Luna ★★★, p. 74
Gelateria Alberto Pica ★★★, p. 74
Il Gelato Bistrò ★★★, p. 60

INTERNATIONAL
Imàgo ★★★, p. 65
La Terrazza dell'Eden ★★★, p. 65

Vatican City & Prati

If you just want a quick, yet very tasty, sandwich to munch on before or after the Vatican safari, **Duecentogradi** is a top-notch panino joint with lots of good choices, right across from the Vatican walls at Piazza Risorgimento 3 (www.duecentogradi.it; ✆ **06-39754239**; Mon–Sat 11–2am; Sun 7pm–2am).

EXPENSIVE

Taverna Angelica ★★ MODERN ITALIAN/SEAFOOD   Considering how close this restaurant is to St. Peter's, it offers surprisingly good value for the money. Specialties include spaghetti with crunchy bacon and leeks, *fettuccine* with king prawns and eggplant (pastas 10€–14€), turbot with crushed almonds, and a delectable black-bread encrusted lamb with potato flan. The seafood is always fresh and simply cooked, from octopus carpaccio to sea bream with rosemary, and everything is beautifully presented. Service is excellent and the wine list carefully selected. Save room for the Moorish chocolate dessert. Reservations are required.

Piazza A. Capponi 6. www.tavernaangelica.it. ✆ **06-6874514.** Main courses 20€–24€. Daily 7pm–midnight; Sun noon–2:30pm. Closed 10 days in Aug. Metro: Ottaviano.

MODERATE

Pizza Rustica ★★★ PIZZA   Known for good reason as the "Michelangelo of pizza," celebrity chef Gabriele Bonci has a cult following in the Eternal City. And since he's been featured on TV shows overseas, as well as written up by influential bloggers, you can expect long lines at his recently expanded pizzeria (once known as Pizzarium). No matter—it's worth waiting for some of the best pizza you'll ever taste, sold by weight. The ingredients are fresh and organic, the crust is perfect, and the toppings often experimental (try the mortadella and crumbled pistachio, or the beguiling roasted potatoes and mozzarella). Hang around, because toppings change on a very quick rotation. There's also a good selection of Italian craft IPAs and wheat beers, and wines by the glass. Note that there are only a handful of benches outside to sit on, and reservations aren't taken.

Via della Meloria 43. www.gabrielebonci.it. ℰ **06-39745416.** Pizza 12€–14€ for large tray. Daily 11am–10pm. Metro: Cipro.

Romeo ★★ MODERN ITALIAN   This collaboration between a famous bakery dynasty and Michelin-star chef Cristina Bowerman of **Glass ★★★** (p. 69) offers a refreshing, contemporary detour from traditional Roman cooking, with American-inspired sandwiches, burgers, and creative pasta dishes served in sleek, modern premises. Musts include foie gras sandwiches served with sweet mango mayonnaise, and ravioli stuffed with asparagus and Castelmagno cheese. The restaurant-proper is at the back, but you can opt for a more casual lunch of pizza or sandwiches from the counters out front.

Via Silla 26/a. www.romeo.roma.it. ℰ **06-32110120.** Main courses 15€–30€. Mon–Sat 9am–midnight, Sun 10am–midnight. Metro: Ottaviano.

INEXPENSIVE

Il Gelato Bistrò ★★★ GELATO   Claudio Torcè's artisanal ice cream shop is credited with starting a natural, gluten-free gelato movement in Rome, but what makes this place really enticing (and why it doesn't really fit on our recommended mainstream gelato list; p. 72) are its savory flavors (out of a total 150). These are especially good during the happy hour *aperitivo* (dubbed *aperigelato*), when wine and cocktails are served. Prepare for gelato made from sweet bell peppers, chili, green tea, and even oyster and smoked salmon, paired with crudités, cold cuts, and even sushi. Purists can still get an incredible chocolate and pistachio, too, plus they offer free Wi-Fi.

Circonvallazione Trionfale 11/13. ℰ **06-39725949.** Cup from 3€. Tues–Thurs 8am–11pm, Fri 8am–midnight, Sat 9am–1am, Sun 9am–midnight. Metro: Cipro.

Panificio Bonci ★★ BAKERY   The newest addition to the Gabriele Bonci empire is not another pizzeria but a traditional bakery, with naturally leavened bread (including seasonal delights such as pumpkin bread), cakes, cookies, croissants, and puffy *pizzette* with tomato sauce, sold by weight. During holiday season, Bonci bakes some of the best panettone in town, characterized by innovative twists on the classic recipe.

Via Trionfale 36. ℂ **06-39734457.** Cakes, pizza 3€–5€. Mon–Sat 7:30–10pm; Sun 9:30am–3pm (July–Aug Mon–Sat 9:30am–3pm and 5–9pm). Closed 1 week in mid-Aug. Metro: Ottaviano.

Ancient Rome, Monti & Celio

If all you need is a snack, there's no beating **Gaudeo,** Via del Boschetto 112 (www.gaudeo.it; ℂ **06-98183689**). A freshly baked roll loaded with the finest prosciutto, mozzarella, salami, and a whole lot more costs between 4€ and 10€.

EXPENSIVE

InRoma al Campidoglio ★ ITALIAN   Once a social club for Rome's film industry, InRoma sits on a cobbled lane opposite the Palatine Hill. The food is consistently good thanks to careful sourcing of premier ingredients from around Italy. Meals might start with *caprese di bufala affumicata* (salad of tomatoes and smoked buffalo mozzarella) followed by *tagliata* (griddled sliced beef) with a red wine reduction. You can eat inside in an understated romantic setting, but we'd recommend you reserve on the terrace for a table to remember. They also serve a 12€ light lunch based around classic Roman pastas like *amatriciana* (cured pork, tomato, and Pecorino cheese).

Via dei Fienili 56. www.inroma.eu. ℂ **06-69191024.** Main courses 18€–30€. Daily noon–4pm and 6:30–11:30pm. Bus: C3, 80D, 81, 160, or 628.

MODERATE

Caffè Propaganda ★ MODERN ITALIAN   An all-day diner—part lively Parisian bistro, part cocktail bar—that's a safe bet for scoring a good meal within eyeshot of the Colosseum. Diners lounge on caramel-colored leather banquettes, choosing from a diverse menu that mixes Roman classics such as *carbonara* (pasta with cured pork, egg, and cheese), with familiar international dishes like Caesar salad (or an 18€ hamburger). When the chef gets whimsical, he offers treats like deep-fried *alici* (whole anchovy) served in a paper bag. Service is relaxed by North American standards, so only eat here if you have time to linger. A good mixology department, led by star bartender Patrick Pistolesi, skillfully assembles Propaganda's signature cocktails.

Via Claudia 15. www.caffepropaganda.it. ℂ **06-94534255.** Main courses 10€–18€. Tues–Sun 12:30pm–12:30am. Metro: Colosseo/Tram: 3.

La Barrique ★★ MODERN ROMAN   This cozy, contemporary *enoteca* (a wine bar with food) has a kitchen that knocks out farm-to-table fresh fare that complements the well-chosen wine list. The atmosphere is lively and informal, with rustic place settings and friendly service, as any proper enoteca should. Dishes come in hearty portions on daily changing menu. Expect the likes of *bocconcini di baccalà* (salt-cod morsels), crispy on the outside and served with a rich tomato dipping sauce; or *crostone* (a giant crostino) topped with grilled burrata cheese, chicory, and cherry tomatoes. Wines are available by the glass, quarter-liter, or half-liter.

Via del Boschetto 41B. ℂ **06-47825953.** Main courses 10€–18€. Mon–Fri 12:30–2:30pm; Mon–Sat 6:30–11:30pm. Metro: Cavour.

4

ROME | Where to Eat

Terre e Domus della Provincia Romana ★★ CONTEMPORARY ROMAN   Located in the stunning Palazzo Valentini, opposite the Trajan Column, with sleek, modern decor and floor-to-ceiling windows that overlook the Vittoriano and Trajan Markets, the newly managed "enoteca" belonging to the county of Rome strictly showcases only the best in local wines and products, plus produce grown at the Rebibbia prison in Rome. The menu lists traditional Roman classics and an abundance of seasonal, vegetable-driven dishes: we loved the gnocchi *cacio e pepe* and classic amatriciana. Don't miss the local artichokes, which are in their prime between February and May; you won't be disappointed.

Foro di Traiano 82–84. www.palazzovalentini.it. ⓒ **06-69940273.** *Main courses 10€–15€. Daily 7:30am-midnight.* Metro: Cavour. Bus: 80, 85, 87, or 175.

INEXPENSIVE

Li Rioni ★★ PIZZA   This fab neighborhood pizzeria is close enough to the Colosseum to be convenient, but just distant enough to avoid the dreaded "tourist" label that applies to so much dining in this part of town. Roman-style pizzas baked in the wood-stoked oven are among the best in Rome, with perfect crisp crusts. There's also a bruschetta list (from around 4€) and a range of salads. Outside tables can be cramped, but there's plenty of room inside. If you want to eat late, reservations are essential or you'll be fighting for a table with hungry locals.

Via SS. Quattro 24. ⓒ **06-70450605.** *Pizzas 6€–9€. Wed–Mon 7:30–11:30pm.* Bus: 53, 85, or 117.

Centro Storico & the Pantheon

Vegetarians looking for massive salads (or anyone who just wants a break from all those heavy meats and starches) can find great food at the neighborhood branch of **Insalata Ricca,** Largo dei Chiavari 85 (www.linsalataricca.it; ⓒ **06-68803656;** daily noon–midnight). It also offers free Wi-Fi.

EXPENSIVE

Da Pancrazio ★ ROMAN   At this traditional Roman restaurant, the premises *almost* outshine the food. The restaurant is built over the ruins of the 1st-century B.C Theatre of Pompey (close to where Julius Caesar was infamously murdered), and its various dining rooms and spaces are decked out with charming historical decor, from Roman-style benches and carved capitals to Belle Epoque paintings and furnishings (the restaurant opened in 1922). As for the menu, go for classic Roman fare such as *abbacchio al forno con patate* (baked lamb with potatoes) or the *spaghetti alla carbonara.*

Piazza del Biscione 92. www.dapancrazio.it. ⓒ **06-6861246.** *Main courses 15€–27€. Thurs–Tues 12:30–3pm and 7:30pm–11pm. Closed 3 weeks in Aug.* Bus: 46, 64, 84, or 916 to Largo di Torre Argentina.

Osteria dell'Antiquario ★ MODERN ITALIAN/ROMAN   A romantic restaurant, where tables are lit by candlelight in the evenings, and in the summer you can sit on the terrace overlooking the Palazzo Lancillotti. The menu is mostly Roman, but there some inventive detours such as lobster soup, linguine with grouper sauce, and gnocchi with clams and wild mushrooms. Fresh fish here is especially good, with tuna, turbot, prawns, and swordfish brought in daily from the coast.

Piazzetta di S. Simeone 26–27, Via dei Coronari. www.osteriadellantiquario.it. ⦿ **06-6879694.** Main courses 15€–30€. Daily 7–11pm; Sept–June also daily noon–2:30pm. Closed 15 days in mid-Aug, Christmas, and Jan 6–30. Bus: 70, 81, or 90.

MODERATE

Alfredo e Ada ★ ROMAN No menus here, just the waiter—usually owner Sergio—explaining, in Italian, what the kitchen is preparing that day. You'll typically be offered Roman trattoria classics like eggplant Parmigiana, artichoke lasagna, excellent carbonara, or tripe. The whole place oozes character, with shared tables, scribbled walls festooned with drawings and paintings, and the house wine poured into carafes from a tap in the wall. With only five tables, try to make a reservation or get here early. This sort of place is becoming rare in Rome—enjoy it while you can.

Via dei Banchi Nuovi 14. ⦿ **06-6878842.** Main courses 10€–18€. Tue–Sat 12:30pm–midnight. Closed Aug. Bus: 46B, 98, 870, or 881.

Armando al Pantheon ★ ROMAN/VEGETARIAN Despite being just a few steps from the Pantheon, this typical Roman trattoria remains an authentic, family-owned business serving as many locals as tourists. Chef Armando Gargioli took over the place in 1961, and his sons now run the business. Roman favorites to look out for include the *pasta e ceci* (pasta and chickpeas, on Fri only), the Jewish-influenced *aliciotti all'indivia* (endive and roasted anchovies, Tues only), and the fabulous *abbacchio* (roast lamb). Another bonus: Vegetarians get their own, fairly extensive, menu. Good wine list with local labels.

Salita dei Crescenzi 31. www.armandoalpantheon.it. ⦿ **06-68803034.** Main courses 10€–24€. Mon–Fri noon–3pm and 7–11pm; Sat noon–3pm. Closed Aug. Bus: 30, 40, 62, 64, 81, or 492.

La Campana ★★ ROMAN/ITALIAN Rome's oldest and most traditional restaurant is located at a stone's throw from Piazza Navona and the Pantheon. Family atmosphere and a classic Roman elegance permeate the spacious, well-lit rooms. The atmosphere is convivial yet refined, with a lovely mixture of regulars and locals. There's a broad selection of vegetable-based *antipasti* displayed on a buffet at the entrance, and the menu (which changes daily) features authentic *cucina romana* classics like pasta with oxtail ragout, tripe, gnocchi, *cacio e pepe,* and myriad vegetarian choices. The wine list includes interesting local labels, and the staff and service are impeccable.

Vicolo della Campana 18. www.ristorantelacampana.com. ⦿ **06-6875273.** Main courses 12€–18€. Tue–Sun noon–3pm and 7:30–11pm. Bus: 30, 70, 81, 87, 186, 492, or 628.

Nonna Betta ★★ JEWISH/ROMAN Though not strictly kosher, this is the only restaurant in Rome's old Jewish quarter historically owned

4

ROME | Where to Eat

and managed by Roman Jews. Traditional "nonna" dishes include delicious *carciofi alla giudia* (deep fried artichokes), stellar tagliolini with mullet roe and chicory, and quintessential homemade baccalà preparations. Leave room for desserts like "pizza ebraica," a sort of nutty fruit cake, and all manner of Middle Eastern honey and pistachio creations. Good Israeli wines are on the wine list.

Via del Portico d'Ottavia 16. www.nonnabetta.it. *©* **06-68806263.** Main courses 10€. Sun–Fri noon–3pm and 7–11pm. Bus: 23, 63, 280, 630, or 780. Tram 8.

INEXPENSIVE

Antico Forno Roscioli ★★ BAKERY   The Rosciolis have been running this celebrated bakery for three generations since the 1970s, though the premises have been knocking out bread since at least 1824. Today, it's home to the finest crusty sourdough in Rome, assorted cakes, and addictive pastries and biscotti, as well as exceptional Roman-style *pizza bianca* and *pizza rossa* sold by weight. Note that this is a take-out joint, with very limited seating inside and only a few stand-up tables out front—and the wider range of pizza toppings is only available from noon to 2:30pm. The phenomenal Roscioli restaurant and *salumeria* deli is around the corner, at Via dei Giubbonari 21.

Via dei Chiavari 34. *www.anticofornoroscioli.it.* *©* **06-6864045.** Pizza from 5€ (sold by weight). Mon–Sat 7am–7:30pm. Tram: 8.

Tridente & the Spanish Steps

The historic cafes near the Spanish Steps are saturated with history, but sadly, tend to be overpriced tourist traps these days, where mediocre cakes or even a cup of coffee or tea will cost 5€. Nevertheless, you may want to pop inside the two most celebrated institutions: **Babington's Tea Room** (www.babingtons.com; *©* **06-6786027;** daily 10am–9:30pm) was established in 1893 at the foot of the Spanish Steps by a couple of English *signore*. **Caffè Greco,** Via dei Condotti 86 (www.anticocaffegreco.eu; *©* **06-6791700;** daily 9am–8pm), is Rome's oldest bar, opened in 1760 and hosting Keats, Ibsen, Goethe, and many other historical *cognoscenti*.

EXPENSIVE

Café Romano ★ CONTEMPORARY ROMAN   The official restaurant of the posh Hotel d'Inghilterra lies on one of Rome's "fashion streets," a suitably upscale temple to fine dining. Chef Antonio Vitale is the current maestro, his seasonal, contemporary menus utilizing fresh produce and riffing on traditional Roman dishes. Starters such as zucchini blossoms stuffed with buffalo mozzarella, burrata cheese, and salmon roe are classic. The pasta with seafood and grated mozzarella adds some of his Neapolitan hometown flavor. For the main course, there's duck leg served with potato pie, and the roasted veal shank with asparagus, which are both refined, tantalizing versions of Roman favorites.

In Hotel d'Inghilterra, Via Borgognona 4. www.niquesahotels.com. *©* **06-69981500.** Main courses 16€–31€. Daily 7–10:30am and noon–10:30pm. Metro: Spagna.

Canova Tadolini ★★ ROMAN   Few restaurants are so steeped in history as this place. Antonio Canova's sculpture studio was kept as a workshop by the descendants of his pupil, Adamo Tadolini, until 1967, explaining why even today it is littered with tools and sculptures in bronze, plaster, and marble. The whole thing really does seem like a museum, with tables squeezed between models, casts, drapes, and bas-reliefs. The Sala Giulio is dominated by a giant copy of Giulio (Adamo's grandson) Tadolini's statue of Pope Leo XIII (the original stands on the Pope's tomb), while the whimsical (and slightly creepy) Sala Anatomia is decorated with odd bits of marble arms, legs, and thighs once attached to complete sculptures. The pasta menu features a tasty version of *spaghetti alle vongole* and *alla carbonara,* while the entrees offer more of interest, from the veal chop grilled with rustic potatoes and rosemary to the sliced skirt steak salad with arugula, cherry tomatoes, and Parmesan.

Via del Babuino 150A–B. www.canovatadolini.com. ℂ **06-32110702.** Main courses 11€–25€. Mon–Sat 8am–8:30pm. Metro: Spagna.

Imàgo ★★★ INTERNATIONAL/MODERN ITALIAN   The views of Rome from this sixth-floor hotel restaurant are jaw-dropping, with a gorgeous panorama of the old city glowing pink and peach as the sun goes down. The food is equally special, with head chef Francesco Apreda's reinterpretation of regional Italian cuisine borrowing heavily from Indian and Japanese culinary schools. Menus are seasonal, but might include duck breast tandoori-style, sake-glazed black cod with purple baby vegetables, or even lavender-flavored casserole of quail and sea scallops. Reservations are essential; jackets required.

In Hotel Hassler, Piazza della Trinità dei Monti 6. www.hotelhasslerroma.com. ℂ **06-69934726.** Main courses 39€–46€; 9-course tasting menu 140€; 6-course vegetarian menu 120€. Daily 7:30–10:30pm. Metro: Spagna.

MODERATE

Il Bacaro ★ MODERN ITALIAN   Although it's housed in a 17th-century *palazzo,* this is a modern Roman bistro with contemporary takes on traditional trattoria dishes. Expect pasta with swordfish or tuna; or skewered prawns wrapped in thin strips of melty lardo pork, served on vegetal velouté; or the Argentine beef dotted with flecks of pâté, or when available, shaved white truffles from Piedmont. The desserts revolve around a sensational selection of mousses paired with Bavarian chocolate, hazelnuts, caramel, and pistachio. The wine list features over 600 labels, many well-priced varietals from all over Italy, and with just as much attention paid to French wines.

Via degli Spagnoli 27 (near Piazza delle Coppelle). www.ilbacororoma.com. ℂ **06-6872554.** Main courses 14€–24€. Daily 10am–1am. Metro: Spagna.

Via Veneto & Piazza Barberini
EXPENSIVE
La Terrazza dell'Eden ★★★ INTERNATIONAL/MODERN ITALIAN   Perched on the top floor of the Hotel Eden, this restaurant offers superb cuisine and breathtaking views that sweep from Villa Borghese all the way to St.

Peter's. Exciting young chef Fabio Ciervo offers an interesting angle on continental classics, with elegant starters like smoked lobster with wild black rice; to be followed by fragrant risotto with cherries, Champagne rosé, and *pigeon de Bresse* and more treats from the tempting list of pastas. Menus change seasonally, but expect a range of fresh fish, such as sea bass, mullet, and turbot dishes, and some heavily enhanced Roman-style meats, from lamb in a crust of mixed herbs with mushrooms and lemon-thyme sauce, to roast venison and sausage with pistachio and a piquant quince and licorice sauce. Forget showing up without an advance reservation.

In Hotel Eden, Via Ludovisi 49. www.dorchestercollection.com. ✆ **06-47812752.** Main courses 35€–55€; 6-course fixed-price gourmet menu, excluding wine 120€. Daily 12:30–2:30pm and 7:30–10:30pm. Metro: Barberini.

MODERATE
Colline Emiliane ★★ EMILIANA-ROMAGNOLA   A family-owned
restaurant tucked in an alley beside the Trevi Fountain, it's been serving traditional dishes from Emilia-Romagna since 1931. Service is excellent and so is the food: Classics include *tortelli di zucca* (pasta pockets stuffed with creamy pumpkin and crumbled amaretto biscuits) and magnificent *tagliatelle alla bolognese*. Save room for the chocolate tart or lemon meringue pie for dessert. Reservations are essential.

Via degli Avignonesi 22 (off Piazza Barberini). ✆ **06-4817538.** Main courses 14€–25€. Tues–Sun 12:30–2:45pm; Tues–Sat 7:30–10:45pm. Closed Aug and Sun in July. Metro: Barberini.

Villa Borghese & Parioli
EXPENSIVE
Al Ceppo ★★ MARCHIGIANA/ROMAN   The setting of this Parioli din-
ing institution is that of an elegant, 19th-century parlor with family portraits on the walls and lit chandeliers, floral arrangements, and an open kitchen whose main feature is the wood-stoked hearth, where various meats are roasted as you watch. Service is palatial, with the grace proper of the two sisters running it. Because Cristina and Marisa are originally from Le Marche region northeast of Rome, the food is a mixture of regional hallmark dishes, with *marchigiana*-style rabbit, fish stews, fresh seafood, and porchetta. But you'll also find veal, pork, and a variety of pastas. If the braised beef cheek is on the menu, don't forego that mystical experience.

Via Panama 2 (near Piazza Ungheria). www.ristorantealceppo.it. ✆ **06-8419696.** Main courses 18€–32€. Tues–Sun 12:30–3pm and 8–11pm. Closed last 2 weeks in Aug. Bus: 52 or 910.

Metamorfosi ★★★ MODERN ITALIAN   This Michelin star–awarded
restaurant is a feast for both eyes and tastebuds. The minimalistic decor (soft tones of chocolate and beige, dotted with subtle floral accents) balances the chef's flair for astonishing creations. At the helm of the kitchen is chef Roy Caceres, native of Colombia, who likes to stir his guests' emotions, spanning beyond smell and taste, and he tells a story with each beautifully crafted dish.

Caceres shines in risotto and pasta preparations, and elegant game, meat, and fish interpretations. Be prepared for creamy soft cheese ravioli mixed with salmon, hazelnut, and smoked pepper; risotto wrapped in a thin saffron film; stellar glazed eel with crumbled farro and sweet onion sorbet; crispy lamb with almonds, eggplant, and gin-juniper ice cream. Guests can also choose between two creative tasting menus, each featuring the restaurant's show-pieces, and diners can benefit from the helpful guidance of a very talented sommelier.

Via Giovanni Antonelli 30/32. www.metamorfosiroma.it. ℂ **06-8076839.** Main courses 25€–30€. Mon–Fri 12:30–3pm and 8–11:30pm; Sat 7:30–midnight. Bus: 168, 223, 910 and 926.

MODERATE

Al Vero Girarrosto Toscano ★★ TUSCAN This classic dolce vita hangout has been popular with celebrities and gourmands since its opening in the '60s. Since then, the restaurant's praised Roman cuisine has been replaced over the years by universally acclaimed Tuscan recipes, for which it now draws the same VIP crowds and carnivores south of the Arno. The decor is as elegant as the menu, with wood paneling, sleek finishings, and a cozy fire-place that doubles as open-hearth grill. When choosing, go for classic Tuscan hors d'oeuvres, like liver crostini and assorted bruschettas, but also focus your attention on equally classic hearty soups, like pasta e fagioli with borlotti beans, and droolsome *ribollita* (a minestrone with kale, cannellini beans, and bread). Grilled meats come center stage, with *girarrosto* (Tuscan barbecue) classics being the Fiorentina (2-lb. T-bone), succulent tenderloin, filet, and a platter of mixed grilled ribs, chops, and sausages.

Via Campania 29. www.alverogirarrostotoscano.it. ℂ **06-4821899.** *Main courses 18€– 35€. Daily 12:30–3pm and 7:30–midnight. Bus: 52, 53, 217, 360 or 910.*

Around Termini
EXPENSIVE

Pipero al Rex ★★★ CONTEMPORARY ROMAN Who said Termini can't be romantic? Located on the ground floor of the Rex Hotel, this tastefully decorated dining room serves a maximum of 16 covers in a room lined with white tablecloths and flooded in warm lighting. Sommelier and consummate host Alessandro Pipero works the front of the Michelin-star dining room, while Chef Luciano Monosilio runs the kitchen. Service is impeccable and never intrusive, and the menu features an interesting selection of classic spaghetti *carbonara* (portion size and price start at 50 grams for only 10€), or more modern chocolate-filled tortellini in bone broth; while mains shine in the duck breast tartare, or the anglerfish served with licorice and Jerusalem artichoke.

Via Torino 149. www.hotelrex.net. ✆ **06-4815702.** *Main courses 30€–25€; 9-course tasting menu 80€. Mon–Sat 12:30–2:30pm and 7:30–10:30pm.* Metro: Termini.

MODERATE

Da Danilo ★★ ROMAN   The general rule is: Don't dine around the train station, but there are a few exceptions. Da Danilo is one of them. Popular with locals on business lunches and *cucina romana* pundits, this intimate trattoria offers authentic Rome and Lazio fare, made with top-notch local products. Don't let the informal setting, homey wood paneling, and soccer celebrity photos on the walls trick you: This restaurant's fine dining, and care for quality, ranks as one of Rome's finest. Mainstays include one of Rome's best *cacio e pepe,* served out of a massive, scooped out Pecorino cheese round; the house *carbonara,* creamy and egg-forward; and homemade gnocchi served, as traditions dictates, exclusively on Thursday. The beef tartare, grilled lamb chops, and lardo-laced rib-eyes are menu strong points, as are all the daily meat specials. The wine list includes a good choice of fine Lazio labels, and there are interesting tastings and events hosted in the small private room downstairs.

Via Petrarca 13. www.trattoriadadanilo.it. ✆ **06-77200111.** *Main courses 12€–17€. Tue–Sat 12:30–3pm and 7:30–midnight. Closed 2 weeks in August.* Metro: Vittorio Emanuele and Manzoni.

Trimani Il Wine Bar ★ MODERN ITALIAN   This small bistro and impressively stocked wine bar attracts wine lovers in a modern and relaxed ambiance, with contemporary place settings, slate flooring, and smooth jazz. Dishes are made to suit the wines: Seasonal pasta *primi* might include a salad of octopus, fava beans, and potato spiked with olives and almonds. Refined entrees can include rabbit stuffed with asparagus and Luganega sausage served with a zucchini velouté. There's a well-chosen wines-by-the-glass list that changes daily. If you just want a snack to accompany your vino, cheese and salami plates range from 9€ to 13€.

Via Cernaia 37B. www.trimani.com. ✆ **06-4469630.** *Main courses 10€–18€. Mon–Sat 11:30am–3pm and 5:30pm–midnight; mid-Jun to mid-Sept also closed Sat. Closed 2 weeks in mid-Aug.* Metro: Repubblica or Castro Pretorio.

INEXPENSIVE

Pinsere ★★ PIZZA   *Pinsa* is not your average pizza, rather an ancient Roman preparation: an oval focaccia made with a blend of four organic flours and olive oil that's left to rise for 2 to 3 days. The result is a fragrant, single-portion, feather-light snack. The small Pinsere bakery bakes pinsa to order, tops each with a variety of ingredients, and sells them over a tiny counter for an even smaller price. Favorites are "Campionessa" with pureed pumpkin, smoked cheese, and pancetta; classic tomato, basil, and buffalo mozzarella; and the summer plain pinsa stuffed with silken slices of prosciutto and fresh figs. Toppings and fillings are seasonal and change in quick rotation. There's also a good choice of salads and soups, plus bottled beers and soft drinks. Note that there is no seating, so plan on grabbing and going.

Via Flavia 98. www.pinsereroma.com. ⓒ **06-42020924.** *Pinsa 1€–4,50€ according to topping.* Mon–Fri 9am–4pm. Bus: 60, 60L, 61, 62, 82, 492, 910.

Trastevere

Popular craft-beer bar **Bir and Fud** (p. 128) also serves pizzas and traditional snacks like *supplì* (fried rice croquettes filled with mozzarella and ragout) to hungry drinkers. It serves food every evening, and at lunchtime Thursday through Sunday.

EXPENSIVE

Glass ★★★ CONTEMPORARY ROMAN   Sleek modernism rules here, in design as well as cuisine. Walls are stark white and floors are polished, and the menu a mix of inventive and cosmopolitan flair. Listings change monthly, but expect the likes of pasta with lemon, black garlic, and wild asparagus, followed by sumac-scented lamb with purple potato chips. Thanks to the skills of Michelin star–awarded chef Cristina Bowerman, this is one of Rome's hottest tables—reservations are essential.

Vicolo del Cinque 58. www.glass-restaurant.it. ⓒ **06-58335903.** Main courses 28€–45€; fixed price menus 70€–90€. Tues–Sun 7:30–11:30pm. Closed 2 weeks in Jan and 2 weeks in July. Bus: 125.

La Gensola ★★★ ROMAN/SEAFOOD   Family-run and little known, this place is however considered among locals as one of the best seafood destinations in town. Warm and welcoming, like a true Trastevere home, the decor here is cozy and intimate, with soft lighting and a life-size wood-carved tree in the middle of the main dining room. Fish-lovers flock here for trademark spaghetti with sea urchin, a fish-forward *amatriciana*, and general traditional Roman cuisine with a marine twist. The incredibly fresh catch is sourced in Lazio's best coastal sea auctions daily. Besides melt-in-your-mouth calamari, shrimp and tuna, ceviche, carpaccios and tartares, the grill also provides succulent beefsteaks and other non-fish-based dishes. Reservations, which are mandatory on the weekend, can also be made online via the restaurant's website, which is in Italian only.

Piazza della Gensola 15. www.osterialagensola.it. ⓒ **06-58332758.** Main courses 15€. Daily 12:30–3pm and 7:30–11:30pm. Bus: 125.

MODERATE

Cacio e Pepe ★ ROMAN   This ultra-traditional trattoria, complete with paper tablecloths, a TV in the background showing the game, the owner chatting up the ladies, and a bustling crowd waiting to be seated outside, is a Trastevere stalwart. On the menu, besides namesake *cacio e pepe* pasta (sheep's milk Pecorino cheese and black pepper), you won't go wrong with other classic Roman pasta dishes such as *amatriciana* (tomato and guanciale pork jowl) and a very good rendition of *carbonara* (egg, Pecorino, and crispy guanciale)—be ready for hearty portions. For *secondo*—if you have room left—keep it simple; *polpette* (stewed meatballs), *saltimbocca alla romana* (veal cutlets with sage and ham), and simple grilled meats offer oodles of flavor at sensible prices. There are few culinary surprises, but it's all cheap, served with a smile, and in the heart of tourist Trastevere.

Vicolo del Cinque 15. www.osteriacacioepepe.it. ℂ **06-89572853.** Main courses 9€–18€. Daily 7pm–midnight; Sun also 12:30–3pm. Bus: 125.

Da Enzo al 29 ★★ ROMAN   This classic and untouristy Trastevere family-run trattoria serves traditional Roman cuisine in a friendly and relaxed atmosphere, with a few outdoor tables looking out on some of Trastevere's quaintest cobbled alleys. *Cucina romana* including classic carbonara, amatriciana, and cacio e pepe win the gold, but also consider the ravioli stuffed with ricotta and spinach, and the meatballs braised in tomato sauce. Local wines can be ordered by the jug or glass, and desserts, including a good mascarpone with wild strawberries, come served in either full or half portions.

Via dei Vascellari 29. www.daenzoal29.com. ℂ **06 5812260.** Main courses 8€–15€. Mon–Sat 12 :30–3pm and 7:30–11:00pm. Bus: 125.

INEXPENSIVE

Dar Poeta ★ PIZZA   Many consider this the best source for pizza (around 8€) in Rome. I wouldn't go that far, but "the poet" does serve up a good pie, with good toppings, all creatively combined. If the lines are long to eat in, you can also walk up to the host and order a pie for takeout. Popular signature pizzas include the *patataccia* (potatoes, zucchini and speck) or the decadent dessert calzone, filled with ricotta and Nutella.

Vicolo del Bologna 45. www.darpoeta.com. ℂ **06-5880516.** Pizzas 5€–9€. Daily noon–11pm. Bus: 125.

Testaccio

Rome's old meatpacking district is a major dining zone. The old slaughter-houses have been transformed into art venues, markets, and museum **MACRO** (p. 114), but restaurants here still specialize in meats from the *quinto quarto* (the "fifth quarter")—the leftover parts of an animal after the slaughter, typically offal like sweetbreads, tripe, tails, and other goodies you won't find on most American menus (although you find the standard cuts here, too). This is an area to eat *quinto quarto*—offal, either in the restaurants recommended below, or from any street-food stall in the **Nuovo Mercato di Testaccio** (p. 125). If you book a food-themed tour of Rome, you will almost certainly end up here.

EXPENSIVE

Checchino dal 1887 ★★ ROMAN   For haute *quinto quarto* fare, Checchino dal 1887 is your best bet. Testaccio has been changing rapidly, but not Checchino. It's a more expensive choice than most of the other restaurants in this area. Still, Romans from all over the city keep coming back here when they want authentic *tonnarelli al sugo di coda* (pasta with a rich oxtail sauce for which Checchino holds a secret recipe) and *pajata* (veal intestines) cooked any number of ways—with *rigatoni* pasta, roasted, or in a stew.

Via di Monte Testaccio 30. www.checchino-dal-1887.com. ℂ **06-5743816.** Main courses 14€–25€; fixed-price menu 42€–63€. Tues–Sat 12:30–2:45pm and 8–11:45pm. Closed Aug and last week in Dec. Bus: 83, 673, or 719.

MODERATE

Flavio al Velavevodetto ★★ ROMAN   Flavio's plain dining room is burrowed out of the side of Rome's most unusual "hill"—a large mound made from amphorae discarded during the Roman era. But this is one of the best places in the city to try well-prepped classic pastas like *cacio e pepe* (Pecorino cheese and black pepper), and *quinto quarto* entrees at fair prices. The *misto umido* is an ideal three-way sampler for first-timers, with portions of *polpette* (meatballs), *coda alla vaccinara* (oxtail), and *involtini* (stuffed rolled veal). Homemade desserts are also tasty, and the tiramisu wins the gold.

Via di Monte Testaccio 97–99. www.ristorantevelavevodetto.it. ℂ **06-5744194.** Main courses 12€–17€. Daily 12:30–3pm and 7:45–11pm. Bus: 83, 673, or 719.

Osteria degli Amici ★★ MODERN ROMAN   This intimate *osteria,* on the corner of nightlife central and the hill of broken anforas, serves everything from traditional *cucina romana* to creative interpretations. Charming best buddies Claudio and Alessandro base their offers on fresh produce sourced at the nearby market and the experience they gathered working in famous kitchens around the world. Signature musts include golden-crusted fried mozzarella "in carrozza," and a wide choice of pastas, ranging from classic *carbonara* to large *paccheri* tubes with mussels, clams, and cherry tomatoes. My favorite remains "gricia coi carciofi," a tomatoless *amatriciana* with added slivers of braised artichoke. Leave room for the apple tartlet with cinnamon gelato.

Via Nicola Zabaglia 25. No website. ℂ **06-5781466.** Main courses 14€–18€. Wed–Mon 12:30–3pm and 7:30–midnight. Bus: 83, 673, or 719.

Porto Fluviale ★ MODERN ITALIAN   This multi-functional dining behemoth—divided into trattoria, street-food stall, buffet, and pizzeria—can accommodate pretty much whatever you fancy, whenever you fancy, any day you like. The decor is modern, vaguely industrial, with a daytime clientele of young families, white collars, and groups of friends—the vibe gets younger after dark. From the various menus, best bets are the 30 or so *ciccheti,* small appetizers that allow you to test and taste the kitchen's range. Share a few platters of *carpaccio di baccalà* (thin slices of salt-cod), *maialino* (suckling pig with pureed apple and rosemary), and *burrata e pomodori* (Apulian mozzarella pouch filled with cream, served with tomatoes). Most of the regular menu (*primi* and *secondi*) also comes in half portions, and there are sub-10€ burgers, too. The pizzas are nondescript, so can be overlooked.

Via del Porto Fluviale 22. www.portofluviale.com. ⓒ **06-5743199.** Main courses 8€–19€; set lunch 12€–20€. Daily 10:30am–2am. Metro: Piramide.

INEXPENSIVE

Da Remo ★★ PIZZA Mentioning "Testaccio" and "pizza" in the same sentence elicits one typical response from locals: Da Remo, which is a Roman institution. In the summer, reservations at least 2 days in advance are wise. Every crisp-crusted pizza is made for all to see behind the open counters. The most basic ones (margherita and marinara) start at around 6€. If it's too crowded on a summer evening, order your pizza as takeout and eat it in the quaint park across the street. No credit cards.

Piazza Santa Maria Liberatrice 44. No website. ⓒ **06-5746270.** Pizzas 7€–15€. Mon–Sat 7pm–1am. Bus: 83, 673, or 719.

La Moderna ★★ PIZZA/MODERN ITALIAN For lovers of Napoli-style pizza (thicker rim), consider this pizzeria and cocktail bar with an unabashed passion for motion pictures. The decor flirts with Paris bistros and New York delis, with lots of vintage posters and furnishings, a warm and cozy atmosphere, and great lighting. In addition to the movie memorabilia, there's even a functioning silver screen in one of the main dining rooms. Besides signature pizzas, the menu may feature spaghetti *aglio, olio e peperoncino,* a classic preparation made with properly assembled garlic, olive oil, and chili pepper flakes. There's also offal, and why not, in Testaccio? So be prepared for braised tongue, liver, and grilled sweetbreads; plus street food with a wide selection of frankfurters, burgers, and delicious all-Roman *trapizzini* (triangular pizza pockets filled with local classics, like tripe or meatballs). An impressive choice of Italian and foreign craft beers and excellent music complete the warm setting.

Via Galvani 89. www.lamoderna-testaccio.com. ⓒ **06-5750123.** Pizzas 7€; main courses 9€–15€. Daily 7:30am–2am. Bus: 83, 673, or 719.

Gelato

Don't leave town without trying one of Rome's outstanding **ice-cream parlors.** However, choose your Italian ice carefully! *Gelaterie* aimed exclusively at tourists are notorious for poor-quality gelato and sky-high prices. Don't buy close to the main piazzas, and avoid places whose vats display heaped, brightly colored, air-pumped gelato. The best gelato is made from only natural ingredients, which impart an often subtle color (if the pistachio gelato is bright green, for example, rather than grayish-green, move on).

You should generally take your cone (*cono*) or small cup (*coppetta*) and walk as you eat—sitting down on the premises or ordering at outside tables could be much more expensive.

Ordering gelato.

Below are some of our favorite spots in the city, each definitely worth a detour. Each generally opens midmorning and closes late—sometimes after midnight on a summer weekend evening.

Come il Latte ★★★ GELATO   *Latte* is Italian for milk, and in this case, the key ingredient in this delightful little gelateria's daily artisan production. Flavors range from salted caramel to mascarpone and crumbled cookies, espresso coffee, and rice with cinnamon; while fruit flavors rotate according to season. Summer delights may include Sorrento lemons and wild strawberries; persimmon, date, and chestnut creams grace the winter menu. Homemade wafer and sugar cones can be filled with dark or white chocolate sauce and then scooped with your flavors of choice, ultimately topped with fresh whipped cream. Sleek design, sustainable short supply chain ingredients, Americana drinking fountain, and old school vat containers complete the charming setting.

Via Silvio Spaventa 24. www.comeillatte.it. ⓒ **06-42903882.** Cups from 3€. Daily noon–midnight and Sat–Sun 4–10pm. Closed 2 weeks in mid-Aug. Metro: Repubblica or Castro Pretorio.

Fatamorgana ★★★ GELATO   Creative flavors are the hallmark of this Monti gelateria. Try the *crema di zenzero* (cream of ginger), *cioccolato Lapsang Souchong* (chocolate with smoked black tea), or a surprising basil-walnut-honey combo. There's a firm commitment to seasonal and organic ingredients in every slurp, and given the founder has celiac disease, all products, cones included, are gluten-free.

Piazza degli Zingari 5. www.gelateriafatamorgana.it. ℂ **06-86391589.** Cones from 2€.
Metro: Cavour. Also at: Via Lago di Lesina 9–11; Via Bettolo 7; Piazza San Cosimato.

Fior di Luna ★★★ GELATO   Trastevere's best artisan gelato, made with
natural and fairtrade produce. The range is small, and there are no cones—but
you won't care. The stars are the intense and incredibly rich chocolate flavors,
spiked with fig or orange, or made with single *cru* cocoa. Fior di Luna also
churns one mean pistachio, one unlike you've ever tasted.
Via della Lungaretta 96. www.fiordiluna.com. ℂ **06-64561314.** Cups from 2€. Bus: H or
780/Tram: 8.

Gelateria Alberto Pica ★★★ GELATO   One of Rome's oldest artisan
gelato makers, it produces top-quality gelato churned with ingredients
sourced locally, including wild strawberries grown on the family's countryside estate. Just a few of our *many* faves include rice with cinnamon, Sicilian
pistachio, honey and orange, and Amalfi lemon.
Via della Seggiola 12. No website. ℂ **06-6868405.** Cups from 2€. Daily 8am-9pm. Bus:
H, 63, 780, or 810; Tram 8.

EXPLORING ROME

Rome's ancient monuments, whether time-blackened or gleaming in the wake
of a recent restoration, are a constant reminder that Rome was one of the
greatest centers of Western civilization. In the heyday of the Empire, all roads
led to Rome, with good reason. It was one of the first cosmopolitan cities,
importing slaves, gladiators, great art, and even citizens from the far corners

No More Lines

The endless lines outside Italian museums and attractions are a fact of life.
But reservation services can help you
avoid the wait, at least for some of the
major museums. Buying a **Roma Pass**
(p. 35) is a good start—holders can use
a special entrance at the Colosseum,
and for your first two (free) museums,
you can skip the line (so be sure to
choose busy ones).

For the **Vatican Museums,** buy an
advance ticket at **www.biglietteriamu-
sei.vatican.va/musei/tickets/do**; you
pay an extra 4€, but will be able to skip
the line at the main entrance (which can
be very, very long). Note that St. Peter's
is not included: There is no way to jump
the line there.

Coopculture (www.coopculture.it)
operates an online ticket office that
allows you to skip the line at several
sites, including the Colosseum and the
Forum, with a reservation fee of 2€ and
2€ to print tickets in advance.

Select Italy also allows you to
reserve your tickets for the Colosseum,
the Roman Forum, Palatine Hill, the Galleria Borghese, plus many other museums in Florence and Venice. The cost
varies depending on the museum—
there's an agency fee on top of ticket
prices—with several combination passes
available. Contact Select Italy at ℂ **800/
877-1755** in the U.S. or buy your tickets
online at **www.selectitaly.com**.

of the world. Despite its carnage, brutality, and corruption, Rome left a legacy of law; a heritage of art, architecture, and engineering; and a canny lesson in how to conquer enemies by absorbing their cultures.

But Ancient Rome is only part of the spectacle. The Vatican has had a tremendous influence on making the city a tourism center. Although Vatican architects stripped down much of the city's ancient glory during the Renaissance, looting ancient ruins (the Forum especially) for their precious marble, they created more treasures and even occasionally incorporated the old into the new—as Michelangelo did when turning the Baths of Diocletian into a church. And in the years that followed, Bernini adorned the city with the wonders of the baroque, especially his glorious fountains.

INDEX OF ATTRACTIONS & SITES

St. Peter's & the Vatican
VATICAN CITY

The world's smallest sovereign state, **Vatican City** is a truly tiny territory, comprising little more than St. Peter's Basilica and the walled headquarters of the Roman Catholic Church. There are no border controls, of course, though the city-state's 800 inhabitants (essentially clergymen and Swiss Guards) have their own radio station, daily newspaper, tax-free pharmacy, petrol pumps, postal service, and head of state—the pope. The pope had always exercised a high degree of political independence from the rest of Italy in the form of the medieval Papal States, and this independence was formalized by the 1929 Lateran Treaty between Pope Pius XI and the Italian government to create the Vatican. The city is still protected by the flamboyantly uniformed (some say by Michelangelo) Swiss Guards, a tradition dating from the days when the Swiss Guards, known as brave soldiers, were often hired out as mercenaries for foreign armies. Today, the Vatican remains at the center of the Roman Catholic world, the home of the pope and—it is believed—the resting place of St. Peter. **St. Peter's Basilica** is obviously one of the highlights, but the only part of the Apostolic Palace itself that you can visit independently are the **Vatican Museums;** with over 100 galleries, it's the biggest and richest museum complex in the world.

The only entrance to St. Peter's for tourists is through one of the glories of the Western world: Bernini's 17th-century **St. Peter's Square (Piazza San**

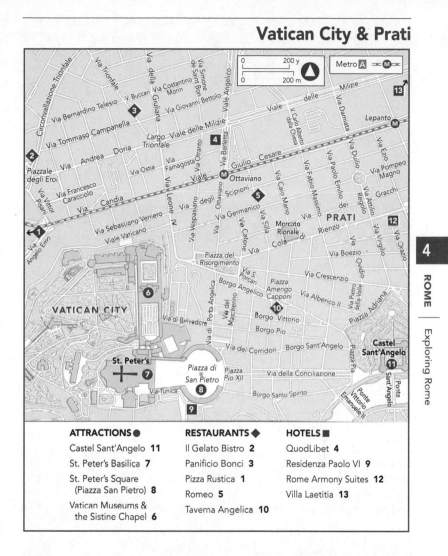

ATTRACTIONS ●

Castel Sant'Angelo **11**

St. Peter's Basilica **7**

St. Peter's Square
(Piazza San Pietro) **8**

Vatican Museums &
the Sistine Chapel **6**

RESTAURANTS ◆

Il Gelato Bistro **2**

Panificio Bonci **3**

Pizza Rustica **1**

Romeo **5**

Taverna Angelica **10**

HOTELS ■

QuodLibet **4**

Residenza Paolo VI **9**

Rome Armony Suites **12**

Villa Laetitia **13**

Pietro). As you stand in the huge piazza, you are in the arms of an ellipse partly enclosed by a majestic **Doric-pillared colonnade.** Stand in the marked disc embedded in the piazza pavement near the fountains to see the columns all lined up in an impressive optical illusion. Straight ahead is the facade of St. Peter's itself (Sts. Peter and Paul are represented by statues in front, with Peter carrying the keys to the kingdom), and to the right, above the colonnade, are the dark brown buildings of the **papal apartments** and the Vatican Museums. In the center of the square is a 4,000-year-old **Egyptian obelisk,** created in the ancient city of Heliopolis on the Nile delta and appropriated by the Romans under Emperor Augustus. Flanking the obelisk are two 17th-century

Vatican City.

fountains. The one on the right (facing the basilica), by Carlo Maderno, who designed the facade of St. Peter's, was placed here by Bernini himself; the other is by Carlo Fontana.

On the left side of Piazza San Pietro is the **Vatican Tourist Office** (www.vatican.va; ✆ **06-69882019;** Mon–Sat 8:30am–7:30pm). It sells maps and guides that will help you make more sense of the riches you will be seeing in the museums, and it also accepts reservations for tours of the Vatican Gardens.

St. Peter's Basilica ★★★

CHURCH The Basilica di San Pietro, or simply **St. Peter's,** is the holiest shrine of the Catholic Church, built on the site of St. Peter's tomb by the greatest Italian artists of the 16th and 17th centuries. One of the lines on the right side of the piazza funnels you into the basilica, while the other two lead to the underground grottoes or the dome. Whichever you opt for first, you must be **properly dressed**—a rule that is very strictly enforced.

In Roman times, the Circus of Nero, where St. Peter is said to have been crucified, was slightly to the left of where the basilica is now located. Peter was allegedly buried here in A.D. 64 near the site of his execution, and in A.D. 324, Emperor Constantine commissioned a church to be built over Peter's tomb. That structure stood for more than 1,000 years, until it verged on collapse. The present basilica, mostly completed in the 1500s and 1600s, is predominantly High Renaissance and baroque. Inside, the massive scale is almost too much to absorb, showcasing some of Italy's greatest artists: Bramante, Raphael, Michelangelo, and Maderno. In a church of such grandeur—overwhelming in its detail of gilt, marble, and mosaic—you can't expect much subtlety. It is meant to be overpowering.

Going straight into the basilica, the first thing you see on the right side of the nave, the longest nave in the world, as clearly marked in the pavement, along with other cathedral measurements is the chapel containing Michelangelo's graceful **"Pietà" ★★★**, one of Rome's greatest treasures. Created in the 1490s when the master was still in his 20s, it clearly shows his genius for capturing the human form. (The sculpture has been kept behind reinforced glass since an act of vandalism in the 1970s.) Note the lifelike folds of Mary's robes and her youthful features; although she would've been middle-aged at the time of the Crucifixion, Michelangelo portrayed her as a young woman to convey her purity.

Farther inside the nave, Michelangelo's dome is a mesmerizing space, rising high above the supposed site of St. Peter's tomb. With a diameter of 41.5m (136 ft.), the dome is Rome's largest, supported by four bulky piers, decorated with reliefs depicting the basilica's key holy relics: St. Veronica's handkerchief (used to wipe the face of Christ); the lance of St. Longinus, which pierced Christ's side; and a piece of the True Cross.

Under the dome is the twisty-columned **baldacchino** ★★, by Bernini, resting over the papal altar. The 29m-high (96-ft.) ornate canopy was created in part, so it is said, from bronze stripped from the Pantheon. Bernini sculpted the face of a woman on the bases of each of the pillars; starting with the face on the left pillar (with your back to the entrance), circle the entire altar to see the progress of expressions from the agony of childbirth through to the fourth pillar, where the woman's face is replaced with that of her newborn baby.

Just before you reach the dome, on the right, the devout stop to kiss the foot of the 13th-century **bronze of St. Peter** ★, attributed to Arnolfo di Cambio. Elsewhere, the church is decorated by more of Bernini's lavish sculptures, including his monument to Pope Alexander VII in the south transept, its winged skeleton writhing under the heavy marble drapes.

An entrance off the nave leads to the Sacristy and beyond to the **Historical Museum (Museo Storico)**, or **treasury** ★, which is crammed with richly jeweled chalices, reliquaries, and copes, as well as the late-15th-century bronze tomb of Pope Sixtus IV by Pollaiuolo.

You can also head downstairs to the **Vatican grottoes** ★★, with their tombs of the popes, both ancient and modern (Pope John XXIII got the most adulation until the interment of **Pope John Paul II** in 2005). Behind a wall of glass is what is assumed to be the tomb of St. Peter.

Visits to the **Necropolis Vaticana** ★★ and St. Peter's tomb itself are restricted to 250 persons per day on guided tours (90 min.) You must send a fax or e-mail 3 weeks beforehand, or apply in advance in person at the Ufficio Scavi (©/fax **06-69873017**; e-mail: scavi@fsp.va; Mon–Fri 9am–6pm, Sat 9am–5pm), which is located through the arch to the left of the stairs up from

A St. Peter's Warning

St. Peter's has a strict dress code: no shorts, no skirts above the knee, and no bare shoulders and arms. *Note: You will not be let in if you come dressed inappropriately.* In a pinch, men and women alike can buy a big, cheap scarf from a nearby souvenir stand and wrap it around their legs as a long skirt or throw it over their shoulders as a shawl. If you're still showing too much skin, a guard hands out blue paper capes similar to what you wear in a doctor's office. Only limited photography is permitted inside.

the basilica. For details, check **www.vatican.va**. Children 14 and under are not admitted to the Necropolis.

After you leave the grottoes, you find yourself in a courtyard and ticket line for the grandest sight in the basilica: the climb to **Michelangelo's dome** ★★★, about 114m (375 ft.) high. You can walk all the way up or take the elevator as far as it goes. The elevator saves you 171 steps, and you *still* have 320 to go after getting off. After you've made it to the top, you'll have a scintillating view over the rooftops of Rome and even the Vatican Gardens and papal apartments.

Piazza San Pietro. www.vatican.va. ⓒ **06-69881662.** Basilica (including grottoes) free admission. Necropolis Vaticana (St. Peter's tomb) 13€. Stairs to the dome 5€; elevator to the dome 7€; sacristy (with Historical Museum) free. Basilica (including the grottoes and treasury) Oct–Mar daily 7am–6:30pm, Apr–Sept daily 7am–7pm. Dome Oct–Mar daily 8am–5pm; Apr–Sept daily 8am–6pm. Metro: Cipro, Ottaviano/San Pietro.

Vatican Museums & the Sistine Chapel ★★★ MUSEUM Nothing else in Rome quite lives up to the awe-inspiring collections of the **Vatican Museums,** a 15-minute walk from St. Peter's out of the north side of Piazza San Pietro. It's a vast treasure store of art from antiquity and the Renaissance gathered by the Roman Catholic Church throughout the centuries, filling a series of ornate papal palaces, apartments, and galleries leading to one of the world's most beautiful buildings, the justly celebrated **Sistine Chapel** (considered part of the museums for admission purposes).

Note that the Vatican dress code also applies to the museums (no sleeveless blouses, no miniskirts, no shorts, no hats allowed), though it tends to be less rigorously enforced than at St. Peter's. Visitors can, however, take photos (no flash) and even, more dubiously, use mobile phones inside (with the exception of the Sistine Chapel). **Guided tours** are a good way to get the best out of a visit, and are the only way to visit the **Vatican Gardens.**

Obviously, one trip will not be enough to see everything here. Below are previews of the main highlights, showstoppers, and masterpieces on display (in alphabetical order).

APPARTAMENTO BORGIA (BORGIA APARTMENTS) ★: Created for Pope Alexander VI (the infamous Borgia pope) between 1492 and 1494, these rooms were frescoed with biblical and allegorical scenes by Umbrian painter Pinturicchio and his assistants. The rooms tend to be dimly lit, but look for what is thought to be the earliest European depiction of Native Americans, painted little more than a year after Columbus had returned from the New World.

MUSEI DI ANTICHITÀ CLASSICHE (CLASSICAL ANTIQUITIES MUSEUMS): The Vatican maintains four classical antiquities museums, the most important being the **Museo Pio Clementino** ★★★, crammed with Greek and Roman sculptures in the small Belvedere Palace of Innocent VIII. At the heart of the complex lies the Octagonal Court, where highlights include the sculpture of Trojan priest **"Laocoön"** ★★★ and his two sons locked in a struggle with sea serpents, dating from around 40 B.C., and the exceptional **"Belvedere Apollo"** ★★★ (a 2nd-c. Roman reproduction of an authentic Greek work from the 4th c. B.C.), the symbol of classic male beauty and a possible inspiration for Michelangelo's "David." Look out also for the impressive gilded bronze statue of **"Hercules"** in the Rotonda, from the late A.D. 2nd century, and the **Hall of the Chariot,** containing a magnificent sculpture of a chariot combining Roman originals and 18th-century work by Antonio Franzoni.

MUSEO GREGORIANO EGIZIO ★: Nine rooms are packed with plunder from Ancient Egypt, including sarcophagi, mummies, pharaonic statuary, votive bronzes, jewelry, cuneiform tablets from Mesopotamia, inscriptions from Assyrian palaces, and Egyptian hieroglyphics.

MUSEO GREGORIANO ETRUSCO ★. The core of this collection is a cache of rare Etruscan art treasures dug up in the 19th century, dating from between the 9th and the 1st century B.C. The Romans learned a lot from the Etruscans, as the highly crafted ceramics, bronzes, silver, and gold on display attest. Don't miss the **Regolini-Galassi tomb** (7th c. B.C.), unearthed at Cerveteri. The museum is housed within the *palazzettos* of Innocent VIII (reigned 1484–92) and Pius IV (reigned 1559–65), the latter adorned with frescoes by Federico Barocci and Federico Zuccari.

PINACOTECA (ART GALLERY) ★★★: The great painting collections of the popes are displayed within the Pinacoteca, including work from all the big names in Italian art, from Giotto and Fra' Angelico, to Perugino, Raphael, Veronese, and Crespi. Early medieval work occupies Room 1, with the most intriguing piece a keyhole-shaped wood panel of the "Last Judgment" by Nicolò e Giovanni dated to the late 12th century. **Giotto** takes center stage in Room 2, with the "Stefaneschi Triptych" (six panels) painted for the old St. Peter's basilica between 1315 and 1320. "Madonna del Magnificat," Bernardo Daddi's masterpiece of early Italian Renaissance art, is also here. **Fra' Angelico** dominates Room 3, his "Stories of St. Nicholas of Bari" and "Virgin with Child," justly praised (check out the Virgin's microscopic eyes in the latter piece). Carlo Crivelli features in Room 6, while decent work by Perugino and Pinturicchio graces Room 7, though most visitors press on to the **Raphael salon** ★★★ (Room 8), where you can view five paintings by the Renaissance master: The best are the "Coronation of the Virgin," the "Madonna of Foligno," and the vast "Transfiguration" (completed shortly before his death). Room 9 boasts Leonardo da Vinci's **"St. Jerome with the Lion"** ★★, as well as Giovanni Bellini's "Pietà." Room 10 is dedicated to Renaissance Venice, with Titian's "Madonna of St. Nicholas of the Frari" and Veronese's "Vision of St. Helen" being paramount. Don't skip the remaining galleries: Room 11 contains Barocci's "Annunciation," while Room 12 is really all about one of the masterpieces of the baroque, Caravaggio's **"Deposition from the Cross"** ★★. Crespi is featured in Room 15; Room 17 is full of Bernini sculpture. The collection ends with an odd ensemble of Russian and Greek Orthodox icons in Room 18.

STANZE DI RAFFAELLO (RAPHAEL ROOMS) ★★: In the early 16th century, Pope Julius II hired the young Raphael and his workshop to decorate his personal apartments, a series of connecting rooms on the second floor of the Pontifical Palace. Completed between 1508 and 1524, the **Raphael Rooms** now represent one of the great artistic spectacles inside the Vatican.

The **Stanza dell'Incendio** served as the Pope's high court room and later, under Leo X, a dining room. Most of its lavish fresco work has been attributed to Raphael's pupils. Leo X himself commissioned much of the artwork here, which explains the themes (past popes with the name Leo). Note the intricate ceiling, painted by Umbrian maestro and Raphael's first teacher, Perugino.

Raphael is the main focus in the **Stanza della Segnatura,** originally used as a papal library and private office and home to the awe-inspiring **"School of Athens"** ★★★ fresco, depicting primarily Greek classical philosophers such as Aristotle, Plato, and Socrates. Many of the figures are thought to be based on portraits of Renaissance artists, including Bramante (on the right as Euclid, drawing on a chalkboard), Leonardo da Vinci (as Plato, the bearded man in the center), and even Raphael himself (in the lower-right corner with a black hat). On the wall opposite stands the equally magnificent "Disputa del Sacramento," where Raphael used a similar technique; Dante Alighieri stands behind the pontiff on the right, and Fra' Angelico poses as a monk (which in fact, he was) on the far left.

The **Stanza d'Eliodoro** was used for the private audiences of the pope and was painted by Raphael immediately after he did the Segnatura. His aim here was to flatter his papal patron, Julius II: The depiction of the pope driving Attila from Rome was meant to symbolize the contemporary mission of Julius II to drive the French out of Italy. Finally, the **Sala di Constantino,** used for papal receptions and official ceremonies, was completed by Raphael's students after the master's death but based on his designs and drawings. It's a jaw-dropping space, commemorating four major episodes in the life of Emperor Constantine.

SISTINE CHAPEL ★★★: Michelangelo labored for 4 years (1508–12) to paint the ceiling of the Sistine Chapel; it is said he spent the entire time on his feet, paint dripping into his eyes. But what a result! The world's most famous fresco is as vibrantly colorful and filled with roiling life as it was in 1512 (thanks to a massive restoration effort in the 1990s). And the chapel is still of central importance to the Catholic Church: The Papal Conclave meets here to elect new popes.

The "Creation of Adam" at the center of the ceiling is one of the best-known and most-reproduced images in history, the outstretched hands of God and Adam—not quite touching—an iconic symbol of not just the Renaissance but the age of Enlightenment that followed. Nevertheless, it is somewhat ironic that this is Michelangelo's best-known work: The artist always regarded himself as a sculptor first and foremost.

The endless waiting in order get into the chapel inevitably makes the sense of expectation all the greater, but despite the tour groups and the crowds, seeing the frescoes in person is a truly magical experience.

The ceiling **frescoes** are obviously the main showstoppers, though staring at them tends to take a heavy toll on the neck. Commissioned by Pope Julius II in 1508 and completed in 1512, they primarily depict nine scenes from the Book of Genesis (including the famed "Creation of Adam"), from the "Separation of Light and Darkness" at the altar end to the "Great Flood" and "Drunkenness of Noah." Surrounding these main frescoes are paintings of twelve people who prophesied the coming of Christ, from Jonah and Isaiah to the Delphic Sibyl. Once you have admired the ceiling, turn your attention to the wall behind the altar. At the age of 60, Michelangelo was summoned to finish the chapel decor 23 years after he finished the ceiling work. Apparently saddened by leaving Florence and depressed by the morally bankrupt state of Rome at that time, he painted these dark moods in his "Last Judgment," where he included his own self-portrait on a sagging human hide held by St. Bartholomew (who was martyred by being flayed alive).

Sistine Chapel.

PAPAL audiences

When the pope is in Rome, he gives a public audience every Wednesday beginning at 10:30am (sometimes at 10am in summer). If you want to get a good seat near the front arrive early, as security begins to let people in between 8 and 8:30am. Audiences take place in the Paul VI Hall of Audiences, although sometimes St. Peter's Basilica and St. Peter's Square are used to accommodate a large attendance in the summer. With the ascension of Pope Francis to the Throne of Peter in 2013, this tradition continues. You can check on the pope's appearances and ceremonies he presides over, including celebrations of Mass, on the Vatican website (www.vatican.va). Anyone is welcome, but you must first obtain a **free ticket;** without a reservation you can try the Swiss Guards by the Bronze Doors located just after security at St. Peter's (8am–8pm in summer and 8am–7pm in winter). You can pick up tickets here up to 3 days in advance, subject to availability.

If you would prefer to reserve a place in advance, download a request form at www.vaticantour.com/images/Vatican_Ticket_request.pdf or www.vatican.va and fax it to the **Prefecture of the Papal Household** at ✆ **06-69885863.** Tickets can be picked up at the office located just inside the Bronze Doors from 3 to 7:30pm on the preceding day or on the morning of the audience from 8 to 10:30am.

At noon on Sundays, the pope speaks briefly from his study window and gives his blessing to the visitors and pilgrims gathered in St. Peter's Square (no tickets are required for this). From about mid-July to mid-September, the Angelus and blessing usually take place at the summer residence at Castelgandolfo, some 26km (16 miles) out of Rome and accessible by Metro and bus, though it is unclear whether Francis will continue to spend his summers there every year.

Yet the Sistine Chapel isn't all Michelangelo. The southern wall is covered by a series of astonishing paintings completed in the 1480s: "Moses Leaving to Egypt" by Perugino, the "Trials of Moses" by Botticelli, "The Crossing of the Red Sea" by Cosimo Rosselli (or Domenico Ghirlandaio), "Descent from Mount Sinai" by Cosimo Rosselli (or Piero di Cosimo), Botticelli's "Punishment of the Rebels," and Signorelli's "Testament and Death of Moses."

On the right-hand, northern wall are Perugino's "The Baptism of Christ," Botticelli's "The Temptations of Christ," Ghirlandaio's "Vocation of the Apostles," Perugino's "Delivery of the Keys," and Cosimo Rosselli's "The Sermon on the Mount" and "Last Supper." On the eastern wall, originals by Ghirlandaio and Signorelli were painted over by Hendrik van den Broeck's "The Resurrection" and Matteo da Lecce's "Disputation over Moses" in the 1570s.

Between April 24 and July 31, and again from September 4 to October 30, Vatican Museum visitors will have the extraordinary opportunity to visit the galleries after sunset on Fridays. Twilight visits will allow access to important collections, including the Pio-Clementine Museum, the Egyptian Museum, the Upper Galleries (candelabra, tapestries, and maps), the Raphael Rooms, the Borgia Apartments, the Collection of Modern Religious Art, and the

Sistine Chapel. Friday twilight visits are 7pm to 11pm (last entrance at 9:30pm). Booking online is mandatory.

Vatican City, Viale Vaticano (a long walk around the Vatican walls from St. Peter's Sq.). www.museivaticani.va. © **06-69884676.** Admission 16€ adults, 8€ children 6–13, free for children 5 and under. Tours of Vatican Gardens (2 hr.) 32€ (Mon, Tues, Thurs–Sat). Mon–Sat 9am–6pm (ticket office closes at 4pm). Apr 24–July 31 and Sept 4–Oct 30, Fri 7–11pm (last admission 9:30); also last Sun of every month 9am–2pm (free admission). Closed Jan 1 and 6, Feb 11, Mar 19, Easter, May 1, June 29, Aug 14–15, Nov 1, and Dec 25–26. Reservations for advance tickets (reservation fee 4€) and guided tours 32€ per person through www.biglietteriamusei.vatican.va. Metro: Ottaviano or Cipro–Musei Vaticani; bus 49 stops in front of the entrance.

NEAR VATICAN CITY

Castel Sant'Angelo ★★ CASTLE/PALACE This bulky cylindrical fortress on the Vatican side of the Tiber has a storied, complex history, beginning life as the tomb of Emperor Hadrian in A.D. 138, and later serving as a castle (Pope Clement VII escaped the looting troops of Charles V here in 1527), papal residence in the 14th century, and military prison from the 17th century (Puccini used the prison as the setting for the third act of "Tosca"). Consider renting an audioguide at the entrance to help fully appreciate its various manifestations. The ashes and urns of Hadrian and his family have long since been looted and destroyed, and most of what you see today relates to the conversion of the structure into a fortress and residence by the popes of the 14th century.

From the entrance, a stone ramp *(rampa elicoidale)* winds its way to the upper terraces, from which you can see amazing views of the city and enjoy a coffee at the outdoor cafe. The sixth floor features the **Terrazza dell'Angelo,** crowned by a florid statue of the Archangel Michael cast in 1752 by the Flemish artist Peter Anton van Verschaffelt (location of the tragic denouement in "Tosca").

From here you can walk back down through five floors, including the Renaissance apartments (levels 3–5) used by some of Rome's most infamous popes: Alexander VI (the Borgia pope) hid away in the castle after the murder of his son Giovanni in 1497, overwhelmed by grief (although his vows of moral reform were short-lived).

Castel Sant'Angelo.

Below the apartments are the grisly dungeons (**"Le Prigioni"**) used as torture chambers in the medieval period, and utilized especially enthusiastically by Cesare Borgia. The castle is connected to St. Peter's Basilica by **Il Passetto di Borgo,** a walled 800m (2,635-ft.) passage erected in 1277 by Pope Nicholas III, used by popes who needed to make a quick escape to the fortress in times of danger, which was fairly often. Note that the dungeons, Il Passetto, and the apartments of Clement VII are only usually open on summer evenings (July–Aug Tues–Sun 8:30pm–1am; free 50-min. tours with admission, English tour at 10:30pm). Classical music and jazz concerts are also held in and around the castle and gardens in summer (Wed, Fri–Sun 9:30pm).

Lungotevere Castello 50. www.castelsantangelo.com. ℂ **06-6819111.** Admission 11€. Tues–Sun 9am–7.30pm. Bus: 23, 40, 62, 271, 982, 280 (to Piazza Pia).

The Colosseum, Forum & Ancient Rome

It will help your sightseeing if you know a little about the history and rulers of Ancient Rome: See p. 18 for a brief rundown.

THE MAJOR SIGHTS OF ANCIENT ROME

Arco di Costantino (Arch of Constantine) ★★ MONUMENT   The photogenic triumphal arch next to the Colosseum was erected by the Senate in A.D. 315 to honor Constantine's defeat of the pagan Maxentius at the Battle of the Ponte Milvio (Milvian Bridge) Battle (A.D. 312). Many of the reliefs have nothing whatsoever to do with Constantine or his works, but they tell of the victories of earlier Antonine rulers.

Historically, the arch marks a period of great change in the history of Rome. Converted to Christianity by a vision on the eve of battle, Constantine ended the centuries-long persecution of the Christians, during which many followers of the new religion had been put to death in a gruesome manner. Although Constantine didn't ban paganism (which survived officially until the closing of the temples more than half a century later), he embraced the Christian belief himself and began the inevitable development that culminated in the conquest of Rome by the Christian religion.

Btw. Colosseum and Palatine Hill. Metro: Colosseo.

Circo Massimo (Circus Maximus) ★ HISTORIC SITE   Today an almost formless ruin, the once-grand race track was pilfered repeatedly by medieval and Renaissance builders in search of marble and stone. But if you squint and take in its elongated oval proportions and missing tiers of benches, visions of "Ben-Hur" may dance before your eyes. At one time, 250,000 Romans could assemble on the marble seats while the emperor observed the games from his box high on the Palatine Hill. What the Romans called a "circus" was a large arena enclosed by tiers of seats on three or four sides, used especially for sports or spectacles.

The circus lies in a valley between the Palatine and Aventine hills. Next to the Colosseum, it was the most impressive structure in Ancient Rome, in one

Ancient Rome, Monti & Celio

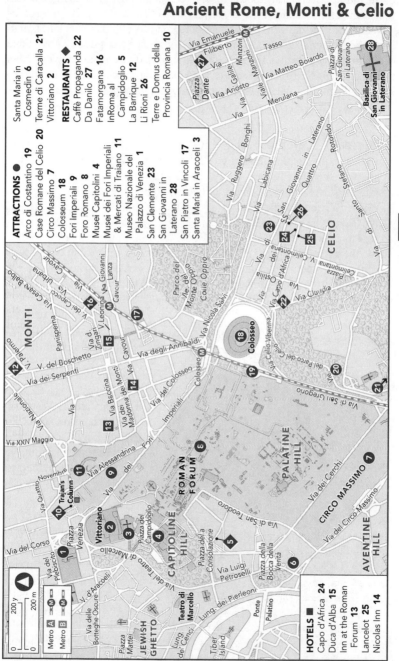

ATTRACTIONS ●
Arco di Costantino **19**
Case Romane del Celio **20**
Circo Massimo **7**
Colosseum **18**
Fori Imperiali **9**
Foro Romano **8**
Musei Capitolini **4**
Musei dei Fori Imperiali & Mercati di Traiano **11**
Museo Nazionale del Palazzo di Venezia **1**
San Clemente **23**
San Giovanni in Laterano **28**
San Pietro in Vincoli **17**
Santa Maria in Aracoeli **3**

Santa Maria in Cosmedin **6**
Terme di Caracalla **21**
Vittoriano **2**

RESTAURANTS ◆
Caffè Propaganda **22**
Da Danilo **27**
Fatamorgana **16**
InRoma al Campidoglio **5**
La Barrique **12**
Li Rioni **26**
Terre e Domus della Provincia Romana **10**

HOTELS ■
Capo d'Africa **24**
Duca d'Alba **15**
Inn at the Roman Forum **13**
Lancelot **25**
Nicolas Inn **14**

4

ROME Exploring Rome

87

of the most exclusive neighborhoods. For centuries, chariot races filled it with the cheers of thousands.

When the dark days of the 5th and 6th centuries fell, the Circus Maximus appeared as a symbol of the ruination of Rome. The last games were held in A.D. 549 on the orders of Totilla the Goth, who had seized Rome twice. After 549, the Circus Maximus was never used again, and the demand for building materials reduced it, like so much of Rome, to a great grassy field.

Btw. Via dei Cerchi and Via del Circo Massimo. www.circo-massimo.it. Metro: Circo Massimo.

Colosseum (Colosseo) ★★★ ICON
No matter how many pictures you've seen, the first impression you'll have of the Colosseum is amazement at its sheer enormity. Its massive bulk looks as if it has been plopped down among the surrounding buildings, and not the other way around.

Your first view of the Flavian Amphitheater (the Colosseum's original name) should be from the outside, and it's important to walk completely around its 500m (1,640-ft.) circumference. It doesn't matter where you start, but do the circle and look at the various stages of ruin before delving in. Note the different column styles on each level. A conservation makeover will run throughout 2016, to consolidate the structure and remove soot and pollution marks.

Once inside, walk onto the partially reconstructed wooden platform flooring that once covered the hypogeum, the place that is, where gladiators and beasts waited their turn in the arena. Vespasian ordered the construction of the elliptical bowl, called the Amphitheatrum Flavium, in A.D. 72; it was inaugurated by Titus in A.D. 80 with a bloody combat, lasting many weeks, between gladiators and wild beasts. The stadium could hold as many as 87,000 spectators by some counts, and seats were sectioned on three levels, dividing the people by social rank and gender. There were 80 entrances, allowing the massive crowds to be seated within a few minutes, historians say. Most events

The Colosseum.

were free, but all spectators had to obtain a terra-cotta disc, called a tessera, to enter.

The Colosseum was built as a venue for gladiator contests and wild animal fights, but when the Roman Empire fell, it was abandoned and eventually overgrown with vegetation. You'll notice on the top of the "good side," as locals call it, that there are a few remaining supports that once held the canvas awning that covered the stadium during rain or for the summer heat. Much of the ancient travertine that once sheathed its outside was used for palaces like the nearby Palazzo Venezia and Palazzo Cancelleria near the Campo de' Fiori.

Note: The same ticket that you buy for the Colosseum includes admission to the Forum and Palatine Hill and is valid for 2 days.

Piazzale del Colosseo. *©* **06-39967700.** www.archeoroma.beniculturali.it. Admission 12€ (includes Roman Forum and Palatine Hill). Nov–Feb 15 daily 8:30am–4:30pm; Feb 16–Mar 15 daily 8:30am–5pm; Mar 16–27 daily 8:30am–5:30pm; Mar 28–Aug daily 8:30am–7:15pm; Sept daily 8:30am–7pm; Oct daily 8:30am–6:30pm. Last admission 1 hr. before closing. Guided tours (45 min.) in English daily at 10:15, 10:45, 11:15, and 11:45am, 12:30, 1:45, and 3pm. Tours 5€. Metro: Colosseo.

Fori Imperiali (Imperial Forums) ★ RUINS   Begun by Julius Caesar as an answer to the overcrowding of Rome's older forums, the Imperial Forums were, at the time of their construction, flashier, bolder, and more impressive than the buildings in the Roman Forum. This site conveyed the unquestioned authority of the emperors at the height of their absolute power.

Alas, Mussolini felt his regime was more important than the ancient one, and issued the controversial orders to cut through centuries of debris and buildings to carve out Via dei Fori Imperiali, thereby linking the Colosseum to the grand 19th-century monuments of Piazza Venezia. Excavations under his Fascist regime began at once (circa 1931), and many archaeological treasures were revealed (and then—argh!—destroyed).

The best view of the Forums is from the railings on the north side of Via dei Fori Imperiali; begin where Via Cavour joins the boulevard. (Visitors are not permitted down into this part of the ruins.) Closest to the junction are the remains of the **Forum of Nerva,** built by the emperor whose 2-year reign (A.D. 96–98) followed the assassination of the paranoid Domitian. You'll be struck by how much the ground level has risen in 19 centuries. The only really recognizable remnant is a wall of the Temple of Minerva with two fine Corinthian columns. This forum was once flanked by that of Vespasian, which is now gone.

The next along is the **Forum of Augustus** ★★, built before the birth of Christ to commemorate the Emperor Augustus's victory over Julius Caesar's assassins, Cassius and Brutus, in the Battle of Philippi (42 B.C.).

Continuing along the railing, you'll see the vast semicircle of **Trajan's Markets** ★★, whose teeming arcades were once stocked with merchandise from the far corners of the Roman world. The shops once covered a multitude of levels, and you can visit the part that has been transformed into the **Museo dei Fori Imperiali** (p. 94).

THREE FREE views TO REMEMBER FOR A LIFETIME

The Forum from the Campidoglio Standing on Piazza del Campidoglio, outside the Musei Capitolini (p. 93), walk around the right side of the Palazzo Senatorio to a terrace overlooking the best panorama of the Roman Forum, with the Palatine Hill and Colosseum as a backdrop. At night, the Forum is dramatically floodlit and its ruins look even more haunting.

The Whole City from the Janiculum Hill From many vantage points in the Eternal City, the views are panoramic. But one of the best spots for a memorable vista is the Janiculum Hill (*Gianicolo*), above Trastevere. Laid out before you are Rome's rooftops, peppered with domes ancient and modern. From up here, you will understand why Romans complain about the materials used to build the Vittoriano (p. 97)—it's a white

shock in a sea of rose- and honey-colored stone. Walk 50 yards north of the famous balcony (favored by tour buses) for a slightly better angle, from the Belvedere 9 Febbraio 1849.

The Aventine Hill & the Priori dei Cavalieri di Malta The mythical site of Remus' original settlement, the Aventine (*Aventino*) is now a leafy, upscale residential neighborhood—but also blessed with some magical views. From Via del Circo Massimo, walk through the gardens along Via di Valle Murcia, and keep walking in a straight line. Along your right side, gardens offer views over the dome of St. Peter's. When you reach Piazza dei Cavalieri di Malta, look through the keyhole of the Priory gate (on the right) for a "secret" view of the Vatican.

The Roman Forum from Campidoglio.

In front of the Markets, the **Forum of Trajan** ★★ is the newest and most beautiful of the Imperial Forums, built between A.D. 107 and 113, and designed by Greek architect Apollodorus of Damascus (who also laid out the adjoining market building). There are many statue fragments and pedestals bearing still-legible inscriptions, but more interesting is the great Basilica Ulpia, whose gray marble columns rise roofless into the sky. This forum was once regarded as one of the architectural wonders of the world. Beyond the Basilica Ulpia is **Trajan's Column** ★★★, in magnificent condition, with an intricate bas-relief sculpture depicting Trajan's victorious campaign.

The **Forum of Julius Caesar** ★★, the first of the Imperial Forums to be built, lies on the opposite side of Via dei Fori Imperiali, adjacent to the Roman Forum. This was the site of the stock exchange, as well as the Temple of Venus.

Along Via dei Fori Imperiali. Metro: Colosseo.

Foro Romano (Roman Forum) & Palatino (Palatine Hill) ★★★

RUINS   When it came to cremating Caesar, sacrificing a naked victim, or just discussing the day's events, the Roman Forum was the place to be. Traversed by the **Via Sacra (Sacred Way)** ★, the main thoroughfare of Ancient Rome, the Forum flourished as the center of Roman life in the days of the Republic, before it gradually lost prestige (but never spiritual draw) to the Imperial Forums (see above).

You'll see only ruins and fragments, an arch or two, and lots of overturned boulders, but with some imagination you can feel the rush of history here. Used for years as a quarry (as was the Colosseum) it eventually reverted to a *campo vaccino* (cow pasture). But excavations in the 19th century and later in the 1930s began to bring to light one of the world's most historic spots.

By day, the columns of now-vanished temples and the stones from which long-forgotten orators spoke are mere shells. Weeds grow where a triumphant Caesar was once lionized. But at night, when the Forum is silent in the moonlight, it isn't difficult to imagine Vestal Virgins still guarding the sacred temple fire.

You can spend at least a morning wandering through the ruins of the Forum. We'd suggest you enter via the gate on Via dei Fori Imperiali. Turn right at the bottom of the entrance slope to walk west along the old Via Sacra toward the arch. Just before it on your right is the large brick **Curia** ★★, the main seat of the Roman Senate, built by Julius Caesar, rebuilt by Diocletian, and consecrated as a church in A.D. 630.

The triumphal **Arch of Septimius Severus** ★★ (A.D. 203), will be your next important sight, displaying time-bitten reliefs of the emperor's victories in what are today Iran and Iraq. During the Middle Ages, Rome became a provincial backwater, and frequent flooding of the nearby river helped bury (and thus preserve) most of the Forum. Some bits did still stick out aboveground, including the top half of this arch.

Just to the left of the arch, you can make out the remains of a cylindrical lump of rock with some marble steps curving off it. That round stone was the **Umbilicus Urbus,** considered the center of Rome and of the entire Roman Empire; the curving steps are those of the **Imperial Rostra ★**, where great orators and legislators stood to speak and the people gathered to listen. Nearby is the iconic trio of fluted columns with Corinthian capitals supporting a bit of architrave form the corner of the **Temple of Vespasian and Titus ★★** (emperors were routinely worshipped as gods even after death).

Start heading to your left toward the eight Ionic columns marking the front of the **Temple of Saturn ★★** (rebuilt in 42 B.C.), which housed the first treasury of republican Rome. It was also the site of one of the Roman year's biggest annual blowout festivals, the December 17 feast of Saturnalia, which (after a bit of tweaking) Christians now celebrate as Christmas. Turn left to start heading back east, past the worn steps and stumps of brick pillars outlining the enormous **Basilica Julia ★★**, built by Julius Caesar. Farther along, on the right, are the three Corinthian columns of the **Temple of the Dioscuri ★★★**, dedicated to the Gemini twins, Castor and Pollux. The founding of this temple dates from the 5th century B.C.

Beyond the bit of curving wall that marks the site of the little round **Temple of Vesta** (rebuilt several times after fires started by the sacred flame within), you'll find the reconstructed **House of the Vestal Virgins** (A.D. 3rd–4th c.). The temple was the home of the consecrated young women who tended the sacred flame in the Temple of Vesta. Vestals were girls chosen from patrician families to serve a 30-year-long priesthood. During their tenure, they were among Rome's most venerated citizens, with unique powers such as the ability to pardon condemned criminals. The cult was quite serious about the "virgin" part of the job description—if one of Vesta's earthly servants was found to have "misplaced" her virginity, the miscreant Vestal was buried alive, because it was forbidden to shed a Vestal's blood. (Her amorous accomplice was merely flogged to death.) The overgrown rectangle of their gardens is lined with broken, heavily worn statues of senior Vestals on pedestals.

The path dovetails back to Via Sacra. Turn right, walk past the so-called "Temple of Romulus," and then left to enter the massive brick remains and coffered ceilings of the 4th-century **Basilica of Constantine and Maxentius ★★** (Basilica di Massenzio). These were Rome's public law courts, with a unique architectural style that was adopted by early Christians for their own houses of worship (the reason so many ancient churches are called "basilicas").

Return to the path and continue toward the Colosseum. Veer right to the Forum's second great triumphal arch, the extensively rebuilt **Arch of Titus ★★** (A.D. 81), on which one relief depicts the carrying off of treasures from Jerusalem's temple. Look closely and you'll see a menorah among the booty. The war that this arch glorifies ended with the expulsion of Jews from the colonized Judea, signaling the beginning of the Jewish Diaspora throughout Europe. You can exit behind the Arch—and there's another exit, accessing the Campidoglio from the opposite end of the Forum.

From here you can climb the **Palatine Hill** ★ (Palatino) on the same ticket. The Palatine, tradition tells us, was the spot on which the first settlers built their huts under the direction of Romulus. In later years, the hill became a patrician residential district that attracted such citizens as Cicero. In time, however, the area was gobbled up by imperial palaces and drew a famous and infamous roster of tenants, such as Livia (some of the frescoes in the House of Livia are in miraculous condition), Tiberius, Caligula (murdered here by members of his Praetorian Guard), Nero, and Domitian.

Only the ruins of its former grandeur remain today, but it's worth the climb for the panoramic views of both the Roman and the Imperial Forums, as well as the Capitoline Hill and the Colosseum. You can also enter from here, and do the entire tour in reverse, historically in proper chronological order.

Via della Salara Vecchia 5/6. ✆ **06-39967700.** Admission 12€ (includes Colosseum). Oct 30–Dec and Jan 2–Feb 15 daily 8:30am–4:30pm; Feb 16–Mar 15 daily 8:30am–5pm; Mar 16–24 daily 8:30am–5:30pm; Mar 25–Aug daily 8:30am–7:15pm; Sept daily 8:30am–7pm; Oct 1–29 daily 8:30am–6:30pm. Last admission 1 hr. before closing. Guided tours are given daily at 11am, lasting 1 hr., costing 4€. Metro: Colosseo.

Musei Capitolini (Capitoline Museums) ★★ MUSEUM   The masterpieces here are considered Rome's most valuable (considering how the Vatican Museums are *not* part of Rome). This is also the oldest public museum *in the world,* with lots to see, so try to schedule adequate time.

First stop is the courtyard of the **Palazzo dei Conservatori** (the building on the right of the piazza designed by Michelangelo, if you enter via the ramp from Piazza Venezia). It's scattered with gargantuan stone body parts. They're the remnants of a massive 12m (39-ft.) statue of the emperor Constantine, including his colossal head, hand, and foot, from the Basilica of Maxentius and Constantine in the Roman Forum. It's nearly impossible to resist snapping a selfie next to the giant foot.

On the *palazzo*'s ground floor, the unmissable works are in the first series of rooms. These include "Lo Spinario" **(Room III),** a lifelike bronze of a young boy digging a splinter out of his foot that was widely copied during the Renaissance; and the "Lupa Capitolina" **(Room IV),** a bronze statue from 500 B.C. of the famous she-wolf that suckled Romulus and Remus, the mythical founders of Rome. The twins were not on the original Etruscan statue; they were added in the 15th century. **Room V** has Bernini's famously pained portrait of "Medusa," even more compelling when you see its writhing serpent hairdo in person.

Before heading upstairs, go toward the new wing at the rear, bathed in natural light thanks to an enormous modern skylight, which houses the original equestrian **statue of Marcus Aurelius** ★★★, dating to around A.D. 180—the piazza outside, where it stood from 1538, now has a copy. There's a giant bronze head from a statue of Constantine (ca. A.D. 337) and the foundations of the original Temple of Jupiter that stood on the Capitoline Hill since its inauguration in 509 B.C.

The second floor is known for its **picture gallery** ★, which is strong on baroque oil paintings, with masterpieces including Caravaggio's "John the Baptist" and "The Fortune Teller" (1595) and Guido Reni's "St. Sebastian" (1615). An underground tunnel takes you under the piazza to the other part of the Capitoline Museums, the **Palazzo Nuovo**, via the **Tabularium** ★. This was built in 78 B.C. to house Ancient Rome's city records, and was later used as a salt mine and then as a prison. The atmospheric stone gallery was opened to the public in the late 1990s to exhibit inscriptions, and also to provide access to one of the best balcony **views** ★★★ in Rome: along the length of the Forum toward the Palatine Hill.

Much of the Palazzo Nuovo is dedicated to statues that were excavated from the forums below and brought in from outlying areas, like Hadrian's Villa in Tivoli (p. 135). If you're running short on time at this point, head straight for the 1st-century **"Capitoline Venus"** ★★, in Room III, admire a modest girl covering up after a bath—and in Room IV, a chronologically arranged row of busts of Roman emperors and their families. Another favorite is the beyond handsome **"Dying Gaul"** ★★, a Roman copy of a lost ancient Greek work. Lord Byron considered the statue so lifelike and moving, he included mention of it in his poem "Childe Harold's Pilgrimage."

Piazza del Campidoglio 1. www.museicapitolini.org.© **060608.** Admission 13€. Tues–Sun 9am–8pm. Last admission 1 hr. before closing. Bus: C3, H, 40, 44, 60, 80B, 190, 780, or 781.

Museo dei Fori Imperiali & Mercati di Traiano (Museum of the Imperial Forums & Trajan's Markets) ★ RUINS/MUSEUM The

museum occupies the ruins of boutiques, food stores, and workshops that formed Emperor Trajan's Market, now home to 172 marble fragments from the Imperial Forums; here are also original remnants from the Forum of Augustus and Forum of Nerva.

Created in A.D. 100 to 110, but having fallen into total ruin, this once-bustling "shopping mall" was built over in the Middle Ages and then extensively excavated under Mussolini. The Imperial Forums, many of which are still being excavated, are hard for ordinary visitors to understand, so the museum uses replicas to help visitors orient themselves, plus galleries housing models and reconstructions of the various forums and temples. It also houses a giant head of Constantine, found in 2005 in an old sewer. Tickets are 11€, so perhaps intended for those with a deeper historical interest in Ancient Rome.

Via IV Novembre 94. www.mercatiditraiano.it. © **060608.** Admission 11€. Tues–Sun 9am–7pm. Last admission 1 hr. before closing. Bus: 53, 80, 85, 87, 175, 186, 271, 571, or 810.

Terme di Caracalla (Baths of Caracalla) ★ RUINS Named for the

emperor Caracalla, the baths were completed in A.D. 217, after Caracalla's death. The richness of decoration has faded, and the lavishness can be judged only from the shell of brick ruins that remain. In their heyday, they sprawled across 11 hectares (27 acres) and could handle 1,600 bathers at one time.

Partially opened to the public in 2012, the tunnels below the complex give an idea of the scale of the hydraulic and heating systems that must have been needed to serve 8,000 or so Romans per day.

The *palestra* (gym) is one setting for summertime outdoor operatic performances in Rome (p. 127).

Via delle Terme di Caracalla 52. www.archeoroma.beniculturali.it. (C) **06-39967700.** Admission 6€ (combined ticket with the Tomb of Cecelia Metella, p. 117). Oct Mon 8:30am–2pm, Tues–Sun 9am–6:30pm; Nov–Feb 15 Mon 8:30am–2pm, Tues–Sun 9am–4:30pm; Feb 16–Mar 15 Mon 8:30am–2pm, Tues–Sun 9am–5pm; Mar 16–Sept Mon 8:30am–2pm, Tues–Sun 9am–7pm. Last admission 1 hr. before closing. Bus: 118 or 628.

OTHER ATTRACTIONS NEAR ANCIENT ROME

Case Romane del Celio ★ RUINS   The 5th-century Basilica of SS. Giovanni e Paolo stands over a residential complex consisting of several Roman houses of different periods. A visit here will provide you with a unique picture of how generations of Romans lived. Preserved at the labyrinthine site is a residence from the A.D. 2nd century, a single home of a wealthy family, and an A.D. 3rd-century apartment building for artisans.

The two-story construction, with some 20 rooms, also contains a small museum room with finds from the site and fragmentary 12th-century frescoes.

Piazza Santi Giovanni e Paolo 13 (entrance on Clivo di Scauro). www.caseromane.it. (C) **06-70454544.** Admission 6€ adults, 4€ ages 12–18. Thurs–Mon 10am–1pm and 3–6pm. Metro: Colosseo or Circo Massimo.

Museo Nazionale del Palazzo di Venezia ★ MUSEUM   Best remembered today as Mussolini's Fascist headquarters in Rome, the palace was built in the 1450s as the Rome outpost of the Republic of Venice—hence the name. It later became the Austrian Embassy, after Venice was dissolved by Napoleon. Today, a few of its rooms are home to a modest collection of exhibits; highlights include Giorgione's enigmatic "Double Portrait" and some early Tuscan altarpieces.

Via del Plebiscito 118. www.museopalazzovenezia.beniculturali.it. (C) **06-6780131.** Admission 5€. Tues–Sun 8:30am–7:30pm. Bus: 30, 40, 46, 62, 70, 87, or 916.

San Clemente ★★★ CHURCH   This isn't just another Roman church—far from it. In this layered church-upon-a-church, centuries of history peel away. In the A.D. 4th century, a church was built over a secular house from the 1st century, beside which stood a pagan temple dedicated to Mithras (god of the sun). Down in the eerie grottoes (which you explore on your own), you'll discover well-preserved frescoes from the 9th to the 11th centuries. The Normans destroyed this lower church, and a new one was built in the 12th century. Its chief attraction is the mosaic adorning the apse, as well as a chapel honoring St. Catherine of Alexandria with 1428 frescoes by Masolino.

Via San Giovanni in Laterano (at Piazza San Clemente). www.basilicasanclemente.com. (C) **06-7740021.** Basilica free admission; excavations 5€. Mon–Sat 9am–12:30pm and 3–6pm; Sun noon–6pm. Last admission 20 min. before closing. Bus: 53, 85, or 117.

4

San Giovanni in Laterano ★ CHURCH   This church (not St. Peter's) is the cathedral of the diocese of Rome, where the pope comes to celebrate Mass on certain holidays. Built in A.D. 314 by Constantine, it has suffered the vicissitudes of Roman history, forcing many overhauls.

The present building is characterized by an 18th-century facade designed by Alessandro Galilei (statues of Christ and the Apostles ring the top)—a 1993 terrorist bomb caused severe damage to this facade. Borromini gets the credit for the interior, built for Pope Innocent X. In a purportedly misguided attempt to redecorate, frescoes by Giotto were destroyed; remains attributed to Giotto were discovered in 1952 and are now on display against the first inner column on the right.

Across the street is the **Santuario della Scala Santa (Palace of the Holy Steps),** Piazza San Giovanni in Laterano 14 (✆ **06-7726641**). Allegedly, the 28 marble steps (now covered with wood for preservation) were originally at Pontius Pilate's villa in Jerusalem, and Christ climbed them the day he was brought before Pilate. According to medieval tradition, these steps were brought from Jerusalem to Rome by Constantine's mother, Helen, in 326, and they've been in this location since 1589. Today pilgrims from all over come here to climb the steps on their knees. This is one of the holiest sites in Christendom, although some historians say the stairs might date only from the 4th century.

Piazza San Giovanni in Laterano 4. ✆ **06-69886433.** Free admission. Daily 7am–6:30pm. Metro: San Giovanni.

San Pietro in Vincoli (St. Peter in Chains) ★ CHURCH   This church was founded in the 5th century to house the supposed chains that bound St. Peter in Palestine (they're preserved under glass below the main altar). But the drawing card is the tomb of Pope Julius II, which features one of the world's most famous sculptures: **Michelangelo's "Moses"** ★★★. Michelangelo was to carve 44 magnificent figures for the tomb. That didn't happen, but the pope was given a great consolation prize—a figure now numbered among Michelangelo's masterpieces. Don't leave without a quick look at the unusual "skeleton tombs" in the left aisle.

Piazza San Pietro in Vincoli 4A. ✆ **06-97844952.** Free admission. Spring–summer daily 8:30am–12:30pm and 3:30–6:30pm (autumn–winter to 5:30pm). Metro: Colosseo or Cavour.

Santa Maria in Aracoeli ★ CHURCH   On the Capitoline Hill, this landmark church was built for the Franciscans in the 13th century. According to legend, Augustus once ordered a temple erected on this spot, where a prophetic sibyl forecast the coming of Christ. In the interior there's a coffered Renaissance ceiling and the tombstone of Giovanni Crivelli (1432) carved by the great Florentine Renaissance sculptor, Donatello. The church is also known for the **Cappella Bufalini** ★ (first chapel on the right), frescoed by Pinturicchio with scenes illustrating the life of St. Bernardino of Siena.

You have to climb a long flight of steep steps to reach the church, unless you're already on neighboring Piazza del Campidoglio, in which case you can cross the piazza and climb the steps on the far side of the Musei Capitolini (p. 93).

Scala dell'Arcicapitolina 12. © **06-69763838.** Free admission. Daily 9am–12:30pm and 2:30–5:30pm. Bus: C3, H, 40, 44, 60, 80B, 190, 780, or 781.

Santa Maria in Cosmedin ★ CHURCH People come to this little church (indeed, stand on line) not for great art treasures, but to see the **"Mouth of Truth,"** a large disk under the portico. It is no longer possible to pull a "Gregory Peck" and actually put your hand in the mouth, like the star did, demonstrating to Audrey Hepburn in the film "Roman Holiday," that the mouth is supposed to chomp down on the hands of liars. The purpose of this disk—which is not of particular artistic interest—is unclear. One hypothesis says that it was one of many Roman "talking statues." If you wanted to rat someone out, you could slip an anonymous note inside the open mouth.

As for the church, it was first erected in the 6th century but was subsequently rebuilt. A Romanesque bell tower was added at the end of the 11th century.

Piazza della Bocca della Verità 18. © **06-6787759.** Free admission. Summer daily 9:30am–5:50pm; winter daily 9:30am–5pm. Bus: 23, 81, 160, 280, or 628.

Vittoriano ★ MONUMENT It's impossible to miss the white Brescian marble Vittorio Emanuele Monument that dominates the corner where Via dei Fori Imperiali meets Piazza Venezia. The city's most flamboyant and, frankly, disliked landmark, it was built in the late 1800s to honor the first king of a united Italy. It has been compared to everything from a wedding cake to a Victorian typewriter, and has been ridiculed because of its harsh white color in a city of honey-gold tones. An eternal flame burns guarded by military. For a panoramic view over the city, a glass lift whisks you to the **Terrazza delle Quadrighe (Terrace of the Chariots)** ★.

Piazza Venezia. © **06-6780664.** Admission to lift 7€. Mon–Thurs 9:30am–5:45pm, Fri–Sun 9:30am–6:45pm. Bus: 53, 80, 85, 87, 175, 186, 271, 571, or 810.

Centro Storico & the Pantheon

Just across the Tiber from the Vatican and Castel Sant' Angelo lies the true heart of Rome, the **Centro Storico** (or "historic center"), roughly the triangular wedge of land that bulges into a bend of the river. Alleys are crammed with piazzas, elegant churches, and lavish fountains, all buzzing with scooters and people.

PIAZZA NAVONA & NEARBY ATTRACTIONS

Rome's most famous square, **Piazza Navona** ★★★, is a gorgeous baroque gem, lined with cafes and restaurants, and often crowded with tourists, street artists, and performers by day and night. Its long, thin shape follows the contours of the old Roman Stadium of Domitian, where chariot races once took place, still a ruin until a mid-17th-century makeover by Pope Innocent X. The

Piazza Navona.

twin-towered facade of 17th-century **Sant'Agnese in Agone** lies on the piazza's western side, while the **Fontana dei Quattro Fiumi (Fountain of the Four Rivers)** ★★★ opposite is one of three great fountains in the square, this one a creation of Bernini, topped with an Egyptian obelisk. The four stone personifications below symbolize the world's greatest rivers: the Ganges, Danube, River Plate, and Nile. It's fun to try to figure out which is which. (*Hint:* The figure with the shroud on its head is the Nile, so represented because the river's source was unknown at the time.) At the south end is the **Fontana del Moro (Fountain of the Moor),** also by Bernini; the **Fontana di Nettuno (Fountain of Neptune)** is a 19th-century addition.

Art lovers should make the short walk from the piazza to **Santa Maria della Pace** ★★ on Arco della Pace, a 15th-century church given the usual baroque makeover by Pietro da Cortona in the 1660s. The real gems are inside, beginning with Raphael's **"Four Sibyls"** ★★ fresco above the arch of the Capella Chigi, and the **Chiostro del Bramante (Bramante cloister)** ★, built between 1500 and 1504, and the first work of the Renaissance master in the city. The church is normally open on Monday, Wednesday, and Saturday from 9am to noon, while the cloister opens Tuesday to Sunday from 10am to 8pm. Admission to the cloister, which hosts temporary art exhibitions, costs 10€.

Palazzo Altemps ★★ MUSEUM Inside this 15th-century *palazzo,* today a branch of the National Museum of Rome, is one of Rome's most charming museums. It's rarely crowded yet houses some of Rome's most famous private and public collections of art. The pieces here are not great in number, but they are individually superb; much of the art was once part of the famed **Boncompagni Ludovisi Collection,** created by Cardinal Ludovico Ludovisi (1595–1632) and sold at auction in 1901.

Among the highlights is the **"Ludovisi Ares"** ★★, a handsome 2nd-century copy of a late-4th-century B.C. Greek statue of Mars (*Ares* to the Greeks). Equally renowned is the **"Ludovisi Gaul"** ★, a marble depiction of a Gaulish warrior plunging a sword into his chest, looking backward defiantly as he

Centro Storico

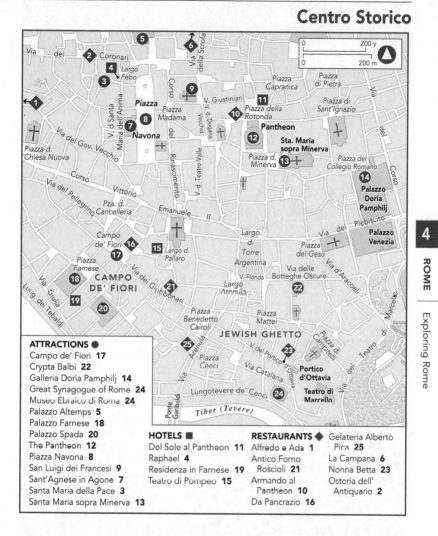

ATTRACTIONS ●
Campo de' Fiori **17**
Crypta Balbi **22**
Galleria Doria Pamphilj **14**
Great Synagogue of Rome **24**
Museo Ebraico di Roma **24**
Palazzo Altemps **5**
Palazzo Farnese **18**
Palazzo Spada **20**
The Pantheon **12**
Piazza Navona **8**
San Luigi dei Francesi **9**
Sant'Agnese in Agone **7**
Santa Maria della Pace **3**
Santa Maria sopra Minerva **13**

HOTELS ■
Del Sole al Pantheon **11**
Raphael **4**
Residenza in Farnese **19**
Teatro di Pompeo **15**

RESTAURANTS ◆
Alfredo e Ada **1**
Antico Forno
Roscioli **21**
Armando al
Pantheon **10**
Da Pancrazio **16**

Gelateria Alberto
Pica **25**
La Campana **6**
Nonna Betta **23**
Osteria dell'
Antiquario **2**

supports a dying woman with his left arm—a 2nd-century Roman copy of a 3rd-century B.C. Hellenistic original. Worth a look is the **"Ludovisi Throne,"** a sculpted block of white marble, thought to date from the 5th century B.C., depicting Aphrodite rising from the sea. Elsewhere, the "Juno Ludovisi" is a massive, 1st-century marble head of the goddess Juno.

Piazza di Sant'Apollinare 46, near Piazza Navona. http://archeoroma.beniculturali.it/en/museums/national-roman-museum-palazzo-altemps. © **06-39967700.** Admission 7€ (also valid at Palazzo Massimo alle Terme, Terme di Diocleziano, and Crypta Balbi for 3 days). Tues–Sun 9am–7:45pm. Last admission 1 hr. before closing. Bus: 87, 70, 492, 30, 130, 81 or 628.

San Luigi dei Francesi ★★ CHURCH   For a painter of such strato-spheric standards as Caravaggio, it is impossible to be definitive in naming his "masterpiece." However, the **"Calling of St. Matthew"** ★★, in the far-left chapel of Rome's French church, has to be a candidate. The panel dramatizes the moment Jesus and Peter "called" the customs officer to join them, in Cara-vaggio's distinct *chiaroscuro* (extreme light and shade) style. Around the same time (1599–1602) Caravaggio also painted the other two St. Matthew panels in the Capella Contarelli—including one depicting the saint's martyr-dom. Other highlights inside include Domenichino's masterful "Histories of Saint Cecilia" fresco cycle.

Via di Santa Giovanna d'Arco 5. www.saintlouis-rome.net. ℂ **06-688271.** Free admis-sion. Mon–Wed and Fri–Sat 10am–12:30pm and 3–7pm; Thurs 10am–12:30pm; Sun 3–7pm. Bus: C3, 30, 70, 81, 87, 116, 186, 492, or 628.

THE PANTHEON & NEARBY ATTRACTIONS

The Pantheon stands on **Piazza della Rotonda,** a lively square with cafes, vendors, and great people watching.

The Pantheon ★★★ HISTORIC SITE   Of all Ancient Rome's great buildings, only the Pantheon ("Temple to All the Gods") remains intact. It was originally built in wood in 27 B.C. by Marcus Agrippa but was entirely recon-structed by Hadrian in the early 2nd century A.D. after it was destroyed in a fire. This remarkable building—once entirely covered in white marble, 43m (142 ft.) wide and 43m (142 ft.) high (a perfect sphere resting in a cyl-inder), and laced with white marble statues of Roman gods in its niches—is among the architectural wonders of the world, even today. Hadrian himself is credited with the basic plan, an architectural design that was unique for the time. There are no visible arches or vaults holding up the dome; instead they're sunk into the concrete of the walls of the building, while the ribbed dome outside is a series of almost weightless cantilevered bricks. Animals were once sac-rificed and burned in the center, and the smoke escaped through the only means of light, the oculus, an opening at the top 5.5m (18 ft.) in diameter.

The Pantheon.

The interior now houses the tombs of two Italian kings (Vittorio Emanuele II and his successor, Umberto I), and the resting place of **Raphael** (fans still bring him flowers), between the second and third chapel on the left. The Pantheon has been used as a Catholic church since the 7th century, the **Santa Maria ad Martyres,** but informally known as "Santa Maria della Rotonda."

Piazza della Rotonda. © **06-68300230.** Free admission. Mon–Sat 8:30am–7:30pm; Sun 9am–6pm. Mass Sat 5pm, Sun 10:30am (only Mass attendees allowed to enter at these times). Bus: 30, 40, 62, 64, 81, or 492 to Largo di Torre Argentina.

Santa Maria sopra Minerva ★ CHURCH   Virtually located behind the Pantheon, Santa Maria sopra Minerva is Rome's most significant Dominican church, and the only Gothic church in the center of town. True, the facade is in the Renaissance style (the church was begun in 1280 but worked on until 1725), but inside, the arched vaulting is pure Gothic. The main art treasures here are the "Statua del Redentore" (1521), a statue of Christ by **Michelangelo** (just to the left of the altar) and a wonderful fresco cycle in the **Cappella Carafa** (on the right before the altar), created by Filippino Lippi between 1488 and 1493 to honor St. Thomas Aquinas. Devout Catholics flock to the venerated tomb of **Saint Catherine of Siena** under the high altar—the room where she died in 1380 was reconstructed behind the Sacristy by Antonio Barberini in 1637 (far-left corner of the church). **Fra' Angelico** also rests here, in the **Cappella Frangipane e Maddaleni-Capiferro** (to the left of the altar).

Piazza della Minerva 42. www.basilicaminerva.it. © **06-69920384.** Free admission. Daily 8am–7pm. Bus: 116.

Crypta Balbi ★ MUSEUM/RUINS   Perhaps most intriguing of all the branches of the National Museum of Rome, the Crypta Balbi houses the archeological remains of the vast portico belonging to the 1st-century B.C. **Theatre of Lucius Cornelius Balbus,** discovered on the premises in 1981. The first floor exhibits chronicle the history of the site through to the medieval period and the construction of the Conservatorio di Santa Caterina della Rosa. The second floor ("Rome from Antiquity to the Middle Ages") explores the transformation of the city between the 5th and 9th centuries, using thousands of ceramic objects, coins, lead seals, bone and ivory implements, precious stones, and tools found on the site.

Via delle Botteghe Oscure 31. www.archeoroma.beniculturali.it. © **06-39967700.** Admission 7€ adults (also valid for Palazzo Massimo alle Terme, Palazzo Altemps, and Terme di Diocleziano for 3 days). Tues–Sun 9am–7:45pm. Bus: 30, 40, 64, 70, 87, 190, 271, 492, 571, 810 or 916.

Galleria Doria Pamphilj ★★ ART MUSEUM   Palazzo Doria Pamhilj, one of the city's finest Rococo palaces, is still privately owned by the aristocratic Doria Pamphilj family, but their stupendous art collection is open to the public. It's a good idea to grab a free audioguide at the entrance.

The *galleria* extends through the old apartments, with paintings displayed floor-to-ceiling amongst antique furniture, drapes, and richly decorated walls. The Dutch and Flemish collection is impressive, with highlights including a rare Italian piece by Pieter Brueghel the Elder, "Battle in the Port of Naples" and his son Jan Brueghel the Elder's "Earthly Paradise with Original Sin." Of the best Italian works are two paintings by Caravaggio, the moving "Repentant Magdalene" and the wonderful "Rest on the Flight into Egypt," hanging near "Salome with the Head of St. John," by Titian. There's also Raphael's "Double Portrait," an "Annunciation" by Filippo Lippi, and a "Deposition from the Cross" by Vasari. The gallery's real treasures, however, occupy a special room: Bernini's bust of the Pamphilj **"Pope Innocent X"** ★, and **Velázquez's celebrated, enigmatic painting** ★★ of the same pope.

Via del Corso 305 (just north of Piazza Venezia). www.dopart.it. ℂ **06-6797323.** Admission 11€ adults, 8€ students. Daily 9am–7pm, last admission 6pm. Bus: 64 to Piazza Venezia.

CAMPO DE' FIORI

The southern section of the Centro Storico, **Campo de' Fiori** is another neighborhood of narrow streets, small piazzas, and ancient churches. Its main focus remains the piazza of **Campo de' Fiori** ★ itself, whose workaday fruit and vegetable stalls are a real contrast to the cafes and street entertainers of Piazza Navona. The excessively expensive open-air food market runs Monday through Saturday from early in the morning until around 2pm (or whenever the food runs out). From the center of the piazza rises a statue of the severe-looking monk **Giordano Bruno,** whose presence is a reminder that heretics were occasionally burned at the stake here: Bruno was executed by the Inquisition in 1600. Curiously, this is the only *piazza* in Rome that doesn't have a church on its perimeter.

Market stalls at Campo de' Fiori.

Palazzo Farnese ★, on Piazza Farnese just to the south of the Campo, built between 1514 and 1589, was designed by Sangallo and Michelangelo, among others, and was an astronomically expensive project for the time. Its famous residents have included a 16th-century member of the Farnese family, plus Pope Paul III, Cardinal Richelieu, and the former Queen Christina of Sweden, who moved to Rome after abdicating. During the 1630s, when the heirs couldn't afford to maintain the *palazzo*, it was inherited by the Bourbon kings of Naples and then purchased by the French government in 1874; the French Embassy is still located here (closed to the public).

Palazzo Spada ★ MUSEUM   Built around 1540 for Cardinal Gerolamo Capo di Ferro, Palazzo Spada was purchased by the eponymous Cardinal Spada in 1632. Most of what you see today dates back to the restoration undertaken by Borromini during the Spada period. Its richly ornate facade, covered in high-relief stucco decorations in the Mannerist style, is the finest of any building from 16th-century Rome. The State Rooms are closed, but it's the richly decorated courtyard and corridor, Borromini's masterful illusion of perspective *(la prospettiva di Borromini)*, and the four rooms of the **Galleria Spada** that draw the most interest. Inside you will also find some notable paintings, such as the "Portrait of Cardinale Bernardino Spada" by Guido Reni, and Titian's "Portrait of a Violinist," plus minor works from Caravaggio, Parmigianino, Pietro Testa, and Giambattista Gaulli.

Piazza Capo di Ferro 13. ℭ **06-6874893.** Admission 5€. Tue–Sun 8:30am–7:30pm. Bus 46, 56, 62, 64, 70, 87, or 492.

THE JEWISH GHETTO

The southern part of Campo de' Fiori merges into the old **Jewish Ghetto,** established near the River Tiber by a Papal Bull in 1555, which required all the Jews in Rome to live in one area. Walled in, overcrowded, prone to floods and epidemics, and on some of the worst land in the city, life here was extremely grim. It was only after the Ghetto was abolished in 1882 that its walls were torn down and the area largely reconstructed. Today the **Via Portico d'Ottavia** lies at the heart of a flourishing Jewish Quarter, with Romans flocking here to soak up the festive atmosphere and sample the stellar Roman-Jewish and Middle Eastern cuisine.

The **Great Synagogue of Rome** (Tempio Maggiore di Roma; www.romae-braica.it; ℭ **06-6840061**) was built from 1901 to 1904 in an eclectic style evoking Babylonian and Persian temples. The synagogue was attacked by terrorists in 1982 and since then has been heavily guarded by *carabinieri*, a division of the Italian police armed with machine guns. On the premises is the **Museo Ebraico di Roma (Jewish Museum of Rome),** Via Catalana (www.museoebraico.roma.it; ℭ **06-6840061**), which chronicles the history of the Jews of Rome and Italy in general, with displays of works of 17th- and 18th-century Roman silversmiths, precious textiles from all over Europe, parchments, and marble carvings saved when the Ghetto synagogues were demolished. Admission includes a guided tour of the synagogue in English and costs 11€ for adults, 4€ for students, children 10 and under admitted free. From mid-June to mid-September, hours are Sunday to Thursday 10am to 7pm, Friday 10am to 4pm. At other times, hours are Sunday to Thursday 10am to 5pm, Friday 9am to 2pm.

The Tridente & the Spanish Steps

The northern half of central Rome is known as the **Tridente** thanks to the trident shape formed by three roads—Via di Ripetta, Via del Corso, and Via del Babuino—leading down from **Piazza del Popolo.** The area around **Piazza di Spagna** and the **Spanish Steps** was once the artistic quarter of the city, attracting English poets Keats and Shelley, German author Goethe, and Italian film director Federico Fellini (who lived on Via Margutta). Institutions such as Caffè Greco and Babington's Tea Rooms are still here, though you will be lucky to see any artists today through the throngs of tourists and shoppers.

PIAZZA DEL POPOLO

Elegant **Piazza del Popolo** ★★ is haunted with memories. According to legend, the ashes of Nero were enshrined here, until 11th-century residents began complaining to the pope about his imperial ghost. The **Egyptian obelisk** dates from the 13th century B.C.; it was removed from Heliopolis to Rome during Augustus's reign (and once stood at the Circus Maximus).

The current piazza was designed in the early 19th century by Napoleon's architect, Valadier. The 15th-century **Santa Maria del Popolo** ★★ is at its northern curve, its facade modified by the great Bernini between 1655 and 1660 in a baroque style. Raphael's mosaic series the "Creation of the World" adorns the interior of the dome of the **Capella Chigi** inside the church (the second chapel on the left), and **Pinturicchio** decorated the main choir vault with frescoes such as the "Coronation of the Virgin." The **Capella Cerasi** (to the left of the high altar), contains gorgeous examples of baroque art: an altarpiece painting of "The Assumption of Mary" by Carracci, and on either side two great works by Caravaggio, "Conversion on the Road to Damascus" and "The Crucifixion of Saint Peter." Opposite Santa Maria del Popolo, standing astride the three roads that form the "trident," are almost-twin baroque churches, **Santa Maria dei Miracoli** (1681) and **Santa Maria di Montesanto** (1679).

MAXXI (National Museum of the XXI Century Arts) ★ MUSEUM

A 10-minute tram ride from Piazza del Popolo allows you to leave the Renaissance far behind and see MAXXI, a masterpiece of contemporary architecture with bending and overlapping oblong tubes designed by Anglo-Iraqi architect Zaha Hadid. The museum is divided into two sections, MAXXI art and MAXXI architecture, primarily serving as a venue for temporary exhibitions of contemporary work in both fields (although it does have a small, growing permanent collection). The building is worth a visit in its own right.

Via Guido Reni 4a. www.fondazionemaxxi.it. ✆ **06-39967350.** Admission 11€, free children 13 and under. Tues–Fri and Sun 11am–7pm; Sat 11am–10pm. Metro: Flaminio, then tram 2.

Tridente & the Spanish Steps

Spanish Steps 16
SS. Vincenzo e
Anastasio 36
Trevi Fountain 35
Trinità dei Monti 17

RESTAURANTS ◆
Al Ceppo 25
Al Vero Girarrosto
Toscano 20
Café Romano 13
Canova Tadolini 9
Colline Emiliane 34
Il Bacaro 7
Imàgo 18
La Terrazza
dell'Eden 19
Metamorfosi 24

HOTELS ■
Adriano 6
Babuino 181 8
Condotti 11
Daphne Trevi 30
Daphne Veneto 33
Deko Rome 27
The Inn at the
Spanish Steps 12
La Residenza 28
Panda 10
Parlamento 14
Villa Spalletti
Trivelli 39

ATTRACTIONS ●
Augustus's Mausoleum
(Mausoleo di Augusto) 5
Galleria Borghese 23
Galleria Nazionale
d'Arte Antica 32
Galleria Nazionale
d'Arte Moderna 22
Keats-Shelley House 15
MACRO Via Nizza 26
MAXXI (National Museum
of the XXI Century Arts) 1
Museo dell'Ara Pacis 4
Museo e Cripta dei Frati
Cappuccini 29
Museo Nazionale Etrusco
di Villa Giulia 21
Palazzo del Quirinale 37
Piazza Barberini 31
Piazza del Popolo 3
Santa Maria del Popolo 2
Scuderie del Quirinale
(Scuderie Papali) 38

Via Nizza 26

Via Aniene

Via Po

Corso d'Italia

Via Puglie

Via Romagna

Piemonte

Via Abruzzi

Sicilia

Via Toscana

Via Marche

LUDOVISI

Via Friuli

Campania

Via

Via d'Italia

Corso d'Italia

Via Pinciana

Via Veneto

Via Vittorio Veneto

Emilia

Via Lazio

Via Ludovisi

Via Lombardia

Via di San Basilio

Via V. Veneto

Via Barberini

Barberini

Piazza
Barberini

Via delle Quattro Fontane

Via del Quirinale

Traforo
Umberto I

Palazzo del
Quirinale

Metro Ⓐ—Ⓜ—Ⓜ

Porta
Pinciana

VILLA BORGHESE

Vle. S. Paolo
del Brasile

Viale del Muro Torto

Viale della Trinità dei Monti

Via di Porta Pinciana

Via degli Artisti

Sistina

Via Francesco Crispi

Via Gregoriana

Spagna

Via d. Due e Case

V. d. Capo e Case

V. d. Due e Case

Via Macelli

Tritone

Via del Traforo

Via d. Via

Rasella

Piazza
Barberini

Ga oppatoio

0   200 y
0   200 m

VILLA BORGHESE

Vle. del Belvedere

Via Margutta

Babuino

Via del Vantaggio

Via Antonio Canova

Via dei Greci

Via Vittoria

Corso

Via della Croce

Condotti

Via Frattina

Via Belsiana

Via della Vite

Via del Mercede

Mario de' Fiori

Piazza de Spagna

Piazza di San Silvestro

Via di Santa
Maria in Via

Via del Corso

Largo
Chigi

Via della Panetteria

Trinità dei Monti

Sebastianello

Via di San

V. di San

Piazza di
San Lorenzo
in Lucina

Via del
Parlamento

Palazzo di
Montecitorio

Piazza di
Montecitorio

Piazzale
Napoleone I

Vle. Gabriele d'Annunzio

Via del Vantaggio

Via di Gesù
e Maria

V. Laurina

Piazza del
Popolo

Via Ferdinando di Savoia

V. N. Ferdinando di Savoia

Flaminio

Ripetta

TRIDENTE

Via Antonio Canova

Via del Vantaggio

Corso

Via

Piazza
Augusto
Imperatore

Piazza N. della Fontanella

Piazza di
Borghese

Via di Ripetta

Lungotevere in Augusta

Ponte
Cavour

Piazza
Nicosia

Lung. Marzio

Via della Scrofa

Tiber (Tevere)

4

ROME | Exploring Rome

105

Museo dell'Ara Pacis ★★ MUSEUM   Set in a very modern glass building, which you can walk around for free, the white marble "Altar of Peace" was created in 9 B.C. to honor the achievements of (soon to be Emperor) Augustus in subduing tribes north of Alps. The marble Altar of Peace, a temple-like monument, was later lost to memory, and though signs of its existence were discovered in the 16th century, it wasn't until the 1930s that the ancient monument was fully excavated. After World War II it lay virtually abandoned until the 1970s; true restoration only began in the 1980s. The current museum building containing it, finished in 2006 and designed by American architect Richard Meier, is one of the most poignant showcases of Imperial Rome.

The exhibit complex housing the *Ara Pacis* provides context, with interactive displays in English and Italian. Note that you get great views of the huge, overgrown ruin of **Augustus's Mausoleum (Mausoleo di Augusto)** from here, but the 1st-century B.C. tomb itself—where the ashes of emperors Augustus, Caligula, Claudius, Nerva, and Tiberius were once stored, is closed to the public.

Lungotevere in Augusta. http://en.arapacis.it. ⓒ **06-060608.** Admission 9€. Tues–Sun 9am–7pm (last admission 6pm). Bus: C3, 70, 81, 87, 186, 492, 628, or 913.

PIAZZA DI SPAGNA

The undoubted highlight of Tridente is **Piazza di Spagna,** which attracts hordes of Romans and tourists alike to lounge on its celebrated **Spanish Steps (Scalinata della Trinità dei Monti)** ★★—the largest stairway in Europe—and enjoy the view onto Bernini's "Fontana della Barcaccia," a fountain shaped like an old boat. The Spanish Steps are especially enchanting in early spring, when they become framed by thousands of blooming azaleas, but they are heaving with flower dealers, trinket sellers, and photographers year-round.

In an odd twist, the monumental stairway of 135 steps and the square take their names from the Spanish Embassy (it used to be headquartered here), but were actually funded, almost entirely, by the French. That's because the Trinità dei Monti church at the top was under the patronage of the Bourbon kings of France at the time. They were built from 1723 to 1725.

Trinità dei Monti itself is a 16th-century church with a stately baroque facade perched photogenically at the top of the Steps, behind yet another Roman obelisk, the "Obelisco Sallustiano." It's worth climbing up just for the views. Inside, the artistic highlights include works by Daniele da Volterra, a pupil of Michelangelo, notably a fresco of the "Assumption" in the third chapel on the right; the last figure on the right is said to be a portrait of the maestro himself. In the second chapel on the left is Volterra's critically acclaimed "Deposition" in monochrome, which imitates a sculpture by clever use of *trompe l'oeil.*

Keats-Shelley House ★ MUSEUM   At the foot of the Spanish Steps is the 18th-century house where the Romantic English poet John Keats died of consumption on February 23, 1821 at age 25. The *palazzo* was bought in 1909

Art in the Pope's Stables

Across from the Palazzo del Quirinale, the **Scuderie del Quirinale** or **Scuderie Papali,** Via XXIV Maggio 16 (www.scuderiequirinale.it; ✆ **06-39967500**), 18th-century stables built for the pope's horses, now serve as remarkably atmospheric art galleries hosting temporary exhibitions. Recent exhibits have included the work of Frida Kahlo and art that depicts Emperor Augustus. The galleries are usually open Sunday through Thursday from 10am to 8pm, and Friday and Saturday 10am to 10:30pm, but often close between exhibitions and throughout the summer months—check the website. Admission is 12€.

by well-intentioned English and American literary types; it has since then been a working library established in honor of Keats and fellow Romantic Percy Bysshe Shelley, who drowned off the coast of Viareggio with a copy of Keats's works in his pocket. The apartment where Keats spent his last months, tended by his close friend Joseph Severn, shelters a death mask of Keats as well as the "deadly sweat" drawing by Severn. Both Keats and Shelley are buried in their beloved Rome, at the Protestant cemetery near the Pyramid of Cestius, in Testaccio.

Piazza di Spagna 26. www.keats-shelley-house.org. ✆ **06-6784235.** Admission 5€. Mon–Sat 10am–1pm and 2–6pm. Metro: Spagna.

Palazzo del Quirinale ★★ HISTORIC SITE   Until the end of World War II, this palace was the home of the king of Italy; before the crown resided here, it was the summer residence of the pope. Since 1946, the palace has been the official residence of the President of Italy, but parts of it are open to the public on Sunday mornings.

Few rooms anywhere are as impressive as the richly decorated, 17th-century **Salone dei Corazzieri,** the **Sala d'Ercole** (once the apartments of Umberto I but completely rebuilt in 1940), and the tapestry covered 17th-century **Sala dello Zodiaco.** Despite its Renaissance origins, this *palazzo* is rich in associations with ancient emperors and deities. The colossal statues of the "Dioscuri," Castor and Pollux, which now form part of the fountain in the piazza, were found in the nearby Baths of Constantine. In 1793, Pius VI had an ancient Egyptian obelisk moved here from the Mausoleum of Augustus. The sweeping view of the city from the piazza, which crowns the highest of the seven ancient hills of Rome, is itself worth the trip.

Piazza del Quirinale. www.quirinale.it. ✆ **06-46991.** Admission 5€, free ages 17 and under and 65 and over. Sun 8:30am–noon. Closed late June to early Sept. Metro: Barberini.

Trevi Fountain (Fontana di Trevi) ★★ MONUMENT   As you elbow your way through the summertime crowds around the **Trevi Fountain,** you'll find it hard to believe that this little piazza was nearly always deserted before the 1950s, when it started starring in films. The first was "Three Coins in the Fountain." It was also the setting for an iconic scene in Federico Fellini's 1960

The baroque Trevi Fountain, a tourist gathering spot in Rome.

masterpiece, "La Dolce Vita," and it's also where the Audrey Hepburn character in "Roman Holiday" gets her signature haircut. To this day, thousands of euros worth of coins are tossed into the fountain every day.

Supplied with water from the Acqua Vergine aqueduct and a triumph of the baroque style, the fountain was based on the design of Nicola Salvi—who's said to have died of illness contracted during his supervision of the project—and was completed in 1762. The design centers on the triumphant figure of Neptune, standing on a shell chariot drawn by winged steeds and led by a pair of tritons. Two allegorical figures in the side niches represent good health and fertility. The fountain is undergoing restoration and should be finished by the time you read this book.

On the southwestern corner of the piazza is an unimpressive-looking church, **SS. Vincenzo e Anastasio,** with a strange claim to fame. Within it survive the relics (hearts and intestines) of several popes. According to legend, the church was built on the site of a spring that burst from the earth after the beheading of St. Paul; the spring is one of the three sites where his head is said to have bounced off the ground.

Piazza di Trevi. Metro: Barberini.

Villa Borghese & Parioli

Villa Borghese ★★, in the heart of Rome, is not actually a villa but one of Europe's most elegant parks, 6km (3¾ miles) in circumference. It provides access to several outstanding museums within. Cardinal Scipione Borghese created the park in the 1600s. Umberto I, king of Italy, acquired it in 1902 and presented it to the city of Rome. With landscaped vistas and manicured gardens, this heart-shaped greenbelt is crisscrossed by roads, but you can escape from the traffic and seek a shaded area under a tree to enjoy a picnic or relax. On a sunny weekend, it's a pleasure to stroll here and see Romans at play, riding bikes, lounging under umbrella pines, or inline skating. There are a few casual cafes and more upscale eateries. In the northeast of the park is a small zoo.

Galleria Borghese ★★★ ART MUSEUM   Occupying the former Villa Borghese Pinciana, the Galleria Borghese was built between 1609 and 1613 for Cardinal Scipione Borghese, who was an early patron of Bernini and an astute collector of work by Caravaggio. Today the gallery is one of Rome's great art treasures. It's also one of Rome's most pleasant sights to tour, thanks to the curators' mandate that only a limited number of people be allowed in at any one time (see the last paragraph of this section for more on that).

The ground floor is a **sculpture gallery** par excellence, housing Canova's famously risqué statue of Paolina Borghese, sister of Napoleon and married to the reigning Prince Camillo Borghese (when asked if she was uncomfortable posing nude, she reportedly replied "No, the studio was heated."). The genius of Bernini permeates the rooms, with his "David" (the face of which is thought to be a self-portrait), and his **"Apollo and Daphne" ★★**, seminal works of baroque sculpture. Next to this room, look out also for Bernini's Mannerist sculpture, "The Rape of Persephone." Caravaggio is represented by the "Madonna of the Grooms," his shadowy "St. Jerome," and his frightening **"David Holding the Head of Goliath" ★★**.

Upstairs lies a rich collection of paintings, including Raphael's ultra-graceful "Deposition" and his sinuous "Lady with a Unicorn." There's also a series of self-portraits by Bernini, and his lifelike busts of Cardinal Scipione and Pope Paul V. One of Titian's best, **"Sacred and Profane Love" ★**, lies in the final rooms. Guided tours of the galleries in English (5€) run 9:10am to 11:10am, but failing that opt for the **audioguides,** as English labeling in the museum is minimal. No photographs are allowed inside the museum.

Galleria Borghese.

Important information: No more than 360 visitors at a time are allowed on the ground floor, and no more than 90 are allowed on the upper floor, during set, 2-hour windows. **Reservations are essential,** so call ✆ **06-32810** (Mon–Fri 9am–6pm; Sat 9am–1pm). You can also make reservations by visiting www.tosc.it, or by stopping by on your first day in Rome to reserve tickets for a later date. If you are having problems making a reservation in advance, ask your hotel to help out.

Piazzale del Museo Borghese 5 (off Via Pinciana). www.galleria borghese.it. ✆ **06-8413979.** Admission 11€ plus 2€ mandatory "service charge." Audioguides 5€. Tues–Sun 8:30am–7:30pm. Bus: 5, 19, 52, 116, 204, 490, or 910.

Galleria Nazionale d'Arte Moderna (National Gallery of Modern Art) ★ ART MUSEUM   Housed in the monumental Palazzo Bazzani and constructed for the exhibition celebrating the 50th anniversary of "United Italy" in 1911, this "modern" art collection ranges from neoclassical and Romantic paintings and sculpture, to better 20th-century works. Quality varies, but art lovers should seek out van Gogh's "Gardener" and "Portrait of Madame Ginoux" in Room 15, the handful of Impressionists in Room 14 (Cézanne, Degas, Monet, and Rodin), and Klimt's harrowing "Three Ages" in Room 16. The Surrealist and Expressionist works by Miró, Kandinsky, and Mondrian appear in Room 22, and Pollock's "Undulating Paths" and Calder's "Mobile" hold court in Room 27. One of Warhol's "Hammer and Sickle" series is tucked away in Room 30.

Frankly, the museum is primarily a showcase for **modern Italian painters.** Be sure to check out especially the rooms dedicated to Giacomo Balla (no. 34), Giacomo Manzù (no. 35), Renato Guttuso (no. 37), and Pino Pascali (no. 40).

Viale delle Belle Arti 131. www.gnam.beniculturali.it. ⓒ **06-322981.** Admission 8€, free children 17 and under. Tues–Sun 8:30am–7:30pm. Bus: 88, 95, 490, or 495.

MACRO Via Nizza ★★ MUSEUM   This is the main branch of Rome's contemporary art museum (the other branch of the museum is housed in a converted slaughterhouse in Testaccio [p. 114]). A recent renovation expanded the museum to occupy an entire block of industrial buildings belonging to the turn-of-the-century Peroni beer factory, located near the Porta Pia gate of the Aurelian walls. Designed by French architect Odile Decq, the museum hosts contemporary art exhibits with edgy installations, visuals, events, and multimedia screenings.

Via Nizza 138. www.museomacro.org. ⓒ **06-671070400.** Admission 15€ (combined ticket with MACRO Testaccio). Tues–Sun 10:30am–7:30pm. Last admission 30 min. before closing. Bus: 38, 89. Tram: 3, 19.

Museo Carlo Bilotti ★ ART MUSEUM   Enthusiasts of Greek-born Italian artist **Giorgio de Chirico** should consider a pilgrimage to this small modern art gallery, created thanks to the generosity of Carlo Bilotti, an Italian-American collector who donated 23 artworks to Rome in 2006. Though long overshadowed by the more famous Surrealists, de Chirico was a major influence on the Surrealist movement in the early 20th century—the themes of loneliness and isolation explored in his "metaphysical" paintings can be compared to American artist Edward Hopper.

Housed in a 16th-century palace in the Villa Borghese, the museum consists of two small rooms, and though the work is good, we recommend it for art aficionados only. Pieces to look out for include a rare restrained piece by the Pop Art master Andy Warhol, the elegant "Portrait of Tina and Lisa Bilotti," and Larry Rivers's depiction of Carlo Bilotti himself. De Chirico dominates Room 2, with 17 paintings representing all his memorable themes depicted in the course of half a century, from the mid-1920s through to the 1970s. Also look out for the beguiling "Summer," an abstract work by Tuscan Gino Severini.

Villa Borghese, at Viale Fiorello La Guardia. www.museocarlobilotti.it. ℗ **060608.** Admission free. June–Sept Tues–Fri 1–7pm; Oct–May Tues–Fri 10am–4pm. Metro: Flaminio.

Museo Nazionale Etrusco di Villa Giulia (National Etruscan Museum) ★★★ MUSEUM The great Etruscan civilization (which gave its name to Tuscany), was one of Italy's most advanced, although it remains relatively mysterious, in part because of its centuries-long rivalry with Rome. Once Rome had absorbed the Etruscans in the 3rd century B.C., it set about eradicating all evidence of their achievements, as it did with most of the people it conquered.

Today this museum, housed in the handsome Renaissance Villa Giulia, built by Pope Julius III between 1550 and 1555, is the best place in Italy to familiarize yourself with the Etruscans, thanks to a cache of precious artifacts, sculptures, vases, monuments, tools, weapons, and jewels. Fans of ancient history could spend several hours here, but for those with less time, here's a quick list of the unmissable sights. The most striking attraction is the stunning **Sarcofago degli Sposi (Sarcophagus of the Spouses)** ★★, a late-6th-century B.C. terra-cotta funerary monument featuring a life-size bride and groom, supposedly lounging at a banquet in the afterlife—there's a similar monument in the Louvre, Paris. Equally fascinating are the **Pyrgi Tablets,** gold-leaf inscriptions in both Etruscan and Phoenician from the 5th century B.C., and the **Apollo of Veii,** a huge painted terra-cotta statue of Apollo dating to the 6th century B.C. The **Euphronios Krater** is also conserved here, a renowned and perfectly maintained red-figured Greek vase from the 6th century B.C. which returned to Italy from the New York Met after a long legal battle won in 2006.

Piazzale di Villa Giulia 9. www.villagiulia.beniculturali.it. ℗ **06-3226571.** Admission 8€. Tues–Sun 8:30am–7:30pm. Bus: 926. Tram: 3, 19.

Via Veneto & Piazza Barberini

Piazza Barberini lies at the foot of several Roman streets, among them Via Barberini, Via Sistina, and Via Vittorio Veneto. It would be a far more pleasant spot were it not for the heavy traffic swarming around its principal feature, Bernini's recently cleaned **Fountain of the Triton (Fontana del Tritone)** ★. For more than three centuries, the strange figure sitting in a vast open clam has been blowing water from his triton. Off to one side of the piazza is the aristocratic side facade of the **Palazzo Barberini,** named for one of Rome's most powerful families; inside hosts the **Galleria Nazionale d'Arte Antica** (see below). The Renaissance Barberini dynasty reached their peak when a son was elected pope as Urban VIII; he encouraged Bernini and gave him patronage.

As you go up **Via Vittorio Veneto,** look for the small fountain on the right corner of Piazza Barberini—it's another Bernini, the **Fountain of the Bees (Fontana delle Api).** At first they look more like flies, but they're the bees of the Barberini crest, complete with the crossed keys of St. Peter above them. The keys were always added to a family crest when a son was elected pope.

Galleria Nazionale d'Arte Antica (National Gallery of Ancient Art) ★★ ART MUSEUM   On the southern side of **Piazza Barberini,** the grand **Palazzo Barberini** houses the Galleria Nazionale d'Arte Antica, a trove of Italian art covering primarily from the early Renaissance to late baroque periods. Some of the works on display are wonderful, but the building itself is the main attraction, a baroque masterpiece begun by Carlo Maderno in 1627 and completed in 1633 by Bernini, with additional work by Borromini (you'll recognize his style in a whimsical spiral staircase). The central **Salone di Pietro da Cortona** is the most captivating space, with a *trompe l'oeil* ceiling frescoed by Pietro da Cortona, a depiction of "The Triumph of Divine Providence."

The initial galleries on the lower two floors cover the early Renaissance, including modest crowd-pleasers like Piero di Cosimo's "St. Mary Magdalene" (Room 10), although most of the devotional work will appeal strictly to aficionados. It's the core of the museum, covering the High Renaissance and baroque periods, which has the most intriguing pieces, including Raphael's "La Fornarina," a baker's daughter thought to have been the artist's mistress (look for Raphael's name on the woman's bracelet); paintings by Tintoretto and Titian (Room 15); a portrait of English King Henry VIII by Holbein (Room 16); and a couple of typically unsettling El Grecos in Room 17, "The Baptism of Christ" and "Adoration of the Shepherds." Caravaggio dominates Room 20 with the justly celebrated "Judith and Holofernes" and the spectacular **"Narcissus"** ★★.

The newer galleries on the top floor cover the less striking, late baroque era, featuring works by painters such as Luca Giordano (Room 25) and other Neapolitans, though Bernini's "Portrait of Urban VIII" certainly stands out in Room 26. If you run out of time, you can skip the final galleries (they cover the even less appealing late 17th and 18th c.), but do slow down to admire the classic Venetian scenes by Canaletto (Room 30), which are always a pleasure.

Via delle Quattro Fontane 13. www.galleriabarberini.beniculturali.it. ℂ **06-4814591.** Admission 7€; combined with Palazzo Corsini 9€. Tues–Sun 8:30am–7pm; last admission 6pm. Metro: Barberini.

Museo e Cripta dei Frati Cappuccini (Museum and Crypt of the Capuchin Friars) ★★ RELIGIOUS SITE/MUSEUM

One of the most mesmerizingly macabre (and therefore hugely popular) sights in all Christendom, this otherwise modest museum dedicated to the Capuchin order ends with an eerie series of six chapels in the crypt, adorned with thousands of skulls and bones woven into mosaic "works of art." To make this allegorical dance of death, the bones of more than 3,700 Capuchin brothers were used. Some of the skeletons are intact, draped with Franciscan habits. The tradition of the friars holds that this was the work of a French Capuchin monk, and literature suggests that you should consider the historical context of its origins: a period when Christians had a rich and creative cult of the dead and great spiritual masters meditated and preached with a skull in hand. Whatever the belief, the experience is undeniably spooky (you can take photographs) so plan wisely if traveling with younger ones. The entrance is halfway up the first staircase on the right of the church of the Convento dei Frati Cappuccini, completed in 1630 and rebuilt in the early 1930s.

Beside the Convento dei Frati Cappuccini, Via Vittorio Veneto 27. www.cappucciniviaveneto.it. © **06-88803695**. Admission 6€, 4€ ages 17 and under. Daily 9am–7pm, last admission 6.30pm. Metro: Barberini.

Around Stazione Termini

Palazzo Massimo alle Terme ★★ MUSEUM   One third of Rome's ancient art canon is conserved at this branch of the Museo Nazionale Romano. Among its treasures are a major coin collection, extensive maps of trade routes (with audio and visual exhibits on the network of traders over the centuries), and a vast sculpture collection that includes portrait busts of emperors and their families, as well as mythical figures like the Minotaur and Athena. But the real draw is on the second floor, where you can see some of Rome's oldens **frescoes** ★★ depicting an entire garden, complete with plants and birds, from the Villa di Livia in the city's northern Prima Porta. (Livia was the wife of Emperor Augustus and was deified after her death in A.D. 29.)

Largo di Villa Peretti. www.archeoroma.beniculturali.it. © **06-39967700**. Admission 7€; ticket valid for Terme di Diocleziano (see below), Palazzo Altemps (p. 98) and Crypta Balbi (p. 101). Tues–Sun 9am–7:45pm. Last admission 1 hr. before closing. Metro: Termini or Repubblica.

Santa Maria della Vittoria ★ CHURCH   This pretty little baroque church showcases a classic Roman travertine facade as well as an ornate interior. But a visit here is all about one unique piece of art: Gian Lorenzo Bernini's **"Ecstasy of St. Teresa"** ★★★. Crafted from marble between 1644 and 1647, it shows the Spanish saint at the moment of her ecstatic encounter with an angel (the so-called "Transverberation"). To suggest Bernini's depiction is a little on the erotic side would be an understatement.

Via XX Settembre 17 (at Largo S. Susanna). www.chiesasantamariavittoriaroma.it. © **06-42740571**. Free admission. Mon–Sat 8:30am–noon and 3:30–6pm, Sun 3:30–6pm. Metro: Repubblica.

Santa Maria Maggiore (St. Mary Major) ★ CHURCH   As one of Rome's four papal basilicas, this majestic church was founded by Pope Liberius in A.D. 358 and rebuilt on the orders of Pope Sixtus III from 432 to 440. Its 14th-century **campanile** (bell tower) is the city's tallest. Much doctored in the 18th century, the church's facade isn't an accurate reflection of the treasures inside. The basilica is noted for its 5th-century Roman mosaics adorning its nave, and for its coffered ceiling, added with gold brought, some say, from the New World. The church also contains the **tomb of Bernini,** Italy's most important baroque sculptor-architect. Ironically, the man who changed the face of Rome with his sensuous shapes and elaborate fountains is buried in a tomb so simple that it takes a sleuth to find it (to the right, near the altar).

Piazza di Santa Maria Maggiore. 📞 **06-69886800.** Free admission. Daily 9am–7pm. Bus: C3, 16, 70, 71, 75, 360, 590, 649, 714, or 717.

Terme di Diocleziano (Baths of Diocletian) ★ MUSEUM/ RUINS   Ancient Roman recycling at its finest. Originally, this spot held the largest of Rome's hedonistic baths (dating back to A.D. 298 at the time of the reign of Emperor Diocletian). During the Renaissance, a church, a vast cloister, and a convent were built around and into the ruins—much of it designed by Michelangelo, no less. Today the entire complex is part of the Museo Nazionale Romano, and this juxtaposition of Christianity, pagan ancient ruins, and exhibit space make for a compelling museum stop that's typically quieter than the city's usual blockbusters. There's a large collection of inscriptions and other stone carvings from the Roman and pre-Roman periods, alongside statuary. Only Aula 10 remains of the vast baths, which accommodated 3,000 at a time when they opened in the early 4th century. They were abandoned in the 6th century, when invading Goth armies destroyed the city's aqueducts.

Note: The museum is undergoing restoration, and only sections may be open.

Viale E. di Nicola 78. www.archeoroma.beniculturali.it. 📞 **06-39967700.** Admission 7€; ticket valid for Palazzo Massimo alle Terme (see above), Palazzo Altemps (p. 98) and Crypta Balbi (p. 101). Tues–Sun 9am–7:45pm. Last admission 1 hr. before closing. Metro: Termini or Repubblica.

Testaccio & Southern Rome

Centrale Montemartini ★★ MUSEUM   In Rome's first thermo-electric plant, named after Giovanni Montemartini, the renovated boiler rooms have been home since 1997 to a grand collection of Roman and Greek statues originally housed in the Museo del Palazzo dei Conservatori, Museo Nuovo, and Braccio Nuovo. This creates a unique juxtaposition of classic and industrial archeology. The powerhouse was the first public plant to produce electricity for the city of Rome, and was founded at the turn of the 19th century on Via Ostiense, where it still occupies a large block between the ex-wholesale markets, the Gazometro (defunct methane gas meter) and the bank of the Tiber River. Striking installations include those in the Boiler Hall, a 10,764 square-foot room where statues share space with an immense steam boiler: an intricate web of pipes, masonry, and metal walkways. Equally striking is the Hall of Machines, where two huge turbines tower opposite the reconstructed pediment of the Temple of Apollo Sosiano, which illustrates a famous Greek battle.

Via Ostiense 106. www.centralemontemartini.org. 📞 **06-0608.** Admission 7€. Tues–Sun 9am–7pm. Last admission 30 min. before closing. Bus: 23, 271, 769, N2, N3. Metro: Garbatella.

MACRO Testaccio ★ MUSEUM   The Testaccio outpost of Rome's contemporary art museum is housed—appropriately for this former meatpacking

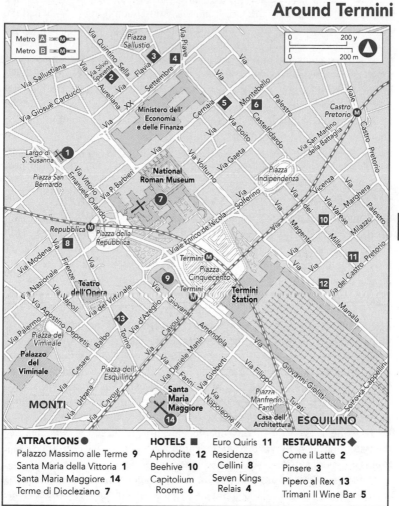

Metro Ⓐ ⬛🇲⬛
Metro Ⓑ ⬛🇲⬛

0　　　　200 y
0　　　　200 m

Piazza Sallustio **3** **4**

Via Piave

Via Sallustiana
Via Giosuè Carducci
Via Quintino Sella
Via Silvio Spaventa
Via Aureliana
XX Settembre
Via Flavia
Via
Via

Ministero dell' Economia e delle Finanze

Cernaia **5** Montebello **6** Palestro
Castelfidardo
Via Goito
Castro Pretorio Ⓜ
Viale
Castro Pretorio

Largo di S. Susanna **1**
Piazza San Bernardo

Via Vittorio Emanuele Orlando
Via P. Barberini
National Roman Museum
Via Volturno
Via Gaeta
Piazza Indipendenza
Via San Martino della Battaglia
Vicenza
Via Marghera
Via Palestro

7

Repubblica Ⓜ **8**
Piazza della Repubblica

Via Modena
Via Nazionale
Via Firenze

Viale Enrico de Nicola
Via Solferino
Via dei
Via Magenta
Via Varese
Via Milazzo
10
11
Via del Castro Pretorio

Termini Ⓜ
Piazza Cinquecento
Termini Station

Teatro dell'Opera
9
Termini Ⓜ

12
Via del Castro Pretorio
Marsala

Via Agostino Depretis
Via Napoli
Via del Viminale
Via d'Azeglio
Via Giovanni
Cavour
Amendola
Via
Giovanni Giolitti
Sforza Cappellini

13
Balbo
Torino
Via Daniele Manin
Via Gioberti
Via Filippo

Piazza del Viminale
Palazzo del Viminale

Via Cesare Balbo
Piazza dell' Esquilino
Via Fanti
Piazza Manfredo Fanti

MONTI
Via Urbana
Via Cavour
Santa Maria Maggiore
Via Napoleone III
Casa dell' Architettura
ESQUILINO
Turati

14

ATTRACTIONS ●
Palazzo Massimo alle Terme **9**
Santa Maria della Vittoria **1**
Santa Maria Maggiore **14**
Terme di Diocleziano **7**

HOTELS ■
Aphrodite **12**
Beehive **10**
Capitolium Rooms **6**
Euro Quiris **11**
Residenza Cellini **8**
Seven Kings Relais **4**

RESTAURANTS ◆
Come il Latte **2**
Pinsere **3**
Pipero al Rex **13**
Trimani Il Wine Bar **5**

neighborhood—in a converted slaughterhouse. The edgy programs and exhibits hosted here are a mix of installations, visuals, events, and special viewings. Opening times are made for night owls: Make a late visit before going on to Testaccio's bars and restaurants.

Piazza Orazio Guistiniani 4. www.museomacro.org. 🕐 **06-671070400.** Admission 15€ (combined ticket with MACRO Via Nizza. Tues–Sun 4–10pm. Last admission 30 min. before closing. Bus: 63, 630, or 719.

San Paolo Fuori le Mura (St. Paul Outside the Walls) ★ CHURCH
The giant Basilica of St. Paul is Rome's fourth great patriarchal church; its origins date from the time of Constantine. It was erected over the tomb of

St. Paul and is the second-largest church in Rome after St. Peter's. The basilica fell victim to fire in 1823 and was subsequently rebuilt—hence the relatively modern look. From the inside, its windows may appear to be stained glass, but they're actually translucent alabaster that illuminates a forest of single-file columns and mosaic medallions (portraits of the various popes). Its most important treasure, however, is a 12th-century marble Easter candelabrum by Vassalletto, the same artist responsible for the remarkable cloisters containing twisted pairs of columns enclosing a rose garden. The baldacchino by Arnolfo di Cambio, dated 1285, miraculously wasn't damaged in the fire, and now shelters the tomb of St. Paul the Apostle.

Via Ostiense 190 (at Piazzale San Paolo). www.basilicasanpaolo.org. © **06-69880800.** Basilica free admission; cloisters 4€. Basilica daily 7am–6:30pm. Cloisters daily 8am–6:15pm. Metro: Basilica di San Paolo.

THE VIA APPIA (APPIAN WAY) & THE CATACOMBS

Of all the roads that led to Rome, **Via Appia Antica** (begun in 312 B.C.) was the most famous. It eventually stretched all the way from Rome to the seaport of Brindisi, through which trade with Greece and the East was funneled. (According to Christian tradition, it was along the Appian Way that an escaping Peter encountered the vision of Christ, causing him to go back into the city to face martyrdom.) The road's initial stretch in Rome is lined with the monuments and ancient tombs of patrician Roman families—burials were forbidden within the city walls as early as the 5th century B.C.—and, below ground, miles of tunnels hewn out of the soft *tufa* stone.

These tunnels, or catacombs, were where early Christians buried their dead and, during the worst times of persecution, held clandestine church services. A few of them are open to the public, so you can wander through musty-smelling tunnels whose walls are gouged out with tens of thousands of burial niches. Early Christians referred to each chamber as a *dormitorio*—they believed the bodies were merely sleeping, awaiting resurrection (which is why the traditional Roman practice of cremation was not tolerated). In some of the tunnels, the remains of early Christian art are visible.

The Appia Antica Park is a popular Sunday lunch picnic site for Roman families and is closed to cars on Sundays, left for the picnickers and bicyclists and inline skaters. See **www.parcoappiaantica.it** for more on the park, including downloadable maps.

To reach the catacombs area, take bus no. 218 from the San Giovanni Metro stop and wait at the bus stop on the opposite side of the road to the Basilica. Around two or three buses run every hour during daylight hours. This bus bumps along the basalt cobbles of the Appia Antica for a bit and then veers right on Via Ardeatina at Domine Quo Vadis church. After a long block, it stops at the square Largo Ardeatina, near the gate to the San Callisto catacombs. From here, you can walk right on Via delle Sette Chiese to the Domitilla catacombs or fork left on Via delle Sette Chiese to the San Sebastiano catacombs. *Insider's tip:* This bus service can be unreliable. If you are in a hurry to accommodate your visit to the catacombs, opt for a taxi (p. 43).

The most impressive of the monuments on the Appian Way itself is the **Tomb of Cecilia Metella** ★, within walking distance of the catacombs. The cylindrical tomb honors the wife of one of Julius Caesar's military commanders from the republican era. Why such an elaborate tomb for a figure of relatively minor historical importance? Simply because Cecilia Metella's tomb has remained and the others have decayed.

Catacombe di Domitilla ★★★ RELIGIOUS SITE/TOUR   The oldest of the catacombs is hands-down the overall winner for most enjoyable experience underground. Groups are relatively small, and guides are entertaining and personable. The catacombs—Rome's longest at 18km (11 miles)—were built below land donated by Domitilla, a noblewoman of the Flavian dynasty who was exiled from Rome for practicing Christianity. They were rediscovered in 1593 after a church abandoned in the 9th century collapsed: The visit begins in this sunken church founded in A.D. 380, the year Christianity became Rome's state religion.

There are fewer "sights" than in the other catacombs, but this is the only funerary burial site where you'll still see bones; the rest have emptied their tombs to rebury the remains in ossuaries on the inaccessible lower levels. Elsewhere in the tunnels, 4th-century frescoes depict some of the earliest representations of Saints Peter and Paul. Notice the absence of crosses: It was only later that Christians replaced the traditional fish symbol with the cross. During this period, Christ's crucifixion was a source of shame to the community. He had been killed like a common criminal.

Via delle Sette Chiese 282. www.domitilla.info. ⓒ **06-5110342**. Admission 8€ adults, 5€ children ages 6–14. Wed–Mon 9am–noon and 2–5pm. Closed mid-Dec to mid-Jan. Bus: 714 (to Piazza Navigatori).

Catacombe di San Callisto (Catacombs of St. Callixtus) ★★ RELIGIOUS SITE/TOUR   These catacombs are often packed with tour-bus groups, and they run perhaps the most standard tour, but the funerary tunnels are phenomenal. They're the first cemetery of the Christian community of Rome, and burial place of 16 popes in the 3rd century. They bear the name of St. Callixtus, the deacon whom Pope St. Zephyrinus put in charge of them and who was later elected pope (A.D. 217–22) himself. The complex is a network of galleries structured in four levels and reaching a depth of about 20m (65 ft.), the deepest in the area. There are many sepulchral chambers and almost half a million tombs of early Christians.

Entering the catacombs, you see the most important crypt, concealing the remains of nine popes. Some of the original marble tablets of their tombs are preserved. Also commemorated is St. Cecilia, patron of sacred music (her relics were moved to her church in Trastevere during the 9th c.; see p. 118). Farther on are the Cubicles of the Sacraments, with 3rd-century frescoes.

Via Appia Antica 110–26. www.catacombe.roma.it. ⓒ **06-5130151**. Admission 8€ adults, 5€ children ages 7–15. Thurs–Tues 9am–noon and 2–5pm. Closed late Jan to late Feb. Bus: 218.

Catacombe di San Sebastiano (Catacombs of St. Sebastian) ★

RELIGIOUS SITE/TOUR   Today the tomb and relics of St. Sebastian are housed in the ground-level basilica, but his original resting place was in the catacombs beneath it. Sebastian was a senior Milanese soldier in the Roman army who converted to Christianity and was martyred in the first decade of the 4th century, during Emperor Diocletian's persecutions, which were especially brutal. From the reign of Valerian to that of Constantine, the bodies of Saints Peter and Paul were also hidden in the catacombs, which were dug from *tufa,* a soft volcanic rock that hardens on exposure to the air.

The underground passages, if stretched out, would reach a length of 11km (6¾ miles). In the tunnels and mausoleums are mosaics and graffiti, along with many other pagan and Christian objects, as well as four Roman tombs with their frescoes and stucco fairly intact. They were found in 1922 after being buried for almost 2,000 years.

Via Appia Antica 136. www.catacombe.org. © **06-7850350.** Admission 8€ adults, 5€ children 6–15. Mon–Sat 10am–4:30pm. Closed Nov 26–Dec 26. Bus: 118

Trastevere

Galleria Nazionale d'Arte Antica in Palazzo Corsini ★ PALACE/ART MUSEUM

Palazzo Corsini first found notoriety as the home of Queen Christina of Sweden, who moved to Rome when she abdicated the Swedish throne after converting to Catholicism. Her most famous epithet is "Queen without a realm, Christian without a faith, and a woman without shame." This stemmed from her open bisexuality, which in the 17th century was frowned upon—at least publicly. Several other big names stayed in this beautiful palace, including Michelangelo as well as Napoleon's mother, Letizia. Today, one wing houses a somewhat attractive museum with a Caravaggio worth note, "St. John the Baptist" (1606), and panels by Luca Giordano, Fra' Angelico, and Poussin, but otherwise the palace history and legend are more interesting than the museum itself.

Via della Lungara 10. www.galleriacorsini.beniculturali.it. © **06-68802323.** Admission 5€, free children 17 and under. Tues–Sun 8:30am–7:30pm. Bus: 125.

San Francesco d'Assisi a Ripa ★ CHURCH

Built on the site of a convent where St. Francis stayed when he came to Rome to see the pope in 1219, his simple cell is preserved inside. It is also yet another small Roman church with a Bernini treasure: The "Tomb of Beata Ludovica Albertoni" (1675) unmistakably bears the hand of the Roman baroque master, with its delicate folds of marble and the ecstatic expression on the face of its subject. Ludovica was a noblewoman who died in 1533 having dedicated her life to the city's poor. The sculpture is in the last chapel on the left.

Piazza di San Francesco d'Assisi 88. © **06-5819020.** Free admission. Mon–Sat 10am–1pm and 2–6:30pm, Sun 2–6:30pm. Bus: 23, 44, 75, or 280.

Santa Cecilia in Trastevere ★ CHURCH

A still-functioning convent built around a peaceful courtyard garden, Santa Cecilia contains the partial

Trastevere & Testaccio

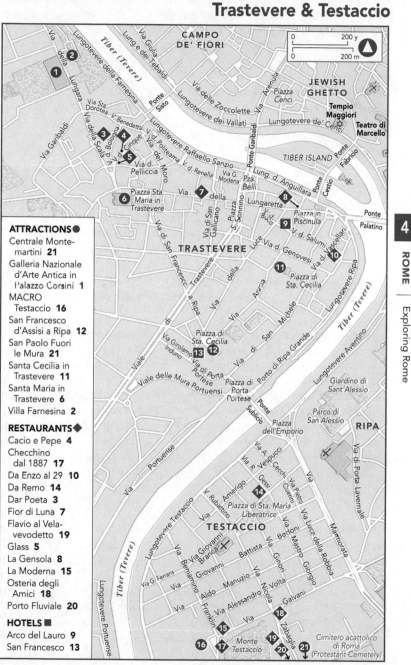

ATTRACTIONS●
Centrale Monte-
martini **21**
Galleria Nazionale
d'Arte Antica in
Palazzo Corsini **1**
MACRO
Testaccio **16**
San Francesco
d'Assisi a Ripa **12**
San Paolo Fuori
le Mura **21**
Santa Cecilia in
Trastevere **11**
Santa Maria in
Trastevere **6**
Villa Farnesina **2**

RESTAURANTS◆
Cacio e Pepe **4**
Checchino
dal 1887 **17**
Da Enzo al 29 **10**
Da Remo **14**
Dar Poeta **3**
Fior di Luna **7**
Flavio al Vela-
vevodetto **19**
Glass **5**
La Gensola **8**
La Moderna **15**
Osteria degli
Amici **18**
Porto Fluviale **20**

HOTELS ■
Arco del Lauro **9**
San Francesco **13**

remains of a masterpiece of Roman medieval painting, the "Last Judgment," by Pietro Cavallini (ca. 1293). Enter to the left of the main doors; a *suora* (nun) will accompany you upstairs to see it. Inside the airy church, over the altar, is a late-13th-century baldacchino by Arnolfo di Cambio. The church is built on the reputed site of Cecilia's ancient palace, and for a small fee you can descend under the church to inspect the ruins of Roman houses, as well as peer through a gate at the faux grotto beneath the altar.

Piazza Santa Cecilia 22. www.benedettinesantacecilia.it. ⓒ **06-45492739.** Church free admission; Cavallini frescoes 3€; excavations 3€. Main church and excavations daily 9:30am–12:30pm and 4–6pm. Frescoes Mon–Sat 10am–12:30pm. Bus: H, 44, or 125/ Tram 8.

Santa Maria in Trastevere ★ CHURCH   This ornate Romanesque church at the colorful heart of Trastevere was founded around A.D. 350 and is one of the oldest in Rome. But parts of it were added around 1100, and more in the early 1700s. The restored mosaics on the apse date from around 1140, and below them are the 1293 mosaic scenes depicting the "Life of the Virgin Mary" by Pietro Cavallini. The faded mosaics on the facade are from the 12th or 13th century, and the octagonal fountain in the piazza is an ancient Roman original that was restored and added to in the 17th century by Carlo Fontana.

Piazza Santa Maria in Trastevere. ⓒ **06-5814802.** Free admission. Daily 9:30am–12:30pm and 3–5:30pm. Bus: H or 125/Tram: 8.

Villa Farnesina ★ HISTORIC HOME   Once called Villa Chigi, this was originally built for Sienese banker Agostino Chigi in 1511, but was acquired (and renamed) by the Farnese family in 1579. With two such wealthy Renaissance patrons, it's hardly surprising that the interior decor is stunning. The villa's architect, Baldassare Peruzzi, began the decoration, with frescoes and motifs rich in myth and symbolism. He was later assisted by Sebastiano del Piombo, Sodoma, and most notably, Raphael. Raphael's **"Loggia of Cupid and Psyche"** ★★ was frescoed to mark Chigi's marriage to Francesca Ordeaschi—though assistants Giulio Romano and Giovanna da Udine did much of the work.

Via della Lungara 230. www.villafarnesina.it. ⓒ **06-68077268.** Admission 6€. Mon–Sat 9am–2pm; 2nd Sun of month 9am–5pm. Bus: 23, 125, 271, or 280.

Organized Tours

Forget the flag-waving guides, leading trance-like crowds around monuments. There's a way of enjoying the abundance of Rome sights minus the unemotional herd-effect. Do consider the advantages of relying on a professionally guided tour, which comes with top-notch insider expertise and focused themes, plus perks like small groups, personalized attention, skipping the lines, and bespoke after-hours experiences.

One of the leading tour operators is **Context Travel** ★ (www.contexttravel. com; ⓒ **800/691-6036** in the U.S., or 06-96727371), a company that, notably, uses local scholars—historians, art historians, preservationists—to lead their tours. Guides offer small-group walking tours, including visits to monuments, museums, and historic piazzas, as well as culinary walks and meals in neighborhood *trattorie*. Custom-designed tours are also available. Prices of the regular tours are high, beginning at 60€ for 2 hours, but most participants consider them a highlight of their trips. Context also offers an excellent family program, which visit sights such as the Vatican and the Colosseum, but do so in a way that's appealing to children.

Walks of Italy (www.walksofitaly.com; ⓒ **06-95583331**) also runs excellent guided walking tours of Rome, with their introductory tour (2½ hr.) just 29€, and more in-depth explorations of the Colosseum, Vatican Museums, and Forum ranging from 59€ to 99€.

Enjoy Rome, Via Marghera 8a (www.enjoyrome.com; ⓒ **06-4451843**), offers a number of "greatest hits" walking tours, like 3-hour overviews of Ancient Rome or the Vatican. Most tours cost 30€ to 45€ per person, exclusive of entrance fees (such as at the Vatican Museums). They also do an early evening tour of the Jewish Ghetto and Trastevere, and a bus excursion to the Catacombs and the Appian Way (50€), with a visit to ruins of an ancient aqueduct that most Romans, let alone tourists, never see.

The self-styled "storytellers of the new millennium" at **Through Eternity** (www.througheternity.com; ⓒ **06-7009336**) are also worth your consideration. Staffed by a group of art historians and architects, what sets them apart is their theatrical delivery, helped along by the dramatic scripts that many of the guides seem to follow. So, on a tour of the Forum, expect your guide to break out into a booming "Friends, romans, countrymen"—it can be a lot of fun, but it's not for everyone. Through Eternity also has the ability to do afterhours tours of the Vatican, allowing you to see its treasures without fighting the crowds (it's a tremendous experience). A 5-hour tour of the Vatican is 67€; other tours range from 39€ to 109€.

Especially for Kids

There's a real "Jekyll and Hyde" quality to exploring Rome with kids. On the one hand, it's a capital city, big, busy, and hot, and with public transportation that doesn't always work too well. On the other, the very best parts of the city for kids—Roman ruins, subterranean worlds, and *gelato*—are aspects you'd want to explore anyway. Seeing Rome with kids doesn't demand an itinerary redesign—at least, if you're willing to skip some of the marquee museums. And despite what you have heard about its famous seven hills, much of the center is mercifully flat and pedestrian. The election of a center-left mayor in 2013 has given the city a more pedestrian-friendly future. His ban of private cars from the roads around the Forum and Colosseum is the first measure aimed at creating a Rome that is friendlier for little visitors, and making its precious ruins even more enjoyable places to visit.

Food is pretty easy too: Roman **pizzas** are some of the best in the world—see "Where to Eat," p. 58, for our favorites. Ditto the ice cream, or *gelato*

(p. 72). Restaurants in pretty much any price category will be happy to serve up a simple *pasta al pomodoro* (pasta with tomato sauce) to a fussy eater.

The city is shorter on green spaces than European cities like London, but the landscaped gardens of the **Villa Borghese** have plenty of space for them to let off steam. Pack a picnic or rent some bikes (p. 43). The **Parco Appia Antica** (www.parcoappiaantica.it) is another family favorite, especially on a Sunday or national holiday when the old cobbled road is closed to traffic. The park's **Catacombs** (p. 116) are eerie enough to satisfy grisly young minds, but also fascinating Christian and historical sites in their own right.

Museums, of course, are trickier. You can probably get kids fired up more easily for the really ancient stuff. The bookshop at the **Colosseum** (p. 88) has a good selection of guides to the city aimed at under-12s, themed on gladiators and featuring funny or cartoonish material. Make that an early stop. We have taken a 6-year-old to the **Musei Capitolini** (p. 93), and she loved hunting down the collection's treasures highlighted on the free museum guide leaflet. It was like a themed treasure hunt, and bought us a couple of hours to admire the exhibits—and the chance to see them from a new and unexpected angle, too. The multiple ground levels below **San Clemente** (p. 95) and the **Case Romane del Celio** (p. 95) are another obvious draw for small visitors.

There are a couple of city museums designed with a specifically child-friendly angle. The best is the **Museo della Civiltà Romana** (http://en.museo civiltaromana.it), which is popular with local schoolchildren for a good reason: Its models of Ancient Rome help bring the old stones to life. Your kids will be able to *see* Rome as it was at its peak. Watch out for the odd opening hours, though, because it is a half-hour Metro journey and walk from the center.

If kids get really into the gladiator angle, enroll them in the **Scuola Gladi-atori Roma (Rome Gladiator School),** where they can spend 2 hours preparing for a duel in a reasonably authentic way. The easiest way to book is through **Viator.com**, but you can find out more about the program at **www. gsr-roma.com**.

Away from the museums, kids will also likely enjoy some of the cheesier city sights—at the very least, these will make some good family photos to share on Facebook or Instagram. Build in some time to place your hands in the Bocca della Verità at **Santa Maria in Cosmedin** (p. 97), to throw a coin in the **Trevi Fountain** (p. 107), and to enjoy watching the feral cats relaxing amid the ruins of **Largo di Torre Argentina.** There is a cat sanctuary here that gives basic healthcare to Rome's many strays.

If you want to delve deeper into the city as a family, check out the tours on **Context Travel**'s family program. Bookable walks and workshops cover mythology, underground Rome, "How Rome Works" (which covers some of the Romans' fiendishly clever engineering), and more. See **www.context-travel.com/rome** for details. Each tour lasts between 2 and 3 hours and costs 255€ to 355€ per family. They are not cheap, but Context's walks and pro-grams are first rate, you will have the docent to yourselves, and it is money well spent if it gets everyone engaged with the city.

SHOPPING

Rome offers temptations of every kind. In our limited space below we've summarized streets and areas known for their shops. The monthly rent on the famous streets is very high, and those costs are passed on to you. Nonetheless, a stroll down some of these streets presents a cross section of the most desirable wares in Rome.

Note that **sales** usually run twice a year, in January and July.

The Top Shopping Streets & Areas

AROUND PIAZZA DI SPAGNA   Most of Rome's haute couture and seriously upscale shopping fans out from the bottom of the Spanish Steps. **Via Condotti** is probably Rome's poshest shopping street, where you'll find Prada, Gucci, Bulgari, and the like. A few more down-to-earth stores have opened, but it's still largely a playground for the superrich. Neighboring **Via Borgognona** is another street where both the rents and the merchandise are chic and ultra-expensive. Like its neighbor, Via Condotti, Via Borgognona is a mecca for wealthy, well-dressed women and men from around the world. It offers a nicer window-browsing experience, however, because it has pedestrian-only access, and storefronts have retained their baroque or neoclassical facades. **Via Frattina** is the third member of this trio of upscale streets. Here the concentration of shops is denser; chic boutiques for adults and kids rub shoulders with ready-to-wear fashions, high-class chains, and occasional tourist tat vendors. It's usually thronged with shoppers who appreciate the lack of motor traffic.

VIA COLA DI RIENZO   The commercial heart of the Prati neighborhood bordering the Vatican, this long, straight street runs from the Tiber to Piazza Risorgimento. Via Cola di Rienzo is known for stores selling a wide variety of merchandise at reasonable prices—from jewelry to fashionable clothes, bags, and shoes. Among the most prestigious is **Bertozzini Profumeria dal 1913,** at no. 192 (© **06-6874662**), the historic Roman perfume store. You will also find the department store **Coin** at no. 173 (with a large supermarket in the basement); the largest branch of venerable gourmet food store **Castroni** at no. 196 (www.castroni.it); and the smaller, more selective gourmet grocery **Franchi** at no. 204 (www.franchi.it), good for Parmigiano cheese.

VIA DEI CORONARI   An antique-lover's souk. If you're shopping (or even window-browsing) for antiques or antique-style souvenir prints, then spend an hour walking the full length of this pretty, pedestrian-only street.

A Pause Before Purchasing

Although Rome has many wonderful boutiques, the shopping is generally better in **Florence.** If you're continuing on to there, you may want to hold off a bit, as you're likely to find a better selection and better prices.

VIA DEL CORSO   Not attempting the stratospheric image or prices of Via Condotti or Via Borgognona, Via del Corso boasts affordable styles aimed at younger consumers. Occasional gems are scattered amid the international shops selling jeans and sporting equipment. In general, the most interesting stores are toward the Piazza del Popolo end of the street (**Via del Babuino** here has a similar profile). Via del Corso also has a branch of department store **La Rinascente,** Piazzale Colonna 357 (www.larinascente.it; © **06-6784209**). Pavements are narrow, so it's not a convenient street to window-browse with a stroller or young children.

VIA MARGUTTA   This beautiful, tranquil street is home to numerous art stalls and artists' studios—Federico Fellini used to live here—though the stores tend to offer the same sort of antiques and mediocre paintings these days. You have to shop hard to find real quality. Highlights include **Bottega del Marmoraro** at no. 53b, the studio of master stonecarver Sandro Fiorentini; and **Valentina Moncada**'s hugely popular contemporary art gallery at no. 54 (www.valentinamoncada.com; © **06-3207956**).

MONTI   Rome's most fashion-conscious central neighborhood has a pleasing mix of indie artisan retailers, hip boutiques, and honest, everyday stores frequented by locals. There's not a brand name in sight. Roam the length of **Via del Boschetto** for one-off fashions, designer ateliers, and unique, gift-sized homewares. In fact, you can roam in every direction from the spot where Via del Boschetto meets **Via Panisperna.** Turn off on nearby **Via Urbana** or **Via Leonina**, where boutiques jostle for shopfront space with cafes that are ideal for a break or light lunch. Via Urbana also hosts the weekly **Mercatomonti** (see below).

Rome's Best Markets

Campo de' Fiori ★   Central Rome's food market has been running since at least the 1800s. It's no longer the place to find a produce bargain, but it is still a genuine slice of Roman life in one of its most attractive squares. The market runs Monday through Saturday from 7am to around 1 or 2pm. Campo de' Fiori. No phone. Bus: H, 23, 63, 116, 271, 280, 780, or 810/Tram: 8.

Eataly ★★   Not strictly a market, but a four-floor homage to Italian ingredients and cooking. Thirty different breads, twenty-five shelving bays of pasta, two aisles of olive oil . . . and that's just scratching the surface of what's here under one roof. Browse the cookbooks, chocolate, local wines and beer and cheese, or stop for a meal in one of the ingredient-themed restaurants and food bars (although prices are a little steep). Eataly is foodie heaven, and open daily from 10am until midnight. Piazzale XII Ottobre 1492. www.roma.eataly.it. © **06-90279201.** Metro: Piramide. Follow signs from Metro exit gates to "Air Terminal," then "Piazza XII Ottobre"; ride up escalator then walk around to the right.

Mercatomonti ★★   Everything from contemporary glass jewelry to vintage cameras, handmade clothes for kids and adults, and one-off designs to wear or admire is on sale here. It takes place in the heart of trendy Monti, in a commandeered parking garage (where else?). The market runs Sundays from 10am to 6pm. Via Leonina 46. www.mercatomonti.com. No phone. Metro: Cavour.

Nuovo Mercato di Testaccio (New Testaccio Market) ★★ In 2012, the old Testaccio market building was replaced by this modern, daringly modernist, sustainably powered market building. It's the best place to go produce shopping with the Romans. There's everything you could want to pack a picnic—cheese, cured meats, seasonal fruit—as well as meat, fish, and fresh vegetables (ideal if you are self-catering in the city). There are also clothes and kitchenware stalls, but the food is the star. For instant gratification, sample the street food at **Mordi e Vai** ★★, Box 15 (www.mordievai.it; ☏ 339-1343344). The likes of a *panino* filled with warm Roman recipes like veal and artichokes in a piquant gravy costs around 4€. The market runs Monday through Saturday from 6am to 2:30pm. Btw. Via Luigi Galvani and Via Aldo Manuzio (at Via Benjamin Franklin). No phone. Bus: 83, 673, or 719.

Nuovo Mercato Trionfale (New Trionfale Market) ★★★ Replacing the old and rickety Via Andrea Doria market, this modern, working class (and rather unattractive) structure houses over 250 stalls, which more than make up for its exterior looks. Vendors sell top choice, local (and value) produce, meat, fish, cheese, eggs, baked goods, and spices, as well as household wares. Keep an eye out for terrific butchers, exquisite fishmongers, and awesome local produce. A handful of stalls specializing in international ingredients sell everything from okra and pomelo to habanero chilis and hopia. If you plan to shop, bring cash; only a few fishmongers and butchers here accept credit cards. The market runs Monday through Saturday from 7am to 2pm; on Tuesdays and Fridays it stays open until 5pm. Via Andrea Doria 3. ☏ **06-39743501.** Tram: 19. Metro: Cipro

Porta Portese ★ Trastevere's vast weekly flea market stretches all the way from the Porta Portese gate along Via di Porta Portese to Viale di Trastevere. Expect to find everything. It runs Sundays from dawn until mid-afternoon. Via di Porta Portese. No phone. Tram: 8.

ENTERTAINMENT & NIGHTLIFE

Even if you don't speak Italian, you can generally follow the listings of special events and evening entertainment featured in **"La Repubblica,"** a leading national newspaper published in Rome. See also the "TrovaRoma" section of its city website, **www.roma.repubblica.it**. **"Wanted in Rome"** (www.wanted inrome.com) has listings of opera, rock, English-language cinema showings, and such and gives an insider look at expat Rome. **"Un Ospite a Roma"** (www.unospitearoma.it), available both online and in print, free at concierge desks and tourist information centers, is full of details on what's happening around the city. Free magazine and website **"Romeing"** (www.romeing.it) is worth consulting for events and lifestyle updates on the contemporary scene. Also check **InRomeNow.com** for monthly updates of cultural events.

ROME, illuminated

When the sun goes down, Rome's palaces, ruins, fountains, and monuments are bathed in a theatrical white light. Few evening occupations are quite as pleasurable as a stroll past the solemn pillars of old temples or the cascading torrents of Renaissance fountains glowing under the blue-black sky.

The **Fountain of the Naiads** (*Fontana delle Naiadi*) on Piazza della Repubblica, the **Fountain of the Tortoises** (*Fontana della Tartarughe*) on Piazza Mattei, the **Fountain of Acqua Paola** (*Fontanone*) at the top of Janiculum Hill, and the **Trevi Fountain** are particularly beautiful at night. The **Capitoline Hill** (or *Campidoglio*) is magnificently lit after dark, with its measured Renaissance facades glowing like jewel boxes. The view of the Roman Forum seen from the rear of Piazza del Campidoglio is perhaps the grandest in Rome (see "Three Free Views to Remember for a Lifetime," p. 90). If you're across the Tiber, **Piazza San Pietro** (in front of St. Peter's) is impressive at night without the crowds. And a combination of illuminated architecture, baroque fountains, and sidewalk shows enlivens **Piazza Navona.**

Unless you're dead set on making the Roman nightclub circuit, try what might be a far livelier and less expensive option—sitting late at night on **Via Veneto, Piazza della Rotonda, Piazza del Popolo,** or one of Rome's other piazzas, all for the (admittedly inflated) cost of an espresso, a cappuccino, or a Campari and soda. For clubbers, it is almost impossible to predict where the next hot venue will appear, but if you like it loud and late—and have an adventurous streak—jump in a cab to **Monte Testaccio** or **Via del Pigneto** and bar-hop wherever takes your fancy. In Trastevere, there's always a bit of life along **Via Politeana** around the spot where it meets **Piazza Trilussa.**

Performing Arts & Live Music

Although Rome's music scene doesn't have the same vibrancy as Florence's—nor the high-quality opera of Milan's La Scala or **La Fenice** in Venice (p. 283)—classical music fans are still well catered for in Rome. As well as the major venues, featured below, you should also look out for concerts and one-off events in churches and salons around the city. Check **www.operainroma.com** for a calendar of opera and ballet staged by the Opera in Roma association at the **Chiesa Evangelica Valdese,** Via IV Novembre 107. Other venues that regularly run classical music and operatic evenings include the **Pontificio Instituto di Musica Sacra,** Piazza Sant'Agostino 20A (www. musicasacra.va; ✆ **06-6638792**) and **All Saints' Anglican Church,** Via del Babuino 153 (www.accademiadoperaitaliana.it; ✆ **06-7842702**).

Alexanderplatz ★ An established stalwart of Rome's jazz scene since the early 1980s. If there's a good act visiting the city, you will find them here. Via Ostia 9. www.alexanderplatzjazzclub.com. ✆ **06-39742171.** Cover 10€. Metro: Ottaviano.

Auditorium–Parco della Musica ★★ Multiple stages showcase a broad range of music—from James Taylor to tango festivals and world music, to the classical chamber and symphonic music of the Accademia Nazionale di Santa Cecilia. The massive, purpose-built complex itself is a postmodern work of art, designed by architect Renzo Piano. Viale Pietro de Coubertin 30. www.auditorium.com. ℂ **02-60060900.** Bus: M, 53, or 910/Tram: 2D.

Teatro dell'Opera di Roma ★★ This is where you will find the marquee operas like "La Traviata," "Carmen" and "Tosca." There's also a full program of classical concerts with top-rank orchestras and ballet. In summer, the action moves outdoors for a short season of unforgettable open-air operatic performances at the ruined **Baths of Caracalla** (p. 94). Piazza Beniamino Gigli 7. www.operaroma.it. ℂ **06-48160255.** Tickets 17€–150€. Metro: Repubblica.

Cafes

Remember: In Rome and everywhere else in Italy, if you just want to drink a quick coffee and bolt, walk up to *il banco* (the bar), order *"un caffè, per favore"* or *"un cappuccino,"* and don't move. They will make it for you to drink on the spot. It will cost more (at least double) to sit down to drink it, and outdoor table service is the most expensive way to go. Even in the heart of the center, a short coffee *al banco* should cost no more than 1€; add around .20€ for a *cappuccino*. Expect to pay up to five times that price if you sit outdoors on a marquee piazza. Most cafes in the city serve a decent cup of coffee, but we have chosen a small selection of places worth hunting down, below.

Bar del Fico ★ With its shabby-chic interior and namesake fig tree backdrop, and charming outdoor seating where locals play chess at tables with mismatched chairs, this is one of Rome's most beloved aperitivo spots and

Coffee "al banco" (standing at the counter).

aperitivo CULTURE

The mass social phenomenon of the *aperitivo* (happy hour—and so much more) can be a great way to meet real Romans, or at least observe their particular ways. It started in hard-working northern cities like Milan, where you'd go to a bar after leaving the office, and for the price of one drink (usually under 10€), you get access to an unlimited buffet of high-quality food—like chunks of Parmigiano, cured meats, fresh green salad, or pasta salads. Luckily for Rome (a decidedly less industrious city), the custom trickled down here, and now the city is filled with casual little places to drop in for a drink (from 6 or 7pm onward) and eat to your heart's content of all these tasty finger foods. Look for signs in the window and follow your nose. The **Monti** neighborhood is a good place to begin. The Terre e Domus **Enoteca Provincia di Roma** (see facing page) also does good *aperitivo*.

coveted see-and-be-seen nightlife destinations. Piazza del Fico 26; www.bardelfico.com. *©* **06 6880 8413.** Bus 116.

Sant'Eustachio il Caffè ★★ This little place roasts its own fairtrade Arabica beans over wood. The unique taste and bitter kick to its brews ensures there's usually a friendly crowd a few deep at the bar. Unless you ask, the coffee comes with sugar. Piazza Sant'Eustachio 82. www.santeustachioilcaffe.it. *©* **06-68802048.** Bus: 46, 64, 84, or 916 to Largo di Torre Argentina.

Tazza d'Oro ★ Debate still rages among Romans as to whether this place—or Sant'Eustachio (above)—serves the best cup of coffee in the city. Close to the Pantheon, it's been a popular spot since it opened in 1946. Via degli Orfani 84. www.tazzadorocoffeeshop.com. *©* **06-6789792.** Bus: 116.

Wine Bars, Cocktail Bars & Craft Beer Bars

For Rome's most creative modern cocktails in a casual environment, visit **Caffè Propaganda** (p. 61).

Ai Tre Scalini ★ This little *bottiglieria* (wine bar) is the soul of Monti. There's a traditional menu, as well as a long wine list with bottles sourced from across Italy. Arrive early or call to reserve a table: This place is usually jammed. Via Panisperna 251. *©* **06-48907495.** Metro: Cavour.

Bir and Fud ★ Around 15 beers on tap (most of them Italian craft brews) as well as carb-heavy snacks like pizza and *supplì* (fried rice balls). It's 5€ for a small beer. Some are brewed as strong as 9%, so drink with care—check the chalkboard for the lowdown on each. Via Benedetta 23. www.birandfud.it. *©* **06-5894016.** Bus: 23, 125, 271, or 280.

Cavour 313 ★★ A wine bar that's as traditional and genuine as you will find this close to the ruins. Walls are racked with bottles, and staff is always happy to help choose the perfect wine/food pairing. There are over 30 wines by the glass (from 4€) as well as cold cuts, cheese, and cured vegetable platters, or excellent carpaccio to partner the wines. A small menu of hot and cold dishes is also available if you fancy something more substantial. Closed Sundays in summer. Via Cavour 313. www.cavour313.it. © **06-6785496.** Metro: Colosseo and Cavour.

Enoteca Provincia Romana ★   A smart, glass-fronted modern wine bar that sells produce and wines from Rome and its surrounding province. Sip as you look out on Trajan's Column, directly opposite. Foro Traiano 82–84. www. enotecaprovinciaromana.it. © **06-69940273.** Bus: 80, 85, 87, or 175.

La Bottega del Caffè ★   Beers, wine, cocktails, *aperitivo*—there's a little of everything at one of Monti's busiest neighborhood bars. Find a seat in the shrub-screened terrace area, or follow the action out onto the piazza and fountain steps. Piazza Madonna dei Monti 5. © **06-64741578.** Metro: Cavour.

Litro ★★   A wonderful addition to Rome's dining and drinking scene: a wine bar located in Monteverde Vecchio (residential area above Trastevere) that serves natural wines, cocktails, and snacks sourced from Lazio-based purveyors of traditional cured meats and cheeses, plus bruschette, and stellar alcoholic sorbets. Via Fratelli Bonnet 5. © **06-45447639.** Bus: 75, 982.

NO.AU ★   Tricked out like a Barcelona cava bar, this place has craft beers from local brewer Birra del Borgo on tap, plus a selection of wines from 5€ a glass. The location is ideal for a pre- or post-dinner drink: Right in the old center, NO.AU (pronounced "knowhow," almost) is set in a narrow alley to provide a little escape from the chaos. Closed Monday. Piazza di Montevecchio 16. www.noauroma.wordpress.com. © **06-45652770.** Bus: 30, 46, 62, 64, 70, 81, 87, 116, or 571.

Open Baladin ★★   If anyone ever tells you that "Italians don't do good beer," send them to this bar near the Ghetto. A 40-long row of taps lines the bar, with beers from their own Piedmont brewery and across Italy (including many local to the Lazio region). There's also a wall of bottles that you would need crampons to climb. Via degli Specchi 5–6. www.openbaladin.com. © **06-6838989.** Tram: 8.

Stravinskij Bar ★   An evening at this award-winning cocktail bar inside one of Rome's most famous grand hotels is always a regal, exclusive affair. Mixology, ingredients, and canapés are all top-notch. Sit inside for a "designer lounge" feel, or choose terrace seating during the warm months. Expect a hefty check. Inside Hotel de Russie, Via del Babuino 9. © **06-32888874.** Metro: Spagna.

DAY TRIPS FROM ROME

I f you only have 3 days or so, you will probably want to spend them in Rome itself. But if you are here for a week— or on your second visit to Rome—head out of the city to see some of the ruins, old towns, and ancient villas that lie beyond, for a true all-around Roman experience.

OSTIA ANTICA ★★

24km (15 miles) SW of Rome

The ruins of Rome's ancient port are a must-see for anyone who can't make it to Pompeii (see p. 132). It's a more comfortable day trip than Pompeii, on a similar theme: the chance to wander around the preserved ruins of an ancient Roman settlement that has been barely touched since its abandonment.

Ostia, at the mouth of the Tiber, was the port of Rome, serving as the gateway for the riches from the far corners of the Empire. Founded in the 4th century B.C., it became a major port and naval base under two later emperors, Claudius and Trajan.

A prosperous city developed, complete with temples, baths, theaters, and patrician homes. Ostia flourished between the 1st and 3rd centuries, and survived until around the 9th century before it was abandoned. Gradually, it became little more than a malaria bed, a buried ghost city that faded into history. A papal-sponsored commission launched a series of digs in the 19th century; however, the major work of unearthing was carried out under Mussolini's orders between 1938 and 1942 (the work had to stop because of World War II). The city is only partially dug out today, but it's believed that all the chief monuments have been uncovered, although digs continue with private sponsorships. There are quite a few impressive ruins—this is no dusty field like the Circus Maximus.

A word to the wise: There is no need for hiking boots, but the Roman streets underfoot are all clad in giant basalt cobblestones. Bear that in mind when choosing footwear.

Essentials
GETTING THERE
Take the Metro to Piramide, changing lines there for the Lido train to Ostia Antica. (From the platform, take the exit for "Air Terminal"

5

and turn right at the top of the steps, where the station name changes to Porta San Paolo.) Departures to Ostia are about every half-hour; the trip takes 25 minutes and is included in the price of a Metro single-journey ticket or Roma Pass (p. 35). It's just a 5-minute walk to the excavations from the Metro stop: Exit the station, walk ahead and over the footbridge, and then continue straight ahead until you reach the car park. The ticket booth is to the left.

VISITOR INFORMATION
The site opens at 8:30am each morning. Closing times vary with the season, ranging from 7:15pm in high season (Apr–Aug) to 4:30pm in off-season (Nov–Feb 15), so check times beforehand at **www.ostiaantica.beniculturali. it** or call ℂ **06-56350215.** Note that the ticket office closes 1 hour before the ruins. Admission costs 8€ (11€ if there's an additional exhibition), free for ages 17 and under and 65 and over. The 2€ map on sale at the ticket booth is a wise investment.

PARKING
The car park, on Viale dei Romagnoli, costs 2.50€ for an unlimited period. Arrive early if you're driving; it is fairly small.

Exploring Ostia Antica
The principal monuments are all labeled. On arrival, visitors first pass the *necropoli* (burial grounds, always outside the city gates in Roman towns and cities). The main route follows the giant cobblestones of the **Decumanus ★**

Roman tile mosaic at Ostia Antica.

(the main street) into the heart of Ostia. The **Piazzale delle Corporazioni ★★** is like an early version of Wall Street. Near the theater, this square contained nearly 75 corporations, the nature of their businesses identified by the patterns of preserved mosaics. Nearby, Greek dramas were performed at the **Teatro,** built in the early days of the Empire. The theater as it looks today is the result of much rebuilding. Every town the size of Ostia had a **Forum ★**, and the layout is still intact: A well-preserved **Capitolium** (once the largest temple in Ostia) faces the remains of the A.D. 1st-century **Temple of Roma and Augustus.**

Elsewhere in the grid of streets are the ruins of the **Thermopolium,** which was a bar; its name means "sale of hot drinks." Of an *insula,* a Roman block of apartments, **Casa Diana** remains, with its rooms arranged around an inner courtyard. Climb the building at the entrance to the **Terme di Nettuno** ★ to look down on the preserved mosaics of this vast baths complex. In addition, in the enclave is a **museum** displaying Roman statuary along with fragmentary frescoes.

Where to Eat

There is no real need to eat by the ruins—a half-day here should suffice, and Ostia is within easy reach of the abundant restaurants of the center. The obvious alternative is a picnic; the well-stocked foodie magnet **Eataly** (p. 124) is located only a couple of minutes from the Lido platform at the Piramide Metro station, making it easy to grab provisions when you make the Metro interchange. There are perfect picnic spots beside fallen columns or old temple walls. If you really crave a sit-down meal, **Allo Sbarco di Enea,** Viale dei Romagnoli 675 (✆ **06-5650034**), has a menu of trattoria staples, a shaded garden, and two-course tourist menus starting at 12€, excluding drinks. There's also a snack and coffee bar outside Ostia's Metro station.

5 POMPEII ★★★

240km (150 miles) SE of Rome

Completely destroyed by Vesuvius on August 24, A.D. 79, the Roman city of Pompeii was one of Italy's most important commercial centers, effectively frozen in time by a thick layer of ash for almost 2,000 years. Today, the excavated ruins provide an unparalleled insight into the everyday life of Roman Italy, especially that of its ordinary citizens and, notoriously, the erotic art that decorated its homes and villas. It is estimated that only 2,000 people actually died in the disaster, with most of the population of 20,000 evacuated before the full eruption. Those that stayed perished horribly: asphyxiated by toxic gases, and buried in several feet of volcanic ash. Pliny the Elder, the celebrated Roman naturalist, was one of the registered casualties. Although parts of the city were rediscovered in 1599, full excavations only began in 1748, starting a process that has never really ended, with new finds still being made.

Making a long day trip to the famous ruins from Rome might seem a little crazy, but on a good day it's only a 3½ hour drive from the capital, and even less by train. Count spending at least 4 or 5 hours wandering the site to do it justice. Remember also to take plenty of water with you as well as **sunscreen,** because there's not much shade anywhere among the ruins, and you'll be doing a lot of walking: Wear flat, comfortable shoes.

Essentials
GETTING THERE

The best option is to take the Trenitalia "Frecciarossa" high-speed **train** from Termini to Naples (1 hr. 10 min.; 70€ one-way), though InterCity trains are cheaper (around 28€) and take just over 2 hours—still doable if you start

Pompeii.

early. The first Frecciarossa usually departs around 7:30am. Once at Napoli Centrale (Naples Central Station), follow the signs to Napoli Piazza Garibaldi station downstairs, where you transfer to the **Circumvesuviana Railway** (www.eavcampania.it; © **800-053939**). Note that this railway is separate to Trenitalia, so you won't be able to buy a through ticket to Pompeii from Rome; just get a return to Naples, and buy the Pompeii portion on arrival in Naples. Trains depart to Pompeii every half-hour from Piazza Garibaldi, but make sure you get on the train headed toward Sorrento and get off at Pompeii/ Scavi (*scavi* means "archaeological excavation"). If you get on the "Pompei" train (toward Poggiomarino), you'll end up in the town of Pompei—which is in a totally different place—and will have to double back to get to the ruins. A ticket costs 3,20€ one-way; trip time is 35 minutes.

To reach Pompeii by **car** from Rome, take the A1 *autostrada* toward Naples, then the A3 all the way to the signposted turnoff for the ruins just after the tollbooth—a straightforward and usually hassle-free drive.

TOURS

Plenty of tour operators run guided tours or transport to Pompeii from Rome. **Enjoy Rome** (www.enjoyrome.com; © **06-4451843**) runs a Pompeii Shuttle (air-conditioned bus) on Tuesday and Friday (Apr–Oct) at 7:30am from its office at Via Marghera 8a (near Termini Station), arriving at the ruins at around 10:45am. You can wander around independently before leaving at 3:30pm (back around 7pm). The shuttle costs 68€ and 58€ for people under 26. This price does not include entrance fees to the ruins. Aggregators such as

www.localrometours.com sell fully guided tours to Pompeii and Vesuvius for around 130€ per person.

VISITOR INFORMATION

Official infopoints (www.pompeiisites.org; ☏ **081-8575347**) can be found at the Porta Marina, Piazza Esedra, and Piazza Anfiteatro entrances. The ruins are open April to October 8:30am to 7:30pm (last entry at 6pm), and November to March 8:30am to 5pm (last entry at 3:30pm). Admission is 13€. Every first Sunday of the month, admission is free. If you wish to visit all five sites (**Pompei, Ercolano, Oplonti, Stabia,** and **Boscoreale**), a special ticket is available for 22€.

PARKING

There is a parking lot at Pompeii, though it is quite small. If you plan on driving, get there early. The charge is 3€ per hour.

Exploring Pompeii

Pompeii covers a large area with a lot to see, so try to be selective. Note that many of the streets run through little more than stone foundations, and although wandering the site is a magical experience, ruin-fatigue can set in by the end of a frenetic day of sightseeing.

Entering through the **Porta Marina,** the **Forum (Foro)** ★ is a long, narrow, open space surrounded by the ruins of the **basilica** (the city's largest single structure), the **Temple of Apollo (Tempio di Apollo)** ★★, the **Temple of Jupiter (Tempio di Giove)** ★★, and a little farther west, the **Terme Stabian (Baths)** ★★, where some skeletons have been preserved.

Walk north along the Via di Mercurio to see some of Pompeii's most famous villas: The **Casa del Poeta Tragico (House of the Tragic Poet)** ★ contains some eye-catching mosaics, notably the CAVE CANEM ("Beware of the Dog") design by the main entrance. The vast **Casa del Fauno (House of the Faun)** ★★ features an amicable *"Ave"* ("welcome") mosaic and the copy of a tiny, bronze faun (the original is in Naples's Archaeological Museum). Nearby, the **Casa dei Vettii** ★★★ is in excellent shape, arranged around a pretty central courtyard and containing celebrated murals, notably an image of Priapus (the fertility god), resting his ludicrously oversized phallus on a pair of scales.

Keep walking beyond the old city walls to the northwest for the **Villa dei Misteri** ★★★, Pompeii's best-preserved insula, a 3rd-century B.C. mansion containing a series of stunning depictions of the Dionysiac initiation rites. The paintings are remarkably clear, bright, and richly colored after all these years.

Walking to the eastern side of Pompeii from the Porta Marina, you'll pass the 5th-century B.C. **Teatro Grande (Grand Theatre)** ★, well-preserved and still used for performances today. Continue west on the Via dell'Abbondanza, passing the **Fullonica Stephanus** (a laundry with a large tiered washtub); and the **Casa della Venere in Conchiglia (House of the Venus in a Shell)** ★★, named after the curious painting on its back wall. At the far western end of the town lies the **Anfiteatro** ★★, one of Italy's most complete amphitheaters and also the oldest, dating from 80 B.C.

Where to Eat

To dine really well around Pompeii, you have to go into (and stay overnight in) Naples. If you're doing Pompeii as a day trip, skip the so-so restaurants around Pompeii itself and pack a picnic from **Eataly** (p. 124), **Panificio Bonci** (p. 60), or **Gina** (p. 67) before you set off from Rome.

TIVOLI & THE VILLAS ★★

32km (20 miles) E of Rome

Perched high on a hill east of Rome, Tivoli is an ancient town that has always been something of a retreat from the city. In Roman times it was known as Tibur, a retirement town for the wealthy; later during the Renaissance, it again became the playground of the rich, who built their country villas out here. To do justice to the gardens and villas that remain—especially if the Villa Adriana is on your list, as indeed it should be—you'll need time, so it's worth setting out early.

Essentials
GETTING THERE

Tivoli is 32km (20 miles) east of Rome on Via Tiburtina, about an hour's drive with traffic (the Rome–L'Aquila *autostrada,* A24, is usually faster). If you don't have a car, take Metro Line B to Ponte Mammolo. After exiting the station, transfer to a Cotral bus for Tivoli (www.cotralspa.it). Cotral buses depart every 15 to 30 minutes during the day (2.20€ one-way). Villa d'Este is in Tivoli itself, close to the bus stop; to get to Villa Adriana, you need to catch another bus (the orange no. 4; buy tickets at a *tabacchi* in the center of Tivoli).

Exploring Tivoli & the Villas

Villa Adriana (Hadrian's Villa) ★★★ HISTORIC SITE/RUINS   The globe-trotting Emperor Hadrian spent the last 3 years of his life in the grandest style. Less than 6km (3¾ miles) from Tivoli, between A.D. 118 and 138 he built one of the greatest estates ever conceived, and he filled acre after acre with some of the architectural wonders he'd seen on his many travels. Hadrian erected theaters, baths, temples, fountains, gardens, and canals bordered with statuary, filling the palaces and temples with sculptures, some of which now rest in the museums of Rome. In later centuries, barbarians, popes, and cardinals, as well as anyone who needed a slab of marble, carted off much that made the villa so spectacular. But enough of the fragmented ruins remain to inspire a real sense of awe. For a glimpse of what the villa used to be, see the accurate plastic reconstruction at the entrance.

The most outstanding remnant is the **Canopo,** a recreation of the town of Canope with its famous Temple of the Serapis. The ruins of a rectangular area, **Piazza d'Oro,** are still surrounded by a double portico. Likewise, the **Edificio**

Villa Adriana.

con Pilastri Dorici (Doric Pillared Hall) remains, with its pilasters with Doric bases and capitals holding up a Doric architrave. The apse and the ruins of some magnificent vaulting are found at the **Grandi Terme (Great Baths),** while only the north wall remains of the **Pecile,** otherwise known as the "Stoà Poikile di Atene" or "Painted Porch," which Hadrian discovered in Athens and had reproduced here. The best is saved for last—the **Teatro Marittimo,** a circular maritime theater in ruins with its central building enveloped by a canal spanned by small swing bridges, said to have been Hadrian's private "studio."

For a closer look at some of the items excavated, you can visit the museum on the premises and a visitor center near the villa parking area.

Largo Marguerite Yourcenar 1, Tivoli. www.villaadriana.beniculturali.it. ℂ **0774-530203.** Admission 11€. Daily 9am–sunset (about 7:30pm in May–Aug, 5pm Nov–Jan, 6pm Feb, 6.30pm Mar, and 7pm Apr and Oct). Bus: 4 from Tivoli.

Villa d'Este ★★ PARK/GARDEN   Like Hadrian centuries before, Cardinal Ippolito d'Este of Ferrara ordered this villa built on a Tivoli hillside in the mid–16th century. The Renaissance structure, with its second-rate paintings, is not that interesting; the big draw for visitors is the **spectacular garden** below (designed by Pirro Ligorio).

As you descend the cypress-studded garden slope, you're rewarded with everything from lilies to gargoyles spouting water; torrential streams; and waterfalls. The loveliest fountain is the **Fontana dell'Ovato,** by Ligorio. But nearby is the most spectacular engineering achievement: the **Fontana dell'Organo Idraulico (Fountain of the Hydraulic Organ),** dazzling with its music and water jets in front of a baroque chapel, with four maidens who look tipsy (the fountain "plays" every 2 hours from 10:30am).

The moss-covered **Fontana dei Draghi (Fountain of the Dragons),** also by Ligorio, and the so-called **Fontana di Vetro (Fountain of Glass),** by Bernini, are also worth seeking out, as is the main promenade, lined with 100 spraying fountains. The garden is worth hours of exploration, but it involves a lot of walking, with some steep climbs.

Piazza Trento 5, Tivoli. www.villadestetivoli.info. © **0774-332920.** Admission 11€ (8€ Nov–Apr). Tues–Sun 8:30am to 1 hr. before sunset. Bus: Cotral service from Ponte Mammolo (Roma–Tivoli); the bus stops near the entrance.

Villa Gregoriana ★ PARK/GARDEN   Villa d'Este dazzles with artificial glamour, but the Villa Gregoriana relies more on nature. Originally laid out by Pope XVI in the 1830s, the gardens were reopened in 2005 after a $5.5-million restoration. The main highlight is the panoramic waterfall of Aniene, with the trek to the bottom on the banks of the Aniene River studded with grottoes and balconies that open onto the chasm. The only problem is that if you do make the full descent, you might need a helicopter to pull you up again (the climb back up is fierce). From one of the belvederes, there's a view of the **Temple of Vesta** on the hill. A former school has been converted into a visitor center designed by architect Gae Aulenti.

Largo Sant'Angelo, Tivoli. www.villagregoriana.it. © **06-39967701.** Admission 6€. Apr–Oct Tues–Sun 10am–6:30pm; Mar, Nov, and Dec Tues–Sun 10am–4pm. Bus: Cotral service from Ponte Mammolo (Roma–Tivoli); the bus stops near the entrance.

Where to Eat

Tivoli's gardens make for a pleasant place for a picnic (see **Eataly,** p. 124), but if you crave a sit-down meal, **Antica Trattoria del Falcone,** Via del Trevio 34 (www.ristoranteilfalcone.it; © **0774-312358**), is a dependable option in Tivoli itself, just off Largo Garibaldi, open since 1918 and specializing in excellent pizza (ask for the pizza menu), Roman pastas, and roast meats. It is open daily 11:30am to 4pm and 6:30 to 11:30pm.

FLORENCE

Botticelli, Michelangelo, and da Vinci all left their mark on Florence, the cradle of the Renaissance. With Brunelleschi's dome as your backdrop, follow the River Arno to the Uffizi Gallery (Florence's foremost art museum) and soak in centuries of great painting. Wander across the Ponte Vecchio, Florence's iconic bridge, taking in the tangle of Oltrarno's medieval streets. Then sample seasonal Tuscan cooking in a Left Bank trattoria. Congratulations! You've discovered the art of fine living in this masterpiece of a city.

Michelangelo's "David" stands tall (literally) behind the doors of the **Accademia,** and nearby are the delicate paintings of Fra' Angelico in the convent of **San Marco.** Works by Donatello, Masaccio, Pontormo, and Ghiberti fill the city's churches and museums. Once home to the Medici, the **Palazzo Pitti** is stuffed with Raphaels and Titians backed by the fountains of the **Boboli Garden.**

Statue of "David" at Galleria dell'Accademia.

But Florence isn't just about art. Florentines love to shop, too. Italy's leather capital strains at the seams with handmade gloves, belts, bags, and shoes sold from workshops, family-run boutiques, and high-end stores, as well as at tourist-oriented **San Lorenzo Market.** You can also splurge on designer wear from fashion houses along **Via de' Tornabuoni**—this city is the home of Gucci, Pucci, and Ferragamo.

As for Florentine cuisine, it's increasingly cosmopolitan, but flavors are often Tuscan at heart. Even in fine restaurants, meals might kick off with country concoctions like *ribollita* (seasonal vegetable stew) before moving onto the chargrilled delights of a *bistecca alla fiorentina* (Florentine beefsteak on the bone), all washed down with a fine **Chianti Classico.** At lunchtime, order a plate of cold cuts and Pecorino cheese, or if you're feeling adventurous, *lampredotto alla fiorentina,* a sandwich of cow's stomach stewed in tomatoes and garlic. When you've dined to your fill, retire to a wine bar in the **Oltrarno,** or to one of the edgier joints of **Santo Spirito** or **San Frediano.** If you're a fan of opera, classical, theater, or jazz, you'll find those here, too.

ESSENTIALS

Getting There

BY PLANE Several European airlines service Florence's **Amerigo Vespucci Airport** (www.aeroporto.firenze.it; ℭ **055-306-15** switchboard, 055-306-1300 for flight info), also called **Peretola,** 5km (3 miles) northwest of town. There are no direct flights to or from North America, but you can make connections through London, Paris, Amsterdam, Frankfurt, and other major European cities. The half-hourly **BusItalia Vola in bus** service to and from the central bus station at Via Santa Caterina da Siena 17 (ℭ **800-424-500**), beside the train station, takes 20 minutes and costs 6€ one-way or 10€ round-trip. Metered **taxis** line up outside the airport's arrival terminal and charge a flat rate of 20€ to the city center (22€ on holidays, 24€ after 10pm, additional 1€ per bag).

The closest international airport with seasonal direct flights to North America is Pisa's **Galileo Galilei Airport** (www.pisa-airport.com; ℭ **050-849-300**), 97km (60 miles) west of Florence. Until the **PisaMover** airport transit service opens (scheduled for Dec 2015), all train connections to Florence involve a short bus journey (1.30€) or taxi ride (10€ approx.) from the airport to Pisa Centrale, where you can catch a state rail service to Florence (60–80 min.; 8€). Alternatively, 17 daily buses operated by **Terravision** (www.terravision.eu) connect downtown Florence directly with Pisa Airport in just over 1 hour. One-way tickets are 5€ adults, 4€ children ages 5 to 12; round-trip fares are 10€ and 8€.

BY TRAIN Florence is Tuscany's rail hub, with regular connections to all of Italy's major cities. To get here from Rome, take the high-speed Frecciarossa or Frecciargento trains (1½ hr.; www.trenitalia.com) or similar high-speed trains operated by **Italo** (www.italotreno.it). High-speed trains run to Venice (2 hr.) via Bologna and Padua.

Most Florence-bound trains roll into **Stazione Santa Maria Novella,** Piazza della Stazione, which you'll see abbreviated as **S.M.N.** The station is an architectural masterpiece, albeit one dating to Italy's Fascist period, rather than the Renaissance. It is on the northwestern edge of the city's compact historic center, a 10-minute walk from the Duomo and a brisk 15-minute walk from Piazza della Signoria and the Uffizi.

BY CAR   The **A1 autostrada** runs north from Rome past Arezzo to Florence and continues to Bologna, and **unnumbered superhighways** run to and from Siena (the *SI-FI raccordo*) and Pisa (the so-called *FI-PI-LI*). To reach Florence from Venice, take the A13 southbound then switch to the A1 at Bologna.

Driving to Florence is easy; the problems begin once you arrive. Almost all cars are banned from the historic center—only residents or merchants with permits are allowed into a camera-patrolled *zona a trafico limitato* (the "ZTL"), which was extended in 2015. Have the name and address of your hotel ready and the traffic police will wave you through. You can drop off baggage there (the hotel will organize a temporary ZTL permit); then you must relocate to a parking lot. Special rates are available through most hotels.

> ### Florence's "City Code"
>
> What was once Florence's city code—055—is now an integral part of every phone number. Always dial it (including the initial zero, even from overseas), even when calling to another local number from within Florence.

Your best bet for overnight or longer-term parking is one of the city-run garages. The best deal—better than many hotels' garage rates—is at the **Parterre parking lot** under Piazza Libertà at Via Madonna delle Tosse 9 (© **055-5030-2209**). It's open around the clock and costs 2€ per hour, or 10€ for the first 24 hours, 15€ for the second, then 20€ per 24 hours thereafter; it's 70€ for up to a week's parking. More info on parking is at **www.firenzeparcheggi.it**.

Don't park your car overnight on the streets in Florence without local knowledge; if you're towed and ticketed, it will set you back substantially—and the headaches to retrieve your car are beyond description. If this happens to you, start by calling the vehicle removal department (the *Recupero Veicoli Rimossi*) at © **055-422-4142**.

Visitor Information

TOURIST OFFICES   The most convenient tourist office is at Via Cavour 1R (www.firenzeturismo.it; © **055-290-832**), 2 blocks north of the Duomo. The office is open Monday through Friday from 9am to 6pm, Saturday 9am to 2pm. Its free map is adequate for navigation purposes; there's no need to upgrade to a paid version.

The train station's nearest tourist office (© **055-212-245**) is opposite the terminus at Piazza della Stazione 5. With your back to the tracks, take the left exit, cross onto the concrete median, and bear right; it's across the busy road junction ahead. The office is usually open Monday through Saturday from 9am to 7pm (sometimes only to 2pm in winter) and Sunday 9am to 2pm. This office gets crowded; unless you're really lost, press onward to the Via Cavour office.

Another helpful office is under the Loggia del Bigallo on the corner of Piazza San Giovanni and Via dei Calzaiuoli (© **055-288-496**); it's open Monday through Saturday from 9am to 7pm (often 5pm mid-Nov to Feb) and

The address system in Florence has a split personality. Private homes, some offices, and hotels are numbered in black (or blue), but businesses, shops, and restaurants are numbered independently in red. (That's the theory anyway; in reality, the division between black and red numbers isn't so clear-cut.) The result is that 1, 2, 3 (black) addresses march up the block numerically oblivious to their 1R, 2R, 3R (red) neighbors. You might find the doorways on one side of a street numbered 1R, 2R, 3R, 1, 4R, 2, 3, 5R.

The color codes occur only in the *centro storico* and other old sections of town; outlying districts didn't bother with this confusing system.

Sunday 9am to 2pm. There is also an information office at airport arrivals (© **055-315-874**), open on the same timetable.

WEBSITES The official Florence tourism website, **www.firenzeturismo.it**, contains a wealth of fairly up-to-date city information. The site also has a downloadable PDF with the latest opening hours for all major city sights (offices will provide a similar printout). The best-informed city **blogs** are written in Italian by locals: **Io Amo Firenze** (www.ioamofirenze.it) is handy for reviews of the latest eating, drinking, and events in town. For one-off exhibitions and culture, **Art Trav** (www.arttrav.com) is an essential bookmark. For more updated Florence info, go to **www.frommers.com/destinations/ florence**. Listings magazines are covered in the "Entertainment & Nightlife" section, p. 203.

City Layout

Florence is a smallish city, sitting on the Arno River and petering out to olive-planted hills rather quickly to the north and south, but extending farther west and east along the Arno valley with suburbs and light industry. It has a compact center that is best negotiated on foot. No two major sights are more than a 25-minute walk apart, and most of the hotels and restaurants in this chapter are in the relatively small *centro storico* (historic center), a compact tangle of medieval streets and *piazze* (squares) where visitors spend most of their time. The bulk of Florence, including most of the tourist sights, lies north of the river, with the **Oltrarno,** an old working artisans' neighborhood, hemmed in between the Arno and the hills on the south side.

The ornate facade of Florence's Duomo.

The Neighborhoods in Brief

The Duomo The area surrounding Florence's gargantuan cathedral is as central as you can get. The Duomo itself is halfway between the two monastic churches of Santa Maria Novella and Santa Croce, as well as at the midpoint between the Uffizi Gallery and the Ponte Vecchio to the south, and San Marco and the Accademia (home of Michelangelo's "David") to the north. The streets south of the Duomo make up a medieval tangle of alleys and tiny squares heading toward Piazza della Signoria. This is one of the oldest parts of town, and the streets still vaguely follow a grid pattern laid down when the city was a Roman colony. The site of the Roman city's forum is today's Piazza della Repubblica.

The Duomo neighborhood is, understandably, one of the most hotel-heavy parts of town, offering a range from luxury inns to student dives and everything in between. However, several places around here rest on the laurels of their sublime location; you need to be choosy. The same goes—even more so—for dining in the area.

Piazza della Signoria This is the city's civic heart and perhaps the best base for museum hounds—the Uffizi Gallery, Bargello sculpture collection, and Ponte Vecchio are all nearby. It's a well-polished part of the tourist zone but still retains the narrow medieval streets where Dante grew up. The few blocks just north of the **Ponte Vecchio** have reasonable shopping, but unappealing modern buildings were planted here to replace those destroyed during World War II. The entire neighborhood can be stiflingly crowded in peak season—**Via Por Santa Maria** is one to avoid—but in those moments when you catch it empty of tour groups, it remains the romantic heart of pre-Renaissance Florence. As with the Duomo neighborhood, you need to be *very* choosy when picking a restaurant or even an ice cream around here.

San Lorenzo & the Mercato Centrale This wedge of streets between the train station and the Duomo, centered on the Medici's old family church of San Lorenzo, is market territory. The vast indoor **Mercato Centrale**

(food market) is here, and many streets are filled daily with stalls hawking leather and other souvenirs at **San Lorenzo Market.** It's a colorful neighborhood, blessed with many budget hotels and a growing range of good, affordable dining spots, but it's not the quietest part of town.

Piazza Santa Trínita This piazza sits just north of the river at the south end of Florence's shopping mecca, Via de' Tornabuoni, home to Gucci, Armani, and more. It's a quaint, well-to-do (and still medieval) neighborhood in which to stay, even if you don't care about haute couture. If you're an upscale shopping fiend, there's no better place to be.

Santa Maria Novella This neighborhood, bounding the western edge of the *centro storico*, has two characters: an unattractive zone around the train station, and a nicer area south of it between the church of Santa Maria Novella and the river. In general, the station area is the least appealing part of town in which to base yourself. Many streets are heavily trafficked and noisy, and you're a little removed from the medieval atmosphere. This area does, however, have more good budget options than any other quarter, especially along Via Faenza and its tributaries. Try to avoid staying on traffic-clogged Via Nazionale.

The situation improves dramatically as you move east into the San Lorenzo area (see above), or you pass Santa Maria Novella church and head south toward the river. **Piazza Santa Maria Novella** and its tributary streets have several stylish boutique-style hotels.

San Marco & Santissima Annunziata On the northern edge of the *centro storico*, these two churches are fronted by *piazze*— **Piazza San Marco,** a busy transport hub, and **Piazza Santissima Annunziata,** the most architecturally unified square in the city. The neighborhood is home to Florence's university, the Accademia, the San Marco paintings of Fra' Angelico, and quiet streets with some hotel gems. The walk back from the heart of the action isn't as far as it looks on a map, and you'll likely welcome the escape from tourist crowds. But it's not (yet) a great dining or nightlife neighborhood.

Santa Croce The art-filled church at the eastern edge of the *centro storico* is the focal point of one of the most genuine neighborhoods left in the center. Few tourists roam too far east beyond **Piazza Santa Croce,** so if you want to feel like a local, stay here. The streets around the **Mercato di Sant'Ambrogio** and **Piazza de' Ciompi** have an especially appealing, local feel, and they get lively after dark. The Santa Croce neighborhood boasts some of the best restaurants and bars in the city—*aperitivo* time is vibrant along **Via de' Benci,** and there is always something going on along **Via Panisperna** and the northern end of **Via de' Macci.**

The Oltrarno, San Niccolò & San Frediano "Across the Arno" is the artisans' neighborhood, still dotted with workshops. It began

as a working-class neighborhood to catch the overflow from the expanding medieval city on the opposite bank, and later became a chic area for aristocrats to build palaces on the edge of the countryside. The largest of these, the **Pitti Palace,** became the home of Tuscany's grand dukes and today houses a set of paintings second only to the Uffizi in scope.

The Oltrarno's lively tree-shaded center, **Piazza Santo Spirito** is lined with bars and close to some great restaurants (and lots of nightlife, too). West of here, the neighborhood of **San Frediano** is becoming ever more fashionable, and **San Niccolò** at the foot of Florence's southern hills has some popular bars. You may not choose to stay around here—the hotel range isn't great— but when evening draws nigh, cross one of Florence's bridges to eat and drink better, and at better prices, than you will generally find in the *centro storico.*

Getting Around

Florence is a **walking** city. You can stroll between the two top sights, Piazza del Duomo and the Uffizi, in 5 to 7 minutes. The hike from the most northerly major sights, San Marco and the Accademia, to the most southerly, the Pitti Palace across the Arno, should take no more than 30 minutes. From Santa Maria Novella eastward across town to Santa Croce is a flat 20- to 30-minute walk. But beware: Flagstones, some of them uneven, are everywhere. Wear sensible shoes with some padding and foot support.

BY BUS & TRAM You'll rarely need to use Florence's efficient **ATAF bus system** (www.ataf.net; ℂ **800-424-500** in Italy) because the city is so compact. Bus tickets cost 1.20€ and are good for 90 minutes, irrespective of how many changes you make. A 24-hour pass costs 5€, a 3-day pass 12€, and a 7-day pass 18€. Tickets are sold at *tabacchi* (tobacconists), some bars, and most newsstands. If you cannot find a machine or vendor near your stop, pay 2€ to buy a ticket onboard, or if you have an Italian cellphone SIM (p. 302), text the word "ATAF" to ℂ **488-0105** to buy a validated ticket for 1.50€ using prepaid phone credit. *Note:* Once on board, validate your ticket in the box near the rear door to avoid a steep fine. Because traffic is restricted in most of the historic center, buses make runs on principal streets only, except for four tiny electric bus lines (*bussini* services C1, C2, C3, and D) that trundle about the *centro storico.* The most useful lines to outlying areas are no. 7 (for Fiesole) and nos. 12 and 13 (for Piazzale Michelangiolo). Buses run from 7am until 8:30 or 9pm daily, with a limited night service on a few key routes (mostly local-focused). Florence's efficient **tram** (line T1) serves the Opera di Firenze, Cascine Park, and southwestern suburbs from its terminus outside Santa Maria Novella Station.

BY TAXI Taxis aren't cheap, and with the city so small and a one-way street system forcing drivers to take convoluted routes, they aren't an economical way to get about. They're most useful to get you and your bags between the train station and a hotel. The standard rate is .91€ per kilometer, with 3.30€ to start the meter (which rises to 5.30€ on Sun; 6.60€ 10pm–6am), plus 1€ per bag. There's a taxi stand outside the train station and another in Piazza Santa Croce (by Via de' Benci); otherwise, call **Radio Taxi** at ☎ **055-4242.** For the latest taxi information, see **www.4242.it.**

BY BICYCLE & SCOOTER Florence is largely flat and increasingly closed to cars, and so is ideal for seeing on 2 wheels. Many of the bike-rental shops in town are located between San Lorenzo and Piazza San Marco, including **Alinari,** Via San Zanobi 38R (www.alinarirental.com; ☎ **055-280-500**), which rents vintage-style city bikes (2.50€ per hour; 12€ per day) and mountain bikes (3€ per hour; 18€ per day). It also hires out 100cc scooters (15€ per hour; 55€ per day). **Florence by Bike,** Via San Zanobi 54R (www.florencebybike.it; ☎ **055-488-992**) has similar prices. Make sure to carry a lock (one will be provided with your rental): Bike theft is common.

BY CAR Trying to drive in the *centro storico* is a frustrating, useless exercise, and moreover, unauthorized traffic is not allowed past signs marked ZTL. On top of that, 2013 saw the introduction of a city charge even for residents to drive into the center to park, and restrictions became even more stringent in 2015. You need a permit to do anything beyond dropping off and picking up bags at your hotel. Park your vehicle in one of the huge underground lots on the center's periphery and pound the pavement. (See "By Car" under "Getting There," p. 140.)

[FastFACTS] FLORENCE

Business Hours Hours mainly follow the Italian norm (see p. 300). In Florence, however, many of the larger and more central shops stay open through the midday *riposo*, or nap (note the sign ORARIO NONSTOP).

Doctors **Medical Service Firenze** is at Via Roma 4, in the center (www.medical service.firenze.it; ☎ **055-475-411**). It's open for walk-ins Monday to Friday 11am to noon, 1 to 3pm, and 5 to 6pm; Saturday 11am to noon and 1 to 3pm only. English-speaking **Dr. Stephen Kerr** is a general practitioner with an office at Piazza Mercato Nuovo 1 (www.dr-kerr.com; ☎ **335-836-1682** or 055-288-055), with office hours Monday through Friday from 3 to 5pm without an appointment (appointments are available 9am–3pm). The consultation fee is 50€, slightly less if you show student ID.

Hospitals The most central hospital is **Santa Maria Nuova,** a block northeast of the Duomo on Piazza Santa Maria Nuova (☎ **055-69-381**), with an emergency room (*pronto soccorso*) open 24 hours. There is a comprehensive guide to medical services, including specialist care, on the official Florence city website: See **www.firenzeturismo.it.**

FLORENCE

Fast Facts: Florence

6

144

Internet Access Every hotel we recommend offers wireless Internet, usually for free but occasionally for a small fee. If you have your own laptop or smartphone, several bars and cafes now offer free Wi-Fi to anyone buying a drink or snack. There is free city Wi-Fi with the Firenze Card (p. 170). There's also free Wi-Fi upstairs at the **Mercato Centrale** (p. 160).

Mail & Postage Florence's **main post office** (📞 **055-273-6428**), at Via Pellicceria 3, off the southwest corner of Piazza della Repubblica, is open Monday through Friday from 8:20am to 7:05pm, Saturday 8:20am to 12:35pm.

Newspapers & Magazines Florence's national daily paper, "La Nazione" is on sale everywhere. "The Florentine" (www.the florentine.net) is the city's English-language publication, widely available at bars and cafes. Overseas English-language newspapers are also available: The newsstands at the station are a safe bet, as is the booth under the arcade on the western side of Piazza della Repubblica, where you will find the "Financial Times," "Wall Street Journal," and "London "Guardian," alongside the usual "International New York Times."

Pharmacies There is a 24-hour pharmacy (also open Sun and state holidays) in **Stazione Santa Maria Novella** (📞 **055-216-761;** ring the bell opposite the taxi rank between 11pm and 7am). On holidays and at night, look for the sign in any pharmacy window telling you which ones are open locally.

Police To report lost property or passport problems, call the *questura* (police headquarters) at 📞 **055-49-771. Note:** It is illegal to knowingly buy fake goods anywhere in the city (and yes, a "Louis Vuitton" bag at 10€ counts as *knowingly*). You may be served a hefty on-the-spot fine if caught.

Safety As in any city, plenty of pickpockets are out to ruin your vacation, and in Florence you'll find light-fingered youngsters (especially around the train station), but otherwise you're safe. Steer clear of the Cascine Park after dark, when you run the risk of being mugged—likewise both the area around Piazza Santo Spirito and the backstreets behind Santa Croce after all the nightlife has gone off to bed. And you probably won't want to hang out with the late-night heroin addicts shooting up on the Arno mud flats below the Lungarno embankments on the edges of town. See chapter 10 for more safety tips.

WHERE TO STAY

Thanks to a rapidly growing stock of hotel beds, as well as national economic crises, the forces of supply and demand have brought hotel prices in Florence down . . . a little. Few hoteliers expect major changes to their rates in coming years. Add to that some recent welcome movement in the euro–dollar and euro–pound exchange rates, and you have a hotel market that is as favorable to visitors as it has ever been. That said, it's still difficult to find a high-season double you'd want to stay in for much less than 100€. In addition, some of those price drops have been added back in taxes: Since 2012, Florence's city government has levied an extra 1€ to 1.50€ per person per night per government-rated hotel star, for the first 10 nights of any stay. The tax rose slightly in 2015. It is payable on arrival, and is not usually included in quoted rates.

Peak hotel season is Easter through early July, September through late October, and the entire Christmas and New Year period. May, June, and September are particularly popular; January, February, and August are months to

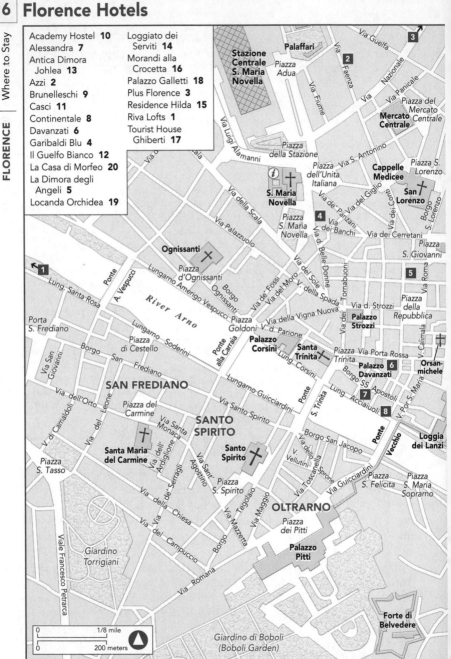

Academy Hostel **10**
Alessandra **7**
Antica Dimora
 Johlea **13**
Azzi **2**
Brunelleschi **9**
Casci **11**
Continentale **8**
Davanzati **6**
Garibaldi Blu **4**
Il Guelfo Bianco **12**
La Casa di Morfeo **20**
La Dimora degli
 Angeli **5**
Locanda Orchidea **19**
Loggiato dei
 Serviti **14**
Morandi alla
 Crocetta **16**
Palazzo Galletti **18**
Plus Florence **3**
Residence Hilda **15**
Riva Lofts **1**
Tourist House
 Ghiberti **17**

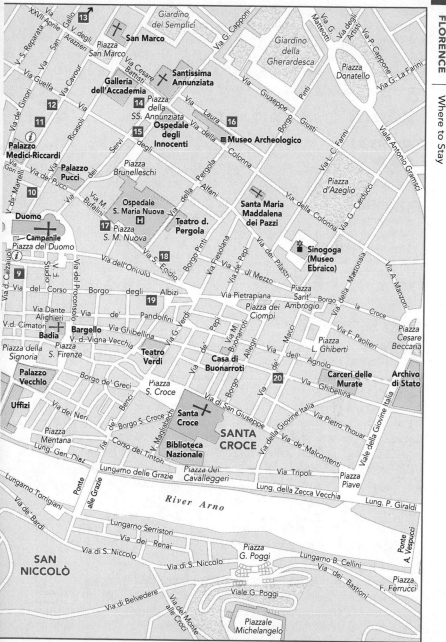

grab a bargain—never be shy to haggle if you're coming then. **Booking direct** using phone, e-mail, or the hotel's own website is often the key to unlocking lower rates, deals, or complimentary extras.

To help you decide where you'd like to base yourself, consult "The Neighborhoods in Brief," p. 142. Note that we have included parking information below only for those places that offer it. And, as indicated, many hotels offer babysitting services. However, these are generally available "on request." At least a couple of days' notice is advisable.

HOTELS BY PRICE

EXPENSIVE
Brunelleschi ★★, p. 148
Continentale★★★, p. 149
Residence Hilda ★★, p. 152

MODERATE
Alessandra ★, p. 150
Antica Dimora Johlea ★★, p. 152
Davanzati ★★, p. 150
Garibaldi Blu ★★, p. 151
Il Guelfo Bianco ★★, p. 149
La Casa di Morfeo ★, p. 153
La Dimora degli Angeli ★★★, p. 148

Loggiato dei Serviti ★★, p. 152
Morandi alla Crocetta ★★, p. 152
Palazzo Galletti ★★, p. 154
Riva Lofts ★★, p. 154
Tourist House Ghiberti ★, p. 153

INEXPENSIVE
Academy Hostel ★, p. 149
Azzi ★, p. 151
Casci ★, p. 150
Locanda Orchidea ★, p. 154
Plus Florence ★★, p. 151

Near the Duomo
EXPENSIVE
Brunelleschi ★★ The Brunelleschi manages to pull off a couple of neat tricks. It exceeds the standards of a 21st-century "design hotel" without losing track of its roots: Rooms and public areas are framed with *pietra serena,* the gray stone used liberally by Florentine architect Brunelleschi. It's big, but feels small, thanks to an entrance on a quiet little piazza and a labyrinthine layout, arranged around the oldest standing building in Florence. Rooms are midsized, with parquet floors and contemporary-classic styling. Although many look onto Via Calzaiuoli, impressive soundproofing means you won't hear the noise. Apparently a favorite of author Dan Brown, the hotel appears in both "The Da Vinci Code" and "Inferno."

Piazza Santa Elisabetta 3 (just off Corso). www.hotelbrunelleschi.it. ⓒ**055-27-370.** 96 units. 234€–919€ double; 287€–929€ superior double. Rates include breakfast. Parking 35€–39€. Bus: C2. **Amenities:** 2 restaurants; bar; concierge; gym; room service; Wi-Fi (free).

MODERATE
La Dimora degli Angeli ★★★ In 2012, this B&B added a new floor, and it now occupies two levels of a grand apartment building in one of the city's busiest shopping districts. Rooms on the original floor are for romantics; bright, modern wallpaper clashes pleasingly with iron-framed beds and traditional furniture. (Corner room Beatrice is the largest, with a view of Brunelleschi's dome—but only just.) The new floor, below, is totally different,

Strolling Piazza del Duomo.

with the kind of decor you find in an interiors magazine, all sharp lines and bespoke leather or wooden headboards throughout. Breakfast is served at a local cafe—though if you prefer, you can grab a morning coffee in the B&B and use your breakfast token for a light lunch instead.

Via Brunelleschi 4. www.ladimoradegliangeli. com. © **055-288-478.** 12 units. 88€–190€ double. Rates include breakfast (at nearby cafe). Parking 26€. Bus: C2. **Amenities:** Wi-Fi (free).

INEXPENSIVE

Academy Hostel ★   If a gated courtyard right in the center appears rather a grand address for a hostel, that is because this is no ordinary student traveler dive. The two private rooms (one with private bathroom) are plainly decorated, certainly, with whitewashed walls and functional furniture. But they are bright and spacious, and include linen and towels in the (bargain) price. Communal areas are comfy, staff is full of advice, and the place is small, spotless, and within a minute's walk of both the Duomo and "David." You will need to book well ahead to bag a room here: They go fast, especially in high season.

Via Ricasoli 9. www.academyhostel.eu. © **055-239-8665.** 10 units. 79€–94€ double. Parking 30€. Bus: C1. **Amenities:** Wi-Fi (free).

Near Piazza della Signoria

EXPENSIVE

Continentale ★★★   Everything about the Continentale is cool, and the effect is achieved without a hint of frostiness. Rooms are uncompromisingly modern, decorated in bright white and bathed in natural light—even the deluxe units built into a medieval riverside tower, which have mighty walls and medieval-sized windows (read: small). Standard rooms are large (for Florence), and there's a 1950s feel to the overall styling. Communal areas are a major hit, too: A relaxation room has a glass wall with a front-row view of the Ponte Vecchio. Top-floor **La Terrazza** (p. 205) mixes Florence's best rooftop cocktails.

Vicolo dell'Oro 6R. www.lungarnocollection.com. © **055-27-262.** 43 units. 180€–730€ double. Parking 35€–37€. Bus: C3 or D. **Amenities:** Bar; concierge; gym; spa; Wi-Fi (free).

Near San Lorenzo & the Mercato Centrale

MODERATE

Il Guelfo Bianco ★★   Decor in this former noble Florentine family home retains its authentic *palazzo* feel, though carpets have been added for comfort and warmth. No two rooms are the same—stone walls this thick cannot just be knocked through—and several have antiques integrated into their individual schemes. Grand rooms at the front (especially 101, 118, and 228) have spectacular Renaissance coffered ceilings and masses of space. Bathrooms are plainer by comparison. Sleep at the back and you'll wake to an unusual sound in Florence: birdsong.

Small adjacent restaurant **Bistrot Il Desco** (www.ildescofirenze.it; ℂ 055-288-330), under the same ownership, serves seasonal Mediterranean dishes made with organic ingredients (many from their own farm), and is open to guests and nonguests alike. Reservations are recommended.

Via Cavour 29 (near corner of Via Guelfa). www.ilguelfobianco.it. ℂ **055-288-330.** 40 units. 99€–300€ double. Rates include breakfast. Valet parking 27€–33€. Bus: C1. **Amenities:** Restaurant; bar; babysitting (prebooking essential); concierge; room service; Wi-Fi (free).

INEXPENSIVE

Casci ★ The front part of the palace now occupied by the Casci was once composer Rossini's Florence digs. This affordable, central hotel has long been a Frommer's favorite, and the partial pedestrianization of Via Cavour now makes it an even more attractive city base. Rooms follow a labyrinthine layout, split between Rossini's old *piano nobile* and a former convent to the rear, where the bigger rooms are located, including a couple of spacious family units. Rooms are simply decorated and some can get a little dark, though a rolling program of modernization has installed new, light-toned furniture to counteract that—now in 16 rooms and counting. The welcome from some of Florence's friendliest family hoteliers is an unchanging feature.

Via Cavour 13 (btw. Via dei Ginori and Via Guelfa). www.hotelcasci.com. ℂ **055-211-686.** 25 units. 80€–150€ double; 100€–190€ triple; 120€–230€ quad. Rates include breakfast. Valet parking 21€–25€. Bus: C1. Closed 2 weeks in Dec. **Amenities:** Bar; babysitting (10€/hr.); concierge; Wi-Fi (free).

Near Piazza Santa Trínita

MODERATE

Alessandra ★ This typical Florentine *pensione* transports you back to the age of the gentleman and lady traveler. Decor has grown organically since the place opened as a hotel in 1950—Alessandra is a place for evolution, not revolution. A pleasing mix of styles is the end result: Some rooms with hefty armoires, carved headboards, gilt frames, and gold damask around the place, others with eclectic postwar furniture, like something from a period movie set. A couple rooms have views of the Arno . . . but then again, Borgo SS. Apostoli, on the front side, is one of the center's most atmospheric streets. There's a small river-view terrace for everyone to share; grab a glass of wine from the honesty bar and kick back.

Borgo SS. Apostoli 17. www.hotelalessandra.com. ℂ **055-283-438.** 27 units. 150€–180€ double. Rates include breakfast. Garage parking 25€. Bus: C3 or D. Closed a few days around Christmas. **Amenities:** Concierge; Wi-Fi (free).

Davanzati ★★ Although installed inside a historic building, the Davanzati never rests on its medieval laurels: There is a laptop in every room for guest use and HD movies streamed to your TV, and lobby newspapers come on an iPad. Rooms are simply decorated in the Tuscan style, with color-washed walls; half-canopies over the beds add a little flourish. Room 100 is probably the best family hotel room in Florence, full of nooks, crannies, and split-levels that give both adults and kids a sense of private space. Complimentary evening drinks remain part of the Davanzati's family welcome.

Via Porta Rossa 5 (at Piazza Davanzati). www.hoteldavanzati.it. © **055-286-666.** 27 units. 122€–211€ double; 152€–243€ superior (sleeping up to 4). Rates include breakfast. Valet parking 26€. Bus: C2. **Amenities:** Bar; babysitting; concierge; Wi-Fi (free).

Near Santa Maria Novella

MODERATE

Garibaldi Blu ★★ The hotels of Piazza Santa Maria Novella are frequented by fashion models, rock stars, and blue-chip businessfolk. You can get a taste of that, for a fraction of the price, at this boutique hotel with attitude that opened in late 2014. Each of the mostly midsize rooms is immaculate, and also reflects the hotel's "warm denim" palette, with modern furnishings, parquet floors, and marble bathrooms. It's well worth paying 30€ extra for a deluxe room at the front: These have much more space and a view over Florence's prettiest church facade, Santa Maria Novella itself.

Piazza Santa Maria Novella 21. www.hotelgaribaldiblu.com. © **055-277-300.** 22 units. 130€–225€ double. Rates include breakfast. Garage parking 35€. Bus: C2, 6, 11, or 22. **Amenities:** Bar; concierge; Wi-Fi (free).

Between Santa Maria Novella & San Lorenzo

INEXPENSIVE

Azzi ★ This quirky, bohemian joint is also known as the Locanda degli Artisti. Each of its original 16 rooms is brightly decorated, and most in the more characterful, original area of the hotel feature an antique piece or colorfully painted wall to add ambience. Floorboards are artfully distressed (both by time and by design), and pictures or wall mirrors have wistfully weathered frames. In short, each is exactly the kind of room you could imagine for a struggling artist to lay his head at night. Refitted in 2013, eight newer rooms have a totally different feel, with laminate flooring, white furniture, and shiny new travertine bathrooms. Frommer's readers booking direct (mention this book) get 10% to 15% off published room rates and 3€ off overnight parking.

Via Faenza 88R. www.hotelazzi.com. © **055-213-806.** 24 units. 54€–130€ double; 95€–140€ triple. Rates include breakfast. Garage parking 22€. Bus: 1, 2, 12, 13, 28, 36, 37, or 57. **Amenities:** Bar; Wi-Fi (free).

Plus Florence ★★ There's simply nowhere in Florence with as many services for your buck—including seasonal indoor and outdoor swimming pools—all in a price bracket where you're usually fortunate to get an en suite bathroom (and Plus has those, too). The best rooms in this large, well-equipped hostel are in the new wing, added in 2013 and housing private rooms only. Units here are dressed in taupe and brown, with subtle uplighting and space (in some) for up to four beds. The only minuses: an un-picturesque building; and the location, between two busy roads (light sleepers should request a room facing the internal courtyard).

Via Santa Caterina d'Alessandria 15. http://plushostels.com/plusflorence. ✆ **055-462-8934.** 187 units. 40€–100€ double; 50€–130€ triple. Bus: 20. **Amenities:** Restaurant; bar; concierge; gym; 2 swimming pools; sauna (winter only); Wi-Fi (free).

Near San Marco & Santissima Annunziata

EXPENSIVE

Residence Hilda ★★ These luxurious mini-apartments are all bright-white decor and designer soft furnishings, with stripped-wood flooring and modern gadgetry to keep everything running. Each is spacious, cool in summer, and totally soundproofed against Florence's permanent background noise. Every apartment also has a mini-kitchen, kitted out just fine for preparing a simple meal, and so ideal if you have kids in tow. In 2015, deluxe units added Nespresso machines, yoga mats, and an exercise bike. Unusually for apartments, all units are bookable by the single night and upward. Staff is some of the friendliest in the city.

Via dei Servi 40 (2 blocks north of the Duomo). www.residencehilda.com. ✆ **055-288-021.** 12 units. 150€–450€ per night for apartments (sleeping 2–4). Valet parking 31€. Bus: C1, 6, 19, 31, or 32. **Amenities:** Airport transfer; babysitting; concierge; room service; Wi-Fi (free).

MODERATE

Antica Dimora Johlea ★★ There is a real neighborhood feel to the streets around this *dimora* (traditional Florentine home) guesthouse—which means evenings are lively and Sundays are silent (although it's under a 10-min. walk to San Lorenzo). Standard-sized rooms are snug; upgrade to an executive room if you need more space, but there is no difference in the standard of decor, a mix of Florentine and earthy, boho styling, with parquet floor, silk drapes, and Persian rugs. Help yourself to coffee, a soft drink, or a glass of wine from the honesty bar and head up to a knockout roof terrace for views over the terra-cotta rooftops to the center and hills beyond. It is pure magic at dusk. No credit cards.

Via San Gallo 80. www.johanna.it. ✆ **055-463-3292.** 6 units. 90€–180€ double. Rates include breakfast. Valet parking 20€. Bus: C1, 1, 6, 11, 14, 17, 23. **Amenities:** Honesty bar; Wi-Fi (free).

Loggiato dei Serviti ★★ Stay here to experience Florence as the gentleman and lady visitors of the Grand Tour did. For starters, the building is a genuine Renaissance landmark, built by Sangallo the Elder in the 1520s. There is a sense of faded grandeur and unconventional luxury throughout—no gadgetry or chromotherapy showers here—but you will find rooms with writing desks and vintage "occasional tables" with lamps. No unit is small, but most of the standard rooms lack a view of either Brunelleschi's dome or the perfect piazza outside: An upgrade to a "superior" represents good value. Air conditioning is pretty much the only concession to the 21st century—and you will love it that way.

Piazza Santissima Annunziata 3. www.loggiatodeiservitihotel.it. ℂ **055-289-592.** 37 units. 120€–330€ double. Rates include breakfast. Valet parking 21€. Bus: C1, 6, 19, 31, or 32. **Amenities:** Babysitting (prebooking essential); concierge; Wi-Fi (free).

Morandi alla Crocetta ★★ Like many in Florence, this hotel is built into the shell of a former convent. Morandi alla Crocetta has retained the original convent layout, meaning some rooms are snug—though that does not apply to the two rooms added in 2014, ranged around an old cloister downstairs. Anyway, what you lose in size, you more than gain in character: Every single one oozes *tipico fiorentino.* Rooms have parquet flooring thrown with rugs and dressed with antique wooden furniture. Original Zocchi prints of Florence, made in 1744, are scattered around the place. It's definitely worth upgrading to a "superior" if you can: These have more space and either a private courtyard terrace or, in one, original frescoes decorating the entrance to the former convent chapel, though the chapel is now permanently sealed off. The hotel is located on a quiet street.

Via Laura 50 (1 block east of Piazza Santissima Annunziata). www.hotelmorandi.it. ℂ **055-234-4747.** 12 units. 100€–167€ double. Rates include breakfast. Garage parking 24€. Bus: 6, 19, 31, or 32. **Amenities:** Bar; babysitting (prebooking essential); concierge; Wi-Fi (free).

Tourist House Ghiberti ★ There is a pleasing mix of the traditional and the modern at this backstreet guesthouse, named after a famous former resident—the creator of the Baptistery's "Gates of Paradise" had workshops on the top floor of the *palazzo.* Rooms have plenty of space, with high ceilings, herringbone terra-cotta floors, whitewashed walls, and painted wood ceilings in a vaguely Renaissance style. There is a sauna and Jacuzzi for communal use, if you need to soak away the aches and pains after a day's sightseeing; new memory-foam mattresses added in 2014 should help with that, too. E-mail direct if you want to bag the best room rate.

Via M. Bufalini 1. www.touristhouseghiberti.com. ℂ **055-284-858.** 6 units. 64€–179€ double. Rates include breakfast. Garage parking 20€–25€. Bus: C1. **Amenities:** Jacuzzi; sauna; Wi-Fi (free).

Near Santa Croce
MODERATE
La Casa di Morfeo ★ For a cheery, affordable room in the increasingly lively eastern part of the center, look no further than this small hotel that opened in 2012 on the second floor of a shuttered palace. There is no huge difference in quality among the guest rooms. Each is midsized, with modern gadgetry, and painted in bright contemporary colors, each individual scheme corresponding to the flower after which the room is named. Our favorite is Mimosa, painted in light mustard, with a ceiling fresco and a frontside view over Via Ghibellina. Colored lighting brings a bit of fun to every unit, too.

Via Ghibellina 51. www.lacasadimorfeo.it. ℂ **055-241-193.** 9 units. 79€–189€ double. Rates include breakfast. Valet parking 25€. Bus: C2 or C3. **Amenities:** Wi-Fi (free).

Palazzo Galletti ★★   Not many hotels within a sensible budget give you the chance to live like a Florentine noble. Rooms here were all refreshed in 2015, and have towering ceilings and an uncluttered arrangement of carefully chosen antiques. Most have frescoed or painted wood showpiece ceilings. Bathrooms, in contrast, have sharp, contemporary lines, and are decked out in travertine and marble. Aside from two street-facing suites, every room has a small balcony, ideal for a predinner glass of wine. If you're here for a once-in-a-lifetime trip, spring for "Giove" or (especially) "Cerere"; both are large suites, and the latter has walls covered in original frescoes from the 1800s. Wi-Fi is free if you book direct and mention this Frommer's guide.

Via Sant'Egidio 12. www.palazzogalletti.it. © **055-390-5750.** 12 units. 100€–170€ double; 170€–240€ suite. Rates include breakfast. Garage parking 30€. Bus: C1 or C2. **Amenities:** Wi-Fi (5€/day).

INEXPENSIVE

Locanda Orchidea ★   Over several visits to Florence, this has been a go-to inn for stays on a tight budget. Rooms range over two floors of a historic *palazzo*—spot the original "wine hole" by the front door, once used by noble owners to sell direct to thirsty Florentines. The best rooms upstairs face a quiet, leafy rear courtyard where wisteria flowers each spring. Furniture is a fun mix of mismatched flea-market finds and secondhand pieces; tiled floors and bold print wallpaper and fabrics keep up the charmingly outmoded feel. Note that bathrooms are shared (they have good water pressure), and there is no air-conditioning or onsite breakfast. But the value, character, and welcome are hard to beat in this price bracket.

Borgo degli Albizi 11 (close to Piazza San Pier Maggiore). www.hotelorchideaflorence. it. © **055-248-0346.** 7 units. 42€–80€ double. Garage parking 18€–22€. Bus: C1 or C2. **Amenities:** Wi-Fi (free).

West of the Center

MODERATE

Riva Lofts ★★   The traditional Florentine alarm call—a morning mix of traffic and tourism—is replaced by birdsong when you awake in one of the stylish rooms here, on the banks of the River Arno. A former stone-built artisan workshop, Riva has had a refit to match its "loft" label: There's a taupe-and-white scheme with laminate flooring, floating staircases, marble bathrooms with rainfall showers, and clever integration of natural materials in such features as original wooden workshop ceilings. Breakfast is served until 11:45am, and noon checkouts as standard are a seriously traveler-friendly touch. The center is a 30-minute walk, or jump on one of Riva's vintage-style bikes and cycle to the Uffizi along the Arno banks. Yet another standout feature in this price bracket: a shaded garden with outdoor plunge pool.

Via Baccio Bandinelli 98. www.rivalofts.com. © **055-713-0272.** 9 units. 165€–255€ double. Rates include breakfast. Garage parking 20€ (or park out front for free). Bus: 6/ Tram: T1 (3 stops from central station). **Amenities:** Bar; bike rental (free); honesty bar; outdoor pool; Wi-Fi (free).

Apartment Rentals & Alternative Accommodations

It's the way of the modern world: Global players in apartment rental have finally overtaken most of the local specialists in Florence. Online agency **Cross Pollinate** ★ (www.cross-pollinate.com; © **06-99369799**) still has a Florence apartment portfolio worth checking. **GoWithOh.com** ★ has a user-friendly website that incorporates verified guest feedback into its wide portfolio of high-quality city apartments. **HomeAway.com,** Tripadvisor-owned **HolidayLettings.co.uk,** and **Airbnb.com** are also very well-stocked with central and suburban apartments.

An alternative budget option is to stay in a religious house. A few monasteries and convents in the center are happy to receive guests for a modest fee, including the **Suore di Santa Elisabetta,** Viale Michelangiolo 46 (near Piazza Ferrucci; www.csse-roma.eu/eng/english.php?zm=5; © **055-681-1884**), in a colonial villa just south of the Ponte San Niccolò. The **Istituto Oblate dell'Assunzione,** Borgo Pinti 15 (© **055-2480-582**), has simple, peaceful rooms in a Medici-era building ranged around a leafy courtyard garden in the lively eastern part of the center. The easiest way to build a monastery and convent itinerary in Florence and beyond is via U.S. based agent **MonasteryStays.com** ★. Remember that most religious houses have a curfew, generally 11pm or midnight; the welcome is always friendly, as you would expect.

Tip: For basic grocery shopping in the center, try **Conad City,** Via dei Servi 56R (© **055-280-110**), or any central branch of **Supermercato il Centro.** Both the **Mercato Centrale** and **Mercato di Sant'Ambrogio** are well stocked with fresh produce (see "Florence's Best Markets," p. 201).

WHERE TO EAT

Florence is awash with restaurants, though many in the most touristed areas (around the Duomo, Piazza della Signoria, Piazza della Repubblica, and Ponte Vecchio) are of low quality, charge high prices, or both. We point out a few below that are worth a visit. The highest concentrations of excellent *ristoranti* and *trattorie* are around **Santa Croce** and across the river in the **Oltrarno** and **San Frediano.** There's also an increasing buzz around **San Lorenzo,** particularly since the top floor of the **Mercato Centrale** (see p. 160) opened in 2014. Bear in mind that menus at restaurants in Florence can change weekly or even (at some of the very best places) daily. The city has also become much more **gluten-savvy.** If you have celiac disease or any sort of food intolerance, don't be afraid to ask.

Reservations are strongly recommended if you have your heart set on eating anywhere, especially at dinner on weekends.

RESTAURANTS BY CUISINE

CAFES
Caffetteria delle Oblate ★, p. 204
Le Murate ★, p. 206
Le Terrazze ★, p. 204
Rivoire★, p. 204

CONTEMPORARY ITALIAN
Il Santo Bevitore ★, p. 164

CONTEMPORARY TUSCAN
iO: Osteria Personale ★★, p. 163
Konnubio ★★★, p. 160
Ora d'Aria ★★★, p. 157

FLORENTINE
Bondi ★★, p. 161
Da Tito ★, p. 162
Il Magazzino ★, p. 163
La Gratella ★★, p. 160
Mario ★, p. 161

GELATO
Carapina ★★, p. 164
Gelateria della Passera ★★, p. 164
Gelateria de' Neri ★, p. 165
Il Gelato Gourmet di Marco Ottaviano
 ★★, p. 165
Il Procopio ★, p. 165
La Carraia ★★, p. 165

GRILL
La Gratella ★★, p. 160

JAPANESE
Kome ★, p. 162

KOSHER
Ruth's ★, p. 163

LIGHT FARE
Bondi ★★, p. 161
I Fratellini ★, p. 156

MODERN ITALIAN
Mercato Centrale ★★★, p. 160
Vagalume ★★, p. 163

PIZZA
GustaPizza ★★, p. 164
Mercato Centrale ★★★, p. 160

SUSHI
Kome ★, p. 162

SEAFOOD
Pescheria San Pietro ★★, p. 161

TUSCAN
Coquinarius ★, p. 156
Da Tito ★, p. 162
Osteria del Porcellino ★, p. 157

VEGETARIAN/VEGAN
Brac ★★, p. 162
Konnubio ★★★, p. 160
Ruth's ★, p. 163

Near the Duomo
MODERATE
Coquinarius ★ TUSCAN   There is a regular menu here—pasta, mains such as wild boar medallions or stuffed pigeon, traditional desserts. But the real pleasure is tucking into a couple of sharing plates and quaffing from the excellent wine list. Go for something from an extensive carpaccio list (beef, boar, octopus, swordfish, and more) or pair a *misto di salumi e formaggi* (mixed Tuscan salami and cheeses) with a full-bodied red wine, to cut through the strong flavors of the deliciously fatty and salty pork and Tuscan sheep's milk cheese, *Pecorino*.

Via delle Oche 11R. www.coquinarius.com. ✆ **055-230-2153.** Main courses 8€–18€. Daily 12:30–3:30pm and 6:30–10:30pm. Bus: C1 or C2.

INEXPENSIVE
I Fratellini ★ LIGHT FARE   This hole-in-the-wall has been serving food to go since 1875. The drill is simple: Choose a filling, pick a drink, then eat

your fast-filled roll on the curb opposite or find a perch in a nearby piazza. There are around 30 fillings to choose from, including the usual Tuscan meats and cheeses—salami, *Pecorino* cheese, cured ham—and more flamboyant combos such as goat cheese and Calabrian spicy salami or *bresaola* (air-dried beef) and wild arugula salad. A glass of wine to wash it down costs from 2€. No credit cards. Lunchtime lines can be long.

Via dei Cimatori 38R (at Via Calzaiuoli). www.iduefratellini.it. *©***055-239-6096.** Sandwiches 3€. Daily 9:30am–7pm (Jul–Aug often closed Sun). Closed 2 weeks in mid-Aug. Bus: C2.

Near Piazza della Signoria
EXPENSIVE

Ora d'Aria ★★★ CONTEMPORARY TUSCAN   If you want to see what the latest generation of Tuscan chefs can do in a kitchen, this place overseen by head chef Marco Stabile should top your list. The mood is modern and elegant, and yet never stuffy. Dishes are subtle and creative, and combine traditional Tuscan ingredients in an original way. The menu changes daily, but expect the likes of spaghetti with extract of peppers, capers, and smoked ricotta or piglet with spiced pear. If you can't stretch the budget for dinner here, book a table at lunch to taste simpler, cheaper (14€–18€) dishes such as cold salad of salt cod with Pratese vermouth and sweet potato, served in full-size or half-price "tapas" portions. Reservations are essential.

Via dei Georgofili 11–13R (off Via Lambertesca). www.oradariaristorante.com. *©* **055-200-1699.** Main courses 32€–45€ (at dinner); tasting menu 70€–75€. Tues–Sat 12:30–2:30pm; Mon–Sat 7:30–10pm. Closed 3 weeks in Aug. Bus: C3 or D.

MODERATE

Osteria del Porcellino ★ TUSCAN   So many characterful restaurants of "old Florence" have dropped standards in the age of mass tourism, but not this place. Traditional Tuscan is what they do best, and pasta dishes such as *pappardelle* (wide pasta ribbons) with wild boar sauce are always tasty. Follow that with a *tagliata* (sliced steak) with arugula and Parmigiano or a mixed grill of four Tuscan meats for a taste of the city's carnivorous traditions. Lighter options include sublime "flan": a potato cake with cured ham, Vin

---

It's All Tripe

New York has the hot dog. London has pie and mash. Florence has . . . cow's intestine in a sandwich. The city's traditional street food, *lampredotto* (the cow's fourth stomach) stewed with tomatoes, has made a big comeback over the last decade, including on the menus of some fine-dining establishments. The best places to sample it are still the city's *trippai*, tripe vendors who sell it from vans around the center, alongside "regular" sandwiches. The most convenient vendors are in **Piazza de' Cimatori** and on **Via de' Macci** at Piazza Sant'Ambrogio. A hearty, nutritious lunch should come to around 4€. Most are open Monday through Saturday but close in August, when Florentines flee the city.

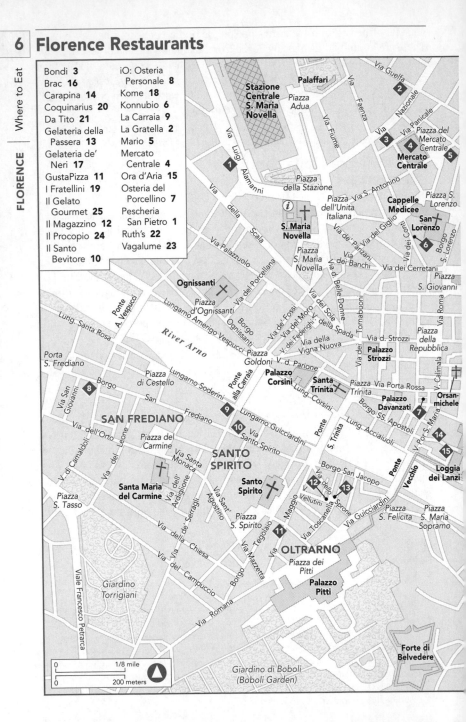

Bondi **3**
Brac **16**
Carapina **14**
Coquinarius **20**
Da Tito **21**
Gelateria della Passera **13**
Gelateria de' Neri **17**
GustaPizza **11**
I Fratellini **19**
Il Gelato Gourmet **25**
Il Magazzino **12**
Il Procopio **24**
Il Santo Bevitore **10**

iO: Osteria Personale **8**
Kome **18**
Konnubio **6**
La Carraia **9**
La Gratella **2**
Mario **5**
Mercato Centrale **4**
Ora d'Aria **15**
Osteria del Porcellino **7**
Pescheria San Pietro **1**
Ruth's **22**
Vagalume **23**

Stazione Centrale S. Maria Novella
Palaffari
Piazza Adua
Via Guelfa
Via Faenza
Via Nazionale
Via Panicale
Piazza del Mercato Centrale
Mercato Centrale
Via Luigi Alamanni
Via della
Via Fiume
Piazza della Stazione
Piazza dell'Unità Italiana
Via S. Antonino
Cappelle Medicee
Piazza S. Lorenzo
San Lorenzo
Via de' Panzani
Via de' Conti
Via del Giglio
Borgo S. Lorenzo
Via Palazzuolo
Scala
S. Maria Novella
Piazza S. Maria Novella
Via de' Banchi
Via dei Cerretani
Piazza S. Giovanni
Ognissanti
Piazza d'Ognissanti
Via del Porcellana
Borgo Ognissanti
Via de' Fossi
Via del Moro
V. della Spada
Via del Sole
Via delle Belle Donne
Via de' Tornabuoni
Piazza della Repubblica
Via Roma
Ponte A. Vespucci
River Arno
Lungarno Amerigo Vespucci
Lung. Santa Rosa
V. dei Federighi
Via della Vigna Nuova
Via d. Strozzi
Palazzo Strozzi
Porta S. Frediano
Piazza di Cestello
Lungarno Soderini
Piazza Goldoni
V. d. Parione
Palazzo Corsini
Santa Trinita
Piazza Trinita
Via Porta Rossa
Palazzo Davanzati
Orsan-michele
Borgo
Via San Giovanni
San Frediano
Ponte alla Carraia
Lung. Corsini
Borgo SS. Apostoli
Lung. Acciaiuoli
V. Por S. Maria
SAN FREDIANO
Via dell'Orto
Via del Leone
Piazza del Carmine
Via Santa Monaca
Lungarno Guicciardini
Via Santo Spirito
Ponte S. Trinita
Loggia dei Lanzi
V. di Camaldoli
Santa Maria del Carmine
Via dell'Ardiglione
Via Sant'Agostino
SANTO SPIRITO
Santo Spirito
Borgo San Jacopo
Via dello Sprone
Ponte Vecchio
Piazza S. Tasso
Via de' Serragli
Piazza S. Spirito
Via Maggio
V. Vellutini
Via Toscanella
Via Guicciardini
Piazza S. Felicita
Piazza S. Maria Soprarno
Via della Chiesa
Via del Campuccio
Borgo
Via Tegolaio
Via Mazzetta
OLTRARNO
Piazza dei Pitti
Giardino Torrigiani
Viale Francesco Petrarca
Via Romana
Palazzo Pitti
Forte di Belvedere
Giardino di Boboli (Boboli Garden)

0   1/8 mile
0   200 meters

158

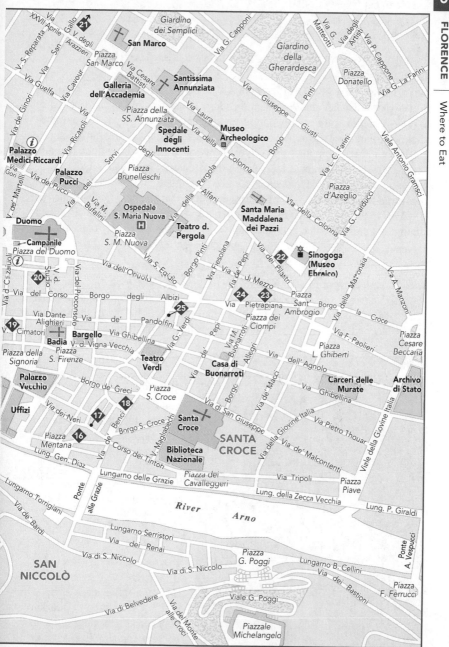

Santo wine, and a *stracchino* cheese sauce. All day dining means you (or the kids) can eat when you like.

Via Val di Limona 7R. www.osteriadelporcellino.com. © **055-264-148.** Main courses 15€–26€. Daily 11:30am–midnight. Bus: C2.

Near San Lorenzo & the Mercato Centrale
MODERATE

Konnubio ★★★ CONTEMPORARY TUSCAN/VEGAN There's a warm glow (candles and low-watt lighting) about this place that opened in 2014—it makes you instantly happy, and the cooking keeps you there. Ingredients are largely Tuscan but combined creatively, such as in warm octopus salad with cherry tomatoes and olives or ravioli stuffed with guinea hen and served with truffle cream sauce. There's an extensive vegan menu, too, including pumpkin with baked tofu, capers, and confit tomato. Under brick vaults and a covered courtyard, it could work for a romantic dinner; but you won't be out of place in a family group either (there's a kids' menu). It feels like refined dining, but at a price that gets you a so-so bowl of pasta in many other places.

Via dei Conti 8R. www.konnubio.it. © **055-238-1189.** Main courses 12€–27€. Daily noon–3pm and 7–11pm. Bus: C1.

La Gratella ★★ FLORENTINE/GRILL It doesn't look like much—a workers' canteen on a nondescript sidestreet—but looks don't matter much when you can source and cook meat like they do here. The star of the show is the *bistecca alla fiorentina*, a large T-bone grilled on the bone and brought to

the table over coals. It's sold by weight and made for sharing; expect to pay about 50€. Pair this, or any market-fresh meat on the menu, with simple Tuscan sides such as *fagioli all'uccelletto* (stewed beans and tomatoes). They cater to celiacs, too.

Via Guelfa 81R. www.trattorialagratella.com. © **055-211-292.** Main courses 12€–18€. Daily noon–3pm and 7–11pm. Bus: 1, 6, 11, 14, 17, or 23.

Mercato Centrale ★★★ MODERN ITALIAN In 2014, the upper floor of Florence's produce market reopened as a bustling shrine to the best modern Italian street food. There are counters selling dishes from all over the

Food stall in the Mercato Centrale, near San Lorenzo.

country, including **Sud,** one of the city's best pizzerias. Don't fancy pizza? There are counters for filled pasta, vegetarian and vegan dishes, cold cuts and cheeses, fresh fish dishes, Chianina burgers and meatballs, and lots more. It works perfectly for families who can't agree on a dinner choice. Or just stop by for a drink and soak up the buzz: There's a beer bar (disappointing) and enoteca (superb).

Piazza Mercato Centrale. www.mercatocentrale.it. © **055-239-9798.** Dishes 5€–13€. Daily 10am–midnight. Bus: C1.

INEXPENSIVE

Bondi ★★ FLORENTINE/LIGHT FARE To label this place opposite the Mercato Centrale a mere sandwich shop is like describing the Super Bowl as "a football game." Bondi is an institution, and specializes in *piadine* (flatbread sandwich) in the Florentine style. Choose from a long list of traditional and unusual combinations, then order at the bar and take a seat on rustic wooden benches to await the arrival of your *piadine* (toasted or cold) filled with any number of combos, including radicchio and mozzarella, salt cod with tomato and pink peppercorns, or eggplant Parmigiana. Wash it down with a glass of Chianti at 2€ a pop. No credit cards.

Via dell'Ariento 85. © **055-287-390.** Sandwiches 2.50€–4€. Daily 11am–11pm. Bus: C1.

Mario ★ FLORENTINE There is no doubt that this traditional market workers' trattoria is now firmly on the tourist trail. But Mario's clings to the traditions and ethos it adopted when it first fired up the burners in its kitchen 60 years ago. Food is simple, hearty, and served at communal tables—"check in" on arrival and you will be offered seats together wherever they come free. Think *zuppa di fagioli* (bean soup) followed by the traditional Tuscan piquant beef stew, *peposo,* or *vitello arrosto* (roast veal). No reservations or credit cards.

Via Rosina 2R (north corner of Piazza Mercato Centrale). www.trattoriamario.com. © **055-218-550.** Main courses 6.50€–14€. Mon–Sat noon–3:30pm. Closed Aug. Bus: C1.

Near Santa Maria Novella
MODERATE

Pescheria San Pietro ★★ SEAFOOD It takes a big serving of confidence to open a seafood restaurant—on two floors no less—in one of Florence's less-fashionable quarters. This place, opened in 2014, has the chops (and the chefs) to pull it off. The fishy focus is unwavering: A route through the menu might take in tuna carpaccio, followed by *tagliatelle* with baby sardines and cherry tomatoes, then a *gran fritto* (mixed fry) of seafood and seasonal vegetables in light tempura batter—though you'd do well to manage that, because portions are generous. With open kitchens, clanking cutlery, brisk service, and a great value "business lunch" (15€ including a glass of wine), San Pietro is classic seafood bistro all over. There's also a 6-item vegetarian menu (dishes 11€–12€).

Via Alamanni 7R. www.pescheriasanpietro.it. © **055-238-2749.** Main courses 16€–24€. Daily 11am–11pm. Bus: C2, D, 29, 30, or 35/Tram: T1.

Near San Marco & Santissima Annunziata

San Marco is the place to head for *schiacciata alla fiorentina,* olive-oil flatbread loaded with savory toppings. You will find the best in the city at **Pugi,** Piazza San Marco 9B (www.focacceria-pugi.it; ✆ **055-280-981**), open 7:45am (Saturday 8:30am) to 8pm Monday to Saturday, but closed most of August.

MODERATE

Da Tito ★★ TUSCAN/FLORENTINE   Sure, they ham it up a little for the tourists, but every night feels like party night at one of central Florence's rare genuine neighborhood trattorias. (And for that reason, it's usually packed—reserve ahead.) The welcome and the dishes are authentically Florentine, with a few modern Italian curveballs: Start, perhaps, with the *risotto con piselli e guanciale* (rice with fresh peas and cured pork cheek) before going on to a traditional grill such as *lombatina di vitella* (veal chop steak). The neighborhood location, a 10-minute walk north of San Lorenzo, and mixed clientele, keep the quality consistent.

Via San Gallo 112R. www.trattoriadatito.it. ✆ **055-472-475.** Main courses 12€–18€. Mon–Sat 12:30–2pm and 7:30–10:30pm. Bus: C1, 1, 7, 20, or 25.

Near Santa Croce

EXPENSIVE

Kome ★ JAPANESE/SUSHI   Perch at the downstairs kaiten restaurant to get the best out of this fashionable joint. The vibe and decor are more 21st century than Medici, with a contoured wooden ceiling sculpture and lots of glass. Grab dishes as they spin around on a conveyor belt; the sashimi, tempura, and *nigiri* are authentically flavored and prepped right in front of you. The set lunch of six sushi plates for 15€, including green tea, is a steal. No reservations at the sushi counter, but there is a Japanese BBQ dining room that accepts prebooking.

Via de' Benci 41R. www.komefirenze.it. ✆ **055-200-8009.** Sushi 3.50€–8€. Mon–Sat noon–3pm and 7pm–midnight. Bus: C3 or 23.

MODERATE

Brac ★★ VEGETARIAN   An artsy cafe/bookshop for most of the day, at lunch and dinner this place turns into one of Florence's best spots for vegetarian and vegan food. There are plenty of seasonal salads and creative pasta dishes, but a *piatto unico* works out to be the best value for hungry diners: one combo plate loaded with three dishes from the main menu, perhaps pear carpaccio with Pecorino cheese and walnuts; potato and broccoli lasagne with ginger and parsley sauce; and an eggplant and mozzarella *pane carasau* (Sardinian flatbread). The atmosphere, with tables ranged around an internal courtyard, is intimate and romantic—yet singletons won't feel at all out of place eating at the counter out front. Reservations at dinner are a must in high season and on weekends.

Via dei Vagellai 18R. www.libreriabrac.net. ✆ **055-094-4877.** Main courses 10€–14€. Mon–Sat 10am–midnight, Sun noon–midnight. Bus: C1, C3, or 23.

Ruth's ★ KOSHER/VEGETARIAN   Ruth's bills itself as a "kosher vegetarian" joint, but you will also find fish on the menu. It's small (around 12 tables), so book ahead if you want to be certain of a table. The interior is cafe-like and informal, the menu likewise. Skip the Italian *primi* and go right for Eastern Mediterranean *secondi* such as vegetarian couscous with harissa or fish *moussaka,* a layered bake of eggplant, tomato, salmon, and spiced rice served with salad and *caponata* (a cold vegetable preserve). A rabbi from the adjacent synagogue oversees the kosher credentials.

Via Farini 2a. www.kosheruth.com. ℂ **055-248-0888.** Main courses 10€–18€. Sun–Fri noon–3pm; Sat–Thurs 7:30–10:30pm. Bus: 6, 19, 31, or 32.

Vagalume ★★ MODERN ITALIAN   The style here is *"tapas fiorentine"* — there are no "courses" and no pasta, and you compile a dinner from a range of good-size dishes in any order you please. Dishes are all seasonal and change daily, but could include a soufflé of Gorgonzola, hazelnuts, and zucchini; rabbit stewed in Vernaccia wine with olives; a "tarte tatin" of beetroot and burrata cheese; or a marinated mackerel salad with fennel and orange. To go with the modern menu, there's stripped-back decor, jazz-funk played in the background on an old vinyl turntable, and an emphasis on beers—three on tap, plus a bottle list that is strong on European styles. The wine list is short, but well chosen.

Via Pietrapiana 40R. ℂ **055-246-6740.** Dishes 7€–14€. Daily 6:30pm–2am. Bus: C2 or C3.

In the Oltrarno, San Niccolò & San Frediano
EXPENSIVE

iO: Osteria Personale ★★ CONTEMPORARY TUSCAN   There's a definite hipster atmosphere, with the brick walls and young staff, and the food ethos here is cutting edge, too. Ingredients are usually familiar Tuscan flavors, but combined in a way you may not have seen before. The menu always has a good range of seafood, meat, and vegetarian dishes: Perhaps tempura artichoke flowers stuffed with Taleggio cheese and marjoram followed by guinea-hen ravioli, then roasted octopus with garbanzo-bean cream and cumin. Reservations are recommended.

Borgo San Frediano 167R (at Piazza di Verzaia). www.io-osteriapersonale.it. ℂ **055-933-1341.** Main courses 17€–20€; tasting menus 40€ for 4 dishes, 55€ for 6 dishes. Mon–Sat 7:30–10pm. Closed 10 days in Jan and all Aug. Bus: D or 6.

MODERATE

Il Magazzino ★ FLORENTINE   A traditional *osteria* that specializes in the flavors of old Florence. It looks the part, too, with its terra-cotta tiled floor and barrel vault, chunky wooden furniture, and hanging lamps. If you dare, this is a place to try tripe or *lampredotto* (intestines), the traditional food of working Florentines, prepared expertly here in ravioli, boiled, or *alla fiorentina* (stewed with tomatoes and garlic). The rest of the menu is carnivore-friendly, too: Follow *tagliatelle al ragù bianco* (pasta ribbons with a "white" meat sauce made with milk instead of tomatoes) with *guancia di vitello in agrodolce* (veal tongue stewed with baby onions in a sticky-sweet sauce).

6

Where to Eat

FLORENCE

Piazza della Passera 3. (?) **055-215-969.** Main courses 9€–18€. Daily noon–3pm and 7:30–11pm. Bus: C3 or D.

Il Santo Bevitore ★ CONTEMPORARY ITALIAN   Sure, this place has lost some of its in-the-know, local buzz. But the commitment to top produce served simply, and the trademark take on Tuscan ingredients, is unwavering: Reservations are still a must. Carefully sourced cold cuts make an ideal sharing antipasto—*prosciutto crudo* from Umbria, *Pecorino* cheese from Pienza, southern Tuscany. Mains are eclectic, seasonal, and come in all appetite sizes, from a whole *burrata* (fresh cheese) served with spinach to pan-fried cockerel or stuffed squid with artichokes. There is a long, expertly compiled wine list, with about 10 offered by the glass, plus craft beers.

Via Santo Spirito 66R (at Piazza N. Sauro). www.ilsantobevitore.com. (?) **055-211-264.** Main courses 10€–24€. Mon–Sat 12:30–2:30pm; daily 7:30–11pm. Closed 10 days in mid-Aug. Bus: C3, D, 6, 11, 36, or 37.

INEXPENSIVE

GustaPizza ★★ PIZZA   Florentines aren't known for their pizza-making skills, so I guess it's just as well this place is run by Calabrians. Pizzas are in the Naples style, with fluffy crusts, doughy bases, and just the classic toppings on a menu that you could write on the back of a napkin: Margherita (cheese, tomato, basil) and Napoli (cheese, tomatoes, anchovies, oregano, capers) are joined by a couple of simple specials, such as mozzarella and basil pesto. It is self-service, but there are a few tables if you want to eat with a knife and fork (no reservations). On warm evenings, eat takeout on the steps of Santo Spirito church, around the corner.

Via Maggio 46R. (?) **055-285-068.** Pizzas 4.50€–8€. Tues–Sun 11:30am–3pm and 7–11pm. Closed 3 weeks in Aug. Bus: C3, D, 11, 36, or 37.

Gelato

Florence has a fair claim to being the birthplace of gelato, and has some of the world's best *gelaterie*—but many, many poor imitations, too. Steer clear of spots around the major attractions, where air-fluffed mountains of ice cream are so full of artificial colors and flavors they glow in the dark. If you can see the Ponte Vecchio or Piazza della Signoria from the front door of the gelateria, you may want to move on. You might only have to walk a block, or duck down a side street, to find a genuine artisan in the gelato kitchen. Trust us, you'll taste the difference. Opening hours tend to be discretionary: When it's warm, many places stay open until 11pm or beyond.

Carapina ★★   Militant seasonality ensures the fruit gelato here is the best in the center. *Note:* This branch usually closes at 7pm.

Via Lambertesca 18R. www.carapina.it. (?) **055-291-128.** Cone from 2.50€. Bus: C3 or D. Also at: Piazza Oberdan 2R ((?) **055-676-930**).

Gelateria della Passera ★★   Milk-free water ices here are some of the most intensely-flavored in the city, and relatively low in sugary sweetness. Try the likes of pink grapefruit or jasmine tea gelato.

164

Via Toscanella 15R (at Piazza della Passera). www.gelaterialapassera.wordpress.com. 🕾 **055-291-882.** Cone from 2€. Bus: C3 or D.

Gelateria de' Neri ★ There's a large range of fruit, *crema* (white cream), and chocolate flavors here, but nothing overelaborate. If the ricotta and fig is available, you're in luck.
Via dei Neri 9R. 🕾 **055-210-034.** Cone from 1.80€. Bus: C1, C3, or 23.

Il Gelato Gourmet di Marco Ottaviano ★★ It's all about the seasonal, produce-led flavors at this spot that opened in 2014. Choices can include Sicilian pistachio or *pastiera*, based on a Neapolitan cake.
Via Palmieri 34R (at Piazza San Pier Maggiore). 🕾 **055-234-1036.** Cone from 2€. Bus: C1 or C2.

Il Procopio ★ Come here for rich, elaborate concoctions, including signature flavor "La Follia," a *crema* gelato with toasted almonds and caramelized figs, and Sachertorte, based on the spiced Austrian cake.
Via Pietrapiana 60R. 🕾 **055-234-6014.** Cone from 2.20€. Bus: C1.

La Carraia ★★ Packed with locals late into the evening on summer weekends—for a good reason. The range is vast, the quality high.
Piazza N. Sauro 25R. www.lacarraiagroup.info. 🕾 **055-280-695.** Cone from 1.50€. Bus: C3, D, 6, 11, 36, or 37. Also at: Via de' Benci 24R (🕾 **329-363-0069**).

EXPLORING FLORENCE

Most museums accept cash only at the door. Staff is usually happy to direct you to the nearest ATM *(un bancomat)*. **Precise opening times can change** without notice, especially at city churches (for example, the Baptistery sometimes remains open until 11pm in summer). The tourist office maintains an up-to-date list of hours. Note, too, that the last admission to the museums and monuments listed is usually between 30 and 45 minutes before the final closing time.

INDEX OF ATTRACTIONS & SITES

Piazza del Duomo

The cathedral square is filled with tourists and caricature artists during the day, strolling crowds in the early evening, and knots of students strumming guitars on the Duomo steps at night. It's always crowded, and the piazza's vivacity and the glittering facade of the cathedral and the Baptistery doors keep it an eternal Florentine sight. The square's closure to traffic in 2009 has made it a more welcoming space than ever.

Battistero (Baptistery) ★★★ RELIGIOUS SITE   In choosing a date to mark the beginning of the Renaissance, art historians often seize on 1401, the year Florence's powerful wool merchants' guild held a contest to decide who would receive the commission to design the **North Doors** ★★ of the Baptistery to match its Gothic **South Doors,** cast 65 years earlier by Andrea Pisano. The era's foremost Tuscan sculptors each cast a bas-relief bronze panel depicting his own vision of the "Sacrifice of Isaac." Twenty-two-year-old Lorenzo Ghiberti, competing against the likes of Donatello, Jacopo della Quercia, and Filippo Brunelleschi, won. He spent the next 21 years casting 28 bronze panels and building his doors.

The result so impressed the merchants' guild—not to mention the public and Ghiberti's fellow artists—that they asked him in 1425 to do the **East Doors** ★★★, facing the Duomo, this time giving him the artistic freedom to realize his Renaissance ambitions. Twenty-seven years later, just before his death, Ghiberti finished 10 dramatic, lifelike Old Testament scenes in gilded bronze, each a masterpiece of Renaissance sculpture and some of the finest examples of low-relief perspective in Italian art. Each illustrates episodes in the stories of Noah (second down on left), Moses (second up on left), Solomon and the Queen of Sheba (bottom right), and others. The panels mounted

Battistero.

here are excellent copies; the originals are in the **Museo Storico dell'Opera del Duomo** (see p. 172). Years later, Michelangelo was standing before these doors and someone asked his opinion. His response sums up Ghiberti's accomplishment as no art historian could: "They are so beautiful that they would grace the entrance to Paradise." They've been nicknamed the Gates of Paradise ever since.

The building itself is ancient. It is first mentioned in city records in the 9th century and was probably already 300 years old by then. Its interior is ringed with columns pilfered from ancient Roman buildings and is a spectacle of mosaics above and below. The floor was inlaid in 1209, and the ceiling was covered between 1225 and the early 1300s with glittering **mosaics ★★**. Most were crafted by Venetian or Byzantine-style workshops, which worked off designs drawn by the era's best artists. Coppo di Marcovaldo drew sketches for the 7.8m-high (26-ft.) "Christ in Judgment" and the "Last Judgment" that fills over a third of the ceiling. Bring binoculars (and a good neck masseuse) if you want a closer look.

Piazza San Giovanni. www.ilgrandemuseodelduomo.it. ℗ **055-230-2885.** Admission included with 10€ Grande Museo del Duomo ticket; see box p. 170. Mon–Wed and Fri–Sat 8:15–10:15am and 11:15am–6:30pm; Thurs 8:15am–6:30pm; Sun 8:15am–1:30pm. Bus: C2.

Campanile di Giotto (Giotto's Bell Tower) ★★ HISTORIC SITE

In 1334, Giotto started the cathedral bell tower but completed only the first two levels before his death in 1337. He was out of his league with the engineering aspects of architecture, and the tower was saved from falling by Andrea Pisano, who doubled the thickness of the walls. Andrea, a master sculptor of the Pisan Gothic school, also changed the design to add statue niches—he even carved a few of the statues himself—before quitting the project in 1348. Francesco Talenti finished the job between 1350 and 1359.

Battistero **4**
Biblioteca delle
    Oblate **25**
Campanile di Giotto **28**
Cappelle Medicee **2**
Cenacolo di
    Sant'Appollonia **30**
Chiostro dello Scalzo **35**
Duomo **27**
Galleria degli Uffizi **21**
Galleria dell'
    Accademia **32**
Giardino Bardini **17**
Giardino di Boboli **16**
Gucci Museo **23**
Museo Archeologico **34**
Museo Marino Marini
    & Cappella Rucellai **9**
Museo Nazionale
    del Bargello **24**
Museo Novecento **5**
Museo dell'Opera **26**
Museo Zoologia
    "La Specola" **12**
Orsanmichele **6**
Palazzo Davanzati **7**
Palazzo Medici-
    Riccardi **29**
Palazzo Pitti **13**
Palazzo Vecchio **22**

Piazzale
    Michelangelo **19**
Ponte Vecchio **14**
San Lorenzo **3**
San Marco **31**
San Miniato
    al Monte **18**
Santa Croce **20**
Santa Felicità **15**
Santa Maria del
    Carmine **10**
Santa Maria
    Novella **1**
Santo Spirito **11**
Santa Trínita **8**
Santissima
    Annunziata **33**

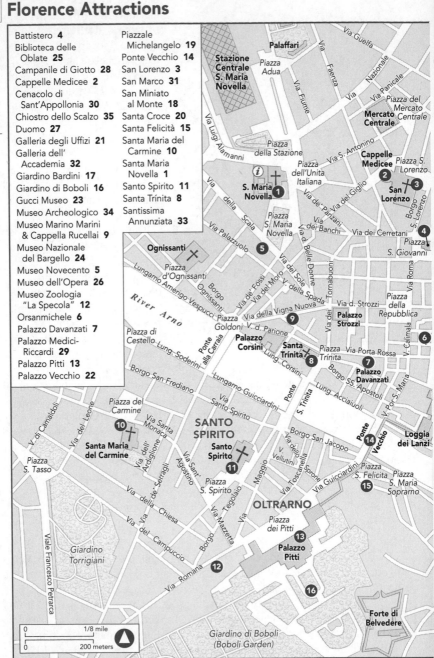

Via XXVII Aprile
Via S. Reparata
Via San Gallo
V. S. Zanobi
Via Arazzieri
Via S. v. degli

35
30
31 San Marco
Piazza San Marco
Via Cesare Battisti
Giardino dei Semplici

Via Guelfa
Via Cavour
Via Ricasoli

32
Galleria dell' Accademia
Piazza della SS. Annunziata

Santissima Annunziata
33

Via G. Capponi
Via G. Matteotti
Via degli Artisti
Via P. Capponi
Via G. La Farini

Giardino della Gherardesca
Piazza Donatello

Via Laura
Via della Colonna

Spedale degli Innocenti
Museo Archeologico
34

Via Giuseppe Giusti
Borgo Pinti
Via L. C. Farini
Viale Antonio Gramsci

29
Via de' Gori
Via dei Pucci

Palazzo Pucci

Piazza Brunelleschi

Via dei Servi
Via M. Bufalini

Ospedale S. Maria Nuova
Piazza S. M. Nuova

Via della Pergola
Via degli Alfani

Teatro d. Pergola

Santa Maria Maddalena dei Pazzi

Piazza d'Azeglio
Via della Colonna
Via G. Carducci

28 Duomo **27**
26

Piazza del Duomo

Via dell'Oriuolo
25

Borgo Pinti
Via Fiesolana
Via de' Pepi
Via de' Pilastri
Via della Mattonaia
Via A. Marzoni

Via d. Cazaiuoli
V. d. Studio
Via del Proconsolo
Via del Corso
Borgo degli Albizi

Via Pietrapiana
Via di Mezzo
Piazza Sant' Ambrogio
Borgo la Croce
Piazza C. Beccaria

✡ Sinogoga (Museo Ebraico)

Via Dante Alighieri
V. Cimatori

Bargello
24
Via Ghibellina
Via de' Pandolfini

Piazza dei Ciompi

Via F. Paolieri

Via del Proconsolo
Badia

V. d. Vigna Vecchia
Via G. Verdi
Via M. Buonarroti
Via de' Pepi
Via de' Macci
Via dell'Agnolo

Piazza L. Ghiberti

Piazza della Signoria **23**
Piazza S. Firenze

22 Palazzo Vecchio
21
Uffizi

Borgo de' Greci
Via dei Neri
Piazza S. Croce

Teatro Verdi

Casa di Buonarroti

Carceri delle Murate
Archivio di Stato

Via Ghibellina

Via de' Benci
Borgo S. Croce
V. Magliabechi

20 Santa Croce

Via di San Giuseppe
Via della Giovine Italia
Via de' Malcontenti
Viale della Giovine Italia

SANTA CROCE

Piazza Mentana
Lung. Gen. Diaz
Via de' Corso dei Tintori

Biblioteca Nazionale

Piazza dei Cavalleggeri
Via Tripoli
Piazza Piave

Via de' Bardi
Lungarno Torrigiani
Ponte alle Grazie
Lungarno delle Grazie
Lung. della Zecca Vecchia
Lung. P. Giraldi

Ponte A. Vespucci

River Arno

Lungarno Serristori
Via dei Renai
Via di S. Niccolo

Piazza G. Poggi
Lungarno B. Cellini
Via dei Bastioni

Piazza F. Ferrucci

17 SAN NICCOLÒ

Via di S. Niccolo
Via di Belvedere
Via del Monte alle Croci

Viale G. Poggi

18
19 Piazzale Michelangelo

Visitors to Florence in mid-2013 got a shock when they went to purchase the discount **Firenze Card** (www.firenzecard. it). Launched in 2011 at 50€ per person, the card was suddenly priced at 72€, still today's price. So, is it a good buy? If you are planning a busy, culture-packed break here, the Firenze Card is a good value. If you only expect to see a few museums, skip it. But for the culture vultures out there, the card (valid for 72 hr.) allows one entrance to each of 60 sites; the list includes a handful that are free anyway, but also the Uffizi, Accademia, Cappella Brancacci, Palazzo Pitti, Brunelleschi's dome, San Marco, and many more. In fact, *everything* we recommend in this chapter except the Gucci Museo is included in the price of the card, as well as some sites in Fiesole (p. 197). It gets you into much shorter lines, taking ticket pre-booking hassles out of the equation—another savings of 3€ to 4€ for busy museums, above all the Uffizi and Accademia. It also includes 3 days' free bus travel (which you likely won't use) and free public Wi-Fi (which you might).

Note: There is no need to buy a Firenze Card for children ages 17 and under; they enter state (e.g., the Uffizi) and civic (e.g., the Palazzo Vecchio) museums free. Private museums and churches have their own pricing policies for children, but admission fees won't add up to anywhere near 72€. One slight gremlin occurs at the Uffizi and Accademia, where in order to skip the longest line and use the Firenze Card entrance, those aged 6 to 17 must pay the 4€ booking fee *but not the ticket price*. However, you can pay on the spot: Join the Firenze Card line together, and be prepared to have to top up your ticket at the teller window. Be sure to carry age-bearing ID for the kids.

Amici degli Uffizi membership (www. amicidegliuffizi.it) is the ticket to choose if you want to delve deeper into a narrower range of Florence museums, especially if you want to make multiple visits to the vast collections at the Uffizi and Palazzo Pitti, or if you plan on visiting Florence more than once in a calendar year. It secures admission (without waiting in line) into 15 or so state museums, including the Uffizi, Accademia, San Marco, Bargello, Cappelle Medicee, and everything at the Palazzo Pitti. It costs 60€ for adults, 40€ ages 18 to 26, 100€ for a family, and is valid for a calendar year (Jan 1–Dec 31). Children 17 and under enter free with a paying adult, and membership permits multiple visits. Join Tuesday to Saturday inside Uffizi entrance no. 2; take photo ID, plus a little patience, because the membership desk is not always manned.

The Opera del Duomo has also dispensed with single-entry tickets to its sites in favor of a value *biglietto cumulativo*, the **Grande Museo del Duomo** ticket. It covers Brunelleschi's dome, the Baptistery, Campanile di Giotto, Museo Storico dell'Opera del Duomo, and crypt of Santa Reparata (inside the cathedral) for 10€, free for accompanied children up to age 14. It also gets you into the Duomo without queuing (in theory). You have 24 hours from first use to enter them all. Buy it at the ticket office almost opposite the Baptistery, on the north side of Piazza San Giovanni. It includes enough to fill a busy half-day, at least, and represents a good value. See **www. ilgrandemuseodelduomo.it** for more details.

The **reliefs** and **statues** in the lower levels—by Andrea Pisano, Donatello, Luca della Robbia, and others—are all copies; the weatherworn originals are housed in the Museo Storico dell'Opera del Duomo (see p. 172). We recommend climbing the 414 steps to the top; the **view ★★** is memorable as you ascend, and offers the best close-up shot in the city of Brunelleschi's dome. Queues are also much shorter than the often-epic lines to climb Brunelleschi's dome itself (see below).

Piazza del Duomo. www.ilgrandemuseodelduomo.it. © **055-230-2885.** Admission included with 10€ Grande Museo del Duomo ticket; see above. Daily 8:15am–6:50pm. Bus: C2, 14, or 23.

Duomo (Cattedrale di Santa Maria del Fiore) ★★★ CATHEDRAL

By the late 13th century, Florence was feeling peevish: Its archrivals Siena and Pisa sported huge, flamboyant new cathedrals while it was saddled with the tiny 5th- or 6th-century cathedral of Santa Reparata. So, in 1296, the city hired Arnolfo di Cambio to design a new Duomo, and he raised the facade and the first few bays before his death (around 1310). Work continued under the auspices of the Wool Guild and architects Giotto di Bondone (who concentrated on the bell tower) and Francesco Talenti (who expanded the planned size and finished up to the drum of the dome). The facade we see today is a neo-Gothic composite designed by Emilio de Fabris and built from 1871 to 1887.

Campanile di Giotto.

The Duomo's most distinctive feature, however, is its enormous **dome ★★★** (or *cupola*), which dominates the skyline and is a symbol of Florence itself. The raising of this dome, the largest in the world in its time, was no mean architectural feat, tackled by Filippo Brunelleschi between 1420 and 1436 (see "A Man & His Dome," p. 172). You can climb up between its two shells for one of the classic panoramas across the city—something that is not recommended for claustrophobes or anyone with no head for heights. **Get there early:** Lines can be extremely long.

The cathedral is rather Spartan inside, but do check out the optical-illusion equestrian "statue" of English mercenary soldier Sir John Hawkwood, painted on the north wall in 1436 by Paolo Uccello.

Piazza del Duomo. www.ilgrandemuseo delduomo.it. © **055-230-2885.** Admission

A MAN & HIS dome

Filippo Brunelleschi, a diminutive man whose ego was as big as his talent, managed in his arrogant, quixotic, and brilliant way to reinvent Renaissance architecture. Having been beaten by Lorenzo Ghiberti in the contest to cast the Baptistery doors (see p. 166), Brunelleschi resolved that he would rather be the top architect than the second-best sculptor, and took off for Rome to study the buildings of the ancients. On returning to Florence, he combined subdued gray *pietra serena* stone with smooth white plaster to create airy arches, vaults, and arcades of perfect classical proportions, in his own variant on the classical orders of architecture. He designed Santo Spirito, the elegant Ospedale degli Innocenti, and a new sacristy for San Lorenzo, but his greatest achievement was erecting the dome over Florence's cathedral.

The Duomo—then the world's largest church—had already been built, but nobody had been able to figure out how to cover the daunting space over its center without spending a fortune. Plus no one was sure whether they could create a dome that would hold up under its own weight. Brunelleschi insisted he knew how, and once granted the commission, revealed his ingenious plan—which may have been inspired by close study of Rome's **Pantheon** (p. 100).

He built the dome in two shells, the inner one thicker than the outer, both shells thinning as they neared the top, thus leaving the center hollow and removing a good deal of the weight. He also planned to construct the dome from giant vaults with ribs crossing them, and with dovetailed stones making up the actual fabric of the dome. In this way, the walls of the dome would support themselves as they were erected. In the process of building, Brunelleschi found himself as much an engineer as architect, constantly designing winches and hoists to carry the materials (plus food and drink) faster and more efficiently up to the level of the workmen.

His finished work speaks for itself, 45m (148 ft.) wide at the base and 90m (295 ft.) high from drum to lantern. For his achievement, Brunelleschi was accorded a singular honor: He is the only person ever buried in Florence's cathedral.

to church free; Santa Reparata and cupola included with 10€ Grande Museo del Duomo ticket; see p. 170. Church Mon–Wed and Fri 10am–5pm; Thurs 10am–4:30pm (July–Sept until 5pm, May until 4pm); Sat 10am–4:45pm; Sun 1:30–4:45pm. Cupola Mon–Fri 8:30am–6:20pm; Sat 8:30am–5pm; Sun 1–4pm; closed during religious festivals. Bus: C1 or C2.

Museo Storico dell'Opera del Duomo (Cathedral Works Museum) ★★ ART MUSEUM   Florence's Cathedral Museum reopened in late 2015 with double the floorspace to show off what is Italy's second-largest collection of devotional art—after Rome's Vatican Museums (p. 76). The site itself is significant: It once housed the workshop where Michelangelo sculpted "David." The museum's prize exhibit is the centerpiece: After a restoration completed in 2012, the original **Gates of Paradise** ★★★ cast by Lorenzo Ghiberti in the early 1400s (see "Baptistery," p. 166) look better than ever. You can see them in a re-creation of their original space on the piazza, and read from interpretation panels that explain the Old Testament scenes.

Also here is a (mostly) Michelangelo **"Pietà" ★★** that nearly wasn't. Early on in the process, he had told students that he wanted this "Pietà" to stand at his tomb, but when he found an imperfection in the marble, he began attacking it with a hammer (look at Christ's left arm). The master never returned to the work, but his students later repaired the damage. The figure of Nicodemus was untouched, legend has it, because this was a self-portrait of the artist—a Michelangelo legend that, for once, is probably true. Elsewhere are works by Donatello, Verrocchio, and others.

Piazza del Duomo 9 (behind cathedral). www.ilgrandemuseodelduomo.it. © **055-230-2885.** Admission included with 10€ Grande Museo del Duomo ticket; see p. 170. Mon–Sat 9am–6:50pm; Sun 9am–1pm. Bus: C1.

Around Piazza della Signoria & Santa Trínita

Galleria degli Uffizi (Uffizi Gallery) ★★★ ART MUSEUM   There is no collection of Renaissance art on the planet that can match the Uffizi. Period. For all its crowds and other inconveniences, the Uffizi remains a must-see.

And what will you see? Some 60-plus rooms and marble corridors—built in the 16th century as the Medici's private office complex, or *uffici*—all jam-packed with famous paintings, among them Giotto's "Ognissanti Madonna," Botticelli's "Birth of Venus," Leonardo da Vinci's "Annunciation," Michelangelo's "Holy Family," and many, many more.

Start with **Room 2** for a look at the pre-Renaissance, Gothic style of painting. Compare teacher and student as you examine Cimabue's "Santa Trínita Maestà" painted around 1280, and Giotto's **"Ognissanti Madonna" ★★★** done in 1310. The similar subject and setting for both paintings allows the viewer to see how Giotto transformed Cimabue's iconlike Byzantine style into something real and human. Giotto's Madonna actually looks like she's sitting on a throne, her clothes emphasizing the curves of her body, whereas Cimabue's Madonna and angels float in space, looking like portraits on coins, with stiff positioning. Also worth a look-see: Duccio's **"Rucellai Madonna" ★** (1285), a founding work of the ethereal Sienese School of painting.

Room 3 showcases the Sienese School at its peak, with Simone Martini's dazzling **"Annunciation" ★★** (1333) and Ambrogio Lorenzetti's "Presentation at the Temple" (1342). The Black Death of 1348 wiped out this entire generation of Sienese painters, and most of that city's population along with them. **Room 6** shows Florentine painting at its most decorative, in the style known as "International Gothic." The iconic work is Gentile da Fabriano's **"Procession of the Magi" ★★★** (1423). The line to see the newborn Jesus is full of decorative and comic elements, and is even longer than the one outside the Uffizi.

Room 8 contains the unflattering profiles of the Duke Federico da Montefeltro of Urbino and his duchess, done by **Piero della Francesca** around 1465. The subjects are portrayed in an unflinchingly realistic way. The duke, in particular, exposes his warts and his crooked nose, which was broken in a tournament. This focus on earthly rather than Christian elements harkens back to the teachings of classical Greek and Roman times, and is made all the more vivid by depiction (on the back) of the couple riding chariots driven by the humanistic virtues of faith, charity, hope, and modesty for her; prudence, temperance, fortitude, and justice for him.

Also here are works by **Filippo Lippi** from the mid–15th century. His most celebrated panel, **"Madonna and Child with Two Angels"** ★★, dates from around 1465. The background, with distant mountains on one side and water on the other, framing the portrait of a woman's face, was shamelessly stolen by Leonardo da Vinci 40 years later for his "Mona Lisa." Lippi's work was also a celebrity scandal. The woman who modeled for Mary was said to be Filippo's lover—a would-be nun called Lucrezia Buti whom he had spirited away from her convent before she could take vows. The child looking toward the viewer is the product of their union. That son, Filippino Lippi, became a painter in his own right, and some of his works hang in the same room. However, it was Filippo's student (who would, in turn, become Filippino's teacher) who would go on to become one of the most famous artists of the 15th century. His name was Botticelli.

Rooms 10 to 14—still collectively numbered as such, even though the partition walls were knocked down in 1978—are devoted to the works of Sandro Filipepi, better known by his nickname "Little Barrels," or Botticelli. Botticelli's 1485 **"Birth of Venus"** ★★ hangs like a highway billboard you have seen a thousand times. Venus's pose is taken from classical statues, while the winds Zephyr and Aura blowing her to shore, and the muse welcoming her, are

Evening at the Galleria degli Uffizi.

from Ovid's "Metamorphosis." Botticelli's 1478 **"Primavera"** ★★★, its dark, bold colors a stark contrast to the filmy, pastel "Venus," defies definitive interpretation (many have tried). But again it features Venus (center), alongside Mercury, with the winged boots, the Three Graces, and the goddess Flora. Next to it, Botticelli's "Adoration of the Magi" contains a self-portrait of the artist. He's the one in yellow on the far right.

Leonardo da Vinci's **"Annunciation"** ★★★ anchors **Room 15.** In this painting, though completed in the early 1470s while Leonardo was still a student in Verrocchio's workshop, da Vinci's ability to orchestrate the viewer's focus is masterful: The line down the middle of the brick corner of the house draws your glance to Mary's delicate fingers, which themselves point along the top of a stone wall to the angel's two raised fingers. Those in turn draw attention to the mountain in the center of the two parallel trees dividing Mary from the angel, representing the gulf between the worldly and the spiritual. Its unusual perspective was painted to be viewed from the lower right.

The art-filled interior of the Galleria degli Uffizi.

The **Tribuna** ★ is an octagonal room added to the Uffizi by Francesco I in the 1580s. Although visitors can no longer walk through it, you can view the mother-of-pearl ceiling and the **"Medici Venus"** ★★, a Roman statue dating from the 1st century B.C., from outside. Note the similarities to Botticelli's painted Venus.

As soon as you cross to the Uffizi's west wing—past picture windows with views of the Arno River to one side and the perfect, Renaissance perspective of the Uffizi piazza to the other—you're walloped with another line of masterpieces. However, it is hard to be certain of the precise layout you'll encounter: The museum is undergoing a major facelift, to create the "New Uffizi." Among the highlights of this "second half" is Michelangelo's 1505–08 **"Holy Family"** ★. The twisting shapes of Mary, Joseph, and Jesus recall those in the Sistine Chapel in Rome for their sculpted nature and the bright colors. The torsion and tensions of the painting (and other Michelangelo works) inspired the next generation of Florentine painters, known as the **Mannerists.** Andrea Del Sarto, Rosso Fiorentino, and Pontormo are all represented in the revamped *Sale Rosse* (**Red Rooms**) downstairs. Here too, the Uffizi has a number of Raphaels, including his recently restored and often-copied **"Madonna of the Goldfinch"** ★★ (Room 66), with a background landscape lifted from Leonardo and Botticelli.

Titian's reclining nude **"Venus of Urbino"** ★★ (Room 83) is another highlight of the Uffizi's later works. It's no coincidence that the edge of the curtain, the angle of her hand and leg, and the line splitting floor and bed all intersect at the "forbidden" part of her body. The Uffizi also owns a trio of paintings by Caravaggio, notably an enigmatic **"Bacchus"** ★, and many by the 17th- to 18th-century *caravaggieschi* artists who aped his *chiaroscuro* (bright light and dark shadows) style of painting. Greatest among them was Artemisia Gentileschi, a rare female baroque painter. Her **"Judith Slaying Holofernes"** ★ (ca. 1612), is one of the more brutal, bloody paintings in the gallery, and shares Room 90 with Caravaggio.

Rooms 46 to 55 opened in 2012 to showcase the works of foreign painters in the Uffizi. The museum owns a vast and varied collection, much of which lay in storage until the opening of these new galleries. The best among these so-called *Sale Blu,* or "Blue Rooms," is the Spanish gallery, with works by Goya, El Greco's "Sts. John the Evangelist and Francis" (1600), and Velázquez's **"Self-Portrait"** ★. **Room 49** displays some of Rembrandt's most familiar portraits and self-portraits.

If you find yourself flagging at any point (it happens to us all), there is a **coffee shop** at the far end of the west wing. Prices are in line with the piazza below, plus you get a great close-up of the Palazzo Vecchio's facade from the terrace. Fully refreshed, you can return to discover works by the many great artists we didn't have space to cover here: Cranach and Dürer; Giorgione, Bellini, and Mantegna (the latter two in Room 20); Uccello, Masaccio, Bronzino, and Veronese. The collection goes on and on—there are multiple original Roman statues and friezes, too, notably in a room dedicated to the Medici's Garden of San Marco. In short, there is nowhere like the Uffizi anywhere in Italy, or the world.

Piazzale degli Uffizi 6 (off Piazza della Signoria). www.uffizi.firenze.it. ✆ **055-238-8651.** (To reserve tickets, see facing page.) Admission 8€ (13€ during compulsory temporary exhibition). Tues–Sun 8:15am–6:50pm. Bus: C1, C2, C3, or D.

Gucci Museo ★ MUSEUM   This private museum tells the story of the Gucci empire, from humble beginnings to worldwide megabrand. Guccio Gucci got his flash of inspiration while working as a "lift boy" at London's Savoy Hotel: His first product designs were for travel luggage to suit the lifestyles of the kinds of people he would meet in the elevator every day.

Of course, as well as the history, the museum's three floors are packed with swag that carries the famous "double-G" logo, including a limited edition 1979 Gucci Cadillac Seville (only 200 were ever made). As well as day bags and duffle bags—and photos of Audrey Hepburn, David Niven, Sophia Loren, and Princess Grace in Gucci gear—there is a room devoted to revering the dresses

If you're not buying a cumulative ticket (see "Discount Tickets for the City," p. 170), you should bypass the hours-long line at the Uffizi by reserving a ticket and an entry time in advance. Call **Firenze Musei** at *C* **055-294-883** (Mon–Fri 8:30am–6:30pm; Sat until 12:30pm) or visit **www.firenzemusei.it** (you may need to have patience with their website, however). You can also reserve for the Accademia (another interminable line, to see "David"), as well as the Galleria Palatina in the Pitti Palace, the Bargello, and several others. There's a 3€ fee (4€ for the Uffizi or Accademia, where a reservation is strongly advised); you can pay by credit card. You can also reserve in person, in Florence, at a kiosk in the facade of Orsanmichele, on Via dei Calzaiuoli (closed Sun), or at a desk inside the bookshop **Libreria My Accademia,** Via Ricasoli 105R (closed Mon; www.myaccademia.com; *C* **055-288-310**), almost opposite the Accademia. You can also reserve, for the Uffizi only, at the Uffizi itself; do so at the teller window inside entrance number 2. Ticket collection point at the Uffizi is across the piazza, at entrance number 3.

that have graced the reddest of red carpets. The museum places Gucci right at the heart of Florence's artisan tradition—which of course, is where it belongs. Piazza della Signoria. www.guccimuseo.com. *C* **055-7592-3302.** Admission 7€ (5€ Thurs 8–11pm). Fri–Wed 10am–8pm, Thurs 10am–11pm. Bus: C1 or C2.

Museo Nazionale del Bargello (Bargello Museum) ★★ MUSEUM This is the most important museum anywhere for Renaissance **sculpture,** and often (inexplicably) quieter than other museums in the city. In a far cry from its original use as the city's prison, torture chamber, and execution site, the Bargello now stands as a three-story art museum containing some of the best works of Michelangelo, Donatello, and Ghiberti, as well as of their most successful Mannerist successor, Giambologna.

In the ground-level Michelangelo room, you'll witness the variety of his craft, from a whimsical 1497 **"Bacchus"** ★★ to the severe, unfinished "Brutus" of 1539. "Bacchus," created when Michelangelo was just 22, really looks like he's drunk, leaning back a little too far, his head off kilter, with a cupid about to bump him over. Nearby is Giambologna's twisting **"Mercury"** ★, who looks like he's about to take off from the ground, propelled by the breath of Zephyr.

Upstairs, an enormous vaulted hall is filled with some of Donatello's most accomplished sculptures, including his original "Marzocco" (from outside the Palazzo Vecchio; p. 180), and **"St. George"** ★ from a niche on the outside of Orsanmichele. Notable among them is his bronze **"David"** ★★ (which some think might actually be Mercury), done in 1440, the first freestanding nude sculpture since Roman times. The classical detail of these sculptures, as well as their naturalistic poses and reflective mood, is the essence of the Renaissance style.

PIAZZA DELLA signoria

When the medieval Guelph party finally came out on top after their political struggle with the Ghibellines, they razed part of the old city center to build a new palace for civic government. It's said the Guelphs ordered architect Arnolfo di Cambio to build what we now call the **Palazzo Vecchio** (see p. 180) in the corner of this space, but to be careful that not 1 inch of the building sat on the cursed former Ghibelline land. This odd legend was probably fabricated to explain Arnolfo's quirky off-center architecture.

The space around the *palazzo* became the new civic center of town, L-shaped **Piazza della Signoria ★★★**, named after the oligarchic ruling body of the medieval city (the "Signoria"). Today, it's an outdoor sculpture gallery, teeming with tourists, postcard stands, horses and buggies, and expensive outdoor cafes. If you want to catch the square at its serene best, come around 8am.

The statuary on the piazza is particularly beautiful, starting on the far left (as you're facing the Palazzo Vecchio) with Giambologna's equestrian "Grand Duke Cosimo I" (1594). To its right is one of Florence's favorite sculptures to hate, the **"Fontana del Nettuno"** ("Neptune Fountain"; 1560–75), created by Bartolomeo Ammannati as a tribute to Cosimo I's naval ambitions but nicknamed by the Florentines "Il Biancone," or "Big Whitey." The **porphyry plaque** set in the ground in front of the fountain marks the site where puritanical monk Savonarola held the Bonfire of the Vanities: With his fiery apocalyptic preaching, he whipped the Florentines into an ascetic frenzy, and hundreds filed into this piazza, arms loaded with paintings, clothing, and other effects that represented their "decadence." They threw it all onto the flames.

To the right of Neptune is a long, raised platform fronting the Palazzo Vecchio known as the *arringheria,* from which soapbox speakers would lecture to crowds before them (we get our word "harangue" from this). On its far left corner is a copy (original in the Bargello; see above) of Donatello's **"Marzocco,"** symbol of the city, with a Florentine lion resting his raised paw on a shield emblazoned with the city's emblem, the *giglio* (lily). To its right is another Donatello replica, **"Judith Beheading Holofernes."** Farther down is a man who needs little introduction, Michelangelo's **"David,"** a 19th-century copy of the original now in the Accademia. Near enough to David to look truly ugly in comparison is Baccio Bandinelli's **"Hercules and Cacus"** (1534). Poor Bandinelli was trying to copy Michelangelo's muscular male form but ended up making his Hercules merely lumpy.

At the piazza's south end is one of the square's earliest and prettiest embellishments, the **Loggia dei Lanzi ★★** (1376–82), named after the Swiss guard of lancers *(lanzi)* whom Cosimo de' Medici stationed here. Andrea Orcagna probably designed the airy loggia—spawning another of its many names, the Loggia di Orcagna (yet another is the Loggia della Signoria). At the front left stands Benvenuto Cellini's masterpiece in bronze, **"Perseus" ★★★** (1545), holding out the severed head of Medusa. On the far right is Giambologna's **"Rape of the Sabines" ★★**, one of the most successful Mannerist sculptures in existence, and a piece you must walk all the way around to appreciate, catching the action and artistry of its spiral design from different angles. Talk about moving it indoors, safe from the elements, continues . . . but for now, it's still here.

Piazza della Signoria.

Side by side on the back wall are the contest entries submitted by Ghiberti and Brunelleschi for the commission to do the Baptistery doors in 1401. Both had the "Sacrifice of Isaac" as their biblical theme, and both displayed an innovative use of perspective. Ghiberti won the contest, perhaps because his scene is more thematically unified. Brunelleschi could have ended up a footnote in the art history books, but instead he gave up the chisel and turned his attentions to architecture, which turned out to be a wise move (see "A Man & His Dome," p. 172).

Via del Proconsolo 4. www.polo museale.firenze.it. 🕐 **055-238-8606.** Admission 4€ (7€ during compulsory temporary exhibition). Daily 8:15am–1:50pm (until 5pm during exhibition). Closed 1st, 3rd, and 5th Sun, and 2nd and 4th Mon of each month. Bus: C1 or C2.

Orsanmichele ★★ RELIGIOUS SITE/ARCHITECTURE This bulky structure halfway down Via dei Calzaiuoli looks more like a Gothic warehouse than a church—which is exactly what it was, built as a granary and grain market in 1337. After a miraculous image of the Madonna appeared on a column inside, however, the lower level was turned into a shrine and chapel. The city's merchant guilds each undertook the task of decorating one of the outside Gothic tabernacles around the lower level with a statue of their guild's patron saint. Masters such as Ghiberti, Donatello, Verrocchio, and Giambologna all cast or carved masterpieces to set here (those remaining are mostly copies, including Donatello's "St. George").

In the dark interior, an elaborate Gothic stone **"Tabernacle"** ★ (1349–59) by Andrea Orcagna protects a luminous 1348 "Madonna and Child" painted by Giotto's student Bernardo Daddi, to which miracles were ascribed during the Black Death of 1348–50.

Tip: Every Monday (9am–5pm) you can access the upper floors, which house many of the original sculptures that once adorned Orsanmichele's exterior niches. Among the treasures of this so-called **Museo di Orsanmichele** ★

are a trio of bronzes: Ghiberti's "St. John the Baptist" (1412–16), the first life-size bronze of the Renaissance; Verrocchio's "Incredulity of St. Thomas" (1483); and Giambologna's "St. Luke" (1602). Climb up one floor farther, to the top, for an unforgettable 360° **panorama ★★** of the city. The Museo is staffed by volunteers, so donate if you are able.

Via Arte della Lana 1. ℗ **055-210-305.** Free admission. Daily 10am–5pm. Bus: C2.

Palazzo Davanzati ★★ PALACE/MUSEUM   One of the best preserved 14th-century palaces in the city is open as a museum dedicated to domestic life in the medieval and Renaissance period. It was originally built for the Davizzi family in the mid-1300s, then bought by the Davanzati clan; check out the latter's family tree, dating back to the 1100s, on the wall of the ground-floor courtyard.

The palace's painted wooden ceilings and murals have aged well (even surviving damage during World War II), but the emphasis is not on the decor but on providing visitors with an insight into medieval life for a noble Florentine family: feasts and festivities in the Sala Madornale; the private, internal well for secure water supply when things got sticky for the family or city; and magnificent bedchamber frescoes dating to the 1350s, which recount, comic-strip style, "The Chatelaine of Vergy," a 13th-century morality tale.

An interesting footnote: In 1916, a New York auction of furnishings from this very palace helped launched a "Florentine style" trend in U.S. interior design circles.

Via Porta Rossa 13. www.polomuseale.firenze.it. ℗ **055-238-8610.** Admission 2€. Daily 8:15am–1:50pm. Closed 2nd and 4th Sun, and 1st, 3rd, and 5th Mon of each month. Bus: C2.

Palazzo Vecchio ★★ PALACE   The core of Florence's fortresslike town hall was built from 1299 to 1302 to the designs of Arnolfo di Cambio, Gothic master builder. The palace was home to the various Florentine republican governments (and is today to the city government). When Duke Cosimo I and his family moved to the *palazzo* in 1540, they redecorated. Michelozzo's 1453 **courtyard ★** was left architecturally intact but frescoed by Vasari with scenes of Austrian cities, to celebrate the 1565 marriage of Francesco de' Medici and Joanna of Austria.

The grand staircase leads up to the **Sala dei Cinquecento,** named for the 500-man assembly that met here in the pre-Medici days of the Florentine Republic. It's also the site of the greatest fresco cycle that wasn't. Leonardo da Vinci was commissioned in 1503–05 to paint one long wall with a battle scene celebrating a Florentine victory at the 1440 Battle of Anghiari. Always trying new methods and materials, he decided to mix wax into his pigments. Leonardo had finished painting part of the wall, but it wasn't drying fast enough, so he brought in braziers stoked with hot coals to try to hurry the process. As others watched in horror, the wax in the fresco melted under the intense heat and the colors ran down the walls to puddle on the floor. The

Palazzo Vecchio.

search for whatever remains of his work continues, and some hope was provided in 2012 with the discovery of pigments used by Leonardo in a cavity behind the current wall.

Michelangelo never even got past making the preparatory drawings for a fresco he was supposed to paint on the opposite wall before Pope Julius II summoned him to Rome to paint the Sistine Chapel. Eventually, Vasari and assistants worked from 1563 to 1565 to cover the bare walls with subservient frescoes exalting Cosimo I and the military victories of his regime, against Pisa (on the near wall) and Siena (far wall). Opposite the door you enter, is Michelangelo's statue of **"Victory" ★**, carved from 1533 to 1534 for Pope Julius II's tomb but later donated to the Medici.

The first series of rooms on the upper floor is the **Quartiere degli Elementi,** frescoed with allegories and mythological characters, again by Vasari. Crossing the balcony overlooking the Sala dei Cinquecento, you enter the **Apartments of Eleonora of Toledo ★**, decorated for Cosimo's Spanish wife. Her small **private chapel ★★★** is a masterpiece of mid–16th-century painting by Bronzino. Farther on, under the coffered ceiling of the **Sala dei Gigli,** are Domenico Ghirlandaio's fresco of "St. Zenobius Enthroned" with figures from Republican and Imperial Rome; and Donatello's original **"Judith and Holofernes" ★** bronze (1455), one of his last works. In late 2014, the palace's basement was opened up for visitors to view the **Scavi del Teatro Romano ★**, the remnants of Roman Florentia's theater, upon which the medieval *palazzo* was built. Remains of the walls and an intact paved street have been uncovered.

Visitors can also climb the **Torre di Arnolfo ★**, the palace's crenellated tower. If you can bear the small spaces and 418 steps, the views from the top of this medieval skyscraper are sublime. The 95m (312-ft.) Torre is closed during bad weather; the minimum age to climb it is 6, and children ages 17 and under must be accompanied by an adult.

The enclosed passageway that runs along the top of Ponte Vecchio is part of the **Corridoio Vasariano (Vasari Corridor)** ★, a private elevated link between the Palazzo Vecchio and Palazzo Pitti, and now hung with the world's best collection of artists' self-portraits. Duke Cosimo I found the idea of mixing with the hoi polloi on the way to work rather distressing—and there was a credible threat of assassination—and so commissioned Vasari to design his VIP route in 1565. He built it in less than a year. It's often possible to walk the corridor, although closures for restoration work are common. Inquire at the tourist office. Among others, **CAF Tours** (p. 199) offers a short walk along the corridor for 65€. Booking in advance for any corridor tour is essential.

Piazza della Signoria. www.museicivicifiorentini.comune.fi.it. ✆**055-276-8325.** Admission to Palazzo or Torre 10€; admission to both or to Palazzo plus Scavi 14€; admission to everything 18€. Palazzo/Scavi Fri–Wed 9am–7pm (Apr–Sept until 11pm); Thurs 9am–2pm. Torre Fri–Wed 10am–5pm (Apr–Sept 9am–9pm); Thurs 9am–2pm. Bus: C1 or C2.

Ponte Vecchio ★ ARCHITECTURE The oldest and most famous bridge across the Arno, the Ponte Vecchio was built in 1345 by Taddeo Gaddi to replace an earlier version. The overhanging shops have lined the bridge since

at least the 12th century. In the 16th century, it was home to butchers until Duke Ferdinand I moved into the Palazzo Pitti across the river. He couldn't stand the stench, so he evicted the meat cutters and moved in classier gold- and silversmiths and jewelers, who occupy it to this day.

The Ponte Vecchio's fame saved it in 1944 from the Nazis, who had orders to blow up all the bridges before retreating out of Florence as Allied forces advanced. They couldn't bring themselves to reduce this span to rubble—so they blew up the ancient buildings on either end instead to block it off. The Great Arno Flood of 1966 wasn't so discriminating, however, and severely damaged the shops.

The Ponte Vecchio spans the River Arno.

A private night watchman saw the waters rising alarmingly and called many of the goldsmiths at home, who rushed to remove their valuable stock before it was washed away.

Via Por Santa Maria/Via Guicciardini. Bus: C3 or D.

Santa Trínita ★★ CHURCH Beyond Bernardo Buontalenti's late-16th-century **facade** lies a dark church, rebuilt in the 14th century but founded by the Vallombrosans before 1177. The third chapel on the right has what remains of detached frescoes by Spinello Aretino, which were found under Lorenzo Monaco's 1424 "Scenes from the Life of the Virgin" frescoes covering the next chapel along.

In the right transept, Domenico Ghirlandaio frescoed the **Cappella Sassetti** ★ in 1483 with a cycle on the "Life of St. Francis," but true to form he set all the scenes against Florentine backdrops and peopled them with portraits of contemporary notables. His "Francis Receiving the Order from Pope Honorius" (in the lunette) takes place under an arcade on the north side of Piazza della Signoria—you'll recognize the Loggia dei Lanzi in the middle, and on its left, the Palazzo Vecchio. (The Uffizi between them hadn't been built yet.)

The south end of the piazza leads to the **Ponte Santa Trínita** ★★, Florence's most graceful bridge. In 1567, Ammannati built a span here that was set with four 16th-century statues of the seasons in honor of the marriage of Cosimo II. After the Nazis blew up the bridge in 1944, it was rebuilt, and all was set into place—save the head on the statue of Spring, which remained lost until a team dredging the river in 1961 found it by accident. If you want to photograph the Ponte Vecchio, head here at dusk.

Piazza Santa Trínita. (🕾 **055-216-912.** Free admission. Mon–Sat 8am–noon and 4–6pm; Sun 8–10:45am and 4–6pm. Bus: C3, D, 6, or 11.

Around San Lorenzo & the Mercato Centrale

Until a controversial—and *perhaps* temporary—move in 2014, the church of San Lorenzo was practically lost behind the leather stalls and souvenir carts of Florence's vast **San Lorenzo street market** (see "Shopping," p. 201). In

---

Catch an Exhibition at the Strozzi

The Renaissance **Palazzo Strozzi** ★★, Piazza Strozzi (www.palazzostrozzi.org; 🕾 **055-264-5155**) and basement **Strozzina**, are Florence's major spaces for temporary and contemporary art shows, and have been experiencing a 21st-century renaissance of their own under energetic directorship. Hits of recent years have included "Americans in Florence: Sargent and the New World

Impressionists" in 2012 and "Power and Pathos: Hellenistic Bronzes" in 2015. There's always plenty going on, including talks, late-night openings (usually Thursday), events, discounted admission (again, usually Thursday), and even discovery trails aimed at 5- to 9-year-olds. Check the website for the latest exhibition news.

fact, the bustle of commerce characterizes this whole neighborhood, centered on both the tourist market and the nearby **Mercato Centrale** food hall, whose upper floor became a popular informal dining destination when it opened in 2014 (see p. 160).

Cappelle Medicee (Medici Chapels) ★ MUSEUM   When Michelangelo built the New Sacristy between 1520 and 1533 (finished by Vasari in 1556), it was to be a tasteful monument to Lorenzo the Magnificent and his generation of relatively pleasant Medici. When work got underway on the adjacent **Cappella dei Principi (Chapel of the Princes)** in 1604, it was to become one of Italy's most god-awful and arrogant memorials, dedicated to the grand dukes, some of Florence's most decrepit tyrants. The Cappella dei Principi is an exercise in bad taste, a mountain of cut marbles and semiprecious stones—jasper, alabaster, mother-of-pearl, agate, and the like—slathered onto the walls and ceiling with no regard for composition and still less for chromatic unity. The pouring of ducal funds into this monstrosity began in 1604 and lasted until the rarely conscious Gian Gastone de' Medici drank himself to death in 1737, without an heir—but teams kept doggedly at the thing, and they were still finishing the floor in 1962.

Michelangelo's **Sagrestia Nuova (New Sacristy)** ★★, built to jibe with Brunelleschi's Old Sacristy in San Lorenzo proper (see facing page), is much calmer. (An architectural tidbit: The windows in the dome taper as they get near the top to fool you into thinking the dome is higher.) Michelangelo was supposed to produce three tombs here (perhaps four) but ironically got only the two less important ones done. So Lorenzo de' Medici ("the Magnificent")—wise ruler of his city, poet of note, grand patron of the arts, and moneybags behind much of the Renaissance—ended up with a mere inscription of his name next to his brother Giuliano's on a plain marble slab against the entrance wall. Admittedly, they did get one genuine Michelangelo sculpture to decorate their slab, a not-quite-finished **"Madonna and Child"** ★.

On the left wall of the sacristy is Michelangelo's **"Tomb of Lorenzo"** ★, duke of Urbino (and Lorenzo the Magnificent's grandson), whose seated statue symbolizes the contemplative life. Below him on the elongated curves of the tomb stretch "Dawn" (female) and "Dusk" (male), a pair of Michelangelo's most famous sculptures. This pair mirrors the similarly fashioned "Day" (male) and "Night" (female) across the way. One additional point "Dawn" and "Night" brings out is that Michelangelo perhaps hadn't seen too many naked women.

Piazza Madonna degli Aldobrandini (behind San Lorenzo, where Via Faenza and Via del Giglio meet). www.polomuseale.firenze.it. ⓒ **055-238-8602.** Admission 6€ (9€ during temporary exhibition). Daily 8:15am–4:50pm. Closed 1st, 3rd, and 5th Mon, and 2nd and 4th Sun of each month. Bus: C1, C2, or 22.

Palazzo Medici-Riccardi ★ PALACE   Built by Michelozzo in 1444 for the Medici "godfather" Cosimo il Vecchio, this is the prototypical Florentine *palazzo,* on which the more overbearing Strozzi and Pitti palaces were later modeled. It remained the Medici's private home until Cosimo I officially declared his power as duke by moving to the city's traditional civic brain center, the Palazzo Vecchio. A door off the courtyard leads up a staircase to the **Cappella dei Magi,** the oldest chapel to survive from a private Florentine palace; its walls are covered with dense and colorful Benozzo Gozzoli **frescoes ★★** (1459–63) in the International Gothic style. Rich as tapestries, the walls depict an extended "Journey of the Magi" to see the Christ child, who's being adored by Mary in the altarpiece.

Via Cavour 3. www.palazzo-medici.it. $©$ **055-276-0340.** Admission 7€ adults, 4€ ages 6 to 12. Thurs–Tues 8:30am–7pm. Bus: C1.

San Lorenzo ★ CHURCH   A rough brick anti-facade hides what is most likely the oldest church in Florence, founded in A.D. 393. It was later the Medici family's parish church, and Cosimo il Vecchio, whose wise behind-the-scenes rule made him popular with the Florentines, is buried in front of the high altar. The plaque marking the spot is inscribed PATER PATRIE— "Father of the Homeland."

Off the left transept is the **Sagrestia Vecchia (Old Sacristy) ★,** one of Brunelleschi's purest pieces of early Renaissance architecture. The focal sarcophagus contains Cosimo il Vecchio's parents, Giovanni di Bicci de' Medici and his wife, Piccarda Bueri. A side chapel is decorated with an early star map showing the night sky above the city in the 1440s (a scene that also features, precisely, in Brunelleschi's Cappella Pazzi, in Santa Croce; see p. 191).

On the wall of the left aisle is Bronzino's huge fresco of the **"Martyrdom of San Lorenzo" ★** (the poor soul was roasted on a grill in Rome).

Left of the church's main door is an entrance to the cloister and inside it a stairwell leading up to the **Biblioteca Laurenziana (Laurentian Library) ★★.** Michelangelo designed this library in 1524 to house the Medici's manuscript collection, and it stands as one of the most brilliant works of Mannerist architecture.

Piazza San Lorenzo. $©$ **055-214-042.** Admission to church 4.50€; admission to library 3€; combined admission 7€. Church: Mon–Sat 10am–5:30pm; Mar–Oct also Sun 1:30–5:30pm. Laurentian Library: Mon–Sat 9:30am–1:30pm. Bus: C1.

Near Piazza Santa Maria Novella

The two squat obelisks in **Piazza Santa Maria Novella ★,** resting on Giambologna tortoises, once served as the turning posts for chariot races held here from the 16th to the mid–19th century. Once a down-at-the-heels part of the center, the area now is home to some of Florence's priciest lodgings.

Museo Marino Marini & Cappella Rucellai ★ MUSEUM   One of Florence's most unusual museums features the work of sculptor Marino Marini (1901–80). A native of nearby Pistoia, Marini worked mostly in bronze, with "horse and rider" a recurring theme in his semi-abstract work. The wide open spaces, thin crowds, monumental sculptures, and fun themes in Marini's work make this museum a good bet with any kids who are becoming weary of the Renaissance.

But they won't escape it entirely . . . because tagged onto the side of the museum is the **Cappella Rucellai,** a Renaissance chapel housing the **Tempietto ★★.** Returned to public view in 2013 after restoration, this polychrome marble tomb was completed by L. B. Alberti for Giovanni de' Rucellai in 1467. Decorated with symbols of both the Rucellai and Medici families, and frescoed on the inside, the tomb was supposedly based on drawings of the Holy Sepulcher in Jerusalem.

Piazza San Pancrazio. www.museomarinomarini.it. ✆**055-219-432.** Mon and Wed–Sat 10am–5pm. Admission 6€. Bus: C3, 6, or 11.

Museo Novecento ★ MUSEUM Opened in 2014, this museum covers 20th-century Italian art through an array of media. Crowds are often sparse—let's face it, you're in Florence to see the 1400s, not the 1900s—but that's no reflection on the quality of the collection, which spans a century of visual arts in reverse chronological order. Exhibits include works by major names such as de Chirico and Futurist Gino Severini, and closer examinations of Florence's role in fashion and Italy's relationship with European avant-garde art. Our favorite spot, though, is a top-floor **screening room** where a 20-minute movie clip montage plays on a loop. It shows Florence as represented by a century of filmmakers, from Arnaldo Ginna's 1916 "Vita Futurista" to more modern films such as "Room with a View" and "Tea with Mussolini."

Piazza Santa Maria Novella 10. www.museonovecento.it. ✆ **055-286-132.** Admission 8€. Apr–Sept Sat–Wed 9am–7pm, Thurs 9am–2pm, Fri 9am–11pm; Oct–Mar Fri–Wed 9am–6pm, Thurs 9am–2pm. Bus: 6 or 11.

Santa Maria Novella ★★ CHURCH Of all Florence's major churches, the home of the Dominicans is the only one with an original **facade ★★** that matches its era of greatest importance. The lower Romanesque half was started in the 14th century by architect Fra' Jacopo Talenti, who had just finished building the church itself (begun in 1246). Renaissance architect and theorist Leon Battista Alberti finished the facade, adding a classically inspired Renaissance top that not only went seamlessly with the lower half, but also created a Cartesian plane of perfect geometry.

Inside, on the left wall, is **Masaccio's "Trinità" ★★★** (ca. 1425), the first painting ever to use perfect linear mathematical perspective. Florentine citizens and artists flooded in to see the fresco when it was unveiled, many remarking in awe that it seemed to punch a hole back into space, creating a chapel out of a flat wall. Frescoed chapels by Filippino Lippi and others fill the **transept.** The **sanctuary ★** behind the main altar was frescoed after 1485 by Domenico Ghirlandaio with the help of his assistants and apprentices, probably including a young Michelangelo. The left wall is covered with a cycle on the "Life of the Virgin" and the right wall with a "Life of St. John the Baptist." (Read from the bottom upward; there are boards that explain the scenes.) The works are not just biblical stories but also snapshots of the era's fashions and personages, full of portraits of the Tornabuoni family who commissioned them. The **Cappella Gondi** to the left of the high altar contains a crucifix carved by Brunelleschi around 1415.

For many years, the church's frescoed cloisters were treated as a separate site; they have been reunited at last, all now accessible on one admission ticket. (Although, confusingly, there are two separate entrances, through the church's garden and via the tourist office at the rear, on Piazza della Stazione.) The **Chiostro Verde (Green Cloister)** ★★ was partly frescoed between 1431 and 1446 by Paolo Uccello, a Florentine painter who became increasingly obsessed with the mathematics behind perspective. His Old Testament scenes include a "Universal Deluge," which ironically was badly damaged by the Great Arno Flood of 1966. Off the cloister, the **Spanish Chapel** ★ is a complex piece of Dominican propaganda, frescoed in the 1360s by Andrea di Bonaiuto. The **Chiostro dei Morti (Cloister of the Dead)** ★ is one of the oldest parts of the convent, dating to the 1200s, and was another area badly damaged in 1966. Andrea Orcagna, Nardo di Cione, and others decorated its low-slung vaults and chapels. It is especially atmospheric early in the morning, with the cloister empty and birdsong at full volume.

Piazza Santa Maria Novella/Piazza della Stazione 4. www.chiesasantamarianovella.it. ⓒ **055-219-257.** Admission 5€. Mon–Thurs 9am–5:30pm; Fri 11am–5:30pm; Sat 9am–5pm; Sun 1–5pm (July–Sept noon–5pm). Bus: C2, 6, 11, or 22.

Near San Marco & Santissima Annunziata

Cenacolo di Sant'Apollonia ★ ART MUSEUM Painter Andrea del Castagno (1421–57) learned his trade painting the portraits of condemned men in the city's prisons, and it's easy to see the influence of his apprenticeship on the faces of the disciples in his version of **"The Last Supper,"** the first painted in Florence during the Renaissance. The giant fresco, completed around 1447, covers an entire wall at one end of a former convent refectory. It is easy to spot Judas, banished to the other side of the communal table and painted as a satyr with a faux-marble panel in turmoil above his head. Above Castagno's "Last Supper," his "Crucifixion," "Deposition," and "Entombment" complete the sequence of the final days of the Christian story.

Via XXVII Aprile 1. ⓒ **055-238-8607.** Free admission. Daily 8:15am–1:50pm. Closed 1st, 3rd, and 5th Sun and 2nd and 4th Mon of each month. Bus: 1, 6, 11, 14, 17, or 23.

Chiostro dello Scalzo ★ ART MUSEUM/ARCHITECTURE You'll need some luck to catch this place open, but it's well worth the short detour from San Marco if you do. Between 1509 and 1526, Mannerist painter Andrea del Sarto frescoed a cloister belonging to a religious fraternity dedicated to St. John the Baptist, and he's the theme of the unusual monochrome (*grisaille*) fresco cycle. This place is usually blissfully empty, too.

Via Cavour 69. No phone. Free admission. Mon; Thurs; 1st, 3rd, and 5th Sat and 2nd and 4th Sun of each month, 8:15am–1:50pm. Bus: 1 or 7.

Galleria dell'Accademia ★★ ART MUSEUM "David" ★★★—"Il Gigante"—is much larger than most people imagine, looming 4.8m (16 ft.) on top of a 1.8m (6-ft.) pedestal. He hasn't faded with time, either; a 2004 cleaning made the marble gleam as if it were the original unveiling day, 1504. Viewing the statue is a pleasure in the bright and spacious room custom-designed for him after the icon was moved to the Accademia in 1873, following 300 years of pigeons perching on his head in Piazza della Signoria. Replicas now take the abuse there, and at Piazzale Michelangiolo. The spot high on one flank of the Duomo, for which he was originally commissioned, stands empty.

But the Accademia is not only about "David"; you will be delighted to discover he is surrounded by an entire museum stuffed with other notable Renaissance works. Michelangelo's unfinished **"Prisoners"** ★★ statues are a contrast to "David," with the rough forms struggling to free themselves from the raw stone. They also provide a unique glimpse into how Michelangelo worked a piece of stone; he famously said that he tried to free the sculpture within from the block, and you can see this quite clearly. Rooms also showcase paintings by Perugino, Filippino Lippi, Giotto, Giovanni da Milano, Andrea Orcagna, and others.

A back room leads to the Academy part of the Accademia, where you'll see a warehouse of old replica **plaster casts** ★, the work of years of students. It's almost as if a Roman assembly line has just stopped for lunch. The best of them were made by Lorenzo Bartolini in the 1800s.

Via Ricasoli 60. www.polomuseale.firenze.it. © **055-238-8609.** (To reserve tickets, see p. 177.) Admission 8€ (13€ with temporary exhibition). Tues–Sun 8:15am–6:50pm. Bus: C1, 1, 6, 14, 19, 23, 31, or 32.

Museo Archeologico (Archaeological Museum) ★ MUSEUM   If you can force yourselves away from the Renaissance, rewind a millennium or two at one of the most important archaeological collections in central Italy, which has a particular emphasis on the **Etruscan** period. You will need a little patience: The collection is not easy to navigate, and displays are somewhat user-unfriendly. Exhibits also have a habit of moving around, but you will easily find the **"Arezzo Chimera"** ★★, a bronze figure of a mythical lion/goat/serpent dating to the 4th century B.C. It is perhaps the most important bronze sculpture to survive from the Etruscan era, and usually shares a room with the "Arringatore," a life-size bronze of an orator dating to the 1st century, just as Etruscan culture was being subsumed by Ancient Rome. On the top

Seeing "David" Without a Reservation

The wait to get in to see "David" can be an hour or more if you didn't reserve ahead or buy a Firenze Card (p. 170).

Try getting there before the museum opens in the morning or an hour or two before closing time.

floor, hunt down the **"Idolino"** ★, an exquisite and slightly mysterious, lithe bronze. The collection is also strong on Etruscan-era *bucchero* pottery and funerary urns, and Egyptian relics including several sarcophagi displayed in a series of eerie galleries.

One bonus: With other visitors so focused on medieval and Renaissance sights around the city, you may have the place almost to yourself.

Piazza Santissma Annunziata 9b. © **055-23-575**. Admission 4€. Tues–Fri 8:30am–7pm; Sat–Mon 8:30am–2pm (Aug closed Sun). Bus: 6, 19, 31, or 32.

San Marco ★★★ ART MUSEUM We have never understood why this place is not mobbed; perhaps it's a mix of the unusual opening hours and because it showcases, almost exclusively, the work of Fra' Angelico, Dominican monk and Florentine painter in the style known as "International Gothic." This is the most important collection in the world of his altarpieces and painted panels, all residing in the former 13th-century convent the artist/monk once called home. Seeing it all in one place allows you to truly appreciate how his decorative impulses and the sinuous lines of his figures mark his work as standing right on the cusp of the Renaissance.

The most moving and unusual work is his **"Annunciation"** ★★★, but a close second are frescoes illustrating scenes from the life of Jesus painted not on one giant wall, but scene by scene, on the individual walls of small monks' cells that honeycomb the upper floor. The idea was that these scenes, painted by Fra' Angelico and his assistants, would aid in the monks' prayer and contemplation. The final cell on the left corridor belonged to fundamentalist firebrand preacher Savonarola, who briefly incited the populace of the most art-filled city in the world to burn their paintings, illuminated manuscripts, and anything else he felt was a worldly betrayal of Jesus' ideals. (Ultimately, he ran afoul of the pope and was burned at the stake.) You'll see his notebooks, rosary, and what's left of the clothes he wore that day in 1498 in his cell, as well as an anonymous panel painted to show the scene when he was burned at the stake in Piazza della Signoria.

There is much more Fra' Angelico secreted around the cloisters, including a **"Crucifixion"** ★ in the Chapter House. The former Hospice is now a gallery dedicated to Fra' Angelico and his contemporaries; look out especially for his **"Tabernacolo dei Linaioli"** ★★, still glowing after a 2011 restoration, and a seemingly weightless **"Deposition"** ★★.

Piazza San Marco 1. www.polomuseale.firenze.it. © **055-238-8608**. Admission 4€ (7€ with compulsory temporary exhibition). Mon–Fri 8:15am–1:50pm; Sat–Sun 8:15am–4:50pm. Closed 1st, 3rd, and 5th Sun and 2nd and 4th Mon of each month. Bus: C1, 1, 6, 7, 11, 14, 17, 19, 20, 23, or 25.

Santissima Annunziata ★ CHURCH In 1233, seven Florentine nobles had a spiritual crisis, gave away all their possessions, and retired to the forests to contemplate divinity. In 1250, they returned to what were then fields outside the city walls and founded a small oratory, proclaiming they were Servants of Mary, or the Servite Order. The oratory was enlarged by Michelozzo (1444–81) and later redesigned in the baroque style. The main art interest is in the **Chiostro dei Voti (Votive Cloister)**, designed by Michelozzo with Corinthian-capitaled columns and decorated with some of the city's finest Mannerist **frescoes** ★★ (1465–1515). Rosso Fiorentino provided an "Assumption" (1513) and Pontormo a "Visitation" (1515) just to the right of the door. Their master, Andrea del Sarto contributed a "Birth of the Virgin" (1513), in the far right corner, one of his finest works. To the right of the door into the church is a damaged but still fascinating "Coming of the Magi" (1514) by del Sarto, who included a self-portrait at the far right, looking out at us from under his blue hat.

Just to the left as you enter the excessively baroque interior is a huge tabernacle hidden under a mountain of *ex votos* (votive offerings). It was designed by Michelozzo to house a small painting of the "Annunciation." Legend holds that this painting was started by a friar who, vexed that he couldn't paint the Madonna's face as beautifully as it should be, gave up and took a nap. When he awoke, he found an angel had filled in the face for him—and the painting became one of a rare group of images known as "acheiropoieta," miraculous objects reputedly made "without hands."

On **Piazza Santissima Annunziata** ★★ outside, flanked by elegant Brunelleschi porticos, is an equestrian statue of "Grand Duke Ferdinand I" by Giambologna. It was his last work, cast in 1608 after his death by his student Pietro Tacca, who also did the two fountains of fantastic mermonkey-monsters. You can stay right on this spectacular piazza, at one of our favorite Florence hotels, the Loggiato dei Serviti (p. 152).

Piazza Santissima Annunziata. ✆ **055-266-181.** Free admission. Cloister: daily 7:30am–12:30pm and 4–6:30pm. Church: daily 4–5:15pm. Bus: 6, 19, 31, or 32.

Around Piazza Santa Croce

Piazza Santa Croce is pretty much like any grand Florentine square—an open space ringed with souvenir and leather shops and thronged with tourists. Once a year during late June, it's covered with dirt and violent, Renaissance-style soccer is played on it in the tournament known as **Calcio Storico Fiorentino.**

Santa Croce ★★ CHURCH The center of Florence's Franciscan universe was begun in 1294 by Gothic master Arnolfo di Cambio in order to rival the church of Santa Maria Novella being raised by the Dominicans across the city. The church wasn't consecrated until 1442, and even then it remained faceless until the neo-Gothic **facade** was added in 1857. This is an art-stuffed complex that demands 2 hours of your time to see properly.

The Gothic **interior** is vast, and populated with the tombs of rich and famous Florentines. Starting from the main door, immediately on the right is the tomb containing the bones of the most venerated Renaissance master, **Michelangelo Buonarroti,** who died in Rome in 1564 at the ripe age of 89.

The pope wanted him buried in the Eternal City, but Florentines managed to sneak his body back to Florence. Two berths along from Michelangelo's monument is a pompous 19th-century cenotaph to **Dante Alighieri**, one of history's great poets, whose "Divine Comedy" effectively codified the Italian language. (Exiled from Florence, Dante is buried in Ravenna.) Elsewhere, seek out monuments to philosopher **Niccolò Machiavelli, Gioacchino Rossini** (1792–1868), composer of "The Barber of Seville," sculptor **Lorenzo Ghiberti,** and scientist **Galileo Galilei** (1564–1642).

The right transept is richly decorated with frescoes. The **Cappella Castellani** was frescoed with stories of saints' lives by Agnolo Gaddi, with a tabernacle by Mino da Fiesole and a "Crucifix" by Niccolò Gerini. Agnolo's father, Taddeo Gaddi, was one of Giotto's closest followers, and the senior Gaddi is the one who undertook painting the **Cappella Baroncelli** ★ (1328–38) at the transept's end. The frescoes depict scenes from the "Life of the Virgin," and include an "Annunciation to the Shepherds," the first night scene in Italian fresco.

Giotto himself frescoed the two chapels to the right of the high altar. The frescoes were whitewashed over during the 17th century but uncovered from 1841 to 1852 and inexpertly restored. The **Cappella Peruzzi** ★, on the right, is a late work and not in the best shape. The many references to antiquity in the styling and architecture of the frescoes reflect Giotto's trip to Rome and its ruins. Even more famous (it's even included in a scene in "A Room with a View,") is the **Cappella Bardi** ★★. Key panels here include the "Trial by Fire Before the Sultan of Egypt" on the right wall (notice the telling subtlety in the expressions and poses of the figures). In one of Giotto's most well-known works, the "Death of St. Francis," monks weep and wail with convincing pathos.

Outside in the cloister is the **Cappella Pazzi** ★, one of Filippo Brunelleschi's architectural masterpieces, faithfully finished after his death in 1446. Giuliano da Maiano probably designed the porch that now precedes the chapel, set with glazed terra cottas by Luca della Robbia. (It was restored in 2015 thanks to an international Kickstarter project run by the church.) The rectangular chapel is one of Brunelleschi's signature pieces, decorated with his trademark *pietra serena* gray stone. It is the defining example of (and model for) early Renaissance architecture. Curiously, the ceiling of the smaller dome depicts the night sky at the same moment as the Old Sacristy in San Lorenzo (p. 185).

From the cloister, you can enter the **Museo dell'Opera** to see the Cimabue **"Crucifix"** ★ that was almost destroyed by the Arno Flood of 1966, and that became an international symbol of the ruination wreaked by the river that November day.

Piazza Santa Croce. www.santacroceopera.it. ☎ **055-246-6105.** Admission 6€ adults, 4€ ages 11–17. Mon–Sat 9:30am–5pm; Sun 2–5pm. Bus: C1, C2, or C3.

The Oltrarno, San Niccolò & San Frediano

Giardino Bardini (Bardini Garden) ★ PARK/GARDEN   Hemmed in to the north by the city's medieval wall, the handsome Bardini Garden is less famous—and so less hectic—than its neighbor down the hill, the Boboli (see below). From its loftier perch over the Oltrarno, it beats the Boboli hands down for views and new angles on the city. Check out the side view of Santa Croce, with the copper dome of the synagogue in the background; see how the church's 19th-century facade was bolted onto a building dating to the 1200s.

Costa San Giorgio 2. www.bardinipeyron.it. © **055-263-8599.** Admission on combined ticket with Boboli; see below. Same hours as Boboli; see below. Bus: C3 or D.

Giardino di Boboli (Boboli Garden) ★★ PARK/GARDEN   The statue-filled park behind the Pitti Palace is one of the earliest and finest Renaissance gardens, laid out mostly between 1549 and 1656 with box hedges in geometric patterns, groves of ilex (holm oak), dozens of statues, and rows of cypress trees. Just above the entrance through the courtyard of the Palazzo Pitti is an oblong **amphitheater** modeled on Roman circuses, with a **granite basin** from Rome's Baths of Caracalla and an **Egyptian obelisk** of Ramses II. In 1589, this was the setting for the reception of Ferdinando de' Medici's marriage to Christine of Lorraine. For the occasion, the Medici commissioned entertainment from Jacopo Peri and Ottavio Rinuccini, who decided to set a

classical story entirely to music and called it "Dafne"— the world's first opera. (Later, they wrote a follow-up hit "Erudice," performed here in 1600; it's the first opera whose score has survived.)

At the south end of the park is the **Isolotto** ★, a dreamy island marooned in a pond full of huge goldfish, with Giambologna's "L'Oceano" sculptural composition at its center. At the north end, down around the end of the Pitti Palace, are some fake caverns filled with statuary, attempting to invoke a classical sacred grotto. The most famous, the **Grotta Grande,** was designed by Giorgio Vasari, Bartolomeo Ammannati, and Bernardo Buontalenti between 1557 and

Boboli Gardens.

1593, dripping with phony stalactites and set with replicas of Michelangelo's unfinished "Prisoners" statues. You can usually get inside on the hour (but not every hour, and not at all on Mon) for 15 minutes.

Entrance via Palazzo Pitti, Piazza de' Pitti. www.polomuseale.firenze.it. (C) **055-238-8791.** Admission (includes Giardino Bardini, Museo degli Argenti, and Museo del Costume) 7€ (10€ during compulsory temporary exhibition). Nov–Feb daily 8:15am–4:30pm; Mar daily 8:15am–5:30pm; Apr–May and Sept–Oct daily 8:15am–6:30pm; June–Aug daily 8:15am–7:30pm. Closed 1st and last Mon of month. Cumulative ticket for everything in Palazzo Pitti and Giardino di Boboli, valid 3 days, 11.50€ (not available during temporary exhibition). Bus: C3, D, 11, 36, or 37.

Museo Zoologia "La Specola" ★ MUSEUM   Several wax anatomical models are one reason this museum may be the only one in Florence where kids eagerly pull their parents from room to room. Vast, impressive, but spooky collections of pickled creepy-crawlies and stuffed specimens from every branch of the animal kingdom kick things off. These transition into rooms filled with lifelike human bodies suffering from dismemberments, flayings, and eviscerations—all in the name of science. These wax models served as anatomical illustrations for medical students studying at this scientific institute from the 1770s. The grisly wax plague dioramas in the final room were created in the early 1700s to satisfy the lurid tastes of Cosimo III.

Via Romana 17. www.msn.unifi.it. (C) **055-275-5100.** Admission 6€ adults, 3€ children 6–14 and seniors 65 and over. Jun–Sept Tues–Sun 10:30am–5:30pm; Oct–May Tues–Sun 9:30am–4:30pm. Bus: D, 11, 36, or 37.

Palazzo Pitti (Pitti Palace) ★★ MUSEUM/PALACE   Although built by and named after a rival of the Medici—merchant Luca Pitti—in the 1450s, this gigantic *palazzo* soon fell into Medici hands. It was the Medici family's principal home from the 1540s, and continued to house Florence's rulers until 1919. The Pitti contains five museums, including one of the world's best collections of canvases by Raphael. Out back are elegant Renaissance gardens, the **Boboli** (see above).

Palazzo Pitti.

In the art-crammed rooms of the Pitti's **Galleria Palatina** ★★, paintings are displayed like cars in a parking garage, stacked on walls above each other in the "Enlightenment" method of exhibition. Rooms are alternately dimly lit or garishly bright; this is how many of the world's great art treasures were seen and enjoyed by their original commissioners.

You will find important historical treasures amid the Palatina's vast and haphazard collection. Some of the best efforts of Titian, Raphael, and Rubens line the walls. Botticelli and Filippo Lippi's **"Madonna and Child"** ★ (1452) are the key works in the **Sala di Prometeo (Prometheus Room)**. Two giant versions of the "Assumption of the Virgin," both by Mannerist painter Andrea del Sarto, dominate the **Sala dell'Iliade (Iliad Room)**. Here you will also find another biblical woman painted by Artemisia Gentileschi, "Judith." The **Sala di Saturno (Saturn Room)** ★ is stuffed with Raphaels and a giant panel by his teacher, Perugino; next door in the **Sala di Giove (Jupiter Room)** you'll find his sublime, naturalistic portrait of **"La Velata"** ★★, as well as **"The Ages of Man"** ★. The painting's current attribution is awarded to Venetian Giorgione, though that has been disputed.

At the **Appartamenti Reali (Royal Apartments)** you get a feeling for the conspicuous consumption of the Medici Grand Dukes and their Austrian and Belgian Lorraine successors—and see some notable paintings in their original, ostentatious setting. The rooms earned their "Royal" label because Italy's first king lived here for several years during Italy's 19th-century unification process—when Florence was Italy's second capital, after Turin—until Rome was finally conquered and the court moved there. Much of the stucco, fabrics, furnishings, and general decoration is in thunderously poor taste, but you should look out for Caravaggio's subtle canvas **"Knight of Malta"** ★.

The Pitti's "modern" gallery, the **Galleria d'Arte Moderna** ★, has a fairly good collection, this time of 19th-century Italian paintings with a focus on Romanticism, Neoclassical works, and the **Macchiaioli**, a school of Italian painters who worked in an "impressionistic style" before the French Impressionists. If you have limited time, make right for the major works of the latter, in Sala 18 through 20, which displays the Maremma landscapes of **Giovanni Fattori** ★ (1825–1908).

The Pitti's pair of lesser museums—the **Galleria del Costume** (Costume Gallery) and **Museo degli Argenti** (Museum of Silverware)—combine to show that wealth and taste do not always go hand in hand. One thing you will notice in the Costume Gallery is how much smaller the locals were a few centuries ago.

Piazza de' Pitti 1. Galleria Palatina, Apartamenti Reali, and Galleria d'Arte Moderna: ✆ **055-238-8614;** to reserve tickets, see p. 177. Admission 8.50€ (13€ during compulsory temporary exhibition). Tues–Sun 8:15am–6:50pm. Museo degli Argenti and Galleria del Costume: ✆ **055-238-8709.** Admission (includes Giardino di Boboli and Giardino Bardini) 7€ (10€ during compulsory temporary exhibition). Same hours as Giardino di Boboli; see p. 192. Cumulative ticket for everything, including Giardino di Boboli (see p. 192), valid 3 days, 11.50€ (not available during temporary exhibition). Bus: D, 11, 36, or 37.

Vista of Florence from Piazzale Michelangiolo.

Piazzale Michelangiolo ★ SQUARE This panoramic piazza is a required stop for every tour bus. The balustraded terrace was laid out in 1869 to give a sweeping **vista** ★★ of the entire city, spread out in the valley below and backed by the green hills of Fiesole beyond. The bronze replica of "David" here points right at his original home, outside the Palazzo Vecchio. Viale Michelangelo. Bus: 12 or 13.

San Miniato al Monte ★★ CHURCH High atop a hill, its gleaming white-and-green facade visible from the city below, San Miniato is one of the few ancient churches of Florence to survive the centuries virtually intact. The current building began to take shape in 1013, under the auspices of the powerful Arte di Calimala guild, whose symbol, a bronze eagle clutching a bale of wool, perches on the **facade** ★★. This Romanesque facade is a particularly gorgeous bit of white Carrara and green Prato marble inlay. Above the central window is a 13th-century mosaic of "Christ Between the Madonna and St. Miniato" (a theme repeated in the apse).

Below the choir is an 11th-century **crypt** with remains of frescoes by Taddeo Gaddi. Off to the right of the raised choir is the **sacristy,** which Spinello Aretino covered in 1387 with cartoonish yet elaborate frescoes depicting the **"Life of St. Benedict"** ★. Off the left aisle of the nave is the 15th-century **Cappella del Cardinale del Portogallo** ★★, a collaborative effort by Renaissance artists built to honor young Portuguese humanist Cardinal Jacopo di Lusitania, who was sent to study in Perugia but died an untimely death at age 25 in Florence.

Note: It's worth timing your visit to come here when the Benedictine monks are celebrating mass in Gregorian chant (usually 5:30pm).

Around the back of the church is San Miniato's **monumental cemetery** ★, one enormous "city of the dead," whose streets are lined with tombs and mausoleums built in elaborate pastiches of every generation of Florentine architecture, with a marked preference for the Gothic and the Romanesque. It's a peaceful spot, soundtracked only by birdsong and the occasional tolling of church bells.

Via Monte alle Croci/Viale Galileo Galilei (behind Piazzale Michelangiolo). ℂ **055-234-2731**. Free admission. Daily 9:30am–1pm and 3pm–dusk (closed some Sun afternoons and often open through *riposo* in summer). Bus: 12 or 13.

Santa Felicità ★ CHURCH   Greek sailors who lived in this neighborhood in the 2nd century brought Christianity to Florence, and this little church was probably the second to be established in the city, the first edition of it rising in the late 4th century. The current version was built in the 1730s. The star works are in the first chapel on the right, the Brunelleschi-designed **Cappella Barbadori–Capponi,** with paintings by Mannerist master Pontormo (1525–27). His **"Deposition" ★★** and frescoed "Annunciation" are rife with his garish color palette of oranges, pinks, golds, lime greens, and sky blues, and exhibit his trademark surreal sense of figure.

Piazza Santa Felicità (on left off Via Guicciardini across Ponte Vecchio). ℂ **055-213-018**. Free admission (take 1€ for lights). Daily 9:30am–12:30pm and 3:30–5:30pm. Bus: C3 or D.

Santa Maria del Carmine ★★★ CHURCH   Following a 1771 fire that destroyed everything but the transept chapels and sacristy, this Carmelite church was almost entirely reconstructed in high baroque style. To see the **Cappella Brancacci ★★★** in the right transept, you have to enter through the cloisters (doorway to the right of the facade) and pay admission. The frescoes here were commissioned by an enemy of the Medici, Felice Brancacci, who in 1424 hired Masolino and his student Masaccio to decorate it with a cycle on the "Life of St. Peter." Masolino probably worked out the cycle's scheme and painted a few scenes along with his pupil before taking off for 3 years to serve as court painter in Budapest, Hungary, while Masaccio kept painting, quietly creating the early Renaissance's greatest frescoes. Masaccio eventually left for Rome in 1428, where he died at age 27. The cycle was completed between 1480 and 1485 by Filippino Lippi.

Masolino was responsible for the "St. Peter Preaching," the upper panel to the left of the altar, and the two top scenes on the right wall, which shows his fastidious, decorative style in a long panel of "St. Peter Healing the Cripple" and "Raising Tabitha," and his "Adam and Eve." Contrast this first man and woman, about to take the bait offered by the snake, with the **"Expulsion from the Garden" ★★★,** opposite it, painted by Masaccio. Masolino's figures are highly posed, expressionless models. Masaccio's Adam and Eve, on the other hand, burst with intense emotion. The top scene on the left wall, the **"Tribute Money" ★★,** is also by Masaccio, and it showcases another of his innovations, linear perspective. The two scenes to the right of the altar are Masaccio's as well: The **"Baptism of the Neophytes" ★★** is among his masterpieces.

Piazza del Carmine 14. www.museicivicifiorentini.comune.fi.it/brancacci. ℭ **055-238-2195.** Free admission to church; Cappella Brancacci 6€. Mon and Wed–Sat 10am–5pm; Sun 1–5pm. Bus: D.

Santo Spirito ★ CHURCH   One of Filippo Brunelleschi's masterpieces of architecture, this 15th-century church doesn't look like much from the outside (no true facade was ever built). But the **interior** ★ is a marvelous High Renaissance space; an expansive landscape of proportion and mathematics worked out in classic Brunelleschi style, with coffered ceiling, lean columns topped with Corinthian capitals, and the stacked perspective of arched arcading. Good late-Renaissance and baroque paintings are scattered throughout, but the best stuff lies in the transepts, especially the **Cappella Nerli** ★, with a panel by Filippino Lippi (right transept). The church's extravagant **baroque altar** has a ciborium inlaid in *pietre dure* around 1607—and frankly, looks a bit silly against the restrained elegance of Brunelleschi's architecture. The sacristy displays a wooden "Crucifix" that has, somewhat controversially, been attributed to Michelangelo. See it (and judge) for yourself.

Piazza Santo Spirito ★ outside is one of the focal points of the Oltrarno, shaded by trees and lined with trendy cafes that see some bar action in the evenings. There are often a few farmers selling their fruit and vegetables on the piazza.

Piazza Santo Spirito. ℭ **055-210-030.** Free admission. Mon–Tues and Thurs–Sat 10am–12:30pm and 4–5:30pm; Sun 4–5:30pm. Bus: C3, D, 11, 36, or 37.

FIESOLE

Although it's only a short city bus ride away from Florence (about 9km or 5½ miles), **Fiesole** ★ is very proud of its status as an independent municipality. In fact, this village high above Florence predates the big city in the valley by centuries.

Etruscans from Arezzo probably founded a town here in the 6th century B.C. on the site of a Bronze Age settlement. *Faesulae* became the most important Etruscan center in the region. Although it eventually became a Roman town—it was first conquered in 90 B.C.—building a theater and adopting Roman customs, it always retained a bit of Etruscan otherness. Following the barbarian invasions, it became part of Florence's administrative district in the 9th century yet continued to struggle for self-government. Medieval Florence settled things in 1125 by attacking and razing the entire settlement, save the cathedral and bishop's palace.

An oasis of cultivated greenery still separates Florence from Fiesole. Even so close to its large neighbor, Fiesole endures as a Tuscan small town, mostly removed from Florence at its feet and hence a perfect escape from summertime crowds. It stays relatively cool all summer long, and while you sit at a cafe on Piazza Mino, sipping an iced cappuccino, the lines at the Uffizi and pedestrian traffic around the Duomo seem very distant indeed.

To get to Fiesole, take bus no. 7 from Florence. It departs from Via La Pira, down the right flank of San Marco. A scenic 25-minute ride through the greenery above Florence takes you to Fiesole's main square, Piazza Mino.

The **tourist office** is at Via Portigiani 3 (www.fiesoleforyou.it; ℂ **055-596-1311**). From March through October it's open daily (Apr–Sept 10am–6:30pm, Mar and Oct 10am–5:30pm); from November through February, it's open Wednesday to Monday from 10am to 1:30pm.

Fiesole's sights all use a single admission ticket, costing 12€ adults, 8€ students age 7 to 25 and seniors 65 and over; a family ticket costs 24€. Prices are 2€ per person lower from Monday to Thursday, when the missable Museo Bandini is closed. All sites are open the same hours as the tourist office, which doubles as the ticket office. For more information, visit **www.museidifiesole.it** or call ℂ **055-596-1293**.

San Francesco ★ MONASTERY/MUSEUM   The ancient high-point of the Etruscan and Roman Fiesole is now occupied by a tiny church and monastery. The 14th-century church has been largely overhauled, but at the end of a small nave hung with devotional works—Piero di Cosimo and Cenni di Francesco are both represented—is a fine "Crucifixion and Saints" altarpiece by Neri di Bicci. Off the cloisters is a quirky little **Ethnographic Museum,** stuffed with objects picked up by Franciscan missionaries, including an Egyptian mummy and Chinese jade and ceramics. Entrance to the church's painted, vaulted **crypt** is through the museum.

To reach San Francesco, you will climb a sharp hill: Pause close to the top where a little balcony provides perhaps the best **view** ★★★ of Florence and the wine hills of the Chianti beyond.

Via San Francesco (off Piazza Mino). ℂ **055-59-175.** Free admission. Daily 9am–noon and 3–5pm (7pm in summer). Bus: 7.

Teatro Romano (Roman Theater) ★ RUINS   Fiesole's archaeological area is romantically overgrown with grasses, amid which sit sections of column, broken friezes, and other remnants of the ancient world. It is also dramatically sited, terraced into a hill with views over the olive groves and forests north of Florence.

Beyond the **Roman Theater** ★ (which seated 1,500 in its day) to the right, recognizable by its three rebuilt arches, are the remains of the 1st-century A.D. **baths.** In Roman times, the baths were a place where all social classes mixed, but the sexes were kept strictly apart. Near the arches, a cement balcony over the far edge of the archaeological park gives you a good look at the best remaining stretch of the 4th-century B.C. **Etruscan town walls.** At the other end of the park from the baths are the floor and steps of a 1st-century B.C. **Roman Temple** built on top of a 4th-century B.C. Etruscan one dedicated to

Minerva. To the left are oblong **Lombard tombs** from the 7th century A.D., when this part of Fiesole was a necropolis.

Via Portigiani 1. ℂ **055-596-1293.** For admission and hours, see "Fiesole Essentials," above. Bus: 7.

ORGANIZED TOURS

To really get under the surface of the city, book an insightful culture tour with **Context Travel ★★** (www.contexttravel.com; ℂ **800/691-6036** in the U.S., or 06-96727371 in Italy). Led by academics and other experts in their field on a variety of themes—from the gastronomic to the archaeological and artistic—the tours are limited to six people and cost around 70€ per person. The quality of Context's walks are unmatched, and well worth the above-average cost.

Offerings from **CAF Tours** (www.caftours.com; ℂ **055-283-200**) include the chance to walk on the cathedral's roof terraces (1½ hr.; 50€), as well as several guided walks and cooking classes costing from 25€ to more than 100€. **ArtViva** (www.italy.artviva.com; ℂ **055-264-5033**) has a huge array of walking tours and museum guides starting at 25€, including the distinctly dark "Sex, Drugs, and the Renaissance" walking tour (2¼ hr.; 39€). **I Just Drive** (www.ijustdrive.us; ℂ **055-093-5928**) offers fully equipped cars (Wi-Fi, iPads, complimentary bottle of Prosecco, cold drinks) plus English-speaking drivers for various themed visits. For example, you can ride in a Bentley limousine up to San Miniato al Monte on the dusk "Gregorian Chant Tour" (1½ hr.), to hear the monks' evening prayers (2 hr.; 99€).

Viator.com and **GetYourGuide.com** also have a vast range of locally organized tours and activities, reviewed by travelers. *Note:* Don't be tempted to book airport or rail station transfers via the tour companies: It is *much* cheaper to call a cab and pay the very reasonable fixed local rates; see "By Taxi" (p. 144).

ESPECIALLY FOR KIDS

You have to put in a bit of work to reach some of Florence's best views—and the climbs, up claustrophobic, medieval staircases, are a favorite with many kids. The dome of **Santa Maria del Fiore** (p. 171), the **Palazzo Vecchio**'s (p. 180) Torre di Arnolfo, and the **Campanile di Giotto** (p. 167) are perfect for any youngster with a head for heights.

Probably the best kids' activities with an educational component are run by the **Museo dei Ragazzi ★★** (www.musefirenze.it; ℂ **055-276-8224**), not a standalone museum but a program that offers child's-eye tours in English around the Palazzo Vecchio, led by guides in period costumes. Lively activities focus on life at the ducal court—pitched at children ages 5 to 10 or 10-plus ("At Court with Donna Isabella")—or take kids into the workshop to learn fresco or tempera painting. Book online, e-mail to inquire on **info@muse.comune.fi.it**, or stop by the desk next to the Palazzo Vecchio ticket window.

Santa Maria del Fiore.

When your youngsters simply need a crowd-free timeout space, head for the children's section of the **Biblioteca delle Oblate,** Via dell'Oriuolo 26 (http://www.biblioteche. comune.fi.it/biblioteca_delle_ oblate; © **055-261-6512**). There's a library with books for little ones (including in English), as well as space to spread out, color, draw, and generally chill out. It's free and open 9am to 6:45pm, except for Monday morning and all day Sunday (and closed for 2 weeks in mid-Aug). The Oblate's **cafe** (p. 204) is an excellent place for anyone to kick back and relax.

There's only one game in town when it comes to spectator sports: *calcio.* To Italians, soccer/football is something akin to a second religion, and an afternoon at the stadium can offer you more insight into local culture than a lifetime in the Uffizi. The Florence team, **Fiorentina** (nicknamed *i viola,* "the purples") plays in Italy's top league, *Serie A.* You can usually catch them alternate Sundays from September through May at the Stadio Comunale Artemio Franchi, Via Manfredo Fanti 4 (www.violachannel.tv). Book tickets online or head for an official ticket office on arrival (take photo ID): There is a sales desk on the Mercato Centrale's upper floor (p. 160) and at Via dei Sette Santi 28R (at Via Giovanni Dupré), open from 9:30am on match days. With kids, get seats in a Tribuna (stand) rather than the Curva, where the fanatical fans sit. To reach the stadium from the center, take bus no. 10 or 20 from San Marco (10–15 min.). **Alè Viola,** Via del Corso 58R (© **055-295-306**), will kit you out in home colors before the match.

You can skip the subtitles at an original 1920s cinema right in the center that shows daily movies in their original language: **Odeon Firenze** ★, Piazza Strozzi (www.odeonfirenze.com; © **055-214-068**). The labyrinthine and well-stocked traditional toy store **Dreoni** is at Via Cavour 31R (www.dreoni giocattoli.eu; © **055-216-611**). **Cycling** is a pleasure in the riverside Parco delle Cascine; see p. 144 for bike rental advice. And remember: You are in the **gelato** capital of the world. At least two scoops per day is the minimum recommended dose; see p. 164.

SHOPPING

After Milan, Florence is **Italy's top shopping city**—beating even the capital, Rome. Here's what to buy: leather, fashion, shoes, marbleized paper, hand-embroidered linens, artisan and craft items including ceramics, Tuscan wines, handmade jewelry, *pietre dure* (known also as "Florentine mosaic," inlaid semiprecious stones), and antiques.

General Florentine **shopping hours** are Monday through Saturday from 9:30am to noon or 1pm and 3 or 3:30 to 7:30pm, although increasingly, many shops are staying open on Sunday and through that midafternoon *riposo* or nap, especially the larger stores and those around tourist sights. Some close Monday mornings instead.

The Top Shopping Streets & Areas

AROUND SANTA TRÍNITA   The cream of the crop of Florentine shopping lines both sides of elegant **Via de' Tornabuoni,** with an extension along **Via della Vigna Nuova** and other surrounding streets. Here you'll find big Florentine fashion names like **Gucci** ★ (at no. 73R; www.gucci.com; ℂ 055-264-011), **Pucci** ★ (at no. 22R; www.emiliopucci.com; ℂ 055-265-8082), and **Ferragamo** ★ (at no. 4R; www.ferragamo.com; ℂ 055-292-123) ensconced in old palaces or minimalist boutiques. Stricter traffic controls have made shopping Via de' Tornabuoni a more sedate experience, though somewhat at the expense of surrounding streets.

AROUND VIA ROMA & VIA DEI CALZAIUOLI   These are some of Florence's busiest streets, packed with storefronts offering mainstream shopping. It is here you will find the city's major department stores, **Coin,** Via dei Calzaiuoli 56R (www.coin.it; ℂ 055-280-531), and **La Rinascente,** Piazza della Repubblica (www.rinascente.it; ℂ 055-219-113) alongside quality clothing chains such as Geox and Zara. **La Feltrinelli RED,** Piazza delle Repubblica 26 (www.lafeltrinelli.it, ℂ 199-151-173), is the center's best bookstore and carries a selection of English titles. A 3-floor branch of upscale food-market minichain **Eataly,** Via de' Martelli 22 (www.eataly.net; ℂ 055-015-3601), is just north of the Baptistery.

AROUND SANTA CROCE   The eastern part of the center has seen a flourishing of one-off stores, with an emphasis on young, independent fashions. **Borgo degli Albizi** and its tributary streets are worth roaming. This is also where you will find the daily flea market, the **Mercato delle Pulci** (see below).

Florence's Best Markets

Mercato Centrale ★★   The center's main food market stocks the usual fresh produce, but you can also browse for (and taste) cheeses, salamis and cured hams, Tuscan wines, takeout food, and more. It is picnic-packing heaven. It runs Monday to Saturday 7am until 2pm (until 5pm Sat for most of the year). Upstairs is street-food nirvana, all day, every day: See p. 160. Btw. Piazza del Mercato Centrale and Via dell'Ariento. No phone. Bus: C1.

Mercato delle Pulci ★★ The little piazza behind the Loggia del Pesce—originally built under Cosimo I for the city's fishmongers—hosts a daily flea market. Rifle through little shanty-style shops in search of costume jewelry, Tiffany lamps, secondhand dolls and books, vintage postcards, weird objects, and other one-off ephemera. The market runs daily, although not every unit is open every day. Piazza de' Ciompi. No phone. Bus: C1, C2, or C3.

Mercato di San Lorenzo ★ The city's tourist street market is a fun place to pick up T-shirts, marbleized paper, notebooks, or a city souvenir. Leather wallets, purses, bags, and jackets are another popular purchase—be sure to assess the workmanship, and haggle shamelessly. The market runs daily. Watch out for pickpockets. In 2014, it was controversially ejected from part of its traditional home, in Piazza San Lorenzo, and now spreads around Piazza del Mercato Centrale; whether it will ever move back is as yet undecided. Via dell'Ariento and Via Rosina. No phone. Bus: C1.

Mercato di Sant'Ambrogio ★ A proper slice of Florentine life, six mornings a week (it's closed on Sun). The piazza outside has fruit, vegetables, costume jewelry, preserves, and end-of-line clothing. Go inside the market building for meat, olive oil, or a budget lunch at "Da Rocco." Piazza Ghiberti. No phone. Bus: C2 or C3.

Crafts & Artisanal Goods

Florence has a longstanding reputation for its craftsmanship. Although storefront display windows along heavily touristed streets are often stuffed with cheap foreign imports and mass-produced goods, you can still find genuine handmade, top-quality items if you search around. To get a better understanding of Florence's artisans, including a visit to a workshop, **Context Travel** (p. 199) runs a guided walk around the Oltrarno, Florence's traditional craft area. This "Made in Florence" walk costs 80€ and lasts 3 hours.

Madova ★ For almost a century, this has been the best city retailer for handmade leather gloves lined with silk, cashmere, or lambs' wool. Expect to pay between 40€ and 60€ for a pair. You may not expect it this close to the Ponte Vecchio, but Madova is the real deal. Closed Sunday. Via Guicciardini 1R. www.madova.com. ☎ **055-239-6526.** Bus: C3 or D.

Masks of Agostino Dessi ★ This little shop is stuffed floor to ceiling with handmade Venetian Carnevale and *commedia dell'arte* masks, made from papier-mâché, leather, and ceramics, and then hand-finished expertly. Via Faenza 72R. ☎ **055-287-370.** Bus: C1 or 4.

Officina Profumo-Farmaceutica di Santa Maria Novella ★★★ A shrine to scents and skincare, and also Florence's most historic herbal pharmacy with roots in the 17th century, when it was founded by Dominicans based in the adjacent convent of Santa Maria Novella. It's not inexpensive, but the perfumes, cosmetics, moisturizers, and other products are made from the finest natural ingredients and packaged exquisitely. Via della Scala 16. www.smnovella.it. ☎ **055-216-276.** Bus: C2.

Parione ★ This traditional Florentine stationer close to the Duomo stocks notebooks, marbleized paper, fine pens, and handmade wooden music boxes. Via dello Studio 11R. www.parione.it. ℭ **055-215-030**. Bus: C1 or C2.

Richard Ginori ★★ Opened in 2014, this is the city-center home for a reborn icon of quality painted porcelain. Nothing is cheap, but Ginori is a piece of Florence history. Via dei Rondinelli 17R. ℭ **055-265-4573**.

Scuola del Cuoio ★★ Florence's leading leather school is also open house for visitors. You can watch trainee artisans at work (Mon–Fri) then visit the small shop to buy the best soft leather. Portable items like wallets and bags are a good purchase. Closed Sundays in off-season. Via San Giuseppe 5R (or enter through Santa Croce, via right transept). www.scuoladelcuoio.com. ℭ **055-244-534**. Bus: C3.

ENTERTAINMENT & NIGHTLIFE

Florence has excellent, mostly free, listings publications. At the tourist offices, pick up the free monthly **"Informacittà"** (www.informacitta.net), which is strong on theater, concerts, and other arts events, as well as markets. Younger and hipper **"Zero"** (http://firenze.zero.eu) is hot on the latest eating, drinking, and nightlife. **"Firenze Spettacolo,"** a 2€ Italian-language monthly sold at newsstands, is the most detailed and up-to-date listing of nightlife, arts, and entertainment. English-language magazine "The Florentine" publishes a weekly events and listings download, at **www.theflr.net/weekly**.

If you just want to wander and see what grabs you, you will find plenty of tourist-oriented action in bars around the city's main squares. For something a little livelier—with a more local focus—check out **Borgo San Frediano, Piazza Santo Spirito,** or the northern end of **Via de' Macci,** close to where it meets Via Pietrapiana. **Via de' Benci** is usually buzzing around *aperitivo* time, and is popular with an expat crowd. **Via de' Renai** and the bars of San Niccolò around the **Porta San Miniato** are often lively too, with a mixed crowd of tourists and locals.

Performing Arts & Live Music

Florence does not have the musical cachet or grand opera houses of Milan, Venice, Naples, or Rome, but there are two symphony orchestras and a fine music school in Fiesole, as well as great expectations for its new opera house (see below). The city's theaters are respectable, and most major touring companies stop in town. Get tickets to all cultural and musical events online; they will e-mail collection instructions, or buy in person at **Box Office,** Via delle Carceri 1 (www.boxofficetoscana.it; ℭ **055-210-804**).

Many performances staged in concert halls and other spaces are sponsored by the **Amici della Musica** (www.amicimusica.fi.it; ℭ **055-607-440**), so check their website to see what is scheduled while you are in town.

Libreria-Café La Cité ★★   A relaxed cafe/bookshop by day, after dark this place becomes a bar and small-scale live music venue. The lineup is eclectic, often offbeat or world music, one night forrò or swing, the next Italian folk or chanteuse. Borgo San Frediano 20. www.lacitelibreria.info. ℂ **055-210-387.** Bus: C3, D, 6, 11, 36, or 37.

Opera di Firenze ★★   This vast new concert hall and arts complex seats up to 1,800 in daring modernist surroundings. Much delayed, the venue co-hosted its first Maggio Musicale Fiorentino in 2014. Piazzale Vittorio Gui. www.operadifirenze.it. ℂ **055-277-9350.** Tickets 10€–100€. Tram: T1.

St. Mark's ★   Operatic duets and full-scale operas in costume are the lure here. The program sticks to crowd pleasers like "Carmen," "La Traviata," and "La Bohème," and runs most nights of the week all year. Via Maggio 18. www.concertoclassico.info. ℂ **340-811-9192.** Tickets 20€–35€. Bus: D, 11, 36, or 37.

Teatro Verdi ★   Touring shows, "serious" popular music, one-off revues, classical music and dance, and the Orchestra della Toscana occupy the stage at Florence's leading theater. Via Ghibellina 97. www.teatroverdionline.it. ℂ **055-212-320.** Closed 2nd half of July and all Aug. Bus: C1, C2, or C3.

Volume ★   By day, it's a laid-back cafe and arts space selling coffee, books, and crepes. By night, a buzzing bar with regular acoustic sets. Piazza Santo Spirito 5R. www.volumefirenze.com. ℂ **055-238-1460.** Bus: D, 11, 36, or 37.

Cafes

Florence no longer has a glitterati or intellectuals' cafe scene, and when it did—from the late-19th-century Italian Risorgimento era through *la dolce vita* of the 1950s—it was basically copying the idea from Paris. Although they're often overpriced tourist spots today—especially around **Piazza della Repubblica**—Florence's high-toned cafes are fine if you want pastries served to you while you sit and people-watch.

Caffetteria delle Oblate ★   A relaxing terrace popular with local families and students, and well away from the tourist crush (and prices) on the streets below. As a bonus, it has unique view of Brunelleschi's dome. Also serves light lunch and *aperitivo*. Top floor of Biblioteca delle Oblate, Via del Oriuolo 26. www.lospaziochesperavi.it. ℂ **055-263-9685.** Bus: C1 or C2.

Le Terrazze ★   The prices, like the perch, are a little elevated (3€–5€ for a coffee). But you get to enjoy your drink on a hidden terrace in the sky, with just the rooftops, towers, and Brunelleschi's dome for company. Top floor of La Rinascente, Piazza della Repubblica. www.larinascente.it. ℂ **055-219-113.** Bus: C3 or D.

Rivoire ★   If you are going to choose one overpriced pavement cafe in Florence, make it this one. The steep prices (6€ a cappuccino, 4.50€ for a small mineral water) help pay for the rent of one of the prettiest slices of real estate on the planet. Piazza della Signoria (at Via Vaccherreccia). www.rivoire.it. ℂ **055-214-412.** Bus: C2.

Wine Bars, Cocktail Bars & Craft Beer Bars

If you want to keep going into the small hours, you will likely find Italian **nightclubs** to be rather cliquey—people usually go in groups to hang out and dance only with one another. There's plenty of flesh showing, but no meat market. Singles hoping to find random dance partners will often be disappointed. Out in the northwestern 'burbs, **Tenax,** Via Pratese 46 (www.tenax. org; ⓒ **335-523-5922**), attracts big-name DJs on Friday and Saturday nights.

Beer House Club ★★   The best artisan beers from Tuscany, Italy, and farther afield. Their own line, brewed for the bar in nearby Prato, includes IPA, Imperial Stout, and Saison styles. Between 5 and 8pm, house beers are 5€ a pint instead of 6€. Corso Tintori 34R. ⓒ **055-247-6763.** Bus: C1, C3, or 23.

Caffè Sant'Ambrogio ★   This fine wine and cocktail bar is in a lively part of the center, northeast of Santa Croce. It is popular with locals without being too achingly hip. In summer, the action spills out onto the little piazza and church steps outside. Piazza Sant'Ambrogio 7R. https://www.facebook.com/pages/Enoteca-SantAmbrogio-Caff%C3%A8/209418819114419. No phone. Bus: C2 or C3.

Cantinetta dei Verrazzano ★★   One of the coziest little wine and food bars in the center is decked out with antique wooden wine cabinets, in genuine *enoteca* style. The wines come from the first-rate Verrazzano estate, in Chianti. Via dei Tavolini 18R. www.verrazzano.com. ⓒ **055-268-590.** Bus: C2.

Diorama ★★   Opened in 2014, this tiny bar has a small terrace, Formica tables, craft beers (5€–7€), hot dogs (3.50€), and a friendly, local vibe. Via Pisana 78R. www.dioramafirenze.com. ⓒ **055-228-6682.** Bus: 6.

Fuori Porta ★★   Friendly San Niccolò wine bar with a terrace at the foot of the climb to Piazzale Michelangiolo. There are cold cuts to accompany the wine, plus the kitchen knocks out excellent pasta and larger dishes. You can order wines by the glass from 3.50€, and a handful of Tuscan craft beers in bottle. It is often open all day in high season (Apr–Oct), without an afternoon closure; otherwise, every lunchtime and evening. Via Monte alle Croci 10R. www.fuoriporta.it. ⓒ **055-234-2483.** Bus: D or 23.

Golden View Open Bar ★   All modernist bright-white Formica and marble, this is one of the city's most elegant *aperitivo* spots. Pay 10€ to 14€ for a cocktail or glass of bubbly and help yourself to the buffet between 7 and 9:30pm every night. There is live jazz 3 nights a week from 9:15pm. Via dei Bardi 58R. www.goldenviewopenbar.com. ⓒ **055-214-502.** Bus: C3 or D.

Il Santino ★★   Tiny wine bar that stocks niche labels from across Italy, and serves exquisite "Florentine tapas" plates to munch while you sip. Via Santo Spirito 60R. ⓒ **055-230-2820.** Bus: D, 11, 36, or 37.

La Terrazza at the Continentale ★★   There are few surprises on the list here—a well-made Negroni, Moscow Mule, Bellini, and the like—and prices are a little steep at around 15€ to 18€ a cocktail. But the setting, on a rooftop right by the Ponte Vecchio, makes them cheap at the price. The atmosphere is fashionable but casual (wear what you like) and staff is supremely welcoming. Arrive at sundown to see the city below start to twinkle. Inside the Continentale Hotel, Vicolo dell'Oro 6R. © **055-27-262.** Bus: C3 or D.

Le Murate ★ It bills itself as a "literary cafe," so the stripped-brick decor and hipster clientele are taken as read. As well as coffee by day—taken in the courtyard of the city's former prison—there are themed food evenings, *aperitivo* (6:30–9:30pm), and a cocktail list as long as your arm. Piazza delle Murate. www.lemurate.it. © **055-234-6872.** Bus: C2 or C3.

Mostodolce ★ Burgers, pizza, Wi-Fi, and sports on the screen: so far, so good. And Mostodolce also has its own artisan beer on tap, brewed just outside Florence at Prato (some are very strong). Happy hour is 3:30 to 7:30pm, when it is .50€ off a beer. Via Nazionale 114R. www.mostodolce.it/firenze. © **055-230-2928.** Bus: C1.

Volpi e L'Uva ★ The wines-by-the-glass list is 30-strong, the atmosphere is relaxed, and the terrace on a little piazza beside Santa Felicità is a delight. It's the kind of place you just sink into. Glasses from 4€. Closed Sundays. Piazza dei Rossi 1. www.levolpieluva.com. © **055-239-8132.** Bus: C3 or D.

DAY TRIPS FROM FLORENCE

lorence is the capital of the region of Tuscany and the hub of its transport network. It is within easy day-trip reach of several of the region's sights, meaning you do not have to switch your accommodation base to see the highlights of central Italy.

SIENA ★★★

70km (43 miles) S of Florence

Siena is a medieval city of brick. Viewed from the summit of the Palazzo Pubblico's tower, its sea of roof tiles blends into a landscape of steep, twisting stone alleys. This cityscape hides dozens of Gothic palaces and pastry shops galore, longstanding neighborhood rivalries, and painted altarpieces of unsurpassed elegance.

Founded as a Roman colony by Emperor Augustus (see p. 19), the city enjoyed its heyday in the 13th and 14th centuries; in 1270, Sienese merchants established the Council of Nine, an oligarchy that ruled over Siena's greatest republican era, when civic projects and artistic prowess reached their heights. Artists like Duccio di Buoninsegna, Simone Martini, and the Lorenzetti brothers invented a distinctive Sienese art, a highly developed Gothic style that was an artistic foil to the emerging Florentine Renaissance. Then in 1348, a plague known as the "Black Death" hit the city, killing perhaps three-quarters of the population, destroying the social fabric and devastating the economy. Siena never recovered, and much of it has barely changed since.

Essentials

GETTING THERE

The **bus** is much more convenient than the train, because Siena's rail station is way outside of town. Siena Mobilità/BusItalia (www. tiemmespa.it) runs express (*rapida;* 75 min.) and slower buses (95 min.) from Florence's main bus station to Siena's Piazza Gramsci. It costs 8€ each way, and there is no need to reserve ahead of time. Buses run at least hourly in the morning. Try not to make the trip on a Sunday, when the bus service is much reduced. The last bus back usually departs around 8:45pm (but check ahead).

Palio (horse race).

If you have a **car,** there's a fast road direct from Florence (it has no route number; follow the green or blue signs toward Siena), or take the scenic route, down the **Chiantigiana wine road,** the SS222. But the bus makes more sense for a day trip.

VISITOR INFORMATION

The **tourist office,** where you can get a useless free map or pay .50€ for a useful one, is inside Santa Maria della Scala, at Piazza del Duomo 1 (www. terresiena.it; ℂ **0577-280-551**). April through October, it is open daily from 9:30am to 6pm. Winter hours are Monday to Saturday 10am to 5pm, Sunday 10am to 1pm.

PARKING

Siena **parking lots** (www.sienaparcheggi.com; ℂ **0577-228-711**) charge between .50€ and 2€ per hour, most at the top end of that scale. All lots are well signposted, with locations just inside the city gates.

Exploring Siena

Be prepared for one *seriously* busy day (and even then you can't see it all). Several stepped alleys lead down into **Piazza del Campo ("Il Campo")** ★★, arguably the most beautiful piazza in Italy. Crafted like a sloping scallop shell, the Campo was first laid out in the 1100s on the former site of the Roman forum. The herringbone brick pavement is divided by white marble lines into nine sections representing the city's medieval ruling body, the Council of Nine.

Overlooking the Campo, the crenellated town hall, the **Palazzo Pubblico** ★★ (built 1297–1310) is the city's (maybe all of Tuscany's) finest Gothic palace, and the **Museo Civico** (ℂ **0577-292-226**) inside is home to Siena's best artworks. Frescoed on the wall of the Sala del Mappamondo is Simone Martini's 1315 **"Maestà"** ★★, following the city's tradition of honoring the Virgin Mary (she is Siena's traditional protector). Next door, in the

Sala della Pace, Ambrogio Lorenzetti covered the walls in his **"Allegories of Good and Bad Government"** ★★★ (1338), full of details of medieval Sienese life and painted to provide encouragement to the city's governing body, which met inside the room. The museum is open daily from 10am to 6pm (mid-March to October until 7pm). Admission costs 9€, 8€ for students and seniors ages 65 and over, free for children ages 10 and under.

Having seen Siena's civic heart, visit the religious monuments of **Piazza del Duomo** (www.operaduomo.siena.it; ✆ **0577-286-300**) on a single ticket: The **Opa Si Pass** costs 12€ and is sold from booths in the piazza. Siena's **Duomo** ★★ is stuffed with art treasures, including Bernini's **Cappella Chigi** ★ (1659) and the **Libreria Piccolomini** ★★, frescoed in 1507 with scenes from the life of Sienese Pope Pius II, by Pinturicchio. If you are visiting between August and October, you will find the cathedral's **floor** ★★★ uncovered; it is a mosaic of 59 etched and inlaid marble panels created between 1372 and 1547 by Siena's top artists, including Domenico di Bartolo, Matteo di Giovanni, Pinturicchio, and especially Domenico Beccafumi. The **Battistero (Baptistery)** ★★ has a baptismal font (1417–30) with gilded brass panels cast by the foremost Sienese and Florentine sculptors of the early Renaissance, including Jacopo della Quercia, Lorenzo Ghiberti, and Donatello. Inside the **Museo dell'Opera del Duomo** ★ is Duccio di Buoninsegna's 1311 **"Maestà"** ★★★, Siena's most precious work of art, which used to sit on the cathedral's high altar. It shows the Virgin and Child in majesty, adored by a

Piazza del Campo ("Il Campo"), one of the most beautiful piazzas in Italy.

litany of saints including St. Paul (holding the sword) and St. John the Baptist (pointing at Jesus and wearing animal skins). From inside the museum, climb to the top of the **Facciatone** ★★ for the best view in Siena, over the rooftops and down into the Campo. Opening hours for most of the Piazza del Duomo sights are 10:30am to 5:30pm, although it stretches to 6 or 7pm in summer. The cathedral is closed to visitors on Sunday mornings.

You also just about have time for **Santa Maria della Scala** ★★ (www.santamaria dellascala.com; ✆ **0577-534-571**), opposite the cathedral. An "old hospital" might not sound too enticing, but this huge building has treasures hidden away in its eerie corridors. The **Pellegrinaio** ★★ was frescoed in the 1440s with sometimes grisly scenes of life in this medieval hospital. The Old Sacristy has an even more gruesome *"***Massacre of the Innocents***"* ★★, painted in 1482 by Matteo di Giovanni. Downstairs is the spooky oratory where Sienese St. Catherine used to pray (and stay) during the night; **Bambimus,** where art is displayed at child's-eye height; and the city's **National Archaeological Museum** on the labyrinthine lower floor. Admission costs 9€ (13€ with the Museo Civico; see p. 208), 8€ students and seniors ages 65 and over. Opening hours are 10:30am to 6:30pm (sometimes closed Tues in winter). It's usually much quieter than other places in the city—and we have no idea why.

Where to Eat

Sienese cooking is rustic and simple, and makes liberal use of sweet meat from the local *Cinta Senese* breed of pig. **L'Osteria** ★, Via de' Rossi 81 (✆ 0577-287-592) does a mean line in local grilled meats, including veal and *Cinta*. Main courses range from 8€ to 21€. It is closed Sunday evenings. At the **Osteria del Gusto** ★, Via dei Fusari 13 (www.osteriadelgusto.it; ✆ 0577-271-076), pasta dishes are a great value and served in filling portions. Think *pici* (hand-rolled, fat spaghetti) served with a *ragù* of *Cinta* and porcini mushrooms for around the 10€ mark.

If you prefer a sandwich to a sit-down meal, walk around the back of the Palazzo Pubblico to **Gino Cacino di Angelo** ★★, Piazza del Mercato 31 (✆ 0577-223-076). Sublime offerings include aged pecorino cheese, Tuscan salami, anchovies, and pretty much anything else that can go on bread, all carefully sourced. It closes at 3:30pm weekdays, 8pm on weekends, and for 3 weeks in August. The best gelato in the city is churned at **Kopa Kabana** ★, Via de' Rossi 52 (www.gelateriakopakabana.it; ✆ 0577-223-744); it's open daily from mid-February through November, 11am to midnight.

PISA ★★

76km (47 miles) W of Florence

On a grassy lawn wedged into the northwest corner of the city walls, medieval Pisans created one of the most dramatic (and now most photographed) squares in the world. Dubbed the **Campo dei Miracoli** (or "Field of Miracles"), Piazza del Duomo contains an array of elegant buildings that heralded the Pisan-Romanesque style—including the *Torre Pendente,* better known as the **Leaning Tower of Pisa.**

The city has its roots long before the Tower went up, as a seaside settlement around 1,000 B.C. that was expanded into a naval trading port by the Romans in the 2nd century B.C. By the 11th century, Pisa had grown into one of Europe's most powerful maritime republics. Its extensive trading in the Middle East helped import Arab ideas—decorative and scientific—to Italy. In 1284, Pisa's battle fleet was destroyed by Genoa at Meloria, off Livorno, a staggering defeat that allowed the Genoese to take control of the Tyrrhenian

Torre Pendente (Tower of Pisa).

Sea and forced Pisa's long slide into twilight. Florence took control in 1406, and despite a few small rebellions, Florence stayed in charge until Italian unification in the 1860s.

Essentials

GETTING THERE

From Florence's Santa Maria Novella station, around 50 daily **trains** make the trip (60–90 min.; 8€) to Pisa Centrale station. The last fast connection back to Florence departs around 10:30pm, but do check **www.trenitalia.com** for timetable updates.

There's also a Florence–Pisa fast, direct, and (for now) free **road**—the so-called *FI–PI–LI*—along the Arno valley. Journey time is usually around 1¼ hours, subject to traffic.

VISITOR INFORMATION

The main **tourist office** is at Piazza Vittorio Emanuele II 16 (www.pisaunica terra.it; © **050-42-291**). It is open daily 10am to 1pm and 2 to 4pm. Another information office in Piazza del Duomo (© **050-550-100**) is open daily 9:30am to 5:30pm.

GETTING AROUND

It is a long walk from the main station to the sights. **CPT** (www.pisa.cttnord. it) runs the city's **buses.** No. 4 and the LAM Rossa bus run from outside the station to near the Tower. Buy tickets from the station newsstand.

PARKING

Much of central Pisa is a controlled traffic zone. However, there is ample street and garage parking (including at Via Cammeo 51) within sight of the Tower. Take loose change for the meters, which range from 1.25€ to 2€ per hour.

Exploring Pisa

The **Campo dei Miracoli** ★★★ is your main destination in Pisa, and its monuments are linked on a combo ticket. The cathedral is free. Any other single admission is 5€; any two sites costs 7€. To access everything except the

Leaning Tower costs 8€. (Children 9 and under enter everything except the Tower for free.) Admission to the Leaning Tower is separate; anyone under 18 must be accompanied by an adult; children 8 and under are not allowed in the tower. It costs 18€ (no discounts); *you should reserve up to 20 days ahead of arrival in peak season or if you are on a tight schedule.* Admission to the Tower is via timed half-hour slots. To book a slot at the Leaning Tower, visit the website at **www.opapisa.it**. The main ticket office is behind the Tower and Duomo, on the north edge of the piazza: If you have no Tower reservation, head there immediately to book for later in the day.

First, spend a moment looking at the layout of **Piazza del Duomo:** A hidden part of the square's appeal is its spatial geometry. If you take an aerial photo of the square and draw connect-the-dot lines between the centers, doors, and other focal points, you'll come up with all sorts of perfect triangles and tangential lines of mathematical grace.

So, why does the **Leaning Tower** ★★★ lean? The main problem—and the bane of local engineers for 8 centuries—is that you can't stack that much heavy marble on shifting subsoil and keep it all upright. Building began in 1173 under Guglielmo and Bonnano Pisano, who also cast the Duomo's doors (see below). They reached the third level in 1185 when they noticed a lean, at that point only about 3.8cm (1½ in.). Work stopped until 1275, under Giovanni di Simone. He tried to correct the tilt by curving the structure back toward the perpendicular, giving the tower its slight banana shape. In 1284, work stopped yet again. In 1360, Tommaso di Andrea da Pontedera capped it off at about 51m (167 ft.) with a vaguely Gothic belfry.

Elsewhere on the piazza, the **Battistero (Baptistery)** ★ has a carved stone **pulpit** ★★ by Nicola Pisano (1255–60), which is perhaps his masterpiece and the prototype for a series he and his son Giovanni carried out over the years (the last is in Pisa's Duomo; the other two are in Pistoia and in Siena's cathedral). Heavily influenced by classical works, Nicola's high-relief panels (a synopsis of Christ's life) include pagan gods converted to Christianity as Madonnas and saints.

Buscheto, the architect who laid the **Cathedral**'s first stone in 1063, kicked off a new era in art by building what was to become the model for the Pisan-Romanesque style. All the key elements are here on the **facade** ★, designed and built by Buscheto's successor, Rainaldo: alternating light and dark banding, rounded blind arches with Moorish-inspired lozenges at the top and colored marble inlay designs, and Lombard-style open galleries of mismatched columns stacked to make the facade much higher than the church roof. The **main door** is one of three cast by students of Giambologna after a 1595 fire destroyed the originals. On the back of the right transept, across from the bell tower, is a 2008 cast of the bronze **Door of San Ranieri** ★★★ (the last original door survives in the **Museo dell'Opera** collection and was cast by Bonnano Pisano in 1180). Inside the Cathedral, on the north side of the nave, is Giovanni Pisano's masterpiece **pulpit** ★★ (1302–11)—it's the last of the Pisano pulpits and, along with the one in Pistoia, the greatest.

The walls of the **Camposanto** ★, or cemetery, were once covered with important 14th- and 15th-century frescoes by Taddeo Gaddi, Spinello Aretino, and Benozzo Gozzoli, among others. On July 27, 1944, however, American warplanes launched an attack against the city (which was still in German hands) and the Camposanto was bombed. The most fascinating panel to survive the bombing is the 1341 **"Triumph of Death"** ★, attributed to Florentine Buonamico Buffalmacco.

Where to Eat

If you want a genuine taste of Pisa, get away from the crowds around the Tower. Head south on Via Santa Maria as far as Piazza Cavalotti, then along Via dei Mille into Piazza dei Cavalieri. Continue through this vast, polygonal square to the center of the "real" city—it is less than 10 minutes' walk away. At **Osteria dei Cavalieri** ★, Via San Frediano 16 (✆ **050-580-858**), there are plenty of grilled meats, fresh fish, and traditional Pisan dishes like rabbit stewed with oregano. Main courses range from 12€ to 18€. Osteria dei Cavalieri is closed Saturday at lunchtime, all-day Sunday, and for 3 weeks in August. Just across the River Arno, at **Da Cucciolo** ★, Vicolo Rosselmini 9 (✆ **050-26-086**), you'll find Pisa residents tucking into dishes using local ingredients such as cuttlefish and Tuscan pulses—and paying local prices. Main courses range 8€ to 13€. It's closed Sunday evenings.

For pizza or *cecina* (warm garbanzo-bean flour flatbread), stop at **Il Montino,** Vicolo del Monte 1 (www.pizzeriailmontino.com; ✆ **050-598-695**), a slice spot often busy with students.

SAN GIMIGNANO ★★

52km (32 miles) SW of Florence

The scene that hits you when you pass through the Porta San Giovanni gate, inside the walls of **San Gimignano,** is thoroughly medieval. The center is peppered with the tall towers that have made *San Gimignano delle Belle Torri* ("of the beautiful towers") the poster child for Italian hill towns everywhere. There were at one time around 70 of the things spiking the sky above this little village, yet only a dozen or so remain. The spires started rising in the bad old days of the 1200s, partly to defend against outside invaders but mostly as command centers for San Gimignano's warring families. Several successive waves of the plague that swept through (1348, 1464, and 1631 were especially bad) caused the economy—based on textiles and hosting pilgrims traveling the Via Francigena to Rome—to crumble. San Gimignano slowly became a provincial backwater. By the time tourism began picking up in the 19th century, visitors found a preserved medieval village of decaying stone towers.

Essentials
GETTING THERE

As with Siena, your best bet is the **bus.** From Florence's main bus station, Siena Mobilità/BusItalia (www.tiemmespa.it) runs buses for most of the day.

The towers of San Gimignano.

It is a 50-minute journey to Poggibonsi, and many of the services are timed to meet the connection to San Gimignano (a further 25 min.). Buy through-tickets for the whole journey in Florence (7€). The last bus back to Florence usually departs around 8pm, but check ahead. Try not to make the day trip on a Sunday, when the bus service is much reduced.

Arriving by **car,** take the Poggibonsi Nord exit off the Florence–Siena highway or the SS2. San Gimignano is 12km (7½ miles) from Poggibonsi, through very pretty country.

VISITOR INFORMATION

The friendly **tourist office** is at Piazza Duomo 1 (www.san gimignano.com; ✆ **0577-940-008**). It's open daily March through October from 9am to 1pm and 3 to 7pm, and November through February from 9am to 1pm and 2 to 6pm.

PARKING

The town is surrounded by well-signposted car parks. The furthest from the town, **P1** is the cheapest (1.50€ per hour; 6€ max. for full day). Drive right up to the town gate, drop any passengers, then return to park—it is a stiff uphill walk of 7 to 10 minutes back.

Exploring San Gimignano

Anchoring the town at the top of Via San Giovanni are its two interlocking triangular *piazze:* **Piazza della Cisterna ★★**, centered on a 1237 well, and **Piazza del Duomo,** flanked by the city's main church and civic palace. It is easy to find them: From any direction, just keep walking uphill.

The town's key art site is the **Collegiata ★★**, Piazza del Duomo (www. duomosangimignano.it; ✆ **0577-286-300**). The right wall of this collegiate church was frescoed from 1333 to 1341—most likely by Lippo Memmi—with three levels of **New Testament scenes** (22 in all) on the life and Passion of Christ. In 1367, Bartolo di Fredi frescoed the left wall with 26 scenes from the **Old Testament,** and Taddeo di Bartolo provided a **"Last Judgment"** peppered with gruesome details (just above and left of the main door) in 1410.

In 1468, Giuliano da Maiano built the **Cappella di Santa Fina** ★★ off the right aisle, and his brother Benedetto carved the relief panels for the altar. Florentine Renaissance painter Domenico Ghirlandaio decorated the tiny chapel's walls with some of his finest, airiest works: In 1475, he frescoed two scenes summing up the life of Santa Fina, a local girl who, although never officially canonized, is one of San Gimignano's patron saints. Admission to the Collegiata costs 4€, 2€ ages 6 to 17. Hours are April through October Monday to Friday 10am to 7:30pm, Saturday 10am to 5:30pm, and Sunday 12:30 to 7:30pm. November to March it's open Monday to Saturday, 10am to 5pm, Sunday 12:30 to 5pm. It is closed altogether in the second half of November and the second half of January.

The town's small **Museo Civico e Pinacoteca (Civic Art Museum)** ★, Piazza del Duomo 2 (www.sangimignanomusei.it; ℭ **0577-286-300**), inside the Palazzo del Popolo, houses a **"Maestà"** ★★ (1317) by Sienese painter Lippo Memmi, and some unique and rather racy medieval "wedding night" frescoes by Lippo's father, Memmo di Filippuccio. Admission costs 6€. The same ticket gets you up the tallest tower still standing, the **Torre Grossa** ★. From 54m (175 ft.) up, you can see for miles. The museum and tower are open daily 9:30am to 7pm April through September, 11am to 5:30pm November to February, and 10am to 5:30pm in March.

At **Sant Agostino,** Piazza Sant'Agostino (ℭ **0577-907-012**), Florentine painter Benozzo Gozzoli spent 2 years frescoing the choir behind the main altar floor-to-ceiling with scenes rich in architectural detail from the **"Life of St. Augustine"** ★★. The church keeps changeable hours, but is generally open daily from 10am to noon and 3 to 7pm (Nov–Mar it closes at 6pm; Jan–Mar it's also closed Mon mornings). Admission is free.

Where to Eat

The best restaurant for a flying visit is **Chiribiri** ★, Piazzetta della Madonna 1 (www.ristorantechiribiri.it; ℭ **0577-941-948**), because it is open all day so you can dine early before heading for the bus or car parks. It is a small place, with a simple, well-executed menu of Italian and Tuscan classics such as lasagna, *osso buco,* or wild boar stew. Main courses are priced fairly— a welcome change from many spots—at 8€ to 12€. No credit cards. For a more snacklike meal, try **diVinorum,** Via degli Innocenti 5 (ℭ **0577-907-192**) for wines by the glass and *bruschettone* (large bruschettas; 5€–9€) loaded with topping combos such as provolone cheese, ham, and radicchio.

The town's essential foodie stop isn't a restaurant, however, but the **Gelateria Dondoli "di Piazza"** ★★, Piazza della Cisterna 4 (www.gelateriadipiazza.com; ℭ **0577-942-244**), for creative combinations like raspberry and rosemary (it works) and the signature *crema di Santa Fina,* made with saffron and pinenuts.

VENICE

Nothing in the world quite looks like Venice. This vast, floating city of grand palazzos, elegant bridges, gondolas and canals is a magnificent spectacle, truly magical when approached by sea for the first time, when its golden domes and soaring bell towers seem to emerge straight from the ocean. Although it can sometimes appear that Venice is little more than an open-air museum, where tourists always outnumber—by a large margin—the locals, it is still surprisingly easy to lose the crowds. Indeed, the best way to enjoy Venice is to simply get lost in its labyrinth of narrow, enchanting streets, stumbling upon a quiet campo (square), market stall, or cafe far off the beaten track, where even the humblest medieval church might contain masterful work by Tiepolo, Titian, or Tintoretto.

The origins of Venice are as muddy as parts of the lagoon it now occupies, but most histories begin with the arrival of refugees from Attila the Hun's invasion of Italy in 453. By the 11th century, Venice had already emerged as a major trading city, with special dispensation from Byzantine taxes granted in 1082, and a seaborne empire (which included Crete, Corfu, and Cyprus) was created by a huge navy and commercial fleet by the 13th century. Though embroiled with wars against Genoa and the Turks for much of the ensuing centuries, these were golden years for Venice, when booming trade with the Far East funded much of its grand architecture and art. Although it remained an outwardly rich city, by the 1700s the good times were over, and in 1797 Napoleon dissolved the Venetian Republic. You'll gain a sense of some of this history touring **Piazza San Marco,** and **St. Mark's Basilica,** or by visiting the **Accademia,** one of Italy's great art galleries, but only when you wander the back *calli* (streets), will you encounter the true, living, breathing side of Venice, still redolent of those glory days.

ESSENTIALS
Getting There
BY PLANE You can fly to Venice nonstop from North America via **Delta Airlines** (www.delta.com) from Atlanta (June–Aug only) via **United Airlines** (www.united.com) from Newark, via

Piazza San Marco (St. Mark's Square).

US Airways (www.usairways.com) from Philadelphia; and via Rome with **Alitalia** (www.alitalia.com) or a number of other airlines year-round. You can also connect through a major European city with European carriers. No-frills **easyJet** (www.easyjet.com) flies direct from Berlin, London-Gatwick, Manchester, and Paris much cheaper than the major airlines, though rival budget carrier **Ryanair** (www.ryanair.com) uses the airport in nearby Treviso (a 1-hr. bus ride to Venice).

Flights land at the **Aeroporto di Venezia Marco Polo,** 7km (4¼ miles) northwest of the city on the mainland (www.veniceairport.it; ✆ 041-2609260). There are two bus alternatives for getting into town. The **ATVO airport shuttle bus** (www.atvo.it; ✆ 0421-594672) connects with Piazzale Roma not far from Venice's Santa Lucia train station (and the closest point to Venice's attractions accessible by car or bus). Buses leave for/from the airport about every 30 minutes, cost 6€ (11€ return), and make the trip in about 20 minutes. Buy tickets at the automatic ticket machines in the arrivals baggage hall, or the Public Transport ticket office (daily 8am–midnight). The local **ACTV bus no. 5** (✆ 041-2424) also costs 6€, also takes 20 minutes, and runs between two and four times an hour depending on the time of day; the best option here is to buy the combined ACTV and "Nave" ticket for 12€, which includes your first *vaporetto* ride at a slight discount (the "vaporetto" is the seagoing streetcar of Venice, which goes to all parts of the city). Buy tickets at machines just outside the terminal. With either bus, you'll have to walk to or from the final stop at Piazzale Roma to the nearby *vaporetto* (water bus) stop for the final connection to your hotel. It's rare to see porters around who'll help with luggage, so pack light.

A **land taxi** from the airport to Piazzale Roma (where you get the *vaporetto*) will run about 45€—the meter starts at 15€.

The most evocative and traditional way to arrive in Venice is by sea. For 15€, 14€ if you buy online, the **Cooperative San Marco/Alilaguna** (www.alilaguna.it; ✆ 041-2401701) operates a large *motoscafo* (shuttle boat) service from the airport (with stops at Murano), arriving after about 1 hour and 15 minutes in Piazza San Marco. The *Linea Blu* (blue line) runs almost every 30 minutes from about 6am to midnight. The *Linea Arancio* (orange line) has the same frequency, costs the same, and takes the same amount of time to arrive at San Marco, but gets there through the Grand Canal, which is much more spectacular and offers the possibility to get off at one of the stops along the way. This might be convenient to your hotel and could save you having to take another means of transportation. The *Linea Rossa* (red line) runs to the Lido and Murano (8€). If you arrive at Piazza San Marco and your hotel isn't in the area, you'll have to make a connection at the *vaporetto* launches. (Your hotel can help you with the specifics if you booked before you left home.)

A good alternative is the newish **Venice Shuttle** (www.venicelink.com; daily 8am–10pm; minimum 2 people for reservations), a shared water taxi (they carry 6–8 people) that will whisk you directly from the airport to many hotels and most of the major locations in the city for 25€ to 30€ (add 6€ after 9pm). You must reserve online in advance.

A **private water taxi** (20–30 min. to/from the airport) is convenient but costly—there is a 110€ fee (discounts available online) to the city for up to four passengers with one bag each (20€ more for each extra person up to a maximum of 8, and another 10€ for 10pm–8am arrivals). It's worth considering if you're pressed for time, have an early flight, are carrying a lot of luggage (a Venice no-no), or can split the cost with a friend or two. It may be able to drop you off at the front (or side) door of your hotel or as close as it can maneuver given your hotel's location (check with the hotel before arriving). Your taxi captain should be able to tell you before boarding just how close he can get you. Try www.venicelink.com, **Corsorzio Motoscafi Venezia** (www. motoscafivenezia.it; ℘ **041-5222303**), or **Venezia Taxi** (www.veneziataxi.it; ℘ **041-723112**).

BY TRAIN Trains from Rome (3¾ hr.), Milan (2½ hr.), Florence (2 hr.), and all over Europe arrive at the **Stazione Venezia Santa Lucia.** To get there, all must pass through (although not necessarily stop at) a station marked Venezia-Mestre. Don't be confused: Mestre is a charmless industrial city that's the last stop on the mainland. Occasionally trains end in Mestre, in which case you have to catch one of the frequent 10-minute shuttles connecting with Venice; it's inconvenient, so when you book your ticket, confirm that the final destination is Venezia Santa Lucia.

On exiting, you'll find the Grand Canal immediately in front of you, with the docks for a number of *vaporetti* lines (the city's public ferries or "water buses") to your left and right. Head to the booths to your left, near the bridge, to catch either of the two lines plying the Grand Canal: the no. 2 express, which stops only at San Marcuola, Rialto Bridge, San Tomà, San Samuele, and Accademia before hitting San Marco (26 min. total); and the slower no. 1, which makes 13 stops before arriving at San Marco (a 33-min. trip). Both leave every 10 minutes or so, but in the mornings before 9am and the evenings after 8pm the no. 2 sometimes stops short at Rialto, meaning you'll have to disembark and hop on the next no. 1 or 2 that comes along to continue to San Marco.

Note: The *vaporetti* go in two directions from the train station: left down the Grand Canal toward San Marco—which is the (relatively) fast and scenic way—and right, which also eventually gets you to San Marco (at the San Zaccaria stop) if you are on the 2, but takes more than twice as long because it goes the long way around Dorsoduro (and serves mainly commuters). If you get the no. 1 going to the right from the train station, it will go only one more stop before it hits its terminus at Piazzale Roma.

A dock for private water taxis is directly in front of the train station. These cost 65€ and offer speedy service directly to your hotel or destination.

BY BUS Although rail travel is more convenient and commonplace, Venice is serviced by long-distance buses from all over mainland Italy and some international cities. The final destination is Piazzale Roma, where you'll need to pick up *vaporetto* no. 1 or no. 2 (as described above) to connect you with stops in the heart of Venice and along the Grand Canal.

BY CAR The only wheels you'll see in Venice are those attached to luggage. Venice is a city of canals and narrow alleys. **No cars are allowed,** or more to the point, no cars could drive through the narrow streets and over the footbridges—even the police, fire department, and ambulance services use boats. Arriving in Venice by car is problematic and expensive—and downright exasperating if it's high season and the parking facilities are full (they often are). You can drive across the Ponte della Libertà from Mestre to Venice, but you can go no farther than Piazzale Roma at the Venice end, where many garages eagerly await your euros. The rates vary with, for example, the public **AVM garage** (www.avmspa.it; ✆ **041-2727301**) charging 26€ for a 24-hour period, while private outfit **Garage San Marco** (www.garagesanmarco.it; ✆ **041-5232213**) costs 30€ for 24 hours.

Vaporetti lines 1 and 2, described above, both stop at Piazzale Roma before continuing down the Grand Canal to the train station and, eventually, Piazza San Marco.

Visitor Information

TOURIST OFFICES The main office is in the Palazzetto Carmagnani, San Marco 2637, 10 minutes from Piazza San Marco (www.turismovenezia.it; ✆ **041-5298711;** *vaporetto:* Giglio). It's open daily from 9am to 7pm. A more convenient office lies in the arcades off Piazza San Marco at Calle de l'Ascension 71/f (daily 8.30am–7pm), and there are smaller offices at the Piazzale Roma garages (daily 8am–2:30pm), Stazione Venezia Santa Lucia (daily 9am–7:30pm), in the arrivals hall at Marco Polo Airport (daily 9am–7:30pm), and at the Venice Pavilion inside the Giardinetti Reali (daily 8:30am–7pm), near Piazza San Marco.

The tourist office's map (2.50€) helps you find only *vaporetto* lines and stops. More useful is the info-packed monthly (every 2 weeks in summer), "Un Ospite di Venezia" (www.unospitedivenezia.it); most hotels have free copies. Also very useful is "VeneziaNews" (www.venezianews.it), published monthly and sold at newsstands all over the city.

City Layout

Even armed with the best map or a hefty smartphone data plan, expect to get a little bit lost in Venice, at least some of the time (GPS directions are

Central Venice refers to the built-up block of islands in the lagoon's center, including St. Mark's, the train station, and everything else in the six main *sestieri* (districts) that make up the bulk of the tourist city. Greater Venice includes all the inhabited islands of the lagoon—central Venice plus Murano, Burano, Torcello, and the Lido. The lagoon comprises everything, from the city to the mud flats to the fish farms to the dozens of abandoned or uninhabited islets.

notoriously unreliable here). Just view it as an opportunity to stumble across Venice's most intriguing corners and vignettes. Keep in mind as you wander seemingly hopelessly among the *calli* (streets) and *campi* (squares) that the city wasn't built to make sense to those on foot but rather to those plying its canals.

Venice lies 4km (2½ miles) from terra firma, connected to the mainland burg of Mestre by the Ponte della Libertà, which leads to Piazzale Roma. Snaking through the city like an inverted *S* is the **Grand Canal,** the wide main artery of aquatic Venice.

The city is divided into six *sestieri* ("sixths," or districts or wards): **Cannaregio, Castello, San Marco, San Polo, Santa Croce,** and **Dorsoduro.** In addition to the six *sestieri* that cluster around the Grand Canal there are a host of other islands in the Venice lagoon. Opposite Piazza San Marco and Dorsoduro is **La Giudecca,** a tranquil, mostly residential and working-class island that offers phenomenal views of Piazza San Marco. The **Lido di Venezia** is the city's sandy beach island, a popular summer destination, while **San Michele** is the cemetery island where such celebrities as Stravinsky and Diaghilev are buried.

Murano, Burano, and **Torcello** are popular islands northeast of the city and easily accessible by *vaporetto.* Since the 13th century, Murano has exported its glass products worldwide. Fishing village Burano is dotted with colorful houses and is famous for its lace, an art now practiced by very few island women. Torcello is the most remote and least populated. The industrial city of **Mestre,** on the mainland, is the gateway to Venice, and while it holds no reason for exploration, in a pinch its host of inexpensive hotels is worth consideration when Venice's are full.

The Neighborhoods in Brief

San Marco The central *sestiere* is anchored by the magnificent Piazza San Marco and St. Mark's Basilica to the south and the Rialto Bridge to the north; it's the most visited (and, as a result, the most expensive) of the *sestieri.* This is the commercial, religious, and political heart of the city and has been for more than a millennium. Although you'll find glimpses and snippets of the real Venice here, ever-rising rents have nudged resident Venetians to look for housing in the outer neighborhoods: You'll be hard-pressed to find a grocery store or dry cleaner, for example. This area is laced with first-class hotels—but we'll give you some suggestions for staying in the heart of Venice without going broke.

Castello This quarter, whose tony waterside esplanade Riva degli Schiavoni follows the Bacino di San Marco (St. Mark's Basin), begins just east of Piazza San Marco, skirting Venice's most congested area to the north and east. Riva degli Schiavoni can sometimes get so busy as to seem like Times Square on New Year's Eve, but if you head farther east in the direction of the Arsenale or inland away from the *bacino*, the crowds thin out, despite the presence of such major sights as Campo SS. Giovanni e Paolo and the Scuola di San Giorgio.

Dorsoduro You'll find the residential area of Dorsoduro on the opposite side of the Accademia Bridge from San Marco. Known for the Accademia and Peggy Guggenheim museums, it is the largest of the *sestieri* and has been known as an artists' haven until recent escalations of rents forced much of the community to relocate elsewhere. Good neighborhood restaurants, a charming gondola boatyard, the lively Campo Santa Margherita, and the sunny quay called le Zattere (a favorite promenade and gelato stop) all add to the character and color that make this one of the city's most-visited areas.

San Polo This mixed-bag *sestiere* of residential corners and tourist sights stretches northwest of the Rialto Bridge to the church of Santa Maria dei Frari, and the Scuola di San Rocco. The hub of activity at the foot of the bridge is due in large part to the Rialto Market—some of the city's best restaurants have flourished in the area for generations, alongside some of its worst tourist traps. The spacious Campo San Polo is the main piazza of Venice's smallest *sestiere*.

Santa Croce North and northwest of the San Polo district and across the Grand Canal from the train station, Santa Croce stretches all the way to Piazzale Roma. Its eastern section is generally one of the least-visited areas of Venice—making it all the more desirable for curious visitors. Less lively than San Polo, it is as authentic and feels light-years away from San Marco. The quiet and lovely Campo San Giacomo dell'Orio is its heart.

Cannaregio Sharing the same side of the Grand Canal with San Marco and Castello, Cannaregio stretches north and east from the train station to include the old Jewish Ghetto. Its outer reaches are quiet, unspoiled, and residential; one-quarter of Venice's ever-shrinking population of 60,000 lives here. Most of the city's one-star hotels are clustered about the train station—not a dangerous neighborhood but not one known for its charm, either. The tourist store–lined Lista di Spagna, which starts just to the left as you leave the train station, morphs into Strada Nova and provides an uninterrupted thoroughfare to the Rialto Bridge.

La Giudecca Located across the Giudecca Canal from the Piazza San Marco and Dorsoduro, La Giudecca is a tranquil working-class residential island where you'll find a youth hostel and a handful of hotels (including the ultra-deluxe Hotel Cipriani, one of Europe's finest).

Lido di Venezia This slim, 11km-long (6¾-mile) island, the only spot in the Venetian lagoon where cars circulate, is the city's beach and separates the lagoon from the open sea. The landmark hotels here serve as a base for the annual Venice Film Festival.

Getting Around

Aside from on boats, the only way to explore Venice is by walking—and by getting lost repeatedly. You'll navigate many twisting streets whose names change constantly and don't appear on any map, and streets that may very well simply end in a blind alley or spill abruptly into a canal. You'll also cross dozens of footbridges. Treat getting bewilderingly lost in Venice as part of the fun, and budget more time than you'd think necessary to get wherever you're going.

A Note on Addresses

Within each *sestiere* is a most original system of numbering the *palazzi*, using one continuous string of 6,000 or so numbers. The format for addresses in this chapter is, where possible, the number with the actual street or *campo* on which you'll find that address. Note that official mailing addresses (and what you'll see written down in most places), is simply the *sestiere* name followed by the building number in that district, which isn't especially helpful—for example, San Marco 1471. Be aware that San Marco 1471 may not necessarily be found close to San Marco 1473 and that many buildings aren't numbered at all.

STREET MAPS & SIGNAGE   The map sold by the tourist office and free maps provided by most hotels don't always show—much less name or index—all the *calli* (streets) and pathways of Venice. For that, pick up a more detailed map (ask for a *pianta della città* at news kiosks—especially those at the train station and around San Marco or most bookstores). The best (and most expensive) is the highly detailed Touring Club Italiano map, available in a variety of forms (folding or spiral-bound) and scales. Almost as good, and easier to carry, is the simple and cheap 1:6,500 folding map put out by Storti Edizioni.

Still, Venice's confusing layout confounds even the best maps and navigators. You're often better off just stopping every couple of blocks and asking a local to point you in the right direction (always know the name of the *campo*/square or major sight closest to the address you're looking for, and ask for that).

As you wander, look for the ubiquitous yellow signs (well, *usually* yellow) whose destinations and arrows direct you toward five major landmarks: **Ferrovia** (the train station), **Piazzale Roma** (the parking garage), **Rialto** (one of the four bridges over the Grand Canal), **San Marco** (the city's main square), and the **Accademia** (the southernmost Grand Canal bridge).

BY BOAT   The various *sestieri* are linked by a comprehensive *vaporetto* (water bus/ferry) system of about a dozen

View of the Grand Canal from Accademia Bridge.

CRUISING THE canals

A leisurely cruise along the **Grand Canal ★★★** (p. 258) from Piazza San Marco to the train station (Ferrovia)—or the reverse—is one of Venice's must-dos. It's the world's most unusual Main Street, a watery boulevard whose *palazzi* have been converted into condos. Lower water-lapped floors are now deserted, but the higher floors are still coveted by the city's titled families, who have inhabited these glorious residences for centuries; others have become the summertime dream homes of privileged expats, drawn here as irresistibly as the romantic Venetians-by-adoption who preceded them—Richard Wagner, Robert Browning, Lord Byron, and (more recently) Woody Allen.

As much a symbol of Venice as the winged lion, the **gondola ★★★** is one of Europe's great traditions, incredibly and inexplicably expensive, but truly as romantic as it looks (detractors who write it off as too touristy have most likely never tried it). The official, fixed rate is 80€ for a 40-minute tour (100€ 7pm–8am), with up to six passengers, and 40€ for every additional 20 minutes (50€ at night). That's not a typo: 150€ for a 1-hour evening cruise. **Note:** Although the price is fixed by the city, a good negotiator at the right time of day (when there is not too much business) can sometimes grab a small discount for a shorter ride. You might also find discounts online. And at these ridiculously inflated prices, there is no need to tip the gondolier.

Aim for late afternoon before sundown, when the light does its magic on the canal reflections (and bring a bottle of Prosecco and glasses). If the gondola price is too high, ask visitors at your hotel or others lingering about at the gondola stations if they'd like to share it. Though the price is "fixed," before setting off establish with the gondolier the cost, time, and route (back canals are preferable to the trafficked and often choppy Grand Canal). They're regulated by the **Ente Gondola** (www.gondola venezia.it; ⓒ **041-5285075**), so call if you have any questions or complaints.

And what of the serenading gondolier immortalized in film? Frankly, you're better off without. But if warbling is de rigueur for you, here's the scoop. An ensemble of accordion player and tenor is so expensive that it's shared among several gondolas traveling together. A number of travel agents around town book the evening serenades for around 35€ per person.

There are 12 gondola stations around Venice, including Piazzale Roma, the train station, the Rialto Bridge, and Piazza San Marco. There are also a number of smaller stations, with *gondolieri* in striped shirts standing alongside their sleek 11m (36-ft.) black wonders looking for passengers. They all speak enough English to communicate the necessary details. Remember, if you just want a quick taster of being in a gondola, you can take a cheap *traghetto* across the Grand Canal.

---

lines operated by the **Azienda del Consorzio Trasporti Veneziano (ACTV;** www.actv.it; ⓒ **041-5287886**). Transit maps are available at the tourist office and most ACTV stations. It's easier to get around on foot, as the *vaporetti* principally serve the Grand Canal, the outskirts, and the outer islands. The crisscross network of small canals is the province of delivery vessels, gondolas, and private boats.

A ticket valid for 1 hour of travel on a *vaporetto* is a steep 7€, while the 24-hour ticket is 20€. Most lines run every 10 to 15 minutes from 7am to midnight, and then hourly until morning. Most *vaporetto* docks (the only place you can buy tickets) have timetables posted. Note that not all docks sell tickets. If you haven't bought a pass or extra tickets beforehand, you'll have to settle up with the conductor onboard (you'll have to find him immediately—he won't come looking for you) or risk a stiff fine of at least 52€, no excuses accepted. Also available are 48-hour tickets (30€) and 72-hour tickets (40€). If you're planning to stay in Venice for a week and intend to use the *vaporetto* service a lot, it might make sense to pick up a Venezia Unica city pass (see "Venice Discounts," on p. 266), with which you can buy 1-hour *vaporetto* tickets for 1.30€. All tickets must be validated in the yellow machines before getting on the *vaporetto*.

Just four bridges span the Grand Canal, and to fill in the gaps, *traghetti* skiffs (oversize gondolas rowed by two standing *gondolieri*) cross the Grand Canal at seven intermediate points (during daylight hours only). You'll find a station at the end of any street named Calle del Traghetto on your map (though not all of them have active ferries today; ask a local before walking to the canal), and are indicated by a yellow sign with the black gondola symbol. The fare is .70€ for locals and 2€ for visitors, which you hand to the gondolier when boarding. Most Venetians cross standing up. For the experience, try the Santa Sofia crossing that connects the Ca' d'Oro and the Pescheria fish market, opposite each other on the Grand Canal just north of the Rialto Bridge—the gondoliers expertly dodge water traffic at this point of the canal, where it's the busiest and most heart-stopping.

BY WATER TAXI *Taxi acquei* (water taxis) charge high prices and aren't for visitors watching their euros. The meter starts at a hefty 15€ and clicks at 2€ per minute. Each trip includes allowance for up to four to five pieces of luggage—beyond that there's a surcharge of 3€ to 5€ per piece (rates differ slightly according to company and how you reserve a trip). Plus there's a 10€ supplement for service from 10pm to 7am, and a 5€ charge for taxis on-call. Those rates cover up to four people; if any more squeeze in, it's another 5€ to 10€ per extra passenger (maximum 10 people). Taking a taxi from the train station to Piazza San Marco or any of the hotels in the area will put you back about 65€ (the Lido is 85€), while there is a fixed 100€ fee (for up to four people) to go or

Gondolas on the small canals.

COME HELL OR high water

During the tidal *acqua alta* (high water) floods, Venice's lagoon rises until it engulfs the city, leaving up to 1.5 to 1.8m (5–6 ft.) of water in the lowest-lying streets. Piazza San Marco, as the lowest point in the city, goes first. As many as 50 floods a year have been recorded since they first started in the late 1700s.

Significant *acqua alta* can begin as early as late September or October, but usually takes place November to March. The waters usually recede after just a few hours. Walkways are set up around town, but wet feet are a given and locals tend to wear high-topped wading boots.

A complex system of hydraulic dams is being constructed out in the lagoon to cut off the highest of these high tides (a controversial project due to its environmental impact), but although the project is well underway, it won't be operational for years.

Note: If you're curious to see *acqua alta* (and it is indeed a wonderful spectacle), but aren't in Venice at the right time, you can still get lucky because very minor occurrences can happen all year round.

come from the airport. Taxis to Burano or Torcello will be at least 120€. Note that only taxi boats with a yellow strip are the official operators sanctioned by the city. You can book trips with Consorzio Moscafi Venezia online at **www. motoscafivenezia.it** or call © **041-5222303.**

Six water-taxi stations serve key points in the city: the Ferrovia, Piazzale Roma, the Rialto Bridge, Piazza San Marco, the Lido, and Marco Polo Airport.

BY GONDOLA If you come all the way to Venice and don't indulge in a gondola ride, you might still be kicking yourself long after you have returned home. Yes, it's touristy, and, yes, it's expensive (see "Cruising the Canals" on p. 223), but only those with a heart of stone will be unmoved by the quintessential Venetian experience. Don't initiate your trip, however, until you have agreed upon a price and synchronized watches. Oh, and don't ask them to sing.

[FastFACTS] VENICE

Consulates See chapter 10.

Doctors & Hospitals The **Ospedale Civile Santi Giovanni e Paolo** (© **041-5294111**), on Campo Santi Giovanni e Paolo, has English-speaking staff and provides emergency service (go to the emergency room, *pronto*

soccorso), 24 hours a day (*vaporetto:* San Tomà).

Emergencies The best number to call in Italy (and the rest of Europe) with a **general emergency** is © **112;** this connects you to the military-trained (and English-speaking) **Carabinieri** who will transfer your

call as needed. For the **police,** dial © **113;** for a medical emergency and to call an **ambulance,** the number is © **118;** for the **fire department,** call © **115.** All are free calls.

Internet Access Venice has traditionally lagged behind the rest of Italy when it comes to Internet speeds and access, though many hotels, hostels, and bars now offer free Wi-Fi, and in 2009 Venice was one of the first cities in the nation to offer citywide Wi-Fi through a network of 200 hotspots. Visitors can buy packages online via www.veneziaunica.it: 5€ for 24 hr., 15€ for 3 days or 20€ for 7 days. Access codes are sent to your e-mail address; once in Venice look for the VeniceConnected network. Alternatively, there are plenty of "Internet points" dotted around the city, particularly in the busy areas around the Rialto, Piazza San Marco, and the railway station. Most charge 6€ to 8€ per hour. Try **ABColor-Internet Point** (((⟨⟩ **041-5244380**), Lista di Spagna

220 in Cannaregio (a 3-min. walk from the train station), open daily 10am to 8pm, or **Venetian Navigator** (((⟨⟩ **041-2771056**), Calle Casselleria 5300 in Castello (a 3-min. walk from Piazza San Marco), open daily 10am to 10pm.

Mail The most convenient post offices are: **Venezia Centro** at Calle de la Acque, San Marco (((⟨⟩ **041-2404149**), open Monday to Friday 8:25pm to 7:10pm and Saturday 8:25am to 12:35pm; **Venezia 4** at Calle de l'Ascension 1241 (((⟨⟩ **041-2446711**), off the west side of Piazza San Marco (Tues–Fri 8:25am–1:35pm, Sat 8:25am–12:35pm); and **Venezia 3** at Campo San Polo 2012

(((⟨⟩ **041-5200315; same** hours).

Pharmacies Venice's pharmacies take turns staying open all night. To find out which one is on call in your area, ask at your hotel or check the rotational duty signs posted outside all pharmacies.

Safety Be aware of petty crime like pickpocketing on the crowded *vaporetti*, particularly the tourist routes, where passengers are more intent on the passing scenery than on watching their bags. Venice's deserted back streets are virtually crime-free, though occasional tales of theft have circulated. Generally speaking, Venice is one of Italy's safest cities.

WHERE TO STAY

Few cities boast as long a high season as that of Venice, beginning with the Easter period. May, June, and September are the best months weather-wise and, therefore, the most crowded. July and August are hot (few of the one- and two-star hotels offer air-conditioning; when they do, it usually costs extra). Like everything else, hotels are more expensive here than in any other Italian city, with no apparent upgrade in amenities. The least special of those below are clean and functional; at best, they're charming and thoroughly enjoyable, with the serenade of a passing gondolier thrown in for good measure. Some may even provide you with your best stay in all of Europe.

It's highly advisable to reserve in advance, even in the off-season. If you haven't booked, come as early as you can on your arrival day, definitely before noon. Another alternative to reserve upon your arrival is through the **A.V.A.** (Venetian Hoteliers Association), online at www.veneziasi.it or ⟨⟩ **041-5222264.** Simply state the price range you want to book, and they'll confirm a hotel while you wait. There are offices at the train station, in Piazzale Roma garages, and in the airport.

SEASONAL CONSIDERATIONS Most hotels observe high- and low-season rates, and the high-end hotels generally adapt their prices to availability. In the prices listed below, **single figures represent rack rates,** because the price varies too widely depending on availability, and you can usually get a room for much less, even in high season.

HOTELS BY PRICE

EXPENSIVE

Al Ponte Antico ★★★, p. 237
Arcadia ★★★, p. 237
Corte Di Gabriela ★★★, p. 230
Giorgione ★★, p. 237
Londra Palace ★★, p. 232
Luna Hotel Baglioni ★★★, p. 230
Metropole ★★★, p. 232

MODERATE

Al Piave ★★, p. 232
American Dinesen ★★, p. 234
Antica Locanda al Gambero ★, p. 231
Antiche Figure ★★★, p. 236
Ca' Barba B&B ★★, p. 235
Casa Verardo ★★★, p. 233

Galleria ★★, p. 234
Locanda Fiorita ★★, p. 231
Locanda Orseolo ★★★, p. 231
Moresco ★★★, p. 234
Pensione Accademia ★★, p. 235
Pensione Guerrato ★★★, p. 235
Violino d'Oro ★★, p. 231

INEXPENSIVE

Ai Due Fanali ★★, p. 236
Ai Tagliapietra ★★★, p. 233
B&B San Marco ★★★, p. 233
Bernardi ★★, p. 238
Falier ★, p. 236
San Geremia ★, p. 238

Self-Catering Apartments

Anyone looking to get into the local swing of things in Venice should stay in a short-term rental apartment. For the same price or less than a hotel room, you could have your own one-bedroom apartment with a washing machine, air-conditioning, and a fridge to keep your wine in. Properties of all sizes and styles, in every price range, are available for stays of 3 nights to several weeks.

ABOUT THE MONEY

It's standard practice for local rental agencies to collect 30% of the total rental amount upfront to secure a booking. When you get to Venice and check in, the balance of your rental fee is normally payable in cash only, so make sure you have enough euros before you leave home. Upon booking, the agency should provide you with detailed "check-in" procedures. Normally, you're expected to call a cell or office phone when you arrive in Venice, and then the keyholder will meet you at the front door of the property at the agreed-upon time. Before the keyholder disappears, make sure you have a few numbers to call in case of an emergency. Otherwise, most apartments come with information sheets that list neighborhood shops and services. Beyond that, you're on your own, which is what makes an apartment stay such a great way to do as the Venetians do.

RECOMMENDED AGENCIES

Airbnb (www.airbnb.com) is now a major player in Venice, with over 1,000 properties listed from just 30€ per night. **Couchsurfing** (www.couchsurfing. com) is also popular and generally safe in Venice, but take the usual precautions using the apartment-swapping service.

Cities Reference (www.citiesreference.com; ✆ **06-48903612**) is the best all-around apartment rental agency for Venice, with over 250 properties listed.

Venice Hotels

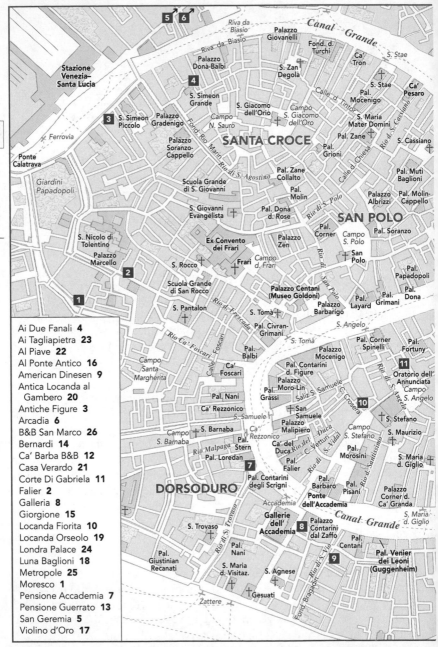

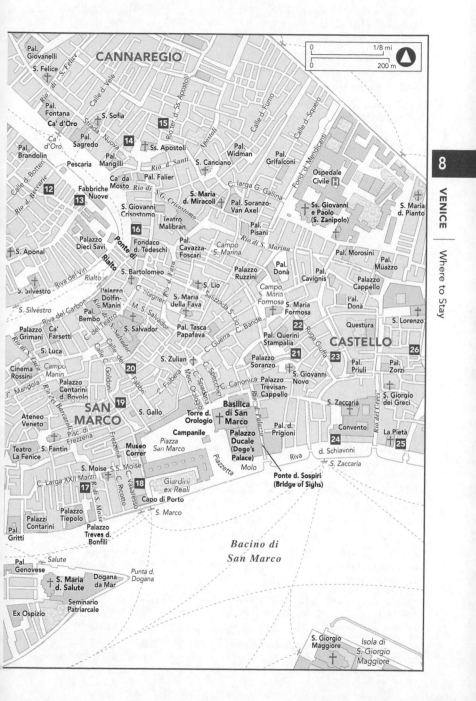

Pal.
Giovanelli
S. Felice
CANNAREGIO

Pal.
Fontana
Ca' d'Oro
S. Sofia

Ca'
d'Oro
Pal.
Sagredo
14
Ss. Apostoli
Pal.
Widman
Pal.
Grifalconi
Ospedale
Civile H

Pal.
Brandolin
Pescaria
Pal.
Mangilli
S. Canciano
S. Maria
d. Pianto

Ca' da
Mosto
Pal. Falier
C. larga G. Gallina
15

12
Fabbriche
Nuove
Rio di S.G. Crisostomo
S. Maria
d. Miracoli
Pal. Soranzo-
Van Axel
Ss. Giovanni
e Paolo
(S. Zanipolo)

13
S. Giovanni
Crisostomo
Teatro
Malibran
16
Pal.
Pisani

S. Aponal
Palazzo
Dieci Savi
Fondaco
d. Tedeschi
Pal.
Cavazza-
Foscari
Campo
S. Marina
Rio di S. Marina
Pal. Morosini
Pal.
Muazzo

S. Silvestro
Riva del Vin
Rialto
S. Bartolomeo
Palazzo
Ruzzini
Pal.
Donà
Pal.
Cavignis
Palazzo
Cappello

S. Silvestro
Riva del Carbon
Palazzo
Dolfin-
Manin
S. Lio
S. Maria
della Fava
Campo
S. Maria
Formosa
S. Maria
Formosa
Pal.
Donà

Palazzo
Grimani
Ca'
Farsetti
Pal.
Bembo
M. S. Salvador
S. Salvador
Pal. Tasca
Papafava
Questura
S. Lorenzo

S. Luca
Cinema
Rossini
Campo
Manin
20
S. Zulian
Pal. Querini
Stampalia
22
CASTELLO
26

Palazzo
Contarini
d. Bovolo
19
S. Gallo
Palazzo
Soranzo
21
23
Pal.
Priuli
Pal.
Zorzi

Ateneo
Veneto
**SAN
MARCO**
Torre d.
Orologio
S. Giovanni
Novo
S. Zaccaria
S. Giorgio
dei Greci

Teatro
La Fenice
S. Fantin
Museo
Correr
Campanile
**Basilica
di San
Marco**
Palazzo
Trevisan-
Cappello
Convento
La Pietà
25

S. Moisè
Piazza
San Marco
**Palazzo
Ducale
(Doge's
Palace)**
Pal. d.
Prigioni
24
d. Schiavoni

17
18
Giardini
ex Reali
Piazzetta
Molo
Riva
S. Zaccaria

Palazzi
Contarini
Palazzo
Tiepolo
Capo di Porto
S. Marco
**Ponte d. Sospiri
(Bridge of Sighs)**

Pal.
Gritti
Palazzo
Treves d.
Bonfili

Pal.
Genovese
Salute
Punta d.
Dogana
*Bacino di
San Marco*

S. Maria
d. Salute
Dogana
da Mar

Ex Ospizio
Seminario
Patriarcale

S. Giorgio
Maggiore
*Isola di
S. Giorgio
Maggiore*

0 — 1/8 mi
0 — 200 m

Their no-surprises property descriptions come with helpful bits of information and lots of photos.

Cross Pollinate (www.cross-pollinate.com; ☎ **06-99369799**) is a multi-destination agency but with a decent roster of personally inspected apartments and B&Bs in Venice. It was created by the American owners of the Beehive Hotel in Rome (p. 56), and they and their staff now travel around and find places that they can recommend.

GowithOh (www.gowithoh.com; ☎ **800/567-2927** in the U.S.) is a hip rental agency that covers 12 European cities, Venice among them. The website is fun to navigate, offers money-saving tips and lists more than 200 apartments for rent in the city.

Rental in Venice (www.rentalinvenice.com; ☎ **041-718981**) has an alluring website—with video clips of the apartments—and the widest selection of midrange and luxury apartments in the prime *San Marco* zone (there are less expensive ones, too).

San Marco
EXPENSIVE

Corte Di Gabriela ★★★ This gorgeous boutique is just a short walk from Piazza San Marco, with an extremely chic combination of contemporary design and classical Venetian style—ceiling murals, marble pillars and exposed brick blend with designer furniture and appliances (including free use of iPads, strong Wi-Fi, and hundreds of satellite TV channels). The fully renovated property dates from 1870, once serving as the home and offices of Venetian lawyers. It's the attention to detail that makes a stay here so memorable, with breakfast one of the highlights and well worth lingering over: fresh pastries made by the owners the night before, decent espresso and a spread of crepes and omelets made on request.

Calle degli Avvocati 3836. www.cortedigabriela.com. ☎ **041-5235077.** 10 units. 320€–440€ double. Rates include buffet breakfast. *Vaporetto:* Sant' Angelo. **Amenities:** Bar; concierge; room service (limited hours); Wi-Fi (free).

Luna Hotel Baglioni ★★★ Perfectly situated on the lagoon just around the corner from the bustle of Piazza San Marco, this is the oldest hotel in Venice, housed in a building from 1118 that was once a church before Napoleon destroyed its sacristy. Today, the boutique property, a member of Leading Hotels of the World, is a cocoon of privacy and comfort; the bright lobby with Murano chandeliers gives way to plush rooms decorated with antique furnishings, brocade, and original artwork from the 1700s. The breakfast room is especially noteworthy: With a room length mural and intricately painted ceiling frescoes created in the 18th century by students of Tiepolo, it makes every cup of coffee feel like a regal break. Staff here is especially attentive and professional.

San Marco, 1243. www.baglionihotels.com. ☎ **041-5289840.** 91 rooms. 250€–750€. *Vaporetto:* San Marco. **Amenities:** Restaurant; lounge; babysitting (with advance notice); concierge; Wi-Fi (free).

MODERATE

Antica Locanda al Gambero ★   The best attribute of this typically cute, small Venetian hotel is the location, just a 2-minute walk from Piazza San Marco. Rooms are dressed in a bright rococo style with modern extras like satellite TV and air-conditioning, and most have lovely views of the local canal (but not all—check when you book to avoid disappointment). No elevator (remember that a "fourth floor" room in Italy is actually on the fifth floor, quite a climb), and small breakfast buffet, but free Internet terminals in the lobby for those without their own devices, and a small rooftop patio with two tables few guests seem to use. Great rates in low season.

Calle dei Fabbri 4687. www.locandaalgambero.com. ⓒ **041-5224384.** 30 units. 75€–320€ double. Rates include continental breakfast. *Vaporetto:* Rialto (turn right along canal, cross small footbridge over Rio San Salvador, and turn left onto Calle Bembo, which becomes Calle dei Fabbri; hotel is about 5 blocks ahead on left). **Amenities:** Restaurant; bar (in restaurant); concierge. Wi-Fi (free).

Locanda Fiorita ★★   Hard to imagine a more picturesque location for this little hotel, a charming, quiet *campiello* draped in vines and blossoms—no wonder it's a favorite of professional photographers. Most of the standard rooms in the hotel are small (bathrooms are tiny), but all are furnished in an elegant 18th-century style, with wooden floors, shuttered windows, and richly patterned fittings (air-conditioning and satellite TV are included). The helpful staff more than make up for any deficiencies, and breakfast is a real pleasure, especially when taken outside on the *campiello*.

Campiello Novo 3457a. www.locandafiorita.com. ⓒ **041-5234754.** 10 units. 80€–160€ double. Rates include continental breakfast. *Vaporetto:* Sant'Angelo (walk to the tall brick building and go around it, turning right into Ramo Narisi; at a small bridge turn left and walk along Calle del Pestrin until you see a small piazza on your right [Campiello Novo]; the hotel is immediately opposite). **Amenities:** Babysitting; concierge; room service; Wi-Fi (free).

Locanda Orseolo ★★★   Enticing inn made up of three elegant guesthouses operated by the friendly Peruch family, located right behind Piazza San Marco. This place really oozes character, with exposed wood beams and heavy drapes giving a medieval feel and rooms lavishly decorated with Venetian-style furniture and tributes to the masks of the Carnevale—a cross between an artist's studio and Renaissance palace. Lounge with an aperitif on the terrace overlooking the Orseolo canal, and enjoy eggs and crepes made to order at breakfast, while watching the gondolas glide by. Limited selection of TV channels, but the Wi-Fi works pretty well throughout.

Corte Zorzi 1083. www.locandaorseolo.com. ⓒ **041-5204827.** 15 units. 150€–220€ double. Rates include buffet breakfast. *Vaporetto:* San Marco. **Amenities:** Babysitting; concierge; Wi-Fi (free).

Violino d'Oro ★★   The relatively spacious rooms in this handsome 18th-century building have been traditionally adorned in a neoclassical Venetian style with exposed wooden beams, crystal chandeliers, and heaps of character.

Most rooms also overlook the romantic San Moisè canal, and Piazza San Marco is just a 5-minute stroll away. At this price point (with incredible deals in low season), it's reassuring to know you get proper air-conditioning, satellite TV, and a decent elevator. Breakfast is an event, with a vast spread of homemade cakes, savory pies, and muffins complementing one of the best cappuccinos in the city.

Calle Larga XXII Marzo 2091. www.violinodoro.com. (C) **041-2770841**. 26 units. 69€–204€ double. Rates include buffet breakfast. *Vaporetto:* San Marco–Vallaresso (walk straight up Calle di Ca' Vallaresso, turn left on Salizada San Moisè, and cross the footbridge; the hotel is across the campiello on the left). **Amenities:** Bar; concierge; room service. Wi-Fi (free).

Castello

EXPENSIVE

Londra Palace ★★ This white-marble beauty, part of the Relais & Chateaux stable, occupies a prime location overlooking the waterfront promenade—get a room with a balcony to make the most of the spectacular views. All rooms are spacious, with lofty ceilings, 19th-century Biedermeier-style furniture (designed by Versace collaborator Rocco Magnoli), and satellite TV (with Sky channels). This is another place with an intriguing history: The core of the hotel dates back to 1853 when it was the Hotel d'Angleterre, beefed up by a "neolombardesque-style" extension in the 1860s. Tchaikovsky was a guest here in December 1877; legend has it he composed the first three movements of his Symphony No. 4 in room no. 106.

Riva degli Schiavoni 4171. www.londrapalace.com. (C) **041-5200533**. 53 units. 240€–440€ double. Rates include buffet breakfast. *Vaporetto:* San Zaccaria. **Amenities:** Restaurant; bar; babysitting; concierge; room service; Wi-Fi (free).

Metropole ★★★ A luxury behemoth with a prime location on the water is part posh hotel, part eclectic art museum, with antiques, Asian artworks, and exhibits of ancient fans, corkscrews, and tapestries dotted throughout. It's no dusty grand dame, however; on the contrary, owner Gloria Beggiato has transformed the hotel into a chic boutique with rooms furnished with a classic Oriental theme. The building has an incredible history, beginning life in the Middle Ages as the Ospedale della Pietà, serving as a charitable institution for orphans and abandoned girls, and later a music school (Vivaldi taught violin here in the early 18th c.). Converted into a hotel in 1895, Sigmund Freud was an early guest along with Thomas Mann in 1900, who allegedly wrote parts of "Death in Venice" here.

Riva degli Schiavoni 4149. www.hotelmetropole.com. (C) **041-5205044**. 67 units. 202€–316€ double. Buffet breakfast 30€ (sometimes included). *Vaporetto:* San Zaccaria (walk along Riva degli Schiavoni to the right; the hotel is next to La Pietà church). **Amenities:** Restaurant; bar; babysitting; concierge; room service; Wi-Fi (free).

MODERATE

Al Piave ★★ Cozy, old-fashioned family-run hotel just 5 minutes from Piazza San Marco. Rooms are simply but attractively furnished with richly woven rugs and carpets, marble floors and some of the original wood beams exposed (some come with a terrace, while the family suites are good value for groups). Bathrooms are relatively big, and the air-conditioning a welcome bonus in the summer, but there are no elevators, so be prepared if you get a higher floor. Outside of peak months (July and Sept), Piave is exceptionally good value given its proximity to the piazza.

Ruga Giuffa 4838. www.hotelalpiave.com. ℭ **041-5285174.** 20 units. 130€–210€ double. Rates include continental breakfast. Closed Jan 7 to Carnevale. *Vaporetto:* San Zaccaria (find Calle delle Rasse beyond Palazzo Danieli, and walk to the end of the street; turn left and then immediately right; continue straight until you get to tiny Ponte Storto, cross and continue until you reach Ruga Giuffa—the hotel is on the left). **Amenities:** Babysitting; concierge; Wi-Fi (free).

Casa Verardo ★★★ Tucked away across a small bridge in the warren of central Castello, this enchanting hotel occupies a 16th-century palazzo, though it's been a hotel since 1911. Rooms (over four floors with an elevator), sport an old-fashioned Venetian style, with Florentine furniture, hand-painted beds and colorful textiles (there are precious antiques and paintings scattered throughout the property), but updated with air-conditioning and satellite TV. Some rooms have a view over a canal, others over the shady courtyard and the city. Don't miss the top floor, where the panoramic terrace is a pleasant spot for an aperitif. They'll also take you to Murano for free (you have to find your own way back).

Calle Drio La Chiesa 4765 (at foot of Ponte Storto). www.casaverardo.it. ℭ **041-5286138.** 25 units. 140€–225€ double. Rates include buffet breakfast. *Vaporetto:* San Zaccaria (walk straight on Calle delle Rasse to Campo SS. Filippo e Giacomo; continue straight through the *campo* to Calle della Sacrestia, then Calle Drio La Chiesa until you reach Ponte Storto, and look for the hotel on the left). **Amenities:** Bar, babysitting; concierge; room service; Wi-Fi (free).

INEXPENSIVE

Ai Tagliapietra ★★★ Cozy B&B run by the amicable Lorenzo (who will bend over backward to make your stay a memorable one), and a real bargain in this part of town. Basic rooms, but spotless, modern and relatively spacious with private showers. The small, shared kitchenette (with refrigerator and free tea) is available for guests to use. Lorenzo will usually meet you at San Zaccaria, will give you a map, print boarding passes, and generally organize your trip (if you desire), making this an especially recommended budget option for first-time visitors.

Salizada Zorzi 4943. www.aitagliapietra.com. ℭ **347-3233166.** 4 units. 75€–100€ double. Rates include breakfast. *Vaporetto:* San Zaccaria (walk straight on Calle delle Rasse to Campo SS. Filippo e Giacomo; continue straight through the *campo* to Calle della Sacrestia, then take the first left; cross Salita Corte Rotta and continue on to Salizada Zorzi). **Amenities:** Wi-Fi (free).

B&B San Marco ★★★ With just three rooms, this exquisite B&B in a peaceful, residential neighborhood fills up fast, so book ahead. This is a comfortable, charming, yet convenient option, the kind of place that makes you feel like a local, but not too far from the main sights. Your hosts are the bubbly Marco and Alice Scurati, who live in the attic upstairs, happy to provide help and advice. Rooms overlook the Schola di San Giorgio degli Schiavoni, offering wonderful views of the canal and streetscapes nearby, and are furnished with original antique family furniture. Two rooms share a bathroom, while the third has a private shower. Breakfast is self-service in the shared kitchen; yogurt, croissants, pastries, punchy espresso, cappuccino, juice, and tea.

Fondamenta San Giorgio dei Schiavoni 3385. www.realvenice.it. ℂ **041-5227589.** 3 units. 70€–125€ double. Rates include breakfast. *Vaporetto:* San Zaccaria (walk straight on Calle delle Rasse to Campo SS. Filippo e Giacomo; continue straight through the *campo* to Calle della Sacrestia, cross the canal and take a left at Campo S Provolo along Fondamenta Osmarin; turn left where the canal ends at a larger canal, and walk up to the bridge that connects to Calle Lion; at the end of the street turn left along the canal; this is Fondamenta San Giorgio dei Schiavoni). **Amenities:** Wi-Fi (free).

Dorsoduro
MODERATE

American Dinesen ★★   Overlooking the San Vio Canal close to the Accademia, this 17th-century Venetian town house offers elegant rooms decorated in a classical Venetian style, with all the usual modern amenities including LCD TV (with Sky TV channels). All the "superior canal" view rooms have picture-perfect views of the San Vio, many with a balcony (make sure you check if this is important to you), and even partial views of the Grand Canal. Note that the cheaper, modern "dependence rooms" are located in the annex next door and don't include breakfast.

San Vio 628 (on Fondamenta Bragadin). www.hotelamerican.it. ℂ **041-5204733.** 30 units. 85€–240€ double. Rates include buffet breakfast. *Vaporetto:* Accademia (veer left around the Accademia, taking the 1st left turn, and walk straight ahead until you cross the 1st small footbridge; turn right along the Fondamenta Bragadin and the hotel is on the left). **Amenities:** Bar; babysitting; concierge; room service; free Murano trips; Wi-Fi (free).

Galleria ★★   Just around the corner from the Accademia, right on the Grand Canal, this hotel occupies a 19th-century *palazzo* in one of the most inviting locations in the city. It's been a hotel since the 1800s, hosting poet Robert Browning in 1878, and maintains a Venetian 18th-century theme in the rooms, with wood furniture and rococo decor. Hosts Luciano and Stefano serve a simple breakfast in your room. Note that the smallest rooms here, really are tiny, and there is no air-conditioning (rooms are supplied with fans when it gets hot), but the fridge of free water and sodas is a lifesaver in summer.

Dorsoduro 878a (at foot of Accademia Bridge). www.hotelgalleria.it. ℂ **041-5232489.** 9 units, 6 with bathroom. 110€–220€ double. Rates include continental breakfast. *Vaporetto:* Accademia (with Accademia Bridge behind you; hotel is just to your left). **Amenities:** Babysitting; concierge; room service; Wi-Fi (free in public areas).

Moresco ★★★   Incredibly attentive staff, a decadent breakfast that includes Prosecco (to mix with orange juice, ahem), and lavish 19th-century Venetian decor away from the tourist hubbub make this a justly popular choice. Rooms seamlessly blend Venetian style with modern design, oak parquet or Venetian terrazzo floors. Some rooms have a terrace (with views over the canal or garden), while others have a spa bathtub; all have flatscreen TVs with satellite channels. If the weather cooperates, take breakfast in the courtyard garden to really soak up the ambience. The hotel is just a 5- to 10-minute walk from Piazzale Roma and the train station, but note there are a number of bridges and stairs to negotiate along the way.

Fondamenta del Rio Novo 3499, Dorsoduro. www.hotelmorescovenice.com. ℭ **041-2440202.** 23 units. 165€–226€ double. Rates include continental buffet breakfast. *Vaporetto:* Ferrovia/Piazzale Roma (from the train station walk south west along Fondamenta Santa Lucia, cross Ponte della Costituzione and turn left onto Fondamenta Santa Chiara; cross Ponte Santa Chiara and turn right onto Fondamenta Papadopoli, continuing across Campiello Lavadori then along Fondamenta del Rio Novo). **Amenities:** Bar; concierge; free trips to Murano; room service; Wi-Fi (free).

Pensione Accademia ★★ Spellbinding hotel with a tranquil blossom-filled garden and a fascinating history. The Gothic-style Villa Maravege was built in the 17th-century as a family residence, but served as the Russian Embassy between World Wars I and II before becoming a hotel in 1950. If that's not enticing enough, the rooms are fitted with Venetian-style antique reproductions, classical hardwood furnishings, handsome tapestries, air-conditioning, and satellite TV, with views over either the Rio San Trovaso or the gardens. Breakfast is served in your room, in the dining hall, or on the garden patio.

Fondamenta Bollani 1058. www.pensioneaccademia.it. ℭ **041-5210188.** 27 units. 140€–300€ double. Rates include buffet breakfast. *Vaporetto:* Accademia (turn right down Calle Gambara, which doglegs 1st left and then right; it becomes Calle Corfu, which ends at a side canal; walk left to cross over the bridge, and then turn right back toward the Grand Canal and the hotel). **Amenities:** Bar; babysitting; concierge; room service; Wi-Fi (free).

San Polo
MODERATE

Ca' Barba B&B ★★ What you'll remember most about Ca' Barba may well be the host, Alessandro, who will usually meet guests at the Rialto *vaporetto* stop; inspire daily wanderings with tips, maps, and books; and provide fresh breads and pastries from the local bakery for breakfast. Of the four rooms (advance reservations essential), no. 201 is the largest and brightest, with a Jacuzzi tub (no. 202 also has one). All rooms come with en suite bathrooms, antique furniture, 19th-century paintings of Venice, wood-beamed ceilings, LCD TVs, air-conditioning, and strong Wi-Fi.

Calle Campanile Castello 1825. www.cabarba.com. ℭ **041-5242816.** 4 units. 140€–180€ double. Rates include breakfast. *Vaporetto:* Rialto (walk back along the Grand Canal, and turn left when you reach Calle Campanile Castello). **Amenities:** Concierge; Wi-Fi (free).

Pensione Guerrato ★★★ Dating, incredibly, from 1227, this is definitely one of the city's most historic places to lay your head. The building's long and complicated history—it was once the "Inn of the Monkey," run by nuns, the original mostly destroyed by fire in 1513—is well worth delving into (the owners have all the details). Rooms are simply but classically furnished, with wood floors, exposed beams, air-conditioning, and private bathrooms—some rooms still contain original frescos, possibly dating from the medieval inn. Note that some rooms are on the sixth floor—and there's no elevator.

Calle Drio La Scimia 240a (near the Rialto Market). www.pensioneguerrato.it. ℂ **041-5227131.** 19 units. 100€–145€ double. Rates include buffet breakfast. Closed Dec 22–26 and Jan 8 to early Feb. *Vaporetto:* Rialto (from the north side of the Ponte Rialto, walk straight through the market until the corner with the UniCredit Banca; go 1 more short block and turn right; the hotel is halfway along Calle Drio La Scimia). **Amenities:** Babysitting; concierge; Wi-Fi (free).

Santa Croce

MODERATE

Antiche Figure ★★★   The most convenient luxury hotel in Venice lies directly across the Grand Canal from the train station, a captivating 15th-century *palazzo* adjacent to an ancient gondola workshop (seriously). History aside, this is a very plush choice, with rooms decorated in a traditional neo-classical Venetian style, with gold leaf, antique furniture, red carpets, silk tapestries, and aging Murano glass and chandeliers, but also LCD satellite TVs and decent Wi-Fi. With the soothing nighttime views across the water it's certainly a romantic choice, and the staff are definitely worth singling out—friendly and very helpful. There is an elevator, just in case you were wondering.

Fondamenta San Simeone Piccolo 687. www.hotelantichefigure.it. ℂ **041-2759486.** 22 units. 105€–264€ double. Rates include buffet breakfast. *Vaporetto:* Ferrovia (from the train station you just need to cross the Scalzi bridge on your left and take a right). **Amenities:** Restaurant; bar; babysitting; concierge; room service; Wi-Fi (free).

INEXPENSIVE

Ai Due Fanali ★★   Originally a wooden oratory frequented by fishermen and farmers (later rebuilt), this beguiling hotel features small but artsy rooms, even for Venice: Headboards have been hand-painted by a local artist, exposed wood beams crisscross the ceiling, and vintage drapes and curtains add a cozy feel (work by Jacopo Palma the Younger, the 16th-c. Mannerist painter, adorns the public areas). The bathrooms are embellished with terra-cotta tiles and Carrera marble. The location is excellent for the train station, while the roof terrace on the third floor is the best place to soak up a panorama of the city (breakfast is served up here). It's incredibly popular—book months ahead.

Campo San Simeon Profeta 946. www.aiduefanali.com. ℂ **041-718490.** 16 units. 95€–125€ double. Rates include buffet breakfast. Closed most of Jan. *Vaporetto:* Ferrovia (cross the Scalzi bridge over the Grand Canal; once you are to the other side, continue straight, taking the 2nd left and keep walking to the Campo San Simeon Profeta). **Amenities:** Bar; concierge; room service. Wi-Fi (free).

Falier ★   Tranquil budget hotel set in a quiet neighborhood, next to the Frari Church and just a 10-minute walk from the train station. Rooms are fairly compact (and could be a little cramped for some), but par for this price point in Venice, and all are air-conditioned and come with free Wi-Fi and satellite TV (although there rarely seems to be any English-language channels). The elegant garden is a great place for breakfast (you can also have it in the dining room), with warm croissants, cheese, and a selection of yogurts and cereals, teas and coffees, and fruit juices. The hotel provides free entrance to the Venice casino and a free tour of a Murano glass factory, but the friendly English-speaking staff will also set you up with all manner of other tour options.

Salizada San Pantalon 130. www.hotelfalier.com. © **041-710882.** 19 units. 85€–160€ double. Rates include continental breakfast. *Vaporetto:* Ferrovia. (From the train station, cross the Scalzi Bridge, turn right along the Grand Canal an walk to the first footbridge; turn left before crossing the bridge and continue along the smaller canal to Fondamenta Minotti; turn left here, and the street becomes Salizada San Pantalon.) **Amenities:** Concierge. Wi-Fi (free).

Cannaregio

EXPENSIVE

Al Ponte Antico ★★★   Yes it's expensive, but this is one of the best, most exclusive hotels in Venice, steps from the Rialto Bridge, with a private wharf on the Grand Canal—forget those giant five-stars, to indulge your James Bond fantasy, look no further. Part of the attraction is size—there are only seven rooms—but the attention to lavish detail is astounding, with opulent rooms and bright rococo wallpaper, rare tapestries, elegant beds, and Louis XV-style furnishings, making this seem like Versailles on the water. The building was originally a 16th-century palazzo; don't miss the charming balcony where breakfast is served, and where fabulous Bellinis are offered in the evenings.

Calle dell'Aseo 5768. www.alponteantico.com. © **041-2411944.** 7 units. 240€–430€ double. *Vaporetto:* Rialto (walk up Calle Large Mazzini, take the 2nd left and then continue to walk through Campo San Bartolomio; continue north along Salizada S.G. Grisostomo until you see Calle dell'Aseo on the left). **Amenities:** Bar; concierge; room service; Wi-Fi (free).

Arcadia ★★★   Sensational, modestly advertised boutique set in a 17th-century *palazzo*, with an appealing blend of old and new: The theme is Byzantium east-meets-west, combining elements of Venetian and Asian style, but the rooms are full of cool, modern touches—rainforest showers, flatscreen satellite TVs, bathrobes, slippers, and posh toiletries, with a lobby crowned with a Murano glass chandelier. This is a sweaty (in summer) 5-minute walk from the train station—thankfully the air-conditioning is excellent.

Rio Terà San Leonardo 1333, Cannaregio. www.hotelarcadia.net. © **041-717355.** 17 units. 130€–300€ double. Rates include continental buffet breakfast. *Vaporetto:* Guglie (take a left into the main street Rio Terà San Leonardo; Arcadia is just 30m on the left). **Amenities:** Bar; concierge; room service; Wi-Fi (free).

Giorgione ★★   Elegant gem of a hotel, located in a grand 18th-century building. Staying here really is like taking a trip back to old Venice. The combination of old and new works well: Rooms are a little worn, but that adds to the historic ambience, with antique furniture and Venetian decor, fabrics, Murano glass chandeliers, and also satellite TV. In the summer, the generous breakfast is served in the pretty fountain courtyard.

Campo SS. Apostoli 4587. www.hotelgiorgione.com. ⓒ **041-5225810.** 76 units. 100€–260€ double. Rates include buffet breakfast. *Vaporetto:* Ca' d'Oro (walk up Calle Ca' d'Oro and turn right onto Strada Nuova, which ends in Campo SS Apostoli). **Amenities:** Bar; babysitting; concierge; room service; Wi-Fi (free).

INEXPENSIVE

Bernardi ★★ This hotel is an excellent deal, with small, basic but spotless rooms in a 16th-century *palazzo* (the "superior" rooms are bigger), owned and managed by the congenial (and English-speaking) Leonardo and his wife Teresa. Most rooms come with one or two classical Venetian touches: Murano chandeliers, hand-painted furniture, exposed wood beams, and tapestries. The shared showers are kept very clean, and fans are provided in the hot summer months for the cheaper rooms (no air-conditioning). Breakfast is very basic, however, and note that the more spacious annex rooms, which have air-conditioning (nearby the main building) don't appear to get good Wi-Fi coverage.

Calle de l'Oca 4366. www.hotelbernardi.com. ⓒ **041-5227257.** 18 units, 11 with private bathroom. 60€–94€ double. Rates include breakfast. *Vaporetto:* Ca' d'Oro (walk straight to Strada Nova, turn right toward Campo SS. Apostoli; in the square, turn left and take the 1st side street on your left, which is Calle de l'Oca). **Amenities:** Babysitting; concierge; room service; Wi-Fi (free).

San Geremia ★ Excellent budget option just 10 minutes from the train station. Rooms are small and simple but adequate, with most featuring air-conditioning and views across the canal or *campo*. Note that there is no elevator, with some rooms up three flights of stairs, and breakfast is not provided (but you get 50% off breakfast next door). No TVs in the rooms, but there is strong Wi-Fi. The dorm rooms are a good deal at just 21€ to 25€ per night (for guests under 35 only). Cash only.

Campo San Geremia 283. www.hotelsangeremia.com. ⓒ **041-715562.** 20 units, 14 with private bathroom. 46€–100€ double. Closed the week of Christmas. *Vaporetto:* Ferrovia (exit the train station, turn left onto Lista di Spagna, and continue to Campo San Geremia). **Amenities:** Babysitting; concierge; room service. Wi-Fi (free).

Giudecca

A quick ferry straight across from the cacophony of Piazza San Marco brings you to the quiet charms of Giudecca island and its spectacular views across the lagoon to Venice. This is where you'll find **Belmond Hotel Cipriani** (Giudecca 10; www.belmond.com/hotelcipriani; ⓒ **041-240801**), the most famous hotel in Venice, if not all of northern Italy, with its enormous saltwater pool, decadent spa, and rambling gardens. It's extremely expensive, but keep an eye out for shoulder-season deals (the hotel is closed during winter months). Or just come for dinner at waterside **The Cip's Club** where dinner comes with a sparkling view of Piazza San Marco.

WHERE TO EAT

Eating cheaply in Venice is not easy, but it's by no means impossible. The city's reputation for mass-produced menus, bad service, and wildly overpriced food is, sadly, well-warranted, and if you've been traveling in other parts of the country, you may be a little disappointed here. Having said that, everything is relative—this is still Italy after all—and there are plenty of excellent options in Venice, listed below. As a basic rule, value for money tends to increase the farther you travel from Piazza San Marco, and anything described as a *menu turistico,* while cheaper than a la carte, is rarely any good in Venice (exceptions noted below). Note also that compared with Rome and other points south, Venice is a city of early meals: You should be seated by 7:30 to 8:30pm. Most kitchens close at 10 or 10:30pm, even though the restaurant may stay open until 11:30pm or midnight.

While most restaurants in Italy include a cover charge *(coperto)* that usually runs 1.50€ to 3€, in Venice they tend to instead tack on 10% to 12% to the bill for "taxes and service." Some places in Venice will very annoyingly charge you the cover and still add on 12%. A menu should state clearly what extras the restaurant charges (sometimes you'll find it in miniscule print at the bottom), and if it doesn't, take your business elsewhere.

VENETIAN CUISINE Venice has a distinguished culinary history, much of it based on its geographical position on the sea. For first courses, both pasta and risotto are commonly prepared with fish or seafood: Risotto *al nero di seppia* or *alle seppioline* (tinted black by the ink of cuttlefish, also called *risotto nero* or black risotto) or *spaghetti alle vongole* (with clams; clams without their shells are not a good sign) are two commonly found specialties. Both appear with *frutti di mare,* "fruit of the sea," which is mixed shellfish.

BACARI & CICCHETTI

One of the essential culinary experiences of Venice is trawling the countless neighborhood bars known as *bacari,* where you can stand or sit with *tramezzini* (small, triangular white-bread half-sandwiches filled with everything from thinly sliced meats and tuna salad to cheeses and vegetables), and *cicchetti* (tapas-like finger foods, such as calamari rings, speared fried olives, potato croquettes, or grilled polenta squares), traditionally washed down with a small glass of wine, Veneto Prosecco, or spritz (a fluorescent cocktail of Prosecco and orange-flavored Aperol). All of the above will cost approximately 1.50€ to 6€ if you stand at the bar, as much as double when seated. Bar food is displayed on the countertop or in glass counters and usually sells out by late afternoon, so though it can make a great lunch, don't rely on it for a light dinner. A concentration of popular, well-stocked bars can be found along the Mercerie shopping strip that connects Piazza San Marco with the Rialto Bridge, the always lively Campo San Luca (look for Bar Torino, Bar Black Jack, or the character-filled Leon Bianco wine bar), and Campo Santa Margherita.

Venice Restaurants

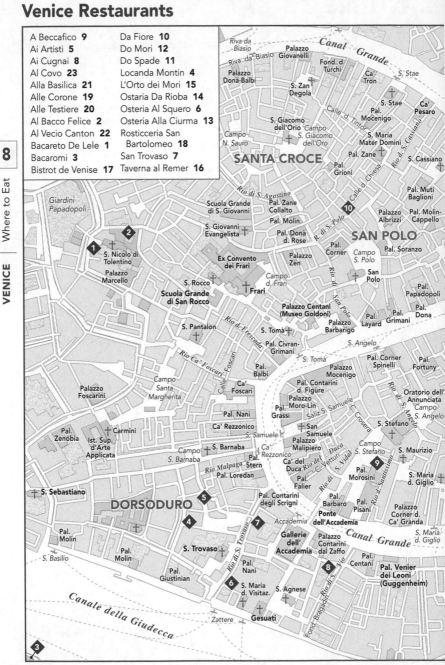

A Beccafico **9**
Ai Artisti **5**
Ai Cugnai **8**
Al Covo **23**
Alla Basilica **21**
Alle Corone **19**
Alle Testiere **20**
Al Bacco Felice **2**
Al Vecio Canton **22**
Bacareto De Lele **1**
Bacaromi **3**
Bistrot de Venise **17**

Da Fiore **10**
Do Mori **12**
Do Spade **11**
Locanda Montin **4**
L'Orto dei Mori **15**
Ostaria Da Rioba **14**
Osteria Al Squero **6**
Osteria Alla Ciurma **13**
Rosticceria San
  Bartolomeo **18**
San Trovaso **7**
Taverna al Remer **16**

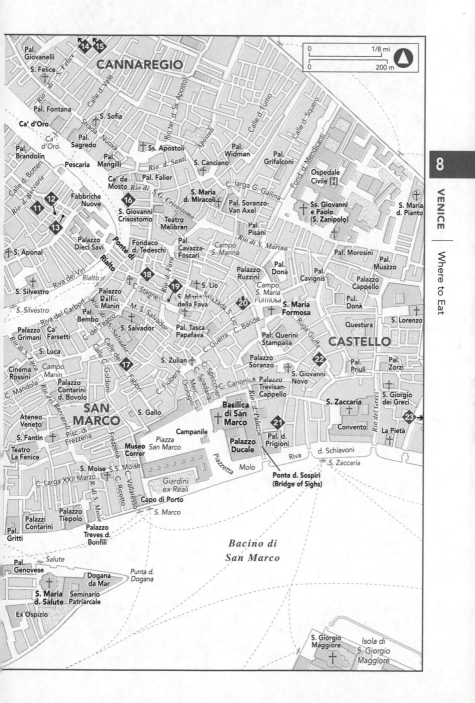

Ciccheti (small snacks) with wine.

Bigoli, a sort of thick spaghetti that's perfect for catching lots of sauce, is a Venetian staple, as is creamy polenta, often served with *gamberetti* (small shrimp) or tiny shrimp called *schie,* or as an accompaniment to *fegato alla veneziana* (calf's liver cooked with onions and white wine). Some of the fish and seafood dishes Venice does particularly well include *branzino* (a kind of sea bass), *rombo* (turbot or brill), *moeche* (small soft-shelled crab) or *granseola* (crab), and *sarde in saor* (sardines in a sauce of onion, vinegar, pinenuts, and raisins).

Try the dry white Tocai and pinot from the Friuli region to the northeast of Venice and the light, sparkling Prosecco that Venetians consume almost like a soft drink. Popular local red wines include Bardolino, Valpolicella, and Soave, all of which come from the surrounding Veneto region. *Grappa,* the local firewater, is an acquired taste and is often offered in many variations.

RESTAURANTS BY CUISINE

CAFE
Caffè dei Frari ★★★, p. 284
Caffè Florian ★★, p. 285
Caffè Lavena ★★, p. 285
Gran Caffè Quadri ★, p. 285
Il Caffè (aka Caffe Rosso) ★★★, p. 286
Marchini Time ★★, p. 286
Pasticceria Nobile ★★, p. 286

DELI
Rosticceria San Bartolomeo ★★, p. 244

GELATO
Gelato Fantasy ★, p. 251
Il Doge ★★, p. 252
La Mela Verde ★★, p. 252
Nico ★, p. 253

ITALIAN
Al Bacco Felice ★, p. 249
Alle Testiere ★★★, p. 245
Al Vecio Canton ★, p. 246
Bacaromi ★★, p. 251
San Trovaso ★, p. 248

San Marco
EXPENSIVE

A Beccafico ★ SICILIAN   Take a trip to Sicily for a refreshing change from Venetian cuisine, with a menu rich in seafood pastas (such as a simple but delicious *spaghetti alle vongole*) and fresh tuna, sea bream, fabulous calamari, and swordfish—the waiters will advise on the fish of the day and specials such as eggplant ragout. For dessert, you'd be remiss to ignore the utterly addictive tiramisu, and the evening is usually rounded off with complimentary *limoncello*. The location is charming; sit outside to enjoy the people watching in Campo Santo Stefano. On the downside, service can be hit and miss, and though the food is good, the high prices reflect the location rather than overall quality.

Campo Santo Stefano 2801. www.abeccafico.com. © **041-5274879.** Reservations recommended. Main courses 24€–28€. Daily noon–3pm and 7–11pm. *Vaporetto:* Accademia (cross bridge to San Marco side and walk straight ahead to Campo Santo Stefano; the restaurant is on your right and toward the back end of the *campo*).

Bistrot de Venise ★★★ VENETIAN   Though it looks a bit like a wood-paneled French bistro, the menu here is primarily old-school Venetian, specializing in rare wines and historical recipes from the 14th to 18th centuries. It's gimmicky, but it works; think old-fashioned fennel soup, an incredible shrimp pie, and cod fillet with almonds in a light ginger and saffron sauce, served with wild berries and garlic pudding. We recommend the "historical" tasting menu as the best introduction. Whatever you opt for, expect service to be top-notch. The restaurant also doubles as an arts center in the winter, with all sorts of live music and poetry readings between October and May. In summer, sit outside in the pleasant side street.

4685 Calle dei Fabbri. www.bistrotdevenise.com. © **041-5236651.** Main courses 26€–34€; classic Venetian tasting menu 65€; historical 5-course Venetian menu 95€.

Daily: bar 10am–midnight, restaurant noon–3pm and 7pm–midnight. *Vaporetto:* Rialto (turn right along canal, cross small footbridge over Rio San Salvador, turn left onto Calle Bembo, which becomes Calle dei Fabbri; Bistrot is about 5 blocks ahead).

Da Fiore ★★ VENETIAN   Classy but laid-back Venetian trattoria (not to be confused with the posher osteria with the same name), with two cozy little rooms and 11 tables. The menu features typical Venetian dishes like squid ink pasta, but the specials here are the most fun, with *moeche* (local soft-shell crab) a particular treat (the two main seasons are March to April and October to November). Desserts are another specialty, with all sorts of sugary *golosessi* on offer, from *buranelli* to *zaletti* (cornmeal cookies, typically eaten dipped in sweet wine or chocolate), and an exceptional *sgroppino al limone* (lemon sherbet). Make sure you visit the associated bar and *cicchetteria* next door, the Bacaro di Fiore (Weds–Mon 9am–10pm), which has been around since 1871, serving cheap wine and snacks like fried fish, fried vegetables (zucchini, pumpkin flowers, and artichokes), meatballs, grilled cuttlefish, sardines, and crostini with creamed cod.

Calle delle Botteghe 3461, off Campo Santo Stefano. www.dafiore.it. ⓒ**041-5235310.** Reservations recommended. Main courses 16€–28€. Wed–Mon noon–3pm and 7–10pm. Closed 2 weeks in Jan and 2 weeks in Aug. *Vaporetto:* Accademia (cross bridge to San Marco side and walk straight ahead to Campo Santo Stefano; as you are about to exit the *campo* at northern end, take a left at Bar/Gelateria Paolin onto Calle delle Botteghe; also close to Sant'Angelo *vaporetto* stop).

MODERATE

Rosticceria San Bartolomeo ★★ DELI/VENETIAN   Also known as Rosticceria Gislon, this no-frills spot has a cheap canteen section popular with locals and a more expensive upstairs sit-down dining room, but don't be fooled by appearances—the downstairs section is just as good, with a range of grilled fish and seafood pastas on offer (lots of scampi, clams, and mussels), a tasty "mozzarella in carrozza" (fried cheese sandwich; 1.70€), and there is a discount if you order to take out. Otherwise just sit at the counter and soak up the animated scene, as the cooks chop, customers chat and people come and go. Order the roast chicken, salt cod, or polenta—typical Venetian fare without all those extra charges.

Calle della Bissa 5424. ⓒ**041-5223569.** Main courses 10€–22€. Daily 9:30am–9:30pm (Mon until 3:30pm). *Vaporetto:* Rialto (with bridge at your back on San Marco side of canal, walk straight to Campo San Bartolomeo; take underpass slightly to your left marked SOTTOPORTEGO DELLA BISSA; the *rosticceria* is at the 1st corner on your right; look for GISLON above the entrance).

Castello

EXPENSIVE

Al Covo ★★ SEAFOOD/VENETIAN   For years, this high-quality Venetian restaurant from Diane and Cesare Benelli has been deservedly popular with American food writers (and TV chefs such as Anthony Bourdain), so expect to be eating with plenty of fellow tourists. It features two cozy dining rooms adorned with art (plus some outdoor seating in summer), but it's the food that takes center stage here: fresh fish from the lagoon or the Adriatic, fruits and vegetables from local farms, and meat sourced from highly regarded Franco Cazzamali Butchers. The pasta, desserts, and sauces are all home-made. Begin with traditional Venetian *saor,* sweet and sour fish and shellfish, or fried zucchini flowers, followed by fresh Adriatic monkfish with pancetta on a celeriac fondue, or deep-fried scampi, calamari, and baby sole. Diane's desserts might include rustic pear and prune cake with grappa-cinnamon sauce or green apple sorbet with Calvados.

Campiello della Pescheria 3968. www.ristorantealcovo.com. (✆ **041-5223812.** Reservations required. Main courses 28€–36€; menu with choice of any combination of 1 *primo,* 1 *secondo,* and 1 dessert 59€. Fri–Tues 12:45–3:30pm (kitchen closes 2pm) and 7:30pm–midnight (kitchen closes at 10pm); Closed usually in Jan and 10 days in Aug. *Vaporetto:* Piazza San Marco; walk along Riva degli Schiavoni toward Arsenale, and take the 3rd narrow street left (Calle della Pescaria) after Hotel Metropole (just before Hotel Gabrielli).

Alle Corone ★★★ SEAFOOD/VENETIAN   One of Venice's finest restaurants, an elegant 19th-century dining room located inside the Hotel Ai Reali overlooking the canal. Start with a selection of classic Venetian cicchetti (21€) before moving on to gnocchi with squid and wild asparagus (19€) or main courses such as baked turbot with black olives, seared tuna with poppy seeds, or roast rack of lamb with thyme, potatoes, and artichokes. To finish, the rosemary panna cotta with apple and ginger jam is spectacular (9€). Reservations recommended.

Campo della Fava 5527 (Hotel Ai Reali). www.hotelaireali.com. (✆ **041-2410253.** Main courses 28€–32€. Daily noon–2:30pm and 7–10:30pm. *Vaporetto:* Rialto (walk east along Calle Larga Mazzini, turn left Merceria then right on Calle Stella until you reach the hotel).

Alle Testiere ★★★ ITALIAN/VENE-TIAN   This tiny restaurant (with only 9 tables, seating for around 22), is the connoisseur's choice for fresh fish and seafood, with a menu that changes frequently and a shrewd selection of wines. Dinner is served at two seatings, where you choose from appetizers such as scallops with cherry tomatoes and orange, and clams that seem to have been literally plucked straight from the sea. The John Dory filet with aromatic herbs is always an exceptional main choice, and the pastas—ravioli with eggplant and pesto, or the ricotta with prawns—are all superb. Finish off with homemade peach pie or

Fish display.

chestnut pudding. In peak season, plan to make reservations at least a month in advance, and note that you'll have a less rushed experience in the second seating.

Calle del Mondo Novo 5801 (off Salizada San Lio). www.osterialletestiere.it. © **041-5227220.** Reservations required for each of 2 seatings. Main courses 26€, and many types of fish sold by weight. Tues–Sat noon–3pm and 2 seatings at 7 and 9:15pm. *Vaporetto:* Equidistant from either the Rialto or San Marco stops. Look for store-lined Salizada San Lio (west of the Campo Santa Maria Formosa), and from there ask for the Calle del Mondo Novo.

MODERATE

Al Vecio Canton ★ ITALIAN/PIZZA Venice is not known for pizza, partly because fire codes restrict the use of traditional wood-burning ovens, but the big, fluffy crusted pies here—made using natural mineral water—are the best in the city. They also do a mean T-bone steak, cooked tableside on a granite slab, accompanied by truffle or red pepper sauce, and some of the pastas are pretty good too—stick with seafood versions like cuttlefish, and the seasonal *moeche* (soft-shell crabs fried in batter), and *schie,* small gray shrimp caught in the lagoon. Wash it all down with the house wine, or for a change, tasty craft beers from Treviso-based 32 Via dei Birrai.

Castello 4738a (at the corner of Calle Ruga Giuffa). www.alveciocanton.com. © **041-5287143.** Reservations not accepted. Main courses 13€–20€. Wed–Mon 11:30am–3pm and 6–10:30pm. *Vaporetto:* San Zaccaria (head down the road that flanks the left side of the Hotel Savoia e Jolanda to Campo San Provolo; take Salizada San Provolo on the north side of the *campo,* cross the 1st footbridge on your left, and the pizzeria is on the 1st corner on the left).

INEXPENSIVE

Alla Basilica ★★ VENETIAN Considering this restaurant is just around the corner from the Doge's Palace and St. Mark's, lunch here is a phenomenally good deal. Don't expect romance—it's a large, noisy, canteenlike place—but the simple, freshly prepared meals comprise a pasta course like creamy lasagna or *spaghetti con ragu,* a meat or fish main (think grilled pork chops or *dentice al vapore con zucchini grigliate,* steamed red snapper with grilled zucchini), and mixed vegetables for just 14€, with bread and bottled water. Add a liter of extremely drinkable house wine for just 10€. Basilica is a favorite of local workers, and English is rarely spoken, so you'll need to practice your Italian skills here.

Calle degli Albanesi 4255, Castello. www.allabasilicavenezia.it. © **041-5220524.** Lunch set menu 14€. Tues–Sun noon–3pm. *Vaporetto:* San Marco (as you disembark, the entrance to Calle degli Albanesi is a short walk to the left).

Dorsoduro

EXPENSIVE

Ai Artisti ★★★ VENETIAN This unpretentious, family-owned osteria enoteca is one of the best dining experiences in Venice, with a menu that changes daily according to what's available at the market (because the fish market is closed on Monday, no fish is served that day). Grab a table by the canal and feast on stuffed squid, pan-fried sardines and an amazing, buttery veal *scallopini,* or opt for one of the truly wonderful pastas. The tiramisu and chocolate torte are standouts for dessert. Something that's likely to stay with you in addition to the food is the impeccable service, with wait staff happy to guide you through the menu, and offer brilliant suggestions for wine pairing. Reservations recommended—it's a tiny place, with seating for just 20.

Fondamenta della Toletta 1169A. www.enotecaartisti.com. © **041-5238944.** Reservations recommended. Main courses 22€–30€. Mon–Sat noon–4pm and 7–10pm. *Vaporetto:* Accademia (walk around Accademia and turn right onto Calle Gambara; when this street ends at Rio di San Trovaso, turn left onto Fondamenta Priuli; take the 1st bridge over the canal and onto a road that soon leads into Fondamenta della Toletta).

Locanda Montin ★★ VENETIAN   Montin was the famous ex-hang-out of Peggy Guggenheim in the 1950s, and was frequented by Jimmy Carter, Robert De Niro, and Brad Pitt, among many other celebrities, but is the food any good? Well, yes. Grab a table in the wonderfully serene back garden (completely covered by an arching trellis), itself a good reason to visit, and sample Venetian classics such as sardines in *soar* (a local marinade of vinegar, wine, onion, and raisins), and an exquisite *seppie in nero* (cuttlefish cooked in its ink). For a main course, it's hard to beat the crispy sea bass *(branzino)* or legendary monkfish, while the lemon sorbet with vodka is a perfect, tangy conclusion to any meal.

Fondamenta di Borgo 1147. www.locandamontin.com. © **041-5227151.** Main courses 22€–30€. Daily 12:30–2:30pm and 5pm–midnight. *Vaporetto:* Ca'Rezzonico (walk straight along Calle Lunga San Barnaba for around 1,000 ft., then turn left along Fondamenta di Borgo).

MODERATE

Ai Cugnai ★★ VENETIAN   The name of this small trattoria means "at the in-laws," and in that spirit the kitchen knocks out solid, home-cooked Venetian food, beautifully prepared and very popular with locals and hungry gondoliers. The classics are done especially well: The *spaghetti vongole* here is crammed with sea-fresh mussels and clams, the *caprese* and baby octopus salad perfectly balanced appetizers, and the house red top value. Our favorite, though, is the sublime spaghetti with scallops, a slippery, salty delight. Just two small tables outside, so get here early if you want to eat alfresco.

Calle Nuova Sant'Agnese 857. © **041-5289238.** Main courses 13€–25€. Tues–Sun noon–3:30pm and 7–10pm. *Vaporetto:* Accademia (head east of bridge and Accademia in direction of Guggenheim Collection; restaurant will be on your right, off the straight street connecting the 2 museums).

Osteria Al Squero ★★★ WINE BAR/VENETIAN   Enticing *osteria* with perhaps the most beguiling view in Venice, right opposite the Squero di San Trovaso (p. 269). Sip coffee and nibble *cicchetti* (from around 1.20€), while observing the activity at this medieval gondola boatyard and workshop, on the other side of the Rio di San Trovaso. It's essentially a place for a light lunch or *aperitivi* rather than a full meal, snacking on delights such as Carnia smoked sausage, baccalà crostini (cod), anchovies, blue cheese, tuna, and sardines in *saor* for a total of around 15€ per person. House wine from 1.50€.

*Fondamenta Nani 943–944. http://osteriaalsquero.wordpress.com. ℂ **335-6007513.** Cicchetti 1.20€ per piece. Tues–Sun 7am–8pm. Vaporetto: Zattere (walk west along the waterside to the Rio di San Trovaso and turn right up Fondamenta Nani).*

San Trovaso ★ ITALIAN/VENETIAN   No-frills tavern perfect for a lunch or dinner of tasty Italian comfort food, with a daily 3-course *menu turistico* (21€) featuring classics such as spaghetti with pesto, *spaghetti vongole* and an utterly addictive *gnocchi ai 4 formaggi* (gnocchi with four cheeses). The seafood menu is huge, with *salmone alla griglia* (grilled salmon) and a delightful *scaloppini* (finely sliced scallops) with lemon sauce in addition to the usual Venetian line-up of scampi, monkfish, and sea bass. Tends to be touristy, of course, but a good value all the same.

*Dorsoduro 1016 (on Fondamenta Priuli). www.tavernasantrovaso.it. ℂ **041-5230835.** Reservations recommended. Main courses 12€–19€. Tues–Sun noon–2:45pm and 7pm–9:45pm. Vaporetto: Accademia (walk to right around Accademia and take a right onto Calle Gambara; when this street ends at small Rio di San Trovaso, turn left onto Fondamenta Priuli).*

San Polo
MODERATE

Do Spade ★ VENETIAN   It's tough to find something so authentic and local this close to the Rialto Bridge these days, but Do Spade has been around since 1415. Most locals come here for the *cicchetti* (you can sit on benches outside if it's too crowded indoors), typical Venetian small plates such as fried calamari, meatballs, mozzarella, salted cod (1€–3€), and decent wines (3€ a glass). The more formal restaurant section is also worth a try, with seafood highlights including a delicately prepared monkfish, scallops served with fresh zucchini, and a rich seafood lasagna. The seasonal pumpkin ravioli is one of the best dishes in the city.

*Sottoportego do Spade 860. www.cantinadospade.com. ℂ **041-5210574.** Main courses 14€–22€. Daily 10am–3pm and 6–10pm. Vaporetto: Rialto Mercato (with your back to Grand Canal, walk straight up Ruga Vecchia San Giovanni and turn right on Ruga dei Spezieri; at the end turn left on Calle de le Beccarie O Panataria, and then take 2nd right onto covered Sottoportego do Spade).*

INEXPENSIVE

Do Mori ★★★ WINE BAR/VENETIAN   Serving good wine and *cicchetti* since 1462 (check out the antique copper pots hanging from the ceiling), Do Mori is above all a fun place to have a genuine Venetian experience, a small, dimly lit *bàcari* that can barely accommodate ten people standing up. Sample the baby octopus and ham on mango, lard-smothered *crostini,* and pickled onions speared with salty anchovies, or opt for the *tramezzini* (tiny sandwiches). Local TV (and BBC) star Francesco Da Mosto is a regular, but note that this institution is very much on the well-trodden tourist trail—plenty of *cicchetti* tours stop by in the early evening. Local wine runs around 3€ to 4€ per glass.

Calle Do Mori 429 (also Calle Galeazza 401). 𝒞 **041-5225401.** *Tramezzini* and *cicchetti* 1.80€–3€ per piece. Mon–Sat 8am–8pm (June–Aug closed daily 2–4:30pm). *Vaporetto:* Rialto Mercato (with your back to Grand Canal, walk straight up Ruga Vecchia San Giovanni and turn right on Calle Galeazza).

Osteria Alla Ciurma ★★★ WINE BAR/VENETIAN With a dining room decked out like a traditional Venetian boat, this *cicchetteria* offers some of the freshest seafood snacks in the city—they source their fresh fish from the daily market just around the corner—washed down with quality wines, spritz, and Prosecco. Mouth-watering *cicchetti* include cod fillets, fried zucchini flowers, fried artichokes, and shrimp wrapped in bacon. More substantial sandwiches (from 3.50€) and lunch specials (noon–3pm) from 5€ are also available.

Calle Galeazza 406. 𝒞 **340-6863561.** *Cicchetti* 1.50€–2€ per piece. Mon–Sat 9am–3pm and 5:30–9pm; Sun 10:30am–3pm (May–Sep only). *Vaporetto:* Rialto Mercato (with your back to Grand Canal, walk straight up Ruga Vecchia San Giovanni and turn right on Calle Galeazza).

Santa Croce
MODERATE
Al Bacco Felice ★ ITALIAN This quaint, friendly neighborhood restaurant is convenient for the train station and popular with locals, with a real buzz most evenings. Stick with the basics and you won't be disappointed—the pizzas, pastas, and fish dishes are always outstanding, with classic standbys *spaghetti alle vongole,* pasta with spicy *arrabbiata,* and *carpaccio* of swordfish especially well done. The meal usually ends with complimentary plates of Venetian cookies, a nice touch.

Santa Croce 197E (on Corte dei Amai). 𝒞 **041-5287794.** Main courses 15€–30€. Mon–Fri noon–3:30pm and 6:30–11pm, Sat and Sun noon–11:30pm. *Vaporetto:* Piazzale Roma (you can walk here in 10 min. from the train station; from the Piazzale Roma *vaporetto* stop keep the Grand Canal on your left and head toward the train station; cross the small canal at the end of the park and immediately turn right onto Fondamenta Tolentini; when you get to Campo Tolentini turn left onto Corte dei Amai).

INEXPENSIVE
Bacareto Da Lele ★★★ WINE BAR/VENETIAN This tiny hole-in-the-wall *bacaro* is worth seeking out for its fresh snacks, sandwiches, and *cicchetti.* Tiny glasses or *ombras* of wine and Prosecco are just 0.60€–1€). There are no seats, so do as the locals do and grab a space on the nearby church steps, outside by the canal, while you sip and nibble. Opt for a tiny porchetta and mustard or the bacon and artichoke panini (around 1€–2€), antipasti plates for 1.20€ (cheese and salami), or a simple, freshly baked crostini for 1€ to 1.60€. Expect long lines here in peak season; the secret is definitely out.

Campo dei Tolentini 183. No phone. *Cicchetti* 1€–2€ per piece. Mon–Fri 6am–8pm, Sat 6am–2pm. *Vaporetto:* Piazzale Roma (walk left along the Grand Canal, past the Ponte della Costituzione, into the Giardino Papadopoli; turn right along Fonadmenta Papa-dopoli then turn left and cut across the park at the first bridge; the next canal you hit should be the Rio del Tolentini, with the campo across the bridge and Bacareto Da Lele on the southwest corner).

Cannaregio

EXPENSIVE

L'Orto dei Mori ★★ VENETIAN   Traditional Venetian cuisine cooked up by a young Sicilian chef, so expect some subtle differences to the usual flavors and dishes. Everything on the relatively small menu is exceptional—the *baccalà* (salted cod) especially so—and the setting next to a small canal is enhanced by candlelight at night. This place can get very busy—the waiters are normally friendly, but be warned, expect brusque treatment if you turn up late or early for a reservation. Don't be confused: The restaurant prefers to serve dinner, broadly, within two seatings, one early (7–9pm) and one late, so that's why waiters will be reluctant to serve those that arrive early for the second sitting—even if there's a table available, you'll be given water and just told to wait.

Campo dei Mori 3386. www.osteriaortodeimori.com. (C) **041-5243677.** Reservations recommended. Main courses 19€–25€. Wed–Mon 12:30–3:30pm and 7pm–midnight, usually in 2 seatings (July–Aug closed for lunch Mon–Fri). *Vaporetto:* Madonna dell'Orto (walk through the *campo* to the canal and turn right; take the 1st bridge to your left, walk down the street and turn left at the canal onto Fondamenta dei Mori; go straight until you hit Campo dei Mori).

Ostaria Da Rioba ★★ SEAFOOD/VENETIAN   Fresh, creative, and absolutely scrumptious Venetian food served right alongside a serene canal in a lively—but not touristy—area. Plenty of locals eat here, enticed by the beau-tifully executed seafood; monkfish, sea bass, scampi, turbot, mackerel, tuna, and lots of cod. Top choices include their lightly grilled scampi (massive prawns sliced down the middle), and their "spaghetti noir," an interpretation of that Venetian classic, spaghetti with cuttlefish ink, but for a real treat order the grilled duck, a rich, sumptuous dish served with seasonal vegetables. Note that there are only 35 seats along the canal, so to watch that gorgeous summer sunset, reservations are a must.

Fondamenta della Misericordia 2553. www.darioba.com. (C) **041-5244379.** Reserva-tions highly recommended. Main courses 20€–25€. Tues–Sun 11am–3pm and 6–10pm. *Vaporetto:* San Marcuola (walk behind the church at the stop, then go straight for 5 blocks to the 1st bridge; cross and turn right on Misericordia).

INEXPENSIVE

Taverna al Remer ★★ VENETIAN   Eating on a budget in Venice doesn't always mean panini and pizza slices. This romantic *taverna* overlooks the Grand Canal from a small, charming piazza, and while the a la carte options can be pricy, the secret is to time your visit for the buffets. The 20€ lunch is a fabulous deal, with a choice of two fresh pastas plus a buffet of antipasto which includes seasonal vegetables, salads, cold cuts, a choice of two or three quality hot dishes (such as Venice-style liver with polenta, or pan-fried squid), a choice of two or three desserts, and coffee, water, and a quarter liter of wine (per person), all included. The evening *aperitivo* is an even better deal, from just 7€ for as much smoked meats, sausage, salads, seafood risotto, and pasta as you can eat, plus one Aperol spritz, Bellini, vino, or Prosecco from 5:30 to 7:30. Normal service resumes (main courses 16€–25€) after the buffet is cleared, with live music (Latin, soul, jazz) most nights at 8:30pm, but as long as you order a few drinks, it's fine to stick around and take in the scene.

Cannaregio 5701 (off Salizada S. Giovanni Grisostomo). www.alremer.it. ℗ **041-5228789.** Lunch buffet 20€; aperitivo (5:30–7:30pm) from 7€, Mon, Tues, and Thurs–Sat noon–2:30pm and 5:30pm–midnight; Sun 5:30pm–midnight. *Vaporetto:* Ca' d'Oro or Rialto; (heading south on Salizada S. Giovanni Grisostomo, look for a narrow passage on the right, just beyond the Ponte S. Giovanni footbridge).

La Giudecca

EXPENSIVE

Bacaromi ★★ ITALIAN/VENETIAN   This hotel restaurant is well worth staying over on Giudecca for, even if you're not spending the night. It's a faux rustic Venetian canteen where you can sample *cicchetti*, and a glass of local wine in the company of welcoming and incredibly helpful English-speaking staff led by the indomitable Giuseppe Russo. Combine that with the views across the canal and this is a pricy but pleasurable experience, especially for those new to Venice. Menus change regularly, but seafood, unsurprisingly, dominates. If available, order the crab and squid ink risotto, mixed fried fish, roasted mackerel, or just a simple pasta with prawns, but don't be afraid to create a meal from several *cicchetti*—these also change regularly, but the *baccala* (cod) mousse is a taste sensation.

Fondamenta San Biagio 810 (in the Hilton Molino Stucky). www.molinostuckyhilton. com. ℗ **041-2723311.** Main courses 18€–30€. Daily 6–10:30pm. *Vaporetto:* Palanca, then walk 5 minutes along the canal (to the right) to the hotel.

Gelato

Is the gelato any good in Venice? Italians might demur, but by international standards, the answer is most definitely yes. As always, though, remember that gelato parlors aimed exclusively at tourists are notorious for poor quality and extortionate prices, especially in Venice. Try to avoid places near Piazza San Marco altogether. Below are some of our favorite spots in the city. Each generally opens midmorning and closes late. Winter hours are more erratic.

Gelato Fantasy ★ GELATO   Since 1998, this tiny gelato shop has been doling out tasty scoops dangerously close to Piazza San Marco, but the quality remains high and portions generous. Fresh, strong flavors, with standouts including the pistachio, tiramisu, and dark chocolate.

Calle dei Fabbri 929, San Marco. www.gelatofantasy.com. ℗ **041-5225993.** Cone from 2€. *Vaporetto:* Rialto or San Marco.

EATING alfresco IN VENICE

You don't have to eat in a fancy restaurant to enjoy good food in Venice. Prepare a picnic, and while you eat alfresco, you can observe the life in the city's *campi* or the aquatic parade on its main thoroughfare, the Grand Canal. Plus, shopping for your food can be an interesting experience because you will probably have to do it in the small *alimentari* (food shops); supermarkets are scarce.

Mercato Rialto Venice's principal open-air market is a sight to see, even for non-shoppers. It has two parts, beginning with the produce section, whose many stalls, alternating with those of souvenir vendors, unfold north on the San Polo side of the Rialto Bridge (behind these stalls are a few permanent food stores that sell delicious cheese, cold cuts, and bread selections). The vendors are here Monday to Saturday 7am to 1pm, with some staying on in the afternoon.

At the market's farthest point, you'll find the covered **fish market,** with its carnival atmosphere, picturesquely located on the Grand Canal opposite the magnificent Ca' d'Oro and still redolent of the days when it was one of the Mediterranean's great fish bazaars. The area is filled with a number of small *bacari* bars frequented by market vendors and

Mercato Rialto.

shoppers, where you can join in and ask for your morning's first glass of Prosecco with a *cicchetto* pick-me-up. The fish

Il Doge ★★ GELATO   A definite contender for best gelato in Venice, with a great location at the southern end of the *campo* since 1986. These guys use only natural, homemade flavors and ingredients, from their exceptional spicy chocolate to their specialty, "Crema de Doge," a rich concoction of eggs, cream, and real oranges. Look for refreshing *granitas* in summer.

Campo Santa Margherita 3058, Dorsoduro. ⓒ **041-5234607.** Cones and cups from 1.50€–5.50€. *Vaporetto:* Ca'Rezzonico.

La Mela Verde ★★ GELATO   The popular rival to Il Doge for best scoop in the city, with sharp flavors and all the classics done sensationally well: pistachio, chocolate, *nocciola* (hazelnut), and the mind-blowing lemon and basil. The overall champions: *mela verde* (green apple), like creamy, frozen fruit served in a cup, and the addictive tiramisu flavor.

merchants take Monday off and work mornings only.

Campo Santa Margherita

On this spacious *campo* in Dorsoduro, Tuesday through Saturday from 8:30am to 1pm, a number of open-air stalls set up shop, selling fresh fruit and vegetables. There's also a conventional supermarket, **Punto SMA,** just off the *campo* in the direction of the quasi-adjacent *campo* San Barnaba, at no. 3019.

San Barnaba

This is where you'll find Venice's heavily photographed **floating market** (mostly fruit and vegetables), operating from a boat moored just off San Barnaba at the Ponte dei Pugni in Dorsoduro. This market is open daily from 8am to 1pm and 3:30 to 7:30pm, except Wednesday afternoon and Sunday.

The Best Picnic Spots

Given its aquatic roots, you won't find much in the way of green space in Venice (if you are really desperate for green, you can walk 30 min. past San Marco along the water, or take a *vaporetto* to the Giardini Pubblici, Venice's only green park, but don't expect anything great). A much more enjoyable alternative is to find some of the larger *campi* that have park benches, such as Campo San Giacomo dell'Orio (in the quiet *sestiere* of Santa Croce). The two most central are **Campo Santa Margherita** (*sestiere* of Dorsoduro) and **Campo San Polo** (*sestiere* of San Polo).

For a picnic with a view, scout out the **Punta della Dogana (Customs House)** near La Salute Church for a prime viewing site at the mouth of the Grand Canal. Pull up on a piece of the embankment here and watch the flutter of water activity against a canvaslike backdrop deserving of the Accademia Museum. In this same area, another superb spot is the small **Campo San Vio** near the Guggenheim, which is directly on the Grand Canal (not many *campi* are) and even boasts two benches as well as the possibility to sit on an untrafficked small bridge.

To go a bit farther afield, you can take the *vaporetto* out to Burano and then no. 9 for the 5-minute ride to the near-deserted island of **Torcello.** If you bring a basketful of bread, cheese, and wine you can do your best to reenact the romantic scene between Katharine Hepburn and Rossano Brazzi from the 1955 film "Summertime."

Fondamenta de L'Osmarin, Castello 4977. © **349-1957924.** Cones or cups from 1.50€. *Vaporetto:* Zaccaria.

Nico ★ GELATO   Founded in 1935, this is one of the city's more historic gelato counters, with a handful of chairs outside on the waterfront (be warned that these are only for "table service," at extra charge). Quality is good (the mint, amaretto, and the signature *gianduiotto,* a chocolate and nut blend, are crazy good), but the lines are always long in the afternoons and evenings, and service can be a little surly.

Fondamenta Zattere al Ponte Longo 922, Dorsoduro. www.gelaterianico.com. © **041-5225293.** Cone from 3€. *Vaporetto:* Zattere.

EXPLORING VENICE

Venice is notorious for changing and extending the opening hours of its museums and, to a lesser degree, its churches. Before you begin your exploration of Venice's sights, ask at the tourist office for the season's list of museum and church hours. During the peak months, you can enjoy extended museum hours—some places stay open until 7 or even 10pm. Unfortunately, these hours are not released until approximately Easter of every year. Even then, little is done to publicize the information, so you'll have to do your own research.

INDEX OF ATTRACTIONS & SITES

San Marco

Basilica di San Marco (St. Mark's Cathedral) ★★★ CATHEDRAL
One of the grandest, most confusing, and certainly the most exotic of all cathedrals in Europe, **Basilica di San Marco** is a grand treasure-heap of Venetian art and all sorts of lavish booty garnered from the eastern Mediterranean. Legend has it that **St. Mark,** on his way to Rome, was told by an angel his body would rest near the lagoon that would one today become Venice. Hundreds of years later, the city fathers were looking for a patron saint of high

The guards at the cathedral's entrance are serious about forbidding entry to anyone in inappropriate attire—shorts, sleeveless shirts (and shirts too short to hide your bellybutton), and skirts above the knee. Note also that you cannot enter the basilica with luggage, and that photos and filming inside are forbidden.

With masses of people descending on the cathedral every day, your best bet for avoiding the long lines is to come early in the morning. Although the basilica is open Sunday morning for anyone wishing to attend Mass, non-worshippers cannot enter merely to tour the site.

stature, more in keeping with their lofty aspirations, and in 828 the prophecy was duly fulfilled when Venetian merchants stole the body of St. Mark from Alexandria in Egypt (the story goes that the body was packed in pickled pork to avoid the attention of the Muslim guards).

Modeled on Constantinople's Church of the Twelve Apostles, the shrine of St. Mark was consecrated in 832, but in 976 the church burned down. The present incarnation was completed in 1094 but extended and embellished over subsequent years, serving as the personal church of the doge. Even today San Marco looks more like a Byzantine cathedral than a Roman Catholic church, with a cavernous interior exquisitely gilded with Byzantine mosaics added over some 7 centuries and covering every inch of both ceiling and pavement. For a closer look at many of the most remarkable ceiling mosaics and a better view of the Oriental carpet–like patterns of the pavement mosaics, pay the admission to go upstairs to the **Museo di San Marco** (the entrance to this is in the atrium at the principal entrance); this was originally the women's gallery, or *matroneum,* and also includes the outside Loggia dei Cavalli (see below). Here you can mingle with the celebrated **"Triumphal Quadriga"** of four gilded bronze horses dating from the 2nd or 3rd century A.D.; originally set on the Loggia, the restored originals were moved inside in the 1980s for preservation. (The word *quadriga* actually refers to a car or chariot pulled by four horses though in this case there are only the horses.) The horses were transported to Venice from Constantinople in 1204 along with lots of other loot from the Fourth Crusade. For centuries, these were symbols of the unrivaled Serene Republic and are the only quadriga to have survived from the classical era. Not to be outdone by looting-prone Venetians, Napoleon carted the horses off to Paris in 1798, though they were returned to Venice in 1815 after the fall of Bonaparte.

A visit to the outdoor **Loggia dei Cavalli** (where replicas of the horses now stand) is an unexpected highlight, providing a panoramic view of the piazza and what Napoleon called "the most beautiful salon in the world" upon his arrival in Venice in 1797. The 500-year-old **Torre dell'Orologio (Clock Tower)** stands to your right; to your left is the **Campanile (Bell Tower)** and, beyond, the glistening waters of the open lagoon and Palladio's **San Giorgio** on its own island. It is any photographer's dream.

Venice Attractions

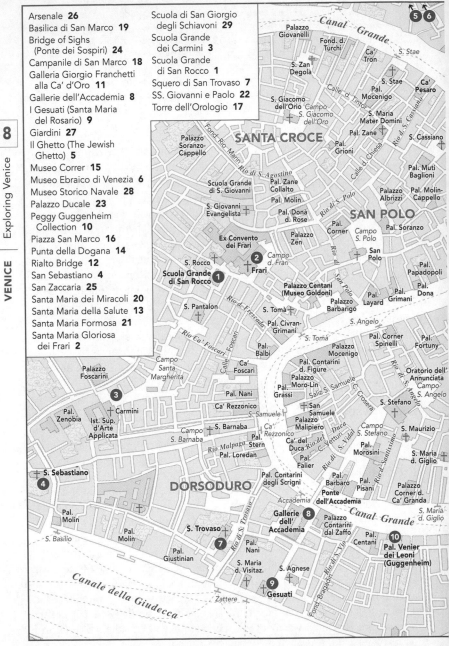

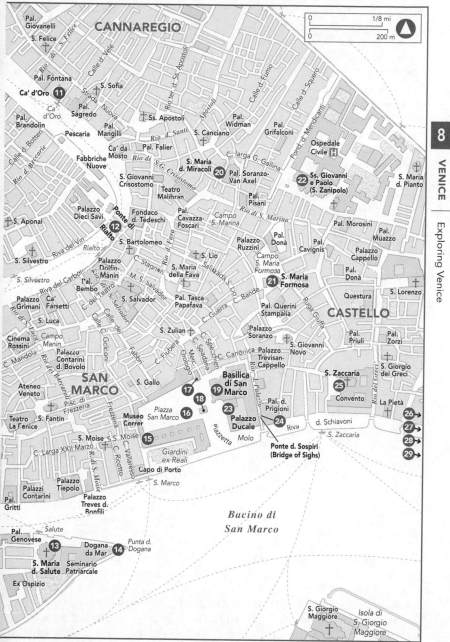

CANNAREGIO

Pal. Giovanelli
S. Felice
Rio di SS. Felice
Pal. Fontana
Ca' d'Oro 11
Ca' d'Oro
Strada Nuova
S. Sofia
Pal. Sagredo
Calle d. Vele
Rio ter. d. SS. Apostoli
Calle di Fumo
Calle d. Squero
Pal. Brandolin
Calle di Botteri
Pescaria
Pal. Mangilli
Ss. Apostoli
Rio d. Santi
S. Canciano
Apostoli
Pal. Widman
Pal. Grifalconi
Ospedale Civile H
Fabbriche Nuove
Ca' da Mosto
Pal. Falier
Rio di S.G. Crisostomo
S. Maria d. Miracoli 20
C. larga G. Gallina
Pal. Soranzo-Van Axel
Ss. Giovanni e Paolo (S. Zanipolo) 22
S. Maria d. Pianto
Calle d. Beccarie
S. Giovanni Crisostomo
Teatro Malibran
Pal. Pisani
Rio di S. Marina
S. Aponal
Palazzo Dieci Savi
Fondaco d. Tedeschi
Pal. Cavazza-Foscari
Campo S. Marina
Pal. Morosini
Pal. Muazzo
Ponte di Rialto 12
Rialto
S. Bartolomeo
Rio d. Fava
S. Lio
Palazzo Ruzzini
Pal. Donà
Pal. Cavignis
Palazzo Cappello
Riva del Vin
S. Silvestro
Palazzo Dolfin-Manin
C. Stagneri
M. S. Salvador
S. Maria della Fava
Campo S. Maria Formosa
S. Maria Formosa 21
Pal. Donà
S. Lorenzo
Rio di S. Silvestro
Pal. Bembo
Pal. Grimani
Ca' Farsetti
S. Salvador
Pal. Tasca Papafava
C. Guerra
Salizada S. Lio
C. Bande
Pal. Querini Stampalia
Questura
CASTELLO
S. Luca
Campo Manin
Calle C. Goldoni
S. Zulian
C. Spadaria
Mercerie
C. Canonica
Palazzo Soranzo
Palazzo Trevisan-Cappello
S. Giovanni Novo
Pal. Priuli
Pal. Zorzi
Cinema Rossini
C. Mandola
Palazzo Contarini d. Bovolo
Fabbri
C. Fiubera
Merc. Orologio
Basilica di San Marco
Pal. d. Palazzo
S. Zaccaria 25
S. Giorgio dei Greci
Ateneo Veneto
SAN MARCO
S. Gallo
17
19
Convento
La Pietà
Teatro La Fenice
S. Fantin
Pisc. di Frezzeria
Frezzeria
18
Museo Correr
Piazza San Marco 16
23
Palazzo Ducale
Pal. d. Prigioni
24
26
27
S. Moise
S.S. Moise
15
Piazzetta
Molo
d. Schiavoni
S. Zaccaria
28
C. Larga XXII Marzo
R. di S. Moise
Giardini ex Reali
Ponte d. Sospiri (Bridge of Sighs)
Riva
29
Palazzo Contarini
Palazzi Tiepolo
Capo di Porto
S. Marco
Pal. Gritti
Palazzo Treves d. Bonfili
Bacino di San Marco
Pal. Genovese
Salute
Dogana da Mar 14
Punta d. Dogana
13
S. Maria d. Salute
Seminario Patriarcale
Ex Ospizio
S. Giorgio Maggiore
Isola di S. Giorgio Maggiore

0 —— 1/8 mi
0 —— 200 m

The church's greatest treasure is the magnificent altarpiece known as the **Pala d'Oro (Golden Altarpiece),** a Gothic masterpiece encrusted with over 2,000 precious gems and 83 enameled panels. It was created in 10th-century Constantinople and embellished by Venetian and Byzantine artisans between the 12th and 14th centuries. It is located behind the main altar, whose green marble canopy on alabaster columns covers the tomb of St. Mark (skeptics contend that his remains burned in the fire of 976). Also worth a visit is the **Tesoro (Treasury),** with a collection of the crusaders' plunder from Constantinople and other icons and relics amassed by the church over the years. Much of the Venetian booty has been incorporated into the interior and exterior of the basilica in the form of marble, columns, capitals, and statuary. Second to the Pala d'Oro in importance is the 10th-century **"Madonna di Nicopeia,"** a bejeweled icon taken from Constantinople and exhibited in its own chapel to the left of the main altar.

In July and August (with much less certainty the rest of the year), church-affiliated volunteers give free tours Monday to Saturday, leaving four or five times daily (not all tours are in English), beginning at 10:30am; groups gather in the atrium, where you'll find posters with schedules.

Piazza San Marco. www.basilicasanmarco.it. © **041-2708311.** Basilica free admission; Museo di San Marco (includes Loggia dei Cavalli) 5€, Pala d'Oro 2€, Tesoro (Treasury) 3€. Basilica, Tesoro, and Pala d'Oro Mon–Sat 9:45am–5pm (Tesoro and Pala d'Oro close at 4pm Nov–Easter), Sun 2–5pm (Nov–Easter all close Sun at 4pm). Museo di San Marco daily 9:45am–4:45pm. *Vaporetto:* San Marco.

Campanile di San Marco (Bell Tower) ★★★ ICON
An elevator will whisk you to the top of this 97m (318-ft.) bell tower, where you get an awe-inspiring view of St. Mark's cupolas. It is the highest structure in the city, offering a pigeon's-eye panorama that includes the lagoon, its neighboring islands, and the red rooftops and church domes and bell towers of Venice—and, oddly, not a single canal. Originally built in the 9th century, the bell tower was then reconstructed in the 12th, 14th, and 16th centuries, when the pretty marble loggia at its base was added by Jacopo Sansovino. It collapsed unexpectedly in 1902, miraculously hurting no one except a cat. It was rebuilt exactly as before, using most of the same materials, even rescuing one of the five historical bells that it still uses today (each bell was rung for a different purpose, such as war, the death of a doge, religious holidays, and so on).

Piazza San Marco. www.basilicasanmarco.it. © **041-2708311.** Admission 8€. Easter to June and Oct daily 9am–7pm; July–Sept daily 9am–9pm; Nov–Easter daily 9:30am–3:45pm. *Vaporetto:* San Marco.

Canal Grande (Grand Canal) ★★★ NATURAL ATTRACTION
A leisurely cruise along the "Canalazzo" from Piazza San Marco to the Ferrovia (train station), or the reverse, is one of Venice's (and life's) must-do experiences. Hop on the **no. 1** *vaporetto* in the late afternoon (try to get one of the coveted outdoor seats in the prow), when the weather-worn colors of the former homes of Venice's merchant elite are warmed by the soft light and reflected in the canal's rippling waters, and the busy traffic of delivery boats,

vaporetti, and gondolas that fills the city's main thoroughfare has eased somewhat. The sheer number and opulence of the 200-odd *palazzi,* churches, and imposing republican buildings dating from the 14th to the 18th centuries is enough to make any boat-going visitor's head swim. Many of the largest canal-side buildings are now converted into imposing international banks, government or university buildings, art galleries, and consulates. Look out for the ornate **Ca' d'Oro** (p. 271), the Ca' Rezzonico, where poet Robert Browning died in 1889 (it's now an art museum), and plaques commemorating the visits of Lord Byron (Palazzo Mociengo) and Richard Wagner (Casinò di Venezia; his rooms now a museum dedicated to the German composer).

Best stations to start/end a tour of the Grand Canal are Ferrovia (train station) or Piazzale Roma on the northwest side of the canal and Piazza San Marco in the southeast. Tickets 7€.

Palazzo Ducale and Ponte dei Sospiri (Ducal Palace and Bridge of Sighs) ★★★ PALACE

The pink-and-white marble Gothic-Renaissance **Palazzo Ducale,** residence and government center of the doges who ruled Venice for more than 1,000 years, stands between the Basilica di San Marco and the sea. A symbol of prosperity and power, it was destroyed by a succession of fires, with the current building started in 1340, extended in the 1420s, and largely redesigned again after a fire in 1483. Forever being expanded, it slowly grew to be one of Italy's greatest civic structures. If you want to understand something of this magnificent place, the fascinating history of the 1,000-year-old maritime republic, and the intrigue of the government that ruled it, take the **Secret Itineraries tour** ★★★ (see "An Insider's Look at the Palazzo Ducale," p. 261). Failing that, at least download the free iPhone/Android app (see the website at the end of this listing) or shell out for the infrared audioguide tour (at entrance, 6€) to help make sense of it all. Unless you can tag along with an English-speaking tour group, you may otherwise miss out on the importance of much of what you're seeing.

The 15th-century **Porta della Carta (Paper Gate),** the entrance adjacent to the basilica where the doges' official proclamations and decrees were posted, opens onto a splendid inner courtyard with a double row of Renaissance arches (today visitors enter through a doorway on the lagoon side of the palace). The self-guided route through the palace begins on the left

Campanile di San Marco.

Palazzo Ducale.

side of the main courtyard, where the **Museo dell'Opera** contains assorted bits of masonry preserved from the Palazzo's exterior. Beyond here, the first major room you'll come to is the spacious **Sala delle Quattro Porte (Hall of the Four Doors),** with a worn ceiling by Tintoretto. The **Sala dell'Anticollegio,** the next main room, is where foreign ambassadors waited to be received by the doge and his council. It is covered in four works by Tintoretto, and Veronese's **"Rape of Europe"** ★★, considered one of the *palazzo's* finest. It steals some of the thunder of Tintoretto's "Mercury & the Three Graces" and **"Bacchus and Ariadne"** ★★—the latter considered one of his best by some critics. The highlight of the adjacent **Sala del Collegio** (the Council Chamber itself) is the spectacular cycle of **ceiling paintings** ★★ by Veronese, completed between 1575 and 1578 and one of his masterpieces. Next door lies the most impressive of the spectacular interior rooms, the richly adorned **Sala del Senato (Senate Chamber),** with Tintoretto's ceiling painting, "The Triumph of Venice." Here laws were passed by the Senate, a select group of 200 chosen from the Great Council. The latter was originally an elected body, but in the 13th century it became an aristocratic stronghold that could number as many as 1,700. After passing again through the Sala delle Quattro Porte, you'll come to the Veronese-decorated **Stanza del Consiglio dei Dieci (Room of the Council of Ten,** the Republic's dreaded security police), of particular historical interest. It was in this room that justice was dispensed and decapitations ordered. Formed in the 14th century to deal with emergency situations, the Ten were considered more powerful than the Senate and feared by all. Just outside the adjacent chamber, in the **Sala della Bussola (the Compass Chamber),** notice the **Bocca dei Leoni (Lion's Mouth),** a slit in the wall into which secret denunciations and accusations of enemies of the state were placed for quick action by the much-feared Council.

The main sight on the next level down—indeed, in the entire palace—is the **Sala del Maggior Consiglio (Great Council Hall).** This enormous space is animated by Tintoretto's huge **"Paradiso"** ★ at the far end of the hall above the doge's seat (the painter was in his 70s when he undertook the project with the help of his son). Measuring 7×23m (23×75 ft.), it is said to be the world's largest oil painting; together with Veronese's gorgeous **"Il Trionfo di Vene-zia" ("The Triumph of Venice")** ★★ in the oval panel on the ceiling, it affirms the power emanating from the council sessions held here. Tintoretto also did the portraits of the 76 doges encircling the top of this chamber; note that the picture of the Doge Marin Falier, who was convicted of treason and beheaded in 1355, has been blacked out—Venice has never forgiven him. Although elected for life since sometime in the 7th century, over time *il doge* became nothing but a figurehead (they were never allowed to meet with foreign ambassadors alone); the power rested in the Great Council. Tours culminate at the enclosed **Ponte dei Sospiri (Bridge of Sighs),** built in 1600 and which connects the Ducal Palace with the grim **Palazzo delle Prigioni (Prison).** The bridge took its current name only in the 19th century, when Lord Byron romantically envisioned the prisoners' final breath of resignation upon viewing the outside world one last time before being locked in their fetid cells. Some, however, attribute the name to Casanova, who, following his arrest in 1755 (he was accused of being a Freemason and spreading antireligious propaganda), crossed this very bridge. One of the rare few to escape, something he achieved 15 months after his imprisonment began, he returned to Venice 20 years later. Some of the stone cells still have the original graffiti of past prisoners, many of them locked up interminably for petty crimes.

San Marco, Piazza San Marco. www.palazzoducale.visitmuve.it. ℂ **041-2715911.** Admission only with San Marco Museum Pass (17€; see "Venice Discounts," p. 266). For an Itinerari Segreti (Secret Itineraries) guided tour in English, see "An Insider's Look at the Palazzo Ducale," below. Daily 8:30am–7pm (Nov–Mar until 5:30pm). *Vaporetto:* San Marco.

AN insider's LOOK AT THE PALAZZO DUCALE

The **Itinerari Segreti (Secret Itineraries)** ★★★ guided tours of the Palazzo Ducale is a must-see for any visit to Venice lasting more than a day. The tours offer an unparalleled look into the world of Venetian politics over the centuries and are the only way to access the otherwise restricted quarters and hidden passageways of this enormous palace, such as the doges' private chambers and the torture chambers where prisoners were interrogated. The story of Giacomo Casanova's imprisonment in, and famous escape from, the palace's prisons is the tour highlight (although a few of the less-inspired guides harp on this aspect a bit too much). It is highly advisable to reserve in advance via the website, by phone (toll-free within Italy ℂ **848-082-000,** or from abroad 041-4273-0892), or in person at the ticket desk. Tours often sell out at least a few days ahead, especially from spring through fall. Tours in English are daily at 9:55am and 11:35am and cost 20€ for adults, 14€ for children ages 6 to 14 and students ages 15 to 25. There are also tours in Italian at 9:30am and 11:10am, and French at 10:20am and noon. The tour lasts about 75 minutes.

Piazza San Marco ★★★

SQUARE Dubbed "The finest drawing-room in Europe" by Napoleon, the San Marco Square is undeniably one of Italy's most beautiful spaces, despite being terribly congested in high season (and often flooded during *acqua alta*). Today, the square is focal point for Carnevale, as well as the spectacular Basilica and the most historic cafes in Venice: venerable **Caffè Florian,** Wagner's **Caffè Lavena,** and **Gran Caffè Quadri** (all on p. 285).
Vaporetto: San Marco.

Rialto Bridge.

Rialto Bridge ★★ ICON

This graceful arch over the Grand Canal, linking the San Marco and San Polo districts, is lined with overpriced boutiques and is teeming with tourists and overflow from the daily market on the San Polo side. Until the 19th century, it was the only bridge across the Grand Canal, originally built as a pontoon bridge at the canal's narrowest point. Wooden versions of the bridge followed; the 1444 incarnation was the first to include shops, interrupted by a drawbridge in the center. In 1592, this graceful stone span was finished to the designs of Antonio da Ponte (whose last name fittingly enough means bridge), who beat out Sansovino, Palladio, and Michelangelo with his plans that called for a single, vast, 28m-wide (92-ft.) arch in the center to allow trading ships to pass.
Ponte del Rialto. *Vaporetto:* Rialto.

Torre dell'Orologio (Clock Tower) ★★ MONUMENT

As you enter the magnificent **Piazza San Marco,** it is one of the first things you see, standing on the north side, next to and towering above the **Procuratie Vecchie** (the ancient administration buildings for the Republic). The Renaissance **Torre dell'Orologio** was built between 1496 and 1506, and the clock mechanism still keeps perfect time (although most of the original workings have been replaced over the years). A lengthy restoration that finished in 2006 has helped keep the rest of the structure in top shape. Two bronze figures, known as "Moors" because of the dark color of the bronze, pivot to strike the hour. The tower is the entryway to the ancient Mercerie (from the word for

Your ticket to the Palazzo Ducale also includes entry to the **Museo Correr** (www.correr.visitmuve.it; © **041-2405211;** Apr–Oct daily 10am–7pm, Nov–Mar daily 10am–5pm) on the other side of Piazza San Marco, a dubious treat most visitors pushed for time wisely skip. But although much of the Correr is undeniably dull (comprising

lesser known artworks, archeological remains, and odd bits and pieces from the later history of the city), there is one spark of gold: the **"Courtesans" ★★**, a captivating painting by **Vittore Carpaccio** depicting severely made up and slightly bitter looking ladies of leisure, lounging on a roof terrace.

"merchandise"), the principal souklike retail street of both high-end boutiques and trinket shops that zigzags its way to the Rialto Bridge. Visits are by guided tour only (included in the price of admission).

Piazza San Marco. www.torreorologio.visitmuve.it. © **848-082000** or 041-42730892. Admission 12€, 7€ for children ages 6–14 and students ages 15–25; the ticket also gets you into the Museo Correr, the Museo Archeologico Nazionale, and the Biblioteca Nazionale Marciana (but not Palazzo Ducale). Tours in English Mon–Wed 10am and 11am, Thurs–Sun 2pm and 3pm (must be reserved in advance); tours start at the Museo Correr ticket office. There are also tours in Italian and French. *Vaporetto:* San Marco.

Castello

Though the highlight of this neighborhood is the huge **Santi Giovanni e Paolo,** within a few minutes' walk from here are two more magnificent Renaissance churches, **Santa Maria Formosa** (Mon–Sat 10am–5pm; 3€) on Campo Santa Maria Formosa, and **San Zaccaria** (Mon–Sat 10am–noon and 4–6pm, Sun 4–6pm; free) at Campo San Zaccaria, which contains Giovanni Bellini's **San Zaccaria Altarpiece ★**, and early work from Tintoretto.

Basilica SS. Giovanni e Paolo ★ CHURCH   This massive Gothic church was built by the Dominican order from the 13th to the 15th century and, together with the Frari Church in San Polo, is second in size only to the Basilica di San Marco. An unofficial Pantheon where 25 doges are buried (a number of tombs are part of the unfinished facade), the church, commonly known as Zanipolo in Venetian dialect, is also home to many artistic treasures.

The brilliantly colored **"Polyptych of St. Vincent Ferrer"** (ca. 1465), attributed to a young Giovanni Bellini, is in the right aisle. You'll also see the foot of St. Catherine of Siena encased in glass near here. Visit the **Cappella del Rosario ★** through a glass door off the left transept to see the three restored ceiling canvases and one oil painting by **Paolo Veronese,** particularly "The Assumption of the Madonna."

Anchoring the large and impressive *campo* outside, a popular crossroads for this area of Castello, is the **statue of Bartolomeo Colleoni ★★**, the Renaissance condottiere who defended Venice's interests at the height of its power and until his death in 1475. The 15th-century work is by the Florentine

Andrea Verrocchio; it is considered one of the world's great equestrian monuments and Verrocchio's best.

Campo Santi Giovanni e Paolo 6363. www.basilicasantigiovanniepaolo.it. *℗* **041-5235913.** Admission 2.50€. Mon–Sat 9am–6pm, Sun noon–6pm. *Vaporetto:* Rialto.

Scuola di San Giorgio degli Schiavoni ★★ MUSEUM   One of the

most mesmerizing spaces in Europe, the tiny main hall of the **Scuola di San Giorgio degli Schiavoni** once served as a meeting house for Venice's Dalmatian community (*schiavoni,* literally "Slavs"), built by the side of their church, San Giovanni di Malta, in the early 16th century. The main reason to visit is to admire the awe-inspiring narrative painting cycle that smothers the walls, created by Renaissance master **Vittore Carpaccio** between 1502 and 1509. The paintings depict the lives of the Dalmatian saints George (of dragon-slaying fame), Tryphon, and Jerome, while in the upper hall (Sala dell'Albergo), there's Carpaccio's masterful "Vision of St. Augustine."

Calle dei Furlani 3259A. *℗* **041-5228828.** Admission 5€. Mon 2:45–6pm, Tues–Sat 9:15am–1pm and 2:45–6pm, Sun 9:15am–1pm. *Vaporetto:* Rialto.

Dorsoduro

Gallerie dell'Accademia (Academy Gallery) ★★★ MUSEUM

Along with San Marco and the Palazzo Ducale, the **Accademia** is one of the highlights of Venice, a magnificent collection of European art and especially Venetian painting from the 14th to the 18th centuries. Visitors are currently limited to 300 at one time, so lines can be long in high season—advance reservations are essential. Things will improve after the long-awaited expansion of the gallery is completed. The core galleries occupy the old Scuola della Carità, dating back to 1343. There's a lot to take in here, so buy a catalogue in the store if you'd like to learn more—the audioguides are a little muddled and not worth 6€. Sadly, da Vinci's iconic **"Vitruvian Man" ★★★**, probably the museum's most famous piece, is an extremely fragile ink drawing and rarely displayed in public.

Rooms are laid out in rough chronological order, though the on-going renovation means some rooms may be closed when you visit (call ahead or check the website to see if any galleries are closed). Room 2 includes **Carpaccio**'s grim "Crucifixion & Glorification of the Ten Thousand Martyrs of Mount Ararat" and his much lighter "Presentation of Jesus in the Temple," but the real showstoppers of the collection reside in Rooms 4 and 5, with a gorgeous "St. George" by Mantegna and a series of Giovanni Bellini "Madonnas." Pride of place goes to **Giorgione**'s enigmatic and utterly mystifying **"Tempest"** ★★.

Rooms 6 to 8 feature Venetian heavyweights Tintoretto, Titian, and Lorenzo Lotto, while Room 10 is dominated by Paolo Veronese's mammoth **"Feast in the House of Levi"** ★★. The story goes that Veronese wanted to call the painting "the Last Supper" but the Inquisition objected to the dogs, dwarfs, and drunks—Veronese simply changed the name and all was well. Tintoretto canvases make up the rest of the room, including his three legends of St. Mark: "St. Mark Rescues a Slave," "The Theft of the Body of St. Mark," and "St. Mark Saves a Saracen." Opposite is Titian's last painting, a "Pietà" intended for his own tomb. Room 11 contains work by **Tiepolo**, the master of 18th-century Venetian painting, but also Tintoretto's "Madonna dei Tesorieri." The next rooms contain a relatively mediocre batch of 17th- and 18th-century paintings, though Canaletto's **"Capriccio: A Colonnade"** ★ (Room 17), which he presented to the Academy when he was made a member in 1763, certainly merits a closer look for its elegant contrast between diagonal, vertical, and horizontal lines.

Room 20 is filled by Gentile Bellini's cycle of **"The Miracles of the Relic of the Cross"** ★, painted around 1500 for the Scuola di San Giovanni Evangelista. The next room contains the monumental cycle of pictures by Carpaccio illustrating the **Story of St. Ursula** ★★. Legend has it that St. Ursula was a British Celtic princess, murdered by the Huns as she was making a pilgrimage to Rome along with her 11,000 virgin attendants. Finally, in Room 24 (the former hostel of the Scuola), there's Titian's "Presentation of the Virgin," actually created to hang in this space along with a triptych by Antonio Vivarini and Giovanni d'Alemagna.

Campo della Carità 1050, at foot of Ponte dell'Accademia. www.gallerieaccademia. org. ⓒ **041-5200345.** Admission 11€ adults (includes Palazzo Grimani); free on Sundays (check in advance). Reservations by phone or online incur a 1.50€ charge. Daily 8:15am–7:15pm (Mon until 2pm). *Vaporetto:* Accademia.

Back to Scuola

Founded in the Middle Ages, the Venetian *scuole* (schools) were guilds that brought together merchants and craftspeople from certain trades (for example, the dyers of Scuola dei Carmini), as well as those who shared similar religious devotions (Scuola Grande di San Rocco). The guilds were social clubs, credit unions, and sources of spiritual guidance. Many commissioned elaborate headquarters and hired the best artists of the day to decorate them. The *scuole* that remain in Venice today house some of the city's finest art treasures.

VENICE discounts

Venice offers a somewhat bewildering range of passes and discount cards. We recommend buying an **ACTV travel card** (p. 217) and combining that with one of the first two museum passes listed below. The more complex Venice Card scheme is convenient once you've worked out what you want online, but doesn't save you much money and its main components are only valid for 7 days. However, the Venice Card website (www.veneziaunica.it) is now also a one-stop shop for all the passes listed below.

The **Museum Pass** (www.vivaticket.it) grants admission to all the city-run museums over a 6-month period. That includes the museums of St. Mark's Square—**Palazzo Ducale, Museo Correr,** Museo Archeologico Nazionale, and the Biblioteca Nazionale Marciana—as well as the Museo di Palazzo Mocenigo (Costume Museum), the Ca' Rezzonico, the Ca' Pesaro, the Museo del Vetro (Glass Museum) on Murano, and the Museo del Merletto (Lace Museum) on Burano. The Museum Pass is available online or at any of the participating museums and costs 24€ for adults, and 18€ for students under 30 and kids ages 6 to 14. There is also a **San Marco Museum Pass** (valid for 3 months) that lets you into the four museums of Piazza San Marco for 17€, and 10€ for students under 30 and kids ages 6 to 14. The **Chorus Pass** (www.chorusvenezia.org) covers every major church in Venice, 16 in all, for 12€ (8€ for students under 30), for up to 1 year. For 24€, the **Chorus Pass Family** gives you the same perks for two adults and their children up to 18 years old.

The **Venice Card,** or Venezia Unica City Pass (www.veneziaunica.it), combines the above passes, transport, discounts, and even Internet access on one card via a "made-to-order" online system, where you choose the services you want. The most useful option is the **Tourist City Pass,** which combines the Museum Pass and Chorus Pass plus free entry to the Jewish Museum and discounts on temporary exhibits for 40€ for 7 days (30€ for ages 6–29). You can also buy various transportation packages and Wi-Fi access (from 5€ for 24hr.). Once you've paid, you'll be able to simply print out a voucher to use at museums and sights in Venice; to use public transport you must collect tickets by entering your booking code at one of the ACTV automatic ticket machines or by visiting one of the official Points of Sale in in the city (there's one in the train station open 7am to 9pm, as well as at the Rialto *vaporetto* stop open 7am to 11pm).

Also, for tourists between the ages of 14 and 29, there is the **Rolling Venice** card (also available at www.veneziaunica.it). It's valid until the end of the year in which you buy it, costs just 4€, and entitles the bearer to significant (20%–30%) discounts at participating restaurants (but only applies to cardholder's meal), and a similar discount on ACTV travel cards (20€ for 3 days). Holders of the Rolling Venice card also get discounts in museums, stores, language courses, hotels, and bars across the city (it comes with a thick booklet listing everywhere that you're entitled to get discounts).

I Gesuati (Santa Maria del Rosario) ★ CHURCH   Built from 1724 to 1743 by Giorgio Massari to mirror the Redentore across the wide Canale della Giudecca, this cavernous Dominican church counters the latter's Palladian sobriety with rococo flair. The interior is graced by airy 1738–39 ceiling frescoes (some of the first in Venice) by **Giambattista Tiepolo.** Tiepolo also created the "Virgin with saints Rosa of Lima, Catherine of Siena, and Agnes of Montepulciano" on the first altar on the right. The third altar on the left has a severe Tintoretto "Crucifixion" (1565).

Fondamenta delle Zattere ai Gesuati. ℭ **041-2750462.** Admission 3€ adults, free for children 5 and under. Mon–Sat 10am–5pm. *Vaporetto:* Zattere.

Peggy Guggenheim Collection ★★ MUSEUM One of the best museums in Italy when it comes to American and European art of the 20th century, the modern art here is a refreshing juxtaposition to a city so heavily associated with the High Renaissance and the baroque. Art aficionados will find fascinating work here, and the galleries occupy Peggy Guggenheim's wonderful former home, the 18th-century Palazzo Venier dei Leoni, right on the Grand Canal. Guggenheim purchased the mansion in 1949 and lived here, on and off, until her death in 1979. The core of the museum remains the personal collection of Guggenheim herself. Highlights include Picasso's extremely abstract "Poet," and his more gentle "On the Beach," several works by Kandinsky ("Landscape with Red Spots No. 2" and "White Cross"), Miró's expressionistic "Seated Woman II," Klee's mystical "Magic Garden," and some unsettling works by Max Ernst ("The Kiss," "Attirement of the Bride"), who was briefly married to Guggenheim in the 1940s. Look also for Magritte's "Empire of Light," Dalí's typically surreal "Birth of Liquid Desires," and a couple of gems from Pollock, his early "Moon Woman," which recalls Picasso, and "Alchemy," a more typical "poured" painting. The Italian Futurists are also well represented here, with a rare portrait from Modigliani ("Portrait of the Painter Frank Haviland"), and lots of work from Balla, Carrà, and Morandi. The cafe overlooks the sculpture garden and is a good spot for a touring break. The museum also runs a number of interactive programs for children, making it a top pick for families.

Calle San Cristoforo 701. www.guggenheim-venice.it. ℭ **041-2405411.** Admission 15€ adults; 12€ 65 and over, and for those who present an Alitalia ticket to or from Venice dated no more than 7 days previous; 9€ students 26 and under and children ages 10–18. Wed–Mon 10am–6pm. *Vaporetto:* Accademia (walk around left side of Accademia, take 1st left, and walk straight ahead following the signs).

Punta della Dogana ★★★ MUSEUM The eastern tip *(punta)* of Dorsoduro is crowned by the distinctive triangle of the 17th-century **Dogana di Mare** (Customs House) that once monitored all boats entering the Grand Canal. Transformed by Tadao Ando into a beautiful exhibition space in 2009, it's now an engaging showcase for the contemporary art collection of French multi-millionaire François Pinault (officially dubbed the **Centro d'Arte Contemporanea Punta della Dogana**). It's pricy, but you can expect to see quality work from Cindy Sherman, Cy Twombly, Jeff Koons, and Marlene Dumas, among many others.

Fondamenta della Dogana alla Salute 2. www.palazzograssi.it. ℭ **041-2719031.** Admission 15€ adults, 20€ with Palazzo Grassi. Wed–Mon 10am–7pm. *Vaporetto:* Salute.

San Sebastiano ★★ CHURCH Lose the crowds as you make a pilgrimage to this monument to **Paolo Veronese,** his parish church and home to some of his finest work. Veronese painted the ceiling of the sacristy with the "Coronation of the Virgin" and the "Four Evangelists," while he graced the nave ceiling with "Scenes from the Life of St. Esther." He also decorated the organ shutters and panels around the high altar in the 1560s, with scenes from the life of St. Sebastian. Although Veronese is the main event here, don't miss Titian's sensitive "St. Nicholas" (left wall of the first chapel on the right).

Campo San Sebastiano. ℂ **041-2750462.** Admission 3€. Mon–Sat 10am–5pm. *Vaporetto:* San Basilio.

Santa Maria della Salute (Church of the Virgin Mary of Good Health) ★ CHURCH Generally referred to as "La Salute," this crown jewel of 17th-century baroque architecture proudly reigns at a commercially and aesthetically important point, almost directly across from the Piazza San Marco, where the Grand Canal empties into the lagoon.

The first stone was laid in 1631 after the Senate decided to honor the Virgin Mary for delivering Venice from a plague that had killed around 95,000 people. They accepted the revolutionary plans of a young, relatively unknown architect, Baldassare Longhena (who would go on to design, among other projects, the Ca' Rezzonico). He dedicated the next 50 years of his life to overseeing its progress (he would die 1 year after its inauguration but 5 years before its completion). Today the dome of the church is an iconic presence on the Venice skyline, recognized for its exuberant exterior of volutes, scrolls, and more than 125 statues. The most revered image inside is the **Madonna della Salute,** a rare black-faced image of Mary brought back from Candia in Crete in 1670 as war booty. The otherwise rather sober interior is livened by the **sacristy,** where you will find a number of important ceiling paintings and portraits of the Evangelists and church doctors by **Titian.** On the right wall of the sacristy, which you have to pay to enter, is

Punta della Dogana.

Tintoretto's **"Marriage at Cana"** ★, often considered one of his best paintings.

Campo della Salute. ℂ **041-5225558.** Free admission to church; sacristy 3€. Daily 9am–noon and 3–6pm. *Vaporetto:* Salute.

Scuola Grande dei Carmini ★★ CHURCH   The former Venetian base of the Carmelites, finished in the 18th century, is now a shrine of sorts to **Giambattista Tiepolo,** who painted the ceiling of the upstairs hall between 1739 and 1744. It's truly a magnificent sight. Tiepolo's elaborate rococo interpretation of "Simon Stock Receiving the Scapular" is now fully restored along with various panels throughout the building.

Campo San Margherita 2617. www.scuolagrandecarmini.it. ℂ **041-5289420.** Admission 5€. Daily 11am–4pm. *Vaporetto:* San Basilio.

Squero di San Trovaso ★★ HISTORIC SITE   One of the most intriguing sights in Venice is this small *squero* (boatyard), which first opened in the 17th century. Just north of the Zattere (the wide, sunny walkway that runs alongside the Giudecca Canal in Dorsoduro), the boatyard lies next to the Church of San Trovaso on the narrow Rio San Trovaso (not far from the Accademia Bridge). It is surrounded by Tyrolean-looking wooden structures (a true rarity in this city of stone built on water) that are home to the multigenerational owners and original workshops for traditional Venetian boats (see "The Art of the Gondola," p. 270). Aware that they have become a tourist site themselves, the gondoliers don't mind if you watch them at work from across the narrow Rio di San Trovaso, but don't try to invite yourself in. *Tip:* It's the perfect midway photo op after a visit to the Accademia and a trip to Gelateria Nico (Zattere 922), whose chocolate *gianduiotto* is every bit as decadent as Venice just before the fall of the Republic.

Dorsoduro 1097 (on the Rio San Trovaso, southwest of the Accademia). *Vaporetto:* Zattere.

San Polo & Santa Croce

Basilica Santa Maria Gloriosa dei Frari (Church of the Frari) ★★ CHURCH   Known simply as "i Frari," this immense 14th-century Gothic church is easily found around the corner from the Scuola Grande di San Rocco—make sure you visit both when you're in this area. Built by the Franciscans (*frari* is a dialectal distortion of *frati,* or "brothers"), it is the largest church in Venice after San Marco. Since St. Francis and the order he founded emphasized prayer and poverty, it is not surprising that the church is austere both inside and out. Yet it houses a number of important works, including two Titian masterpieces. The more striking is his **"Assumption of the Virgin"** ★★ over the main altar, painted when the artist was only in his late 20s. His "Virgin of the Pesaro Family," is in the left nave; for this work commissioned by one of Venice's most powerful families, Titian's wife posed for the figure of Mary (and then died soon afterward in childbirth). Don't miss Giovanni Bellini's **"Madonna & Child"** ★★ over the altar in the sacristy; novelist Henry James was struck dumb by it, writing: "It is as solemn as it is gorgeous."

THE ART OF THE gondola

Putting together one of these sleek black boats is a fascinatingly exact science that is still done in the revered traditional manner at boatyards such as the **Squero di San Trovaso** (see p. 269). Gondolas have been painted black since a 16th-century sumptuary law—one of many passed by the local legislators as excess and extravagance spiraled out of control. Whether regarding boats or baubles, laws were passed to restrict the gaudy outlandishness that, at the time, was commonly used to "outdo the Joneses."

Propelled by the strength of a single *gondoliere*, these boats, unique to Venice, have no modern equipment. They move with no great speed but with unrivaled grace. The right side of the gondola is lower because the *gondoliere* always stands in the back of the boat on the left. Although the San Trovaso *squero*, or boatyard, is the city's oldest and one of only three remaining (the other two are immeasurably more difficult to find), its predominant focus is on maintenance and repair. They will occasionally build a new gondola (which takes some 40–45 working days), carefully crafting it from the seven types of wood—mahogany, cherry, fir, walnut, oak, elm, and lime—necessary to give the shallow and asymmetrical boat its various characteristics. After all the pieces are put together, the painting, the *ferro* (the iron symbol of the city affixed to the bow), and the woodcarving that secures the oar are commissioned out to various local artisans.

Although some 10,000 of these elegant boats floated on the canals of Venice in the 16th century, today there are around 425, almost all catering to the tourist trade. The job of *gondoliere* remains a coveted profession, passed down from father to son over the centuries, but nowadays it's open to anyone that can pass 400 hours of rigorous training—Giorgia Boscolo passed the exam in 2010, becoming the first ever *gondolier;* her father was also in the profession.

The grand **mausoleum of Titian** is on the right as you enter the church, opposite the oddly incongruous 18th-century monument to sculptor **Antonio Canova,** shaped like a pyramid; designed by Canova himself, this was originally supposed to be Titian's tomb.

Campo dei Frari 3072. www.basilicadeifrari.it. ℂ **041-2728611.** Admission 3€, audioguide 2€. Mon–Sat 9am–6pm; Sun 1–6pm. *Vaporetto:* San Tomà (walk straight ahead on Calle del Traghetto and turn right and immediately left across Campo San Tomà; walk straight ahead, on Ramo Mandoler then Calle Larga Prima, and turn right when you reach beginning of Salizada San Rocco).

Scuola Grande di San Rocco (Confraternity of St. Roch) ★★★

MUSEUM   Like many medieval saints, French-born St. Rocco (St. Roch) died young, but thanks to his work healing the sick in the 14th-century, his cult became associated with the power to cure the plague and other serious illnesses. When the saint's body was brought to Venice in 1485, this *scuola* began to reap the benefits, and by 1560 the current complex was completed, work beginning soon after on more than 50 major paintings by Tintoretto. Today the *scuola* is primarily a shrine to the skills of **Tintoretto.** You enter at

Gondoliers.

the **Ground Floor Hall (Sala Terrena),** where the paintings were created between 1583 and 1587, led by one of the most frenzied "Annunciations" ever made, while "The Flight into Egypt" is undeniably one of Tintoretto's greatest works. Upstairs is the **Great Upper Hall (Sala Superiore),** where Old Testament scenes such as "Moses Striking Water From the Rock" cover the ceiling. The paintings around the walls, based on the New Testament, are generally regarded as a master class of perspective, shadow, and color. Off this main hall is the **Sala dell'Albergo,** where an entire wall is adorned by Tintoretto's mind-blowing "Crucifixion" (as well as his "Glorification of St. Roch," on the ceiling, the painting that actually won him the contract to paint the *scuola*). Way up in the loft, the newly opened **Tesoro** (Treasury) is a tiny space dedicated primarily to gold reliquaries containing venerated relics such as the fingers of St. Peter and St. Andrew, and one of the thorns that crowned Christ during the cruxifixion.

Across the piazza **San Rocco** church (daily 9:30am–5pm; free) was built 1489–1507, its interior adorned with more Tintorettos and with St. Roch himself buried under the altar.

Campo San Rocco 3052, adjacent to Campo dei Frari. www.scuolagrandesanrocco.it. *©* **041-5234864.** Admission 10€ adults (includes audioguide); 8€ ages 18–26; 18 and under free. Daily 9:30am–5:30pm. *Vaporetto:* San Tomà (walk straight ahead on Calle del Traghetto and turn right and immediately left across Campo San Tomà; walk straight ahead on Ramo Mandoler, Calle Larga Prima, and Salizada San Rocco, which leads into the *campo* of the same name—look for crimson sign behind Frari Church).

Cannaregio

Galleria Giorgio Franchetti alla Ca' d'Oro ★★ MUSEUM   This magnificent *palazzo* overlooking the Grand Canal, the "golden house," was built between 1428 and 1430 for the noble Contarini family. Baron Giorgio Franchetti bought the place in 1894, and it now serves as an atmospheric art gallery for the exceptional collection he built up throughout his lifetime. The highlight here is **"St. Sebastian"** ★★ by Paduan artist Andrea Mantegna, displayed in its own marble chapel built by the overawed baron. The so-called "St. Sebastian of Venice" was the third and final painting of the saint by Mantegna, created around 1490 and quite different to the other two (in Vienna and

Paris respectively); it's a bold, deeply pessimistic work, with none of Mantegna's usual background details to detract from the suffering of the saint. The rest of the collection will appeal primarily to aficionados, with Renaissance sculpture on the first floor including "Young Couple" by Tullio Lombardo, and work by Jacopo Sansovino, Andrea Riccio, and Jacopo Bonaccolsi. The paintings on the second floor are relatively mediocre, with Titian's "Venus at the Mirror," two landscapes by Francesco Guardi, and, unexpectedly, some decent Flemish work: the mini "Crucifixion" attributed to Jan Van Eyck, and the "Portrait of Marcello Durazzo" by Van Dyck.

Strada Nuova 3932. www.cadoro.org. ℰ **041-520-0345.** Admission 6€, plus 1.50€ reservation fee (price increases during special exhibitions). Mon 8:15am–2pm; Tues–Sun 8:15am–7:15pm. *Vaporetto:* Ca' d'Oro.

Museo Ebraico di Venezia (Jewish Museum of Venice) ★

MUSEUM/SYNAGOGUE   In the heart of the Ghetto Nuovo, the Jewish Museum contains a small but precious collection of artifacts related to the long history of the Jews in Venice, beginning with an exhibition on Jewish festivities in the first room; chandeliers, goblets, and spice-holders used to celebrate Shabbat, Shofàrs (ram's horns) and a Séfer Torà (Scroll of Divine Law). The second room contains a rich collection of historic textiles, including Torah covers, and a rare marriage contract from 1792. A newer exhibition area explores the immigration patterns of Jews to Venice, and their experiences once here. For many the real highlight, though, is the chance to tour three of the area's five historic synagogues (ladies must have shoulders covered and men must have heads covered; no photos): German (Scuola Grande Tedesca), founded in 1528; Italian (Scuola Italiana), founded in 1575; Sephardic (Scuola Levantina), founded in 1541 but rebuilt in the second half of 17th century; Spanish (Scuola Spagnola), rebuilt in the first half of 17th century; and the baroque-style Ashkenazi (Scuola Canton), largely rebuilt in the 18th century. It's difficult to predict which three you'll visit on any given day, as it depends on which synagogues are being used (and on the whim of your guide); the Levantina and the Spanish are the most lavishly decorated, with one usually included on the tour.

Cannaregio 2902B (on Campo del Ghetto Nuovo). www.museoebraico.it. ℰ **041-715359.** Museum 4€ adults, 3€ children; museum and synagogue tour 10€ adults, 8€ children. Museum Sun–Fri 10am–7pm (Oct–May until 5:30pm); synagogue guided tours in English hourly 10:30am–5:30pm (Oct–May last tour 4:30pm). Closed on Jewish holidays. *Vaporetto:* Guglie.

Santa Maria dei Miracoli ★

CHURCH   Hidden in a quiet corner of the residential section of Cannaregio northeast of the Rialto Bridge, the small and exceedingly attractive 15th-century Miracoli has one side of its precious polychrome-marbled facade running alongside a canal, creating colorful and shimmering reflections. It was built 1481 to 1489 by Pietro Lombardo, a local artisan whose background in monuments and tombs is obvious, and would go on to become one of the founding fathers of the **Venetian Renaissance.**

Jews began settling in Venice in great numbers in the 15th century (originally on the island of Giudecca, thought to be named after a corruption of the Latin "Judaica"), and the Republic soon came to value their services as moneylenders, physicians, and traders. In 1516 however, fearing their growing influence, the Venetians forced the Jewish population to live on an island where there was an abandoned 14th-century foundry (*ghetto* is old Venetian dialect for "foundry"), and drawbridges were raised to enforce a nighttime curfew. By the end of the 17th century, as many as 5,000 Jews lived in the Ghetto's cramped confines. Napoleon tore down the Ghetto gates in 1797, but it wasn't until the unification of Italy in 1866 that Jews achieved equal status with their fellow citizens. It remains the spiritual center for Venice's ever-diminishing

community of Jewish families, with two synagogues and Chabad House. Although accounts vary widely, it's said that anywhere from 500 to 2,000 Jews live in all of Venice and Mestre, though very few live in the Ghetto.

Aside from its historic interest, this is also one of the less touristy neighborhoods in Venice (although it has become something of a nightspot) and makes for a pleasant and scenic place to stroll. Venice's first kosher restaurant, **Gam Gam,** has operated here in 1996, at 1122 Ghetto Vecchio right on the canal (www.gamgamkosher.com; © **366-2504505**), close to the Guglie *vaporetto* stop. Owned and run by Orthodox Jews, it is open Sunday to Thursday noon to 10pm, noon to 2 hours before Shabbat (sunset on Fri evening), and on Saturday from 1 hour after Shabbat, until 11pm (excluding summer).

The less romantic are inclined to compare it to a large tomb with a dome, but the untold couples who have made this perfectly proportioned jewel-like church their choice for weddings will dispel such insensitivity. The small square in front is the perfect place for gondolas to drop off and pick up the newly betrothed. The inside is intricately decorated with early Renaissance marble reliefs, its pastel palette of pink, gray, and white marble making an elegant venue for all those weddings. The church was constructed for a venerated image of the Virgin Mary (created in 1408 by Zanino di Pietro), credited with working miracles. including bringing back to life someone who spent half an hour at the bottom of the Giudecca Canal. The icon is now displayed over the main altar.

Campiello di Miracoli, Rio d. Miracoli. No phone. Admission 3€. Mon–Sat 10am–5pm. *Vaporetto:* Rialto (located midway btw. the Rialto Bridge and the Campo SS. Giovanni e Paolo).

Giudecca & San Giorgio

Il Redentore ★★ CHURCH   Perhaps the masterpiece among Palladio's churches, Il Redentore was commissioned by Venice to give thanks for being delivered from the great plague (1575–77), which claimed over a quarter of the population (some 46,000 people). The doge established a tradition of visiting this church by crossing a long pontoon bridge made up of boats from the

Dorsoduro's Zattere on the third Sunday of each July, a tradition that survived the demise of the doges and remains one of Venice's most popular festivals.

The interior is done in grand, austere, painstakingly classical Palladian style. The artworks tend to be workshop pieces (from the studios or schools, but not the actual brushes, of Tintoretto and Veronese), but there is a fine "Baptism of Christ" by Veronese himself in the sacristy, which also contains Alvise Vivarini's "Madonna with Child & Angels" alongside works by Jacopo da Bassano and Palma il Giovane, who also did the "Deposition" over the right aisle's third chapel (be warned, however, that the sacristy is often closed).

Campo del Redentore, La Giudecca. ℰ **041-523-1415.** Admission 3€. Mon–Sat 10am–5pm. *Vaporetto:* Redentore.

San Giorgio Maggiore ★★ CHURCH   This church sits on the little island of San Giorgio Maggiore across from Piazza San Marco. It is one of the masterpieces of Andrea Palladio, the great Renaissance architect from nearby Padua. Most known for his country villas built for Venice's wealthy merchant families, Palladio was commissioned to build two churches (the other is the Redentore on the neighboring Giudecca island), beginning with San Giorgio, designed in 1565 and completed in 1610. To impose a classical front on the traditional church structure, Palladio designed two interlocking facades, with repeating triangles, rectangles, and columns that are harmoniously proportioned. Founded as early as the 10th century, the interior of the church was reinterpreted by Palladio with whitewashed stucco surfaces, stark but majestic, an unadorned but harmonious space. The main altar is flanked by two epic paintings by an elderly Tintoretto, "The Fall of Manna," to the left, and the more noteworthy **"Last Supper"** ★★ to the right, famous for its chiaroscuro. Through the doorway to the right of the choir leading to the Cappella dei Morti (Chapel of the Dead), you will find Tintoretto's "Deposition."

To the left of the choir is an elevator that you can take to the top of the campanile (6€) to experience an unforgettable view of the island, the lagoon, and the Palazzo Ducale and Piazza San Marco across the way.

San Giorgio Maggiore.

On the island of San Giorgio Maggiore, across St. Mark's Basin from Piazza San Marco. © **041-5227827.** Free admission. Mon–Sat 9:30am–12:30pm; daily 2:30–6pm (Oct–Apr to 4:30pm). *Vaporetto:* Take the Giudecca-bound *vaporetto* (no. 2) on Riva degli Schiavoni (San Marco/San Zaccaria) and get off at the 1st stop, San Giorgio Maggiore.

Exploring Venice's Islands

Venice shares its lagoon with three other principal islands: Murano, Burano, and Torcello. Guided tours of the three are operated by a dozen agencies with docks on Riva degli Schiavoni/Piazzetta San Marco (all interchangeable). The 3- and 4-hour tours run 25€ to 35€, usually include a visit to a Murano glass factory (you can easily do that on your own, with less of a hard sell), and leave daily around 9:30am and 2:30pm (times change; check in advance).

You can also visit the islands on your own conveniently and easily using the *vaporetti.* Line nos. 4.1 and 4.2 make the journey to Murano from Fondamente Nove (on the north side of Castello). For Murano, Burano, and Torcello, Line no. 12 departs Fondamente Nove every 30 minutes; for Torcello change to the shuttle boat (Line 9) that runs from Burano, timed to match the arrivals from Venice. The islands are small and easy to navigate, but check the schedule for the next island-to-island departure (usually hourly) and your return so that you don't spend most of your day waiting for connections.

MURANO ★★

The island of **Murano** has long been famous throughout the world for the products of its glass factories. A visit to the **Museo del Vetro (Museum of Glass)** ★★, Fondamenta Giustinian 8 (www.museovetro.visitmuve.it; © **041-739586**), provides context, charting the history of the island's glassmaking

Glass blowing in Murano.

and is definitely worthwhile if you intend to buy a lot of glassware. Daily hours are 10am to 6pm (Nov–Mar to 5pm), and admission is 10€ for adults and 5.50€ children 6 to 14 and students 30 and under.

Dozens of *fornaci* (kilns) offer free shows of mouth-blown glassmaking, almost invariably hitched to a hard-sell tour of their factory outlet. These retail showrooms of delicate glassware can be enlightening or boring, depending on your frame of mind. Almost all the places will ship their goods, but that often doubles the price. On the other hand, these pieces are instant heirlooms.

Murano also has two worthy churches (both free): the largely 15th-century **San Pietro Martire** ★ (Mon–Sat 9am–5:30pm, Sun noon–5:30pm), with its paintings by Veronese and Giovanni Bellini, and the ancient **Santa Maria e Donato** ★ (Mon–Sat 9am–6pm, Sun 12:30–6pm), with its intricate Byzantine exterior apse, 6th-century pulpit, stunning mosaic of Mary over the altar, and a fantastic 12th-century inland floor.

BURANO ★★★

Lace is the claim to fame of tiny, historic **Burano,** a craft kept alive for centuries by the wives of fishermen waiting for their husbands to return from the sea. Sadly, most of the lace sold on the island these days is made by machine elsewhere. It's still worth a trip if you have time to stroll the back streets of the island, whose canals are lined with the brightly colored, simple homes of the Buranesi fishermen—it's quite unlike anything in Venice or Murano. The local government continues its attempt to keep its centuries-old lace legacy alive with subsidized classes.

Visit the **Museo del Merletto (Museum of Lace Making)** ★, Piazza Galuppi 187 (www.museomerletto.visitmuve.it; ✆ **041-730034**), to understand why something so exquisite should not be left to fade into extinction. It's open Tuesday to Sunday 10am to 6pm (Nov–Mar to 5pm), and admission is 5€ adults, 3.50€ children 6 to 14 and students 29 and under.

TORCELLO ★★

Torcello is perhaps the most charming of the islands, though today it consists of little more than one long canal leading from the *vaporetto* landing to a clump of buildings at its center.

Torcello boasts the oldest Venetian monument, the **Basilica di Santa Maria dell'Assunta** ★★★, whose foundation dates from the 7th century (✆ **041-2702464**). It's justly famous for its spectacular 11th- to 12th-century Byzantine mosaics—a "Madonna and Child" in the apse and a monumental "Last Judgment" on the west wall—rivaling those of Ravenna's and St. Mark's basilicas. The cathedral is open daily 10:30am to 6pm (November through February to 5pm), and admission is 5€ (audioguide an extra 2€). Also of interest is the adjacent 11th-century church of **Santa Fosca** (free admission), though it's a simple Byzantine brick church with a plain interior, and the **Museo di Torcello** (✆ **041-730761**) with two small galleries showcasing archeological artifacts from the Iron Age to medieval period, many found on the island. The church closes 30 minutes before the basilica, and the museum is open Tuesday to Sunday 10:30am to 5:30pm (Nov–Feb to 5pm). Museum admission is 3€. You must buy tickets for all attractions at the Basilica entrance.

Peaceful Torcello is uninhabited except for a handful of families (plus a population of feral cats), and is a favorite picnic spot. You'll have to bring the food from Venice—there are no stores on the island and only a handful of bars/trattorias plus one destination restaurant, **Locanda Cipriani** ★★★ (open Mar–Dec, Wed–Mon, noon–3pm; www.locandacipriani.com) of Hemingway fame, which opened in 1935 and is definitely worth a splurge. Once the tour groups have left, the island offers a very special moment of solitude and escape.

THE LIDO ★

Although a convenient 15-minute *vaporetto* ride away from San Marco, Venice's **Lido beaches** are not much to write home about and certainly no longer a chic destination. For bathing and sun-worshipping there are much better beaches nearby—in Jesolo, to the north, for example. But the parade of wealthy Italian and foreign tourists (plus a good number of Venetian families with children) who still frequent this coastal area throughout summer is an interesting sight indeed, although you'll find many of them at the elitist beaches affiliated with such deluxe hotels as the legendary Excelsior (in a sign of the times, the equally storied de Bains hotel went out of business in 2010 and now serves as luxury apartments).

There are two main beach areas at the Lido. **Bucintoro** is at the opposite end of Gran Viale Santa Maria Elisabetta (referred to as the Gran Viale) from the *vaporetto* station Santa Elisabetta. It's a 10-minute stroll; walk straight ahead along Gran Viale to reach the beach. **San Nicolò,** about 1.5km (1 mile) away, can be reached by bus B. Renting loungers and parasols can cost from 10€–20€ per person (per day) depending on the time of year (it's just 1€ to use the showers and bathrooms). Keep in mind that if you stay at any of the hotels on the Lido, most of them have some kind of agreement with the different *bagni* (beach establishments).

Beach going on the Lido.

carnevale A VENEZIA

Venetians once more are taking to the open *piazze* and streets for the pre-Lenten holiday of Carnevale. The festival traditionally was the celebration preceding Lent, the period of penitence and abstinence prior to Easter; its name is derived from the Latin *carnem levare*, meaning "to take meat away."

Today, Carnevale builds for 10 days until the big blowout, Shrove Tuesday (Fat Tuesday), when fireworks illuminate the Grand Canal, and Piazza San Marco is turned into a giant open-air ballroom for the masses. Book your hotel months ahead, especially for the 2 weekends prior to Shrove Tuesday. In the 18th-century heyday of Carnevale in La Serenissima Republic, well-heeled revelers came from all over Europe to take part in festivities that began months prior to Lent and reached a raucous climax at midnight on Shrove Tuesday. As the Venetian economy declined and its colonies and trading posts fell to other powers, the Republic of Venice in its swan song turned to fantasy and escapism. The faster its decline, the longer, and more licentious, became its anything-goes merrymaking. Masks became ubiquitous, affording anonymity and the pardoning of a thousand sins. Masks permitted the fishmonger to attend the ball and dance with the baroness, the properly married to carry on as if they were not. The doges condemned it and the popes denounced it, but nothing could dampen the Venetian Carnevale spirit until Napoleon arrived in 1797 and put an end to the festivities.

Resuscitated in 1980 by local tourism powers to fill the empty winter months when tourism comes to a screeching halt, Carnevale is calmer nowadays, though just barely. The born-again festival got off to a shaky start, met at first with indifference and skepticism, but in the years since has grown in popularity and been embraced by the locals. In the 1980s, Carnevale attracted an onslaught of what was seemingly the entire student population of Europe, backpacking young people who slept in the *piazze* and train station. Politicians and city officials adopted a middle-of-the-road policy that helped establish Carnevale's image as neither a backpacker's free-for-all outdoor party nor a continuation of the exclusive private balls in the Grand Canal *palazzi* available to a very few.

Carnevale is now a harlequin patchwork of musical and cultural events, many of them free of charge, which appeals to all ages, tastes, nationalities, and budgets. Musical events are staged in some of the city's dozens of *piazze*—from reggae and zydeco to jazz and baroque. Special art exhibits are mounted at museums and galleries.

The city is the perfect venue; Hollywood could not create a more evocative location. This is a celebration of history, art, theater, and drama that one would expect to find in Italy, the land that gave us the Renaissance and Zeffirelli—and Venice, an ancient and wealthy republic that gave us Casanova and Vivaldi. Venice and Carnevale were made for each other. Visit **www.carnevalevenezia.com** for details on upcoming events.

Vaporetto line nos. 1, 2, 5.1, 5.2, and LN cross the lagoon to the Lido from the San Zaccaria–Danieli stop near San Marco. Note that the Lido becomes chilly, windswept, and utterly deserted between October and April.

Venice during Carnevale, with masked revelers.

Organized Tours

Because of the sheer number of sights to see in Venice, some first-time visitors like to start out with an organized tour. Although few things can really be covered in any depth on these overview tours, they're sometimes useful for getting your bearings. **Avventure Bellissime** (www.tours-italy.com; ☏ **041-970499**) coordinates a plethora of tours (in English), by boat and gondola, though the walking tours are the best value, covering all the main sights around Piazza San Marco in 2 hours for 25€. For something with a little more bite, try **Urban Adventures** (www.urbanadventures.com; ☏ **348-9808566**), which runs enticing *cicchetti* tours (2½ hr.) for 75€.

For those with more energy, learn to "row like a Venetian" (yes, literally standing up), at **Row Venice** (www.rowvenice.com; ☏ **347-7250637**), where 1½-hour lessons take place in traditional, hand-built "shrimp-tail" or *batele coda di gambero* boats for 80€ for up to 2 people. Or you could abandon tradition altogether and opt for a **Venice Kayak** tour (www.venicekayak.com; ☏ **346-4771327**), a truly enchanting way to see the city from the water. Day trips are 120€ per person for two to six people with a guide (10am–4 or 5pm).

Especially for Kids

It goes without saying that a **gondola ride** (p. 223) will be the thrill of a lifetime for any child (or adult). If that's too expensive, consider the convenient and far less expensive alternative: a **ride on the no. 1** *vaporetto* (p. 258). They offer two entirely different experiences: The gondola gives you the chance to see Venice through the back door (and ride past Marco Polo's house); the *vaporetto* provides a utilitarian—but no less gorgeous—journey down Venice's aquatic Main Street, the Grand Canal. Look for the ambulance boat, the garbage boat, the firefighters' boat, the funeral boat, even the Coca-Cola delivery boat. Best sightings are the special gondolas filled with flowers and rowed by *gondolieri* in livery delivering a happy bride and groom from the church.

Judging from the squeals of delight, **feeding the pigeons in Piazza San Marco** (purchase a bag of corn and you'll be draped in pigeons in a nanosecond; p. 262) could be the epitome of your child's visit to Venice, and it's the ultimate photo op. Be sure your child won't be startled by all the fluttering and flapping.

A jaunt to the neighboring **island of Murano** (p. 275) can be as educational as it is recreational—follow the signs to any *fornace* (kiln), where a glassblowing performance of the island's thousand-year-old art is free entertainment. But be ready for the guaranteed sales pitch that follows.

Before you leave town, take the elevator to the **top of the Campanile di San Marco** (the highest structure in the city; p. 258) for a scintillating view of Venice's rooftops and church cupolas, or get up close and personal with the four bronze horses on the facade of the Basilica San Marco. The view from its **outdoor loggia** is something you and your children won't forget. Climbing the **Torre dell'Orologio** (p. 262) or the bell tower at **San Giorgio Maggiore** (p. 274) should also be lots of fun.

Some children enjoy the **Museo Storico Navale (Naval History Museum)** and **Arsenale** (Arsenal; http://arsenale.comune.venezia.it; ℂ 041-274-8151) with its ship models and old vessels, and the many historic artifacts in the **Museo Correr** (**Correr Civic Museum;** p. 263); tangible vestiges of a time when Venice was a world unto itself.

The **Peggy Guggenheim Collection** (p. 267) offers family programs every weekend, and the bright paintings and outdoor sculpture gardens are often a welcome break for Renaissance-weary kids.

The **winged lion,** said to have been a kind of good luck mascot to St. Mark, patron saint of Venice, was the very symbol of the Serene Republic and to this day appears on everything from cafe napkins to T-shirts. Who can spot the most flying lions? They appear on facades, atop columns, over doorways, as pavement mosaics, on government stamps, and on the local flag.

SHOPPING

In a city that for centuries has thrived almost exclusively on tourism, remember this: **Where you buy cheap, you get cheap.** Venetians, centuries-old merchants, aren't known for bargaining. You'll stand a better chance of getting a good deal if you pay in cash or buy more than one item. In our limited space below, we've listed some of the more reputable places to stock up on classic Venetian items.

Shopping Streets & Markets

A mix of low-end trinket stores and middle-market-to-upscale boutiques line the narrow zigzagging **Mercerie** running north between Piazza San Marco and the Rialto Bridge. More expensive clothing and gift boutiques make for great window-shopping on **Calle Larga XXII Marzo,** the wide street that begins west of Piazza San Marco and wends its way to the expansive Campo Santo Stefano near the Accademia. The narrow **Frezzeria,** just west of Piazza San Marco and running north-south, offers a grab bag of bars, souvenir shops, and tony clothing stores like Louis Vuitton and Versace. There are few bargains to be had; the non-produce part of the **Rialto Market** is as good as it gets for basic souvenirs, where you'll find cheap T-shirts, glow-in-the-dark plastic gondolas, and tawdry glass trinkets. The **Mercatino dei Miracoli** (*©*041-2710022), held only six times a year in Campo Santa Maria Nova (Cannaregio), is a fabulous flea market with all sorts of bric-a-brac and antiques sold by ordinary Venetians—haggling, for once, is acceptable. It usually takes place on the second Saturday or Sunday of March, April, May, September, October, and December, between 8:30am and 8pm. There's also the **Mercatino dell'Antiquariato** (www.mercatinocamposanmaurizio.it), a professional antiques market in Campo San Maurizio, San Marco, which takes place four times a year (usually Mar–Apr, May, Sept, Oct, and Dec; see the website for dates).

Arts & Crafts

Venice is uniquely famous for local crafts that have been produced here for centuries and are hard to get elsewhere: the **glassware** from Murano, the **delicate lace** from Burano, and the *cartapesta* (**papier-mâché**) **Carnevale masks** you'll find in endless *botteghe* (shops), where you can watch artisans paint amid their wares.

Now here's the bad news: There's such an overwhelming sea of cheap glass gewgaws that buying Venetian glass can become something of a turnoff (shipping and insurance costs make most things unaffordable; the alternative is to hand-carry anything fragile). There are so few women left on Burano willing to spend countless tedious hours keeping alive the art of lace-making that the few pieces you'll see not produced by machine in China are sold at stratospheric prices; ditto the truly high-quality glass (although trinkets can be cheap and fun). The best place to buy glass is Murano itself—only ever buy items with the **"Vetro Artistico Murano"** trademark, and expect to pay as much as 60€ for just a wine glass.

Anticlea Antiquariato ★ This shop specializes in the shiny glass beads known as *perle Veneziane* ("Venetian pearls"), with drawers full of every conceivable type and color, as well as ready-to-wear rings, necklaces, and bracelets. It's open Monday to Saturday 10am to 1:30pm and 2 to 7pm. Calle San Provolo 4719A, Castello (just off Campo San Provolo). ℭ**041-5224045.** Vaporetto: San Zaccaria.

Atelier Segalin di Daniela Ghezzo ★★ Founded in 1932 by master cobbler Antonio Segalin and his son Rolando, this old leather shoe store is now run by Daniela Ghezzo (the star apprentice of Rolando), maker of exuberant handmade shoes and boots, from basic flats to crazy footware designed for Carnevale (shoes from 650€–1,800€). It's open Monday to Friday 10am to 1pm and 3 to 7pm, and Saturday 10am to 1pm. Calle dei Fuseri 4365, San Marco. www.danielaghezzo.it. ℭ**041-5222115.** Vaporetto: San Marco.

La Bottega dei Mascareri ★★ High-quality, creative masks—some based on Tiepolo paintings—crafted by the brothers Sergio and Massimo Boldrin since 1984. Basic masks start at around 15€ to 20€, but you'll pay over 75€ for a more innovative piece. The original branch lies at the foot of the Rialto Bridge (San Polo 80; ℭ 041-5223857). Both locations tend to open daily 9am to 6pm. Calle dei Saoneri 2720, San Polo. www.mascarer.com. ℭ **041-5242887.** Vaporetto: Rialto.

Ca' del Sol Maschere ★★ Another treasure trove of Venetian masks, run by a group of artists since 1986 (prices range from 15€–250€). They also make elaborate 18th-century costumes and even run mask-making courses. It opens daily 10am to 8pm. Fondamenta de l'Osmarin 4964, Castello. www.cadelsolmascherevenezia.com. ℭ**041-5285549.** Vaporetto: San Zaccaria.

Il Canovaccio ★ Remember the creepy orgy scenes in Stanley Kubrick's film *Eyes Wide Shut*? The ornate masks used in the movie were made by the owners of this vaunted store. All manner of traditional, feathered and animal masks are knocked out of their on-site workshop. It's open daily 10am to 7:30pm. Calle delle Bande 5369 (near Campo Santa Maria Formosa), Castello. www.ilcanovaccio.com. ℭ**041-5210393.** Vaporetto: San Zaccaria.

Il Grifone ★★★ Toni Peressin's handmade leather briefcases, satchels, bound notebooks, belts, and soft-leather purses have garnered quite a following, and justly so—his craftsmanship is truly magnificent (he makes everything in the workshop out back). Items start at around 15€. It's usually open Tuesday to Friday 9am to 12:30pm and 4 to 7:30pm, and Saturday 10am to noon. Fondamenta del Gaffaro 3516, Dorsoduro. www.ilgrifonevenezia.it. ℭ **041-5229452.** Vaporetto: Piazzale Roma.

Marco Polo International ★ This vast showroom, just west of the Piazza San Marco, displays quality glass direct from Murano (although it's more expensive than going to the island yourself), including plenty of easy to carry items such as paperweights and small dishes. It opens daily 10am to 7pm. Frezzeria 1644, San Marco. www.marcopolointernational.it. ℂ **041-5229295.** Vaporetto: San Marco.

Venini ★ Convenient, classy, but incredibly expensive, Venini has been selling quality glass art since 1921, supplying the likes of Versace and many other designer brands. Their **workshop** on Murano is at Fondamenta Vetrai 50 (ℂ **041-2737211**). Both locations tend to open Monday to Saturday 9:30am to 5:30pm. Piazzetta Leoncini 314, San Marco. www.venini.it. ℂ**041-5224045.** Vaporetto: San Marco.

ENTERTAINMENT & NIGHTLIFE ■8

If you're looking for serious nocturnal action, you're in the wrong town—Verona and Padua are far more lively. Your best bet is to sit in the moonlit Piazza San Marco and listen to the cafes' outdoor orchestras, with the illuminated basilica before you—the perfect opera set—though this pleasure comes with a hefty price tag. Other popular spots to hang out include **Campo San Bartolomeo,** at the foot of the Rialto Bridge (although it is a zoo here in high season), and nearby **Campo San Luca.** In late-night hours, for low prices and low pretension, the absolute best place to go is **Campo Santa Margherita,** a huge open *campo* about halfway between the train station and the Accademia Bridge.

Visit one of the tourist information centers for current English-language schedules of the month's special events. The monthly *Ospite di Venezia* is distributed free or online at **www.unospitedivenezia.it** and is extremely helpful, but it's usually available only in the more expensive hotels.

Performing Arts & Live Music

Venice has a long and rich tradition of classical music, and there's always a concert going on somewhere. Several churches and confraternities (such as San Stae, the Scuola di San Giovanni Evangelista, and the Scuola di San Rocco) regularly host classical music concerts (with an emphasis on the baroque) by local and international artists. This was, after all, the home of Vivaldi. People dressed in period costumes stand around in heavily trafficked spots near San Marco and Rialto passing out brochures advertising classical music concerts, so you'll have no trouble finding up-to-date information.

Santa Maria della Pietà ★★ The so-called "Vivaldi Church," built between 1745 and 1760, holds concerts throughout the year; check the website for specific dates. Lauded ensemble **I Virtuosi Italiani** gives a concert series here every September. Full price tickets are usually around 25€. Riva degli Schiavoni 3701, Castello. www.chiesavivaldi.it. ℂ **041-5221120.** Vaporetto: San Zaccaria.

Teatro La Fenice ★★★ One of Italy's most famous opera houses (it officially ranks third after La Scala in Milan and San Carlo in Naples), La Fenice opened in 1836, but was rebuilt after a devastating fire and reopened in 2003. The opera season runs late November through June, but there are also

Teatro La Fenice.

ballet performances and classical concerts. Tickets are expensive for the major productions; around 70€ for the gallery, and 110€ to 220€ for a decent seat. Those on a budget can opt for obstructed-view seats (25€) or listening-only seats (15€). Campo San Fantin 1965, San Marco. www.teatrolafenice.it. © **041-2424.** Vaporetto: Giglio.

Cafes

For tourists and locals alike, Venetian nightlife mainly centers on the many cafes in one of the world's most remarkable *piazze:* Piazza San Marco. It is also the most expensive and touristed place to linger over a spritz or anything else for that matter, but it's a splurge that should not be dismissed too readily. For those on a particularly tight budget, you can hang out near the cafes and listen to the sometimes quite surprisingly good live classical music (you won't be alone). If you're looking for some scrumptious ice cream to slurp as you admire the piazzas by night, see "Gelato," p. 251.

Caffè dei Frari ★★★ Established in 1870, the walls of this inviting bar and cafe overlooking the Frari church are still adorned with the original murals, an antique wooden bar, and a wrought-iron balcony upstairs. The seafood is especially good here, and there are usually at least three excellent German beers on tap. The laid-back owner doubles as DJ on Friday and Saturday evenings (he's pretty good). Open Tuesday to Saturday 9am to 10pm, and Sunday and Monday 9am to 4pm. Fondamenta dei Frari 2564, San Polo. © **041-5241877.** Vaporetto: San Tomà.

Caffè Florian ★★ Occupying prime *piazza* real estate since 1720, this is one of the world's oldest coffee shops, with a florid interior of 18th-century mirrors, frescoes, and statuary. Sitting at a table expect to pay 9€ for a cappuccino, 19€ for a Bellini (Prosecco and fresh peach nectar in season) and 13€ for a spritz, and then add another 6€ if the orchestra plays (Mar to Nov). It's pricy, but remember you're paying for the experience, and the entertainment factor is worth the price if you linger. Standing at the bar is much cheaper (5€ for a cappuccino, 8.50€ for a Bellini). Open Monday to Thursday 10am to 9pm, Friday and Saturday 9am to 11pm, and Sunday 9am to 9pm. Piazza San Marco 56. www.caffeflorian.com. ℂ **041-5205641.** Vaporetto: San Marco.

Caffè Lavena ★★ Said to be Wagner's favorite cafe (look for the plaque inside), and the hangout of fellow composer Franz Liszt, Lavena lies on the opposite side of the *piazza* to Florian and was founded just a few decades later in 1750. Expect the same high prices and surcharges here (a famous case in 2013 saw seven tourists charged 100€ for four coffees and three liqueurs), though as with Florian, if you stand and drink at the bar you'll pay much less than sitting at a table (coffee is just 1€). Open daily 9:30am to midnight (closed Tues in winter). Piazza San Marco 133–134. www.lavena.it. ℂ **041-5224070.** Vaporetto: San Marco.

Gran Caffè Quadri ★ The final member of the San Marco "big three," Quadri opened in 1638 as "Il Rimedio" ("The Remedy"), but it was more of a retail coffee operation at first, with the restaurant upstairs added in 1830. It's been revitalized by chef Max Alajmo of Le Calandre restaurant in Padua, with a fancy restaurant upstairs (Ristorante Quadri). Most coffees are 7.50€ to 11€,

Orchestra at Caffè Florian.

with breakfast from 27€ to 31€. Beer is 13€ and Bellinis are 18€. April to October, guests are serenaded by the 121 St. Mark's Band (an extra 6€). Open daily 9am to midnight (closed Mon in winter). Piazza San Marco 121. www.alajmo. it. © **041-5222105.** Vaporetto: San Marco.

Il Caffè (aka Caffe Rosso) ★★★ Established in the late 19th century, Il Caffè has a history almost as colorful as its clientele, a mixture of students, aging regulars, and lost tourists. This is an old-fashioned, no-nonsense Venetian cafe/bar, with reasonably priced drinks and sandwiches, and plenty of seating on the *campo*. Open Monday to Saturday 7am to 1am. Campo Santa Margherita 2963, Dorsoduro. www.cafferosso.it. © **041-5287998.** Vaporetto: Ca'Rezzonico.

Marchini Time ★★ Plush modern cafe that acts as the outlet for the famed Marchini *pasticcerie* (almost 50 years old), offering a range of addictive pastries, *biscotti*, chocolates, coffees, cakes, and savory *pizzette*. It's open Monday to Saturday 7am to 8:30pm. Campo San Luca 4589, San Marco. © **041-2413087.** Vaporetto: Rialto.

Pasticceria Nobile ★★ The most happening cafe in this section of town, founded in the 1930s and celebrated for its tempting range of sweets, snacks, *pizzette*, pastries, and chocolate. Locals congregate here for breakfast and for *aperitivo* after work. Open Tuesday to Sunday 7am to 8:30pm (closed July). Calle del Pistor 1818, Cannaregio. www.pasticcerianobile.it. © **041-720731.** Vaporetto: San Marcuola.

Birreria, Wine & Cocktail Bars

Although Venice boasts an old and prominent university, dance clubs barely enjoy their 15 minutes of popularity before changing hands or closing down (some are open only in the summer months). Young Venetians tend to go to the Lido in summer or mainland Mestre. Evenings are better spent lingering over a late dinner, having a pint in a *birrerie*, or nursing a glass of Prosecco in one of Piazza San Marco's or Campo Santa Margherita's overpriced outdoor bars and cafes. (*Note:* Most bars are open Mon–Sat 8pm–midnight.)

Al Prosecco ★★ Get acquainted with all things bubbly at this smart enoteca, a specialist, as you'd expect, in Veneto Prosecco. It features plenty of tasty *cicchetti* to wash down the various brands, and a gorgeous terrace from which to observe the *campo* below. Drinks run 3€ to 5€. Open Monday to Saturday 10am to 10:30pm (closes at 8pm in winter; closed Aug and Jan). Campo San Giacomo da l'Orio 1503, Santa Croce. www.alprosecco.com. © **041-5240222.** Vaporetto: San Stae.

Caffè Centrale ★★ Not really a cafe but a super hip bar and restaurant (with iPad menus), this spot is located within the 16th-century Palazzo Cocco Molin, just a short walk from Piazza San Marco. It's got an intriguing selection of local and foreign beers (5.50€–7.50€), and a huge cocktail list (10€–12€)—a spritz is 7.50€ (cover is an extra 5€ per person). Get a table by the canal or lounge on one of the super comfy leather sofas. Open daily 7pm to

Bellini at Harry's Bar.

1am. Piscina Frezzeria 1659, San Marco. www.caffecentralevenezia.com. ℰ**041-8876642.** Vaporetto: Vallaresso.

Harry's Bar ★ Possibly the most famous bar in Venice (and now a global chain), Harry's was established in 1931 by Giuseppe Cipriani and frequented by the likes of Ernest Hemingway, Charlie Chaplin, and Truman Capote. The Bellini was invented here in 1948 (along with *carpaccio* 2 years later), and you can sip the signature concoction of fresh peach juice and Prosecco for a mere 16€. Go for the history but don't expect a five-star experience—most first-timers are surprised just how ordinary it looks inside. It also serves very expensive food, but just stick to the drinks. Open daily 10:30am to 11pm. Calle Vallaresso 1323, San Marco. www.harrysbar venezia.com. ℰ**041-5285777.** Vaporetto: Vallaresso.

Margaret DuChamp ★★ This popular student and *fashionista* hangout has plenty of chairs on the *campo* for people-watching, cocktails, and a spritz or two (most cocktails are just 5€–7€). It also serves decent panini (7€) and *tramezzini* (2€ at the table, or 1.50€ at the bar), and has free Wi-Fi. Open Wednesday to Monday 9am to 2am. Campo Santa Margherita 3019, Dorsoduro. ℰ**041-5286255.** Vaporetto: Ca' Rezzonico.

Paradiso Perduto ★★ "Paradise Lost" is the most happening bar in this neighborhood, crammed with students most nights and featuring the occasional live music set (full concerts every Mon and every first Sun of the month), great *cicchetti* (piled in mountains at the bar) and cheap(ish) wine. Some people come to dine on the tasty seafood, but it's usually too busy and noisy to enjoy a proper meal here—stick to the drinks and the snacks. Open Thursday to Monday noon to midnight (closed Tues–Wed). Fondamenta della Misericordia 2540, Cannaregio. www.ilparadisoperduto.com. ℰ**041-720581.** Vaporetto: Madonna dell'Orto.

DAY TRIPS FROM VENICE

I f you only have 3 days or so, you will probably want to spend them in the center of Venice. However, if you are here for a week—or on your second visit to the city—head over to the mainland to see some of the old towns that lie within the historic Veneto region.

PADUA ★★★

40km (25 miles) W of Venice

Tucked away within the ancient heart of **Padua** lies one of the greatest artistic treasures in all Italy, the precious Giotto frescoes of the **Cappella degli Scrovegni.** Although the city itself is not especially attractive (it was largely rebuilt after bombing during World War II), don't be put off by the urban sprawl that now surrounds it; central Padua is refreshingly bereft of tourist crowds, a workaday Veneto town with a large student population and a small but intriguing ensemble of historic sights.

Like much of the region, Padua prospered in the Middle Ages, and Italy's second oldest university was founded here in 1222. Its fortunes grew further when St. Antony of Padua died in the city in 1231, making it a place of pilgrimage ever since. In the 14th century, the da Carrara family presided over the city's golden age, but in 1405 Padua was conquered and absorbed by Venice, losing its independence. With the fall of the Venetian Republic in 1797, the city was ruled by Napoleon and then became part of the Austrian Empire in 1814. Finally annexed to Italy in 1866, the city boomed again after World War II, becoming the industrial dynamo of northeast Italy.

Essentials

GETTING THERE

The most efficient way to reach Padua is to take the train from the Santa Lucia station. Trains depart every 10 to 20 minutes, and take 25 to 50 minutes depending on the class (tickets range from 4.05€– 13€ one-way). The main station in Padua is a short walk north up Corso del Popolo from the Cappella degli Scrovegni and the old city.

VISITOR INFORMATION

The tourist office at the train station is usually open Monday to Saturday 9am to 7pm, and Sunday 9:15am to 12:30pm (www.

turismopadova.it; (C) **049-8752027**), while the office in the old city at Piazetta Pedrocchi ((C) **049-8767927**) is open Monday to Saturday 9am to 1:30pm and 3 to 7pm.

Exploring Padua

The one unmissable sight in Padua is the **Cappella degli Scrovegni** ★★★ (www.cappelladegliscrovegni.it; (C) **049-2010020;** daily 9am–7pm) at Piazza Eremitani, an outwardly unassuming chapel commissioned in 1303 by Enrico Scrovegni, a wealthy banker. Inside, however, the chapel is gloriously decorated with an astonishing cycle of frescoes completed by Florentine genius **Giotto** 2 years later. The frescoes depict the life of the Virgin Mary and the life of Jesus, culminating with the Ascension and Last Judgment. Seeing Giotto's powerful work in the flesh is spine-tingling; this is where he makes the decisive break with Byzantine art, taking the first important steps toward the realism and humanism that would characterize the Renaissance in Italy.

Entrance to the chapel is limited, involving groups of 25 visitors spending 15 minutes in a climate-controlled airlock, used to stabilize the temperature, before going inside for another 15 minutes. To visit the chapel you must **make a reservation at least 24 hours in advance.** You must then arrive 45 minutes before the time on your ticket. Tickets cost 13€ (6€ for kids ages 6–17 and students under 27).

If you have time, try to take in Padua's other historic highlights. The vast **Palazzo della Ragione** on Piazza del Erbe (Tues–Sun Feb–Oct 9am–7pm, Nov–Jan 9am–6pm; 4€) is an architectural marvel, completed in 1219, and decorated by frescoes completed by Nicola Miretto in the 15th century. Pay a visit also to the **Basilica di Sant'Antonio** (www.basilica delsanto.org; (C) **049-8225652;** daily Apr–Sept 6:20am–7pm, Oct–Mar 6:20am–7:45pm; free admission) on the Piazza del Santo, the stately resting place of **St. Anthony of Padua,** the Portuguese Franciscan best known as the patron saint of finding things or lost people. The exterior is a bizarre mix of Byzantine, Romanesque, and Gothic styles (largely completed in the 14th c.), while the interior is richly adorned with statuary and murals. Don't miss

Cappella degli Scrovegni.

Donatello's stupendous equestrian statue of the Venetian *condottiere* **Gattamelata** (Erasmo da Narni) in the piazza outside, raised in 1453 and the first large bronze sculpture of the Renaissance.

Where to Eat

Padua offers plenty of places to eat, and you'll especially appreciate the overall drop in prices compared to Venice. It's hard to match the location of **Bar Nazionale ★★**, Piazza del Erbe 40 (Mon–Sat 9am–11:30pm), on the steps leading up to Palazzo della Ragione, though it's best for drinks and snacks (excellent *tramezzini*) rather than a full meal. For that, make for **Osteria dei Fabbri ★**, Via dei Fabbri 13, just off Piazza del Erbe (www.osteriadeifabbri. it; ℭ **049-650336**), open Monday to Saturday noon to 3pm and 7 to 11pm, which cooks up cheap, tasty pasta dishes for under 10€.

VERONA ★★

115km (71 miles) W of Venice

The affluent city of **Verona,** with its gorgeous red- and peach-colored medieval buildings and Roman ruins, is one of Italy's major tourist draws, though its appeal owes more to **William Shakespeare** than real history. He immortalized the city in his (totally fictional) "Romeo and Juliet," "The Two Gentlemen of Verona," and partly, "The Taming of the Shrew." Though it does attract its fair share of tourism, Verona is not Venice; this is a booming trading center, with vibrant science and technology sectors.

Verona emerged as a city-state in the 12th century, ruled primarily by the bloodthirsty (and, in Renaissance tradition, art-loving) Scaligeri family until 1387. After a brief period of Milanese rule, Verona fell under the control of Venice in 1405. Like the rest of the region, the city fell to Napoleon in 1797, then Austria, becoming part of Italy in 1866.

Essentials

GETTING THERE

The best way to reach Verona from Venice is by **train.** Direct services depart every 30 minutes and take anywhere from 1 hour and 10 minutes to 2 hours and 20 minutes, depending on the type of train you catch (tickets range from 8.60€–23€ one-way). From Verona station (Verona Porta Nuova), it's a 15-minute walk to the historic center.

VISITOR INFORMATION

The tourist office is off Piazza Bra at Via Degli Alpini 9 (www.tourism. verona.it; ℭ **045-8068680;** Mon–Sat 9am–7pm, Sun 10am–4pm), and can supply maps, hotel reservations, discount cards, and guided tour information.

Exploring Verona

"Two households, both alike in dignity, in fair Verona . . ." So go the immortal opening lines of "Romeo and Juliet," ensuring that the city has been a target for love-sick romantics ever since. Though Verona is crammed with genuine historic goodies, one of the most popular sites is the ersatz **Casa di Giulietta,** Via Cappello 23 (Mon 1:30–7:30pm, Tues–Sun 8:30am–7:30pm; adults 6€; 4.50€ seniors over 60 and students ages 14–30), a 14th-century house (with balcony, naturally), claiming to be the Capulets' home. In the courtyard, the chest of a bronze statue of Juliet has been polished to a gleaming sheen thanks to a legend claiming that stroking her right breast brings good fortune. **Juliet's Wall,** at the entrance, is quite a spectacle, covered with the scribbles of star-crossed lovers; love letters placed here are taken down and, along with 5,000

"Juliet" statue at Casa di Giulietta.

letters annually, are answered by the Club di Giulietta (a group of locally based volunteers). There's not much to see inside the house.

Once you've made the obligatory Juliet pilgrimage, focus on some really amazing historic ruins: the 1st-century **Roman Arena** (Mon 1:30–7:30pm, Tues–Sun 9am–7:30pm; 6€), in the spacious Piazza Bra, is the third-largest classical arena in Italy after Rome's Colosseum and the arena at Capua—it could seat some 25,000 spectators and today it remains a celebrated venue for large-scale opera performances (www.arena.it). To the northwest on Piazza San Zeno, the **Basilica di San Zeno Maggiore** (Mar–Oct Mon–Sat 8:30am–6pm, Sun 12:30–6pm; Nov–Feb Mon–Sat 10am–1pm and 1:30–5pm, Sun 12:30–5pm; 3€) is the greatest Romanesque church in northern Italy. The present structure was completed around 1135, over the 4th-century shrine to Verona's patron saint, St. Zeno (who died 380). Its massive rose window represents the Wheel of Fortune, while the impressive lintels above the portal represent the months of the year. The highlight of the interior is "Madonna and Saints" above the altar, by Mantegna.

Where to Eat

Even in chic Verona, you'll spend less on a meal than in Venice. The most authentic budget Verona restaurant is **Osteria Sottoriva,** Via Sottoriva 9

Roman Arena.

(📞 **045-8014323;** Thurs–Tues 11am–10:30pm), one of the most popular places in town for lunch or dinner; try the *trippa alla Parmigiana* (braised tripe) or the hopelessly rich Gorgonzola melted over polenta (main courses 8€–12€). The **Caffè Monte Baldo,** Via Rosa 12 (📞 **045-8030579**), is an old-fashioned cafe transformed into trendy osteria, serving classic pastas, and scrumptious *crostini* with wine in the evenings (many bottles from nearby vineyards).

PLANNING YOUR TRIP

This chapter provides a variety of planning tools, including information on how to get there, how to get around, and the inside track on local resources.

If you do your homework on special events, pick the right place for the right season, and pack for the climate, preparing for a trip to Italy should be pleasant and uncomplicated. See also "When to Go," p. 30.

GETTING THERE

By Plane

If you're flying across an ocean, you'll most likely land at Rome's **Leonardo da Vinci–Fiumicino Airport** (FCO; www.adr.it/fiumicino), 40km (25 miles) from the center. Rome's much smaller **Ciampino Airport** (CIA; www.adr.it/ciampino) serves low-cost airlines connecting to European cities and other destinations in Italy. For information on getting to central Rome from its airports, see p. 33.

FLYING DIRECTLY TO VENICE, BOLOGNA, OR PISA

Carriers within Europe fly direct to several smaller Italian cities. Among the most convenient are Venice's **Marco Polo Airport** (VCE; www.veniceairport.it), Bologna's **Marconi Airport** (BLQ; www.bologna-airport.it), and Pisa's **Galileo Galilei Airport** (PSA; www.pisa-airport.com).

For information on getting into central Venice from the airport, see p. 216. For reaching Florence from Pisa Airport, see p. 139. Florence is also connected with Bologna Airport, by the **Appennino Shuttle** (www.appenninoshuttle.it; © 055/585-271). The direct bus runs 10 times each day and the journey takes between 80 and 90 minutes. Tickets cost 25€, 10€ ages 5 to 10, free ages 4 and under; book online ahead of time for a 5€ per passenger discount. Buses arrive at and depart from Piazzale Montelungo, close to Florence's Santa Maria Novella rail station.

By Train

Italy's major cities are well connected to Europe's rail hubs. You can arrive in Milan on direct trains from France—including Nice,

Paris, and Lyon—by TGV; on night trains from Munich, Germany, and Vienna, Austria; or intercity services from Zurich, Switzerland; and connect to Venice or Rome (see p. 297). Direct trains from central Europe also arrive at Verona and Venice. **Loco2.com** is good for finding and booking trains into and out of Italy.

Thello (www.thello.com) also operates an overnight service connecting Paris with Venice. After crossing the Alps in the dead of night, the train calls at Milan, Brescia, Verona, Vicenza, and Padua before arriving in Venice around 9:30am. For Florence, Rome, and points south, alight at Milan (around 6am) and switch to Italy's national high-speed rail lines; see p. 297. Accommodation on the Thello train is in sleeping cars, as well as in six- and four-berth couchettes. Prices range from 35€ per person for the cheapest fare in a 6-berth couchette to a maximum of 290€ for sole occupancy of a sleeping car. It's worth paying the extra for private accommodations if you can.

You can book in advance online or with **Rail Europe** (www.raileurope. com; ℂ **800/622-8600**) or **International Rail** (www.internationalrail.com; ℂ **0871/231-0790**).

GETTING AROUND
By Car

Much of Italy is accessible by public transportation, but to explore vineyards, countryside, and smaller towns, a car is essential. You'll get the **best rental rate** if you book your car far ahead of arrival. Try such websites as **Kayak. com, CarRentals.co.uk, Skyscanner.net**, and **Momondo.com** to compare prices across multiple rental companies and agents. Car-rental search companies usually report the lowest rates available between 6 and 8 weeks ahead of arrival. Rent the smallest car possible and request a diesel rather than petrol engine to minimize fuel costs. You must be 25 or older to rent from many agencies (although some accept ages 21 and up, at a premium price).

The legalities and contractual obligations of renting a car in Italy (where accident rates are high) are more complicated than those in almost any other country in Europe. You must have nerves of steel, a sense of humor, and a valid driver's license or **International Driver's Permit.** Insurance on all vehicles is compulsory. *Note:* If you're planning to rent a car in Italy during high season, you should **book well in advance.** It's not unusual to arrive at the airport in Rome in June or July to find that every last agent is all out of cars, perhaps for the whole week.

It can sometimes be tricky to get to the *autostrada* (fast highway) from the city center or airport, so consider renting or bringing a GPS-enabled device or installing an offline satellite/navigation app on your smartphone. In bigger cities you will first have to get to the *tangenziale,* or "beltway," which will eventually lead to your highway of choice. The beltway in Rome is known as the Grande Raccordo Anulare, or "Big Ring Road."

The going can be slow almost anywhere, especially on Friday afternoons leaving the cities and Sunday nights on the way back into town, and rush hour around the cities any day of the week can be epic. See **www.autostrade.it** for live traffic updates and a road-toll calculator. Autostrada tolls can get expensive, costing about 1€ for every 14km (8½ miles), which means that it would cost about 18€ for a trip from Rome to Florence. Add in the high price of fuel (averaging over 1.60€ *per liter* at time of writing) and car rental, and it's often cheaper to take the train, even for two people.

Before leaving home, you can apply for an **International Driving Permit** from the American Automobile Association (AAA; www.aaa.com; ℂ **800/622-7070** or 650/294-7400). In Canada, the permit's available from the Canadian Automobile Association (www.caa.ca; ℂ **416/221-4300**). Technically, you need this permit and your actual driver's license to drive in Italy, though in practice your license itself often suffices. Visitors from within the EU need only take their domestic driver's license.

Italy's equivalent of AAA is the **Automobile Club d'Italia (ACI;** www.aci. it). They're the people who respond when you place an emergency call to ℂ **803-116** for road breakdowns, though they do charge for this service if you're not a member.

DRIVING RULES Italian drivers aren't maniacs; they only appear to be. Spend any time on a highway and you will have the experience of somebody driving up insanely close from behind while flashing headlights. Take a deep breath and don't panic: This is the aggressive signal for you to move to the right so he (invariably, it's a he) can pass, and until you do he will stay mind-bogglingly close. On a two-lane road, the idiot passing someone in the opposing traffic who has swerved into your lane expects you to veer obligingly over toward the shoulder so three lanes of traffic can fit—he would do the same for you. Probably. Many Italians seem to think that blinkers are optional, so be aware that the car in front could be getting ready to turn at any moment.

Autostrade are toll highways, denoted by green signs and a number prefaced with an *A,* like the A1 from Milan to Florence, Rome, and Naples. A few fast highways aren't numbered and are simply called a *raccordo,* a connecting road between two cities (such as Florence–Siena and Florence–Pisa).

Strade statali (singular is *strada statale*) are state roads, sometimes without a center divider and two lanes wide (although sometimes they can be a divided four-way highway), indicated by blue signs. Their route numbers are prefaced with an *SS,* as in the SS11 from Milan to Venice. On signs, however, these official route numbers are used infrequently. Usually, you'll just see blue signs listing destinations by name with arrows pointing off in the appropriate directions. It's impossible to predict which of all the towns that lie along a road will be the ones chosen to list on a particular sign. Sometimes the sign gives only the first minuscule village that lies past the turnoff. At other times it lists the first major town down that road. Some signs mention only the major city the road eventually leads to, even if it's hundreds of kilometers away. It pays to study the map before coming to an intersection, carry a GPS device, or download an offline GPS app for your smartphone. Because they bisect countless towns, the *strade statali* can be frustratingly slow: When feasible, pay for the autostrada.

The **speed limit** on roads in built-up areas around towns and cities is 50 kmph (31 mph). On two-lane roads it's 90 kmph (56 mph) and on the highway its 130 kmph (81 mph). Italians have an astounding disregard for these limits. However, police can ticket you and collect a fine on the spot. The blood-alcohol limit in Italy is 0.05%, often achieved with just two drinks; driving above the limit can result in a fine, driving ban, or imprisonment. The blood-alcohol limit is set at zero for anyone who has held a driver's license for under 3 years. Safety belts are obligatory in both the front and the back seats; ditto child seats or special restraints for minors under 1.5 meters (5 ft.) in height—though this latter regulation is often ignored. Drivers may not use a cellphone while driving, but this is yet another law that locals seem to consider optional.

PARKING   On streets, **white lines** indicate free public spaces, **blue lines** are pay spaces, and **yellow lines** mean only residents are allowed to park. Meters don't line the sidewalk; rather, there's a machine on the block where you punch in how long you want to park. The machine spits out a ticket for placing on your dashboard. If you park in an area marked *parcheggio disco orario,* root around in your rental car's glove compartment for a cardboard parking disc (or buy one at a gas station). With this device, you dial up the hour of your arrival and display it on your dashboard. You're allowed *un'ora* (1 hr.) or *due ore* (2 hr.), according to the sign. If you do not have a disk, write your arrival time clearly on a sheet of paper and leave it on the dash.

Parking lots have ticket dispensers, but exit booths are not usually manned. When you return to the lot to depart, first visit the office or automated payment machine to exchange your ticket for a paid receipt. You then use this to get through the exit gate.

ROAD SIGNS   Here's a brief rundown of the road signs you'll most frequently encounter. A **speed limit** sign is a black number inside a red circle on a white background. The **end of a speed zone** is just black and white, with a black slash through the number. A red circle with a white background, a black arrow pointing down, and a red arrow pointing up means **yield to oncoming traffic,** while a point-down, red-and-white triangle means **yield ahead.**

Many city centers are closed to traffic, and a simple white circle with a red border, or the words *zona pedonale* or *zona traffico limitato,* denotes a **pedestrian zone** (you can sometimes drive through to drop off baggage at your hotel); a white arrow on a blue background is used for Italy's many **one-way streets;** a mostly red circle with a horizontal white slash means **do not enter.** Any image in black on a white background surrounded by a red circle means that image is **not allowed** (for instance, if the image is two cars next to each other, it means no passing; and so on). A circular sign in blue with a red circle-slash means **no parking.**

Gasoline (gas or petrol), *benzina,* can be found in pull-in gas stations along major roads and on the outskirts of towns, as well as in 24-hour stations along the autostrada. Almost all are closed for the *riposo* and on Sundays (except on the autostrada), but most have an automatic machine that accepts cash. Unleaded gas is *senza piombo.* Diesel is *gasolio.*

By Train

Travel Times Between the Major Cities

CITIES	DISTANCE (FASTEST)	TRAIN TRAVEL TIME	DRIVING TIME
Florence to Venice	261km/162 miles	1 hr., 50 min.	3 hr.
Rome to Florence	277km/172 miles	1½ hr.	3 hr.
Rome to Naples	219km/136 miles	1 hr., 10 min.	2½ hr.
Rome to Venice	528km/327 miles	3hr., 20 min.	5¼ hr.

Italy, especially the northern half, has one of the best train systems in Europe with most destinations connected—the train is an excellent option if you're looking to visit the major sites without the hassle of driving. The vast majority of lines are run by the state-owned **Ferrovie dello Stato,** or **FS** (www.tren italia.com; ✆ **89-20-21**). A private operator, **Italo** (www.italotreno.it; ✆ **06-07-08**) operates on the Milan–Florence–Rome–Naples high-speed line, and the branch from Bologna to Padua and Venice.

Travel durations and the price of tickets vary considerably depending on what type of train you are traveling on. The country's principal north–south, high-speed line links Turin and Milan to Bologna, Florence, Rome, Naples, and Salerno. Milan to Rome, for example, takes under 3 hours on the fast train, and costs 86€—though you can find tickets as low as 25€ if you buy ahead and travel in off-peak hours. Rome to Naples takes 70 minutes and costs 43€ (walk-up fare) on the fast train, or you can spend 12€ for a trip on a slower train that takes just over twice as long. If you want to bag the cheapest fares on high-speed trains, try to **book around 100 to 120 days before your travel dates.**

TYPES OF TRAINS The speed, cleanliness, and overall quality of Italian trains vary. **High-speed trains** usually have four classes: Standard, Premium,

Business, and Executive on the state railway; Smart, eXtra Large, First, and Club Executive on Italo. The cheapest of these, on both operators, is perfectly comfortable, even on long legs of a journey (though Business on the state railway is worth paying a little extra for). These are Italy's premium rail services. The **Frecciarossa,** Italo's rival train, is the fastest of the fast (Italy's bullet train). These trains operate on the Milan–Florence–Rome–Naples line, and run up to 300 kmph (186 mph). The **Frecciargento** uses similar hardware, but is a bit slower; it links Naples, Rome, Florence, Verona, and Venice at speeds of up to 250 kmph (155 mph). Speed and cleanliness come at a price, with tickets for the high-speed trains usually costing around three times the cheapest "regional" train. On high-speed services you **must make a seat reservation** when you buy a ticket. If you are traveling with a rail pass (see facing page), you must pay a 10€ reservation fee to ride. Passes are not accepted, for now, on Italo.

Intercity (IC) trains are one step down, in both speed and comfort; specific seat reservations are also compulsory on IC services. The slower *Regionale* **(R)** and *Regionale Veloce* **(RV)** make many stops and can sometimes be on the grimy side of things, but they are also very cheap: A Venice–Verona second-class ticket will put you back only 8.60€ compared with 23€ on the high-speed service. There's no need to book R or RV trains ahead of time, and no price advantage in doing so.

Overcrowding is often a problem on standard services (that is, not the prebookable trains) Friday evenings, weekends, and holidays, especially in and out of big cities, or just after a strike. In summer, the crowding escalates, and any train going toward a beach in August bulges like an overstuffed sausage.

TRAIN TRAVEL TIPS If you don't have a ticket with a reservation for a particular seat on a specific train, then you must **validate you ticket by stamping it in the little yellow box** on the platform before boarding the train. If you board a train without the correct ticket, or without having validated your ticket, you'll have to pay a hefty fine on top of the ticket or supplement, which the conductor will sell you. If you knowingly board a train without a ticket or realize once onboard that you have the wrong type of ticket, your best bet is to search out the conductor, who is likely to be more forgiving because you made it clear you weren't trying to ride for free.

Schedules for all trains leaving a given station are printed on yellow posters tacked up on the station wall (the equivalent white poster lists arrivals). These are good for getting general information, but keep your eye on the electronic boards and screens that are updated with delays and track *(binario)* changes. You can get official schedules (also in English) and buy tickets at www.trenitalia.com and www.italotreno.it, or at an online agent like **Loco2.com.**

In the big cities (especially Milan and Rome) and the tourist destinations (above all Venice and Florence), ticketing lines can be dreadfully long. There is a solution though: **automatic ticket machines.** They are easy to navigate, allow you to follow instructions in English, accept cash and credit cards, and can cut down on the stress that comes with waiting on an interminably slow line. *Note:* You can't buy international tickets at automatic machines. Rail **apps** for state and Italo services offer paperless ticketing for high-speed trains. You can also just show a copy (paper or electronic) of your booking confirmation email, which has a unique PNR code.

SPECIAL PASSES & DISCOUNTS   To buy the **Eurail Italy Pass,** available only outside Italy and priced in U.S. dollars, contact **Rail Europe** (www.raileurope.com). You have a month in which to use the train a set number of days; the base number of days is 3, and you can add up to 5 more. For adults, the first-class pass costs $230, second class is $185. Additional days cost roughly $30 to $35 more for first class, $25 for second class. For youth tickets (25 and under), a 3-day second-class pass is $151 and additional days about $20 each. Saver passes are available for groups of two to five people traveling together *at all times,* and amount to a savings of about 15% on individual tickets. There are also Italy–Greece, Italy–Spain, and Italy–France rail pass combinations.

When it comes to regular tickets, if you're **25 and under,** you can buy a 40€ **Carta Verde (Green Card)** at any Italian train station that gets you a 10% discount on walk-up fares for domestic trips and 25% on international connections for 1 year. Present it each time you buy a ticket. A similar deal is available for anyone **61 and over** with the **Carta d'Argento (Silver Card):** 15% off domestic walk-ups and 25% off international, for 30€ (the Carta d'Argento is free for those 76 and over). **Children 11 and under always ride half-price** and kids 3 and under don't pay, although they also do not have the right to their own seat. On state railways, there are sometimes free tickets for children 14 and under traveling with a paying adult; ask about "Bimbi gratis" when buying your ticket (this option will also appear automatically when it's available on the automatic ticket machines).

By Bus

Although trains are quicker and easier, you can get just about anywhere on a network of local, provincial, and regional bus lines. Keep in mind that in smaller towns, buses exist mainly to shuttle workers and schoolchildren, so the most runs are on weekdays, early in the morning, and usually again in midafternoon.

In a big city, the **bus station** for trips between cities is usually near the main train station. A small town's **bus stop** is usually either in the main square, on the edge of town, or the bend in the road just outside the main town gate. You should always try to find the local ticket vendor—if there's no office, it's invariably the nearest newsstand or *tabacchi* (signaled by a sign with a white T), or occasionally a bar—but you can usually also buy tickets on the bus. You can sometimes flag down a bus as it passes on a country road, but try to find an official stop (a sign tacked onto a telephone pole).

For details on urban bus transportation, see individual chapters on Rome, Florence, and Venice. Perhaps the only long-distance buses you will want to take while you are in Italy are the efficient **Florence–Siena** service and slightly more awkward **Florence–San Gimignano** run. See "Siena," p. 207, and "San Gimignano," p. 213.

[Fast FACTS] ITALY

Area Codes The **country code** for Italy is **39. City codes** (for example, Florence is 055, Venice is 041, Rome is 06) are incorporated into the numbers themselves. Therefore, you must dial the entire number, *including the initial zero,* when calling from *anywhere* outside or inside Italy and even within the same town. To call Florence from the United States, you must dial **011-39-055,** then the local phone number. Phone numbers in Italy can range anywhere from 6 to 12 digits.

ATMs The easiest and best way to get cash away from home is from an ATM (automated teller machine), referred to in Italy as a *bancomat.* ATMs are very prevalent in Italian cities, and while every town usually has one, it's good practice to fuel up on cash in urban centers before traveling to small towns.

Be sure to confirm with your bank that your card is valid for international withdrawal and that you have a four-digit PIN. (Some ATMs in Italy will not accept any other number of digits.) Also, be sure you know your daily withdrawal limit before you depart. *Note:* Many banks impose a fee every time you use a card at another bank's ATM, and that fee can be higher for international transactions

(up to $5 or more) than for domestic ones. In addition, the bank from which you withdraw cash may charge its own fee, although this is not common practice.

If at the ATM you get a message saying your card isn't valid for international transactions, don't panic: It's most likely the bank just can't make the electronic connection (occasionally this can be a citywide epidemic). Try another ATM or another town.

Business Hours General open hours for **stores, offices,** and **churches** are from 9:30am to noon or 1pm and again from 3 or 3:30pm to 7:30 or 8pm. The early afternoon shutdown is the *riposo,* the Italian siesta (in the downtown area of large cities, stores don't close for *riposo*). Most stores close all day Sunday and many also on Monday (morning only or all day). Some services and business offices are open to the public only in the morning. Traditionally, **state museums** are closed Mondays. Most of the large museums stay open all day long otherwise, though some close for *riposo* or are only open in the morning (9am–2pm is popular). Some churches open earlier in the morning, and the largest often stay open all day. **Banks** tend to be open Monday through

Friday 8:30am to 1:30pm and 2:45 to 4:15pm.

Customs Foreign visitors can bring along most items for personal use duty-free, including goods up to 450€.

Disabled Travelers Most of the top museums and churches have installed ramps at their entrances, and some hotels have converted first-floor rooms into accessible units. Other than that, expect to find some of the most charming parts of Italy a little tricky to tackle. Builders in the Middle Ages and the Renaissance didn't have wheelchairs or mobility impairments in mind when they built narrow doorways and spiral staircases, and heritage preservation laws keep Italians from being able to do much about this.

Public transportation is improving, however. There is generally access for passengers in wheelchairs on modern local buses and new developments like Florence's tram. There are usually dedicated seats or areas for those with disabilities, and Italians are quick to give up their place for somebody who looks like they need it. **Trenitalia** has a special number that disabled travelers should call for assistance on the rail network: ✆ **199/303-060. Italo** has a couple of dedicated wheelchair spaces on every service: Call ☏ **06/ 07-08.**

Accessible Italy (www. accessibleitaly.com; ☏ **378-0549-941-111**) provides travelers with information about accessible tourist sites and places to rent wheelchairs, and also sells organized "Accessible Tours" around Italy.

Doctors & Hospitals
See individual chapters for details of walk-in medical services in Rome, Florence, and Venice.

Drinking Laws People of any age can legally consume alcohol in Italy, but a person must be 16 years old in order to be served alcohol in a restaurant or a bar. Noise is the primary concern to city officials, and so bars generally close around 2am, though alcohol is commonly served in clubs after that. Supermarkets carry beer, wine, and spirits.

Electricity Italy operates on a 220-volt AC (50 cycles) system, as opposed to the U.S. 110-volt AC (60 cycles) system. You'll need a simple adapter plug to make the American flat pegs fit Italian round holes and, unless your appliance is dual-voltage (as some hair dryers, travel irons, and almost all laptops are), an electrical currency converter.

Embassies & Consulates
The **Australian Embassy** is in Rome at Via Antonio Bosio 5 (www.italy. embassy.gov.au; ☏ **06-852-721**). The **Canadian Embassy** is in Rome at Via Zara 30 (www.italy.gc.ca;

☏ **06-854-443-937**). The **New Zealand Embassy** is in Rome at Via Clitunno 44 (www.nzembassy.com/italy; ☏ **06-853-7501**). The **U.K. Embassy** is in Rome at Via XX Settembre 80a (www. gov.uk/government/world/ italy.it; ☏ **06-4220-0001**). The **U.S. Embassy** is in Rome at Via Vittorio Veneto 121 (http://italy.usembassy. gov; ☏ **06-46-741**). The **U.S. Consulate General in Florence** is at Lungarno Vespucci 38 (http://florence. usconsulate.gov; ☏ **055-266-951**).

Emergencies The best number to call with a **general emergency** is ☏ **112,** which connects you to the **carabinieri,** who will transfer your call as needed. For the **police,** dial ☏ **113;** for a **medical emergency** and to call an **ambulance,** the number is ☏ **118;** for the **fire department,** call ☏ **115.** If your car breaks down, dial ☏ **116** for **roadside aid** courtesy of the Automotive Club of Italy. All are free calls.

Family Travel Italy is a family-oriented society. A crying baby at a dinner table is greeted with a knowing smile rather than with a stern look. Children almost always receive discounts, and maybe a special treat from the waiter, but the availability of such accoutrements as child seats for dinner tables is more the exception than the norm. There are plenty of parks, offbeat museums, markets, ice-cream parlors, and vibrant streetlife to

amuse even the youngest children. **Prénatal** (www. prenatal.com) is the principal toddler and baby chain store in Italy.

Health There are no special health risks you'll encounter in Italy. The country's public healthcare system is generally well-regarded. The richer north tends to have better **hospitals** than the south. Italy offers universal health care to its citizens and those of other European Union countries (U.K. nationals should remember to carry an EHIC: See **www.nhs.uk/ehic**). Others should be prepared to pay medical bills upfront. Before leaving home, find out what medical services your **health insurance** covers. *Note:* Even if you don't have insurance, you will be treated in an emergency room.

Pharmacies offer essentially the same range of generic drugs available in the United States. Pharmacies are ubiquitous (look for the green cross) and serve almost like miniclinics, where pharmacists diagnose and treat minor ailments, like flu symptoms and general aches and pains, with over-the-counter drugs. Carry the generic name of any prescription medicines, in case a local pharmacist is unfamiliar with the brand. Pharmacies in cities take turns doing night shift; normally there is a list posted at the entrance of each pharmacy informing customers which is open each night of the week.

Insurance   Italy may be one of the safer places you can travel in the world, but accidents and setbacks can and do happen, from lost luggage to car crashes. For information on traveler's insurance, trip cancellation insurance, and medical insurance while traveling, please visit **www.frommers.com/tips**.

Internet Access   Internet cafes are in healthy supply in most Italian cities, though don't expect to find them in every small town. If you're traveling with your own computer or smartphone, you'll find wireless access in almost every hotel, but if this is key for your stay, make sure you ask before booking and certainly don't always expect to find a connection in a rural *agriturismo* (disconnecting is part of their appeal). In a pinch, hostels, libraries, and some cafes and bars have web access. Several spots around Venice, Florence, Rome, and other big cities are covered with free Wi-Fi access provided by the local administration, but at these and any other Wi-Fi spots around Italy, antiterrorism laws make it obligatory to register before you can log on. Take your passport or other photo ID if you go looking for an Internet point. Rome's Leonardo da Vinci–Fiumicino Airport offers free Wi-Fi. Florence's discount **Firenze Card** (p. 170) comes with 72 hours of free Wi-Fi included. High-speed trains often have free Wi-Fi (but throttle video streaming, Skype, and similar services).

LGBT Travelers   Italy as a whole, and northern Italy in particular, is gay-friendly. Homosexuality is legal, and the age of consent is 16. Italians are generally more affectionate and physical than North Americans in all their friendships, and even straight men occasionally walk down the street with their arms around each other—however, kissing anywhere other than on the cheeks at greetings and goodbyes will draw attention. As you might expect, smaller towns tend to be less permissive than cities and beach resorts.

Italy's national associations and support networks for gays and lesbians are **Arcigay and Arcilesbica.** The national websites are **www.arcigay.it** and **www.arcilesbica.it**, and most cities have a local office. See **www.arcigay.it/comitati** for a searchable directory of local organizations.

Mail & Postage   Sending a postcard or letter up to 20 grams, or a little less than an ounce, costs .95€ to other European countries, 2.50€ to North America, and a whopping 3€ to Australia and New Zealand. Full details on Italy's postal services are available at **www.poste.it** (some in English).

Mobile Phones   GSM (Global System for Mobile Communications) is a cellphone technology used by most of the world's countries that makes it possible to turn on a phone with a contract based in Australia, Ireland, the U.K., Pakistan, or almost any other corner of the world and have it work in Italy without missing a beat. (In the U.S., service providers like Sprint and Verizon use a different technology—CDMA—and many phones on those networks won't work in Italy.) Also, if you are coming from the U.S. or Canada, you may need a multiband phone. All travelers should activate "international roaming" on their account, so check with your home service provider before leaving.

But—and it's a *big* but—using roaming can be very expensive, especially if you access the Internet on your phone. It is much cheaper, once you arrive, to buy an Italian SIM card (the removable plastic card found in all GSM phones that is encoded with your phone number). This is not difficult, and is an especially good idea if you will be in Italy for more than a week. You can **buy a SIM card** at one of the many cellphone shops you will pass in every city. The main service providers are TIM, Vodafone, Wind, and 3 *(Tre)*. If you have an Italian SIM card in your phone, local calls may be as low as .10€ per minute, and incoming calls are free. Prepaid data packages are available for each, as are micro- and nano-SIMs, as well as prepaid deals for iPads and other tablets. If you want 4G data speeds, you will often pay a little more. Deals on each network change regularly; for the latest, see the website of one of this guide's authors: **www.donald strachan.com/data roamingitaly**. *Note:* Contract cellphones are often "locked" and will only work with a SIM card provided by the service provider back home, so check to see that you have an unlocked phone.

Buying a phone is another option, and you shouldn't have too much trouble finding one for under 30€. Use it, then recycle it or eBay it when you get home. It will save you a fortune versus alternatives such as roaming or using hotel room telephones.

Money & Costs Frommer's lists exact prices in the local currency. The currency conversions quoted below were correct at press time. However, rates fluctuate, so before departing, consult a currency exchange website, such as **www.oanda.com/ currency/converter**, to check up-to-the-minute rates. Like many European countries, Italy uses the **euro** as its currency. Euro coins are issued in denominations of .01€, .02€, .05€, .10€, .20€, and .50€, as well as 1€ and 2€; bills come in denominations of 5€, 10€, 20€, 50€, 100€, 200€, and 500€. You'll get the best rate if you **exchange money** at a bank or take

cash out from one of its **ATMs** (see p. 300). The rates at "cambio/change/ wechsel" exchange booths are invariably less favorable but still better than what you'd get exchanging money at a hotel or shop (a last-resort tactic).

In any case, the evolution of international computerized banking has led to the triumph of plastic throughout Italy—even if cold cash is still the most trusted currency, especially in small towns and mom-and-pop joints. (It remains a good idea to carry some cash, because small businesses may accept only cash or may claim that their credit card machine is broken to avoid paying fees to the card companies.) **Visa** and **MasterCard** are almost universally accepted, and some businesses take **American Express. Diners Club** tends not to be accepted in Italy. Be sure to let your bank know that you'll be traveling abroad to avoid having your card blocked after a few days of big purchases far from home. *Note:* Many banks assess a 1% to 3% "transaction fee" on **all** charges you incur abroad, whether you're using the local currency or your native currency.

One additional note: Traveler's checks have gone the way of the Stegosaurus.

Newspapers & Magazines The "International New York Times" and "USA Today" are available at most newsstands in the big cities, and sometimes even in smaller towns. You can find the "Wall Street Journal Europe," European editions of "Time," the "Economist," and most of the major European newspapers and magazines at the larger kiosks in the bigger cities.

Police For emergencies, call ℂ **112** or ℂ **113.** Italy has several different police forces, but there are only two you'll likely ever need to deal with. The first is the *carabinieri* (ℂ **112**) who normally only concern themselves with serious crimes, but point you in the right direction. The *polizia* (ℂ **113**), whose city headquarters is called the *questura,* is the place to go for help with lost and stolen property or petty crimes.

Safety Italy is a remarkably safe country. The worst threats you'll likely face are the pickpockets who sometimes frequent touristy areas and public buses; keep your hands on your camera at all times and your valuables in an under-the-clothes money belt or inside zip-pocket. Don't leave anything valuable in a rental car overnight, and leave nothing visible in it at any time. If you are robbed, you can fill

THE VALUE OF THE EURO VS. OTHER POPULAR CURRENCIES

€	Aus$	Can$	NZ$	UK£	US$
1	A$1.45	C$1.39	NZ$1.62	£0.71	$1.12

WHAT THINGS COST IN FLORENCE (HOTEL PRICES ARE HIGH SEASON)

Bus ticket (from/to anywhere in the city)	1.20€
Double room at Continentale (expensive)	450.00€
Double room at Antica Dimora Johlea (moderate)	180.00€
Double room at Locanda Orchidea (inexpensive)	80.00€
Continental breakfast (cappuccino and croissant standing at a bar)	2.30€
Dinner for one, with wine, at Ora d'Aria (expensive)	85.00€
Dinner for one, with wine, at Konnubio (moderate)	35.00€
Dinner for one, with wine, at GustaPizza (inexpensive)	12.00€
Small gelato at Gelateria della Passera	2€
Glass of wine at a bar	2.50€–7.00€
Coca-Cola (standing/sitting in a bar)	2.50€/4.50€
Cup of espresso (standing/sitting in a bar)	1.00€/2.50€
Admission to the Uffizi	8€–12.50€

out paperwork at the nearest police station (questura), but this is mostly for insurance purposes and perhaps to get a passport issued—don't expect them to spend any resources hunting down the perpetrator.

In general, avoid public parks at night. The areas around rail stations are often unsavory, but rarely worse. Other than that, there's a real sense of security in Italy.

Senior Travel Seniors and older people are treated with a great deal of respect and deference, but there are few specific programs, associations, or concessions made for them. The one exception is on admission prices for museums and sights, where those ages 60 or 65 and older will often get in at a reduced rate or even free. There are

also special train passes and reductions on bus tickets and the like in many towns (see "Getting Around," p. 294). As a senior in Italy, you're un anziano (if you're a woman: un'anziana)—it's a term of respect, and you should let people know you're one if you think a discount may be due.

Smoking Smoking has been eradicated from inside restaurants, bars, and most hotels. Many smokers remain, and they tend to take outside tables at bars and restaurants. If you pick an outdoor table, you are essentially choosing a seat in the smoking section, and requesting that your neighbor not smoke may not be politely received.

Student Travelers An **International Student Identity Card (ISIC)** qualifies students for savings on

rail passes, plane tickets, entrance fees, and more. The card is valid for 1 year. You can apply for the card online at **www.myisic.com** or in person at **STA Travel** (www.statravel.com; ✆ **800/781-4040** in North America), the biggest student travel agency in the world. If you're no longer a student but are still 25 or under, you can get an **International Youth Travel Card (IYTC)** and an **International Teacher Identity Card (ITIC)** from the same agency, which entitles you to some discounts.

Taxes There's no sales tax added onto the price tag of purchases in Italy, but there is a 22% value-added tax (in Italy: IVA) automatically included in just about everything except basic foodstuffs like milk and bread. For major purchases, you can get this refunded if you live outside the EU. Several cities also recently introduced an **accommodation tax.** For example, in Florence, you will pay 1.50€ per person per night for a 1-star hotel plus 1€ per night per additional government-star rating of the hotel, up to a maximum of 10 nights. So, in a 4-star joint, the tax is an extra 4.50€ per person per night. Children 9 and under are exempt. Venice, Rome, and several other localities impose their own taxes. These are rarely included in any published room rate.

Tipping In **hotels,** a service charge is usually included in your bill. In family-run operations, additional tips are unnecessary and sometimes considered rude. In fancier places with a hired staff, however, you may want to leave a .50€ daily tip for the maid and pay the bellhop or porter 1€ per bag. In **restaurants,** a 1€ to 3€ per person "cover charge" is automatically added to the bill, and in some tourist areas, especially Venice, another 10% to 15% is tacked on (except in the most unscrupulous of places, this will be noted on the menu somewhere; if unsure, you should ask, è incluso il servizio?). It is not necessary to leave any extra money on the table, though it is not uncommon to leave up to 5€, especially for good service. Locals generally leave nothing. At **bars and cafes,** you can leave something very small on the counter for the barman (maybe 1€ if you have had several drinks), though it is not expected; there is no need to leave anything extra if you sit at a table, as they are probably already charging you double or triple the price you'd have paid standing at the bar. It is not necessary to tip **taxi** drivers, though it is common to round up the bill to the nearest euro or two.

Toilets Aside from train stations, where they cost about .50€ to use, and gas/petrol stations, where they are free (with perhaps a basket seeking donations for the cleaners), public toilets are few and far between. Standard procedure is to enter a cafe, make sure the bathroom is not fuori servizio (out of order), and then order a cup of coffee before bolting to the facilities. It is advisable to always make use of toilets in a hotel, restaurant, museum, or bar before setting off around town.

USEFUL ITALIAN PHRASES

English	Italian	Pronunciation
Thank you	Grazie	**graht-tzee-yey**
You're welcome	Prego	**prey-go**
Please	Per favore	**pehr fah-vohr-eh**
Yes	Si	**see**
No	No	**noh**
Good morning or Good day	Buongiorno	**bwohn-djor-noh**
Good evening	Buona sera	**bwohn-ah say-rah**
Good night	Buona notte	**bwohn-ah noht-tay**
It's a pleasure to meet you.	Piacere di conoscerla.	**pyah-cheh-reh dee koh-nohshehr-lah**
My name is ____.	Mi chiamo ____.	**mee kyah-moh**
And yours?	E lei?	**eh lay**
Do you speak English?	Parla inglese?	**pahr-lah een-gleh-seh**

English	Italian	Pronunciation
How are you?	Come sta?	*koh*-may **stah**
Very well	Molto bene	*mohl*-toh *behn*-ney
Goodbye	Arrivederci	ahr-ree-vah-*dehr*-chee
Excuse me (to get attention)	Scusi	*skoo*-zee
Excuse me (to get past someone)	Permesso	pehr-*mehs*-soh

GETTING AROUND

English	Italian	Pronunciation
Where is . . . ?	Dovè . . . ?	*doh*-vey
the station	la stazione	lah stat-tzee-*oh*-neh
a hotel	un albergo	oon ahl-*behr*-goh
a restaurant	un ristorante	oon reest-ohr-*ahnt*-eh
the bathroom	il bagno	eel *bahn*-nyoh
I am looking for . . .	Cerco . . .	*chehr*-koh
the check-in counter	il check-in	eel check-in
the ticket counter	la biglietteria	*lah beel-lyeht-teh-ree-ah*
arrivals	l'area arrivi	*lah*-reh-ah ahr-*ree*-vee
departures	l'area partenze	*lah*-reh-ah pahr-*tehn*-tseh
gate number	l'uscita numero	loo-*shee*-tah *noo*-meh-roh
the restroom	la toilette	lah twa-*leht*
the police station	la stazione di polizia	lah stah-*tsyoh*-neh dee poh-lee-*tsee*-ah
the smoking area	l'area fumatori	*lah*-reh-ah foo-mah-*toh*-ree
the information booth	l'ufficio informazioni	loof-*fee*-choh een-*fohr*-mah-*tsyoh*-nee
a public telephone	un telefono pubblico	oon teh-*leh*-foh-noh *poob*-blee-koh
an ATM/cash-point	un bancomat	oon *bahn*-koh-maht
baggage claim	il ritiro bagagli	eel ree-*tee*-roh bah-*gahl*-lyee
a cafe	un caffè	oon kahf-*feh*
a restaurant	un ristorante	oon ree-stoh-*rahn*-teh
a bar	un bar	oon bar
a bookstore	una libreria	*oo*-nah lee-breh-*ree*-ah
To the left	A sinistra	ah see-*nees*-tra
To the right	A destra	ah *dehy*-stra
Straight ahead	Avanti (or sempre diritto)	ahv-*vahn*-tee (*sehm*-pray dee-*reet*-toh)

DINING

English	Italian	Pronunciation
Breakfast	Prima colazione	*pree*-mah coh-laht-tzee-*ohn*-ay
Lunch	Pranzo	*prahn*-zoh
Dinner	Cena	*chay*-nah
How much is it?	Quanto costa?	*kwan*-toh *coh*-sta
The check, please	Il conto, per favore	eel kon-toh *pehr* fah-*vohr*-eh

A MATTER OF TIME

English	Italian	Pronunciation
When?	Quando?	*kwan*-doh
Yesterday	Ieri	ee-*yehr*-ree
Today	Oggi	*oh*-jee
Tomorrow	Domani	doh-*mah*-nee
What time is it?	Che ore sono?	kay *or*-ay *soh*-noh
It's one o'clock.	È l'una.	*eh loo*-nah
It's two o'clock.	Sono le due.	*soh*-noh leh *doo*-eh
It's two-thirty.	Sono le due e mezzo.	*soh*-noh leh *doo*-eh eh *mehd*-dzoh
It's noon.	È mezzogiorno.	*eh* mehd-dzoh-*johr*-noh
It's midnight.	È mezzanotte.	*eh* mehd-dzah-*noht*-teh
in the morning	al mattino	ahl maht-*tee*-noh
in the afternoon	al pomeriggio	ahl poh-meh-*reed*-joh
at night	alla notte	dee *noht*-the

DAYS OF THE WEEK

English	Italian	Pronunciation
Monday	Lunedì	loo-nay-*dee*
Tuesday	Martedì	mart-ay-*dee*
Wednesday	Mercoledì	mehr-cohl-ay-*dee*
Thursday	Giovedì	joh-vay-*dee*
Friday	Venerdì	ven-nehr-*dee*
Saturday	Sabato	*sah*-bah-toh
Sunday	Domenica	doh-*mehn*-nee-kah

MONTHS & SEASONS

English	Italian	Pronunciation
January	gennaio	jehn-*nah*-yoh
February	febbraio	fehb-*brah*-yoh
March	marzo	*mahr*-tso
April	aprile	ah-*pree*-leh
May	maggio	*mahd*-joh
June	giugno	*jewn*-nyo

English	Italian	Pronunciation
July	luglio	*lool*-lyo
August	agosto	ah-*gohs*-toh
September	settembre	seht-*tehm*-breh
October	ottobre	oht-*toh*-breh
November	novembre	noh-*vehm*-breh
December	dicembre	dee-*chehm*-breh
spring	la primavera	lah pree-mah-*veh*-rah
summer	l'estate	lehs-*tah*-teh
autumn	l'autunno	low-*toon*-noh
winter	l'inverno	leen-*vehr*-noh

NUMBERS

English	Italian	Pronunciation
1	uno	*oo*-noh
2	due	*doo*-ay
3	tre	tray
4	quattro	*kwah*-troh
5	cinque	*cheen*-kway
6	sei	say
7	sette	*set*-tay
8	otto	*oh*-toh
9	nove	*noh*-vay
10	dieci	dee-*ay*-chee
11	undici	*oon*-dee-chee
20	venti	*vehn*-tee
21	ventuno	vehn-*toon*-oh
22	venti due	*vehn*-tee *doo*-ay
30	trenta	*trayn*-tah
40	quaranta	kwah-*rahn*-tah
50	cinquanta	cheen-*kwan*-tah
60	sessanta	sehs-*sahn*-tah
70	settanta	seht-*tahn*-tah
80	ottanta	oht-*tahn*-tah
90	novanta	noh-*vahnt*-tah
100	cento	*chen*-toh
1,000	mille	*mee*-lay
5,000	cinque milla	*cheen*-kway *mee*-lah
10,000	dieci milla	dee-*ay*-chee mee-lah

Useful Italian Phrases

PLANNING YOUR TRIP

Index

Photo Credits